A TEXT BOOK OF

THERMAL SCIENCE

For
S.E. SEMESTER – III

SECOND YEAR DEGREE COURSES IN MECHANICAL & AUTOMATION ENGINEERING

As Per New Revised Syllabus of Shivaji University Kolhapur.
(Effective From, 2014)

Dr. S. N. Sapali
B.E. (Mech), M.E. (Mech) Ph.D. (IIT) Kharagpur
Professor & Head of Mechanical Engg. Dept.,
College of Engineering (COEP), Pune.
(An Autonomous Insitute of Govt. of Maharashtra)

P. B. Joshi
Professor and Head
Dept. of Mechanical Engg.
Maharashtra Insitutte of Technology,
Pune

S. S. Ghorpade
B.E. (Mech.), M.E. (Mech.)
Assistant Professor, Sinhagad Academy of Engg.
Kondhwa (Bk.) Pune.

U. S. Tumne
Asst. Professor in Mech. Engg. (Retd.)
Maharashtra Institute of Technology,
Pune.

THERMAL SCIENCE (S.E. SEM. III MECH. & AUTO. – SU) **ISBN : 978-93-5164-222-0**
First Edition : August 2014
© :

The text of this publication, or any part thereof, should not be reproduced or transmitted in any form or stored in any computer storage system or device for distribution including photocopy, recording, taping or information retrieval system or reproduced on any disc, tape, perforated media or other information storage device etc., without the written permission of Authors with whom the rights are reserved. Breach of this condition is liable for legal action.

Every effort has been made to avoid errors or omissions in this publication. In spite of this, errors may have crept in. Any mistake, error or discrepancy so noted and shall be brought to our notice shall be taken care of in the next edition. It is notified that neither the publisher nor the authors or seller shall be responsible for any damage or loss of action to any one, of any kind, in any manner, therefrom.

Published By : **Printed at**
NIRALI PRAKASHAN **Repro Knowledgecast Limited**
Abhyudaya Pragati, 1312, Shivaji Nagar, **India**
Off J.M. Road, PUNE – 411005
Tel - (020) 25512336/37/39, Fax - (020) 25511379
Email : niralipune@pragationline.com

DISTRIBUTION CENTRES
PUNE

Nirali Prakashan *Nirali Prakashan*
119, Budhwar Peth, Jogeshwari Mandir Lane S. No. 28/25, Dhyari,
Pune 411002, Maharashtra Near Pari Company, Pune 411041
Tel : (020) 2445 2044, 66022708, Fax : (020) 2445 1538 Tel : (022) 24690204 Fax : (020) 24690316
Email : bookorder@pragationline.com Email : dhyari@pragationline.com
 bookorder@pragationline.com

MUMBAI
Nirali Prakashan
385, S.V.P. Road, Rasdhara Co-op. Hsg. Society Ltd.,
Girgaum, Mumbai 400004, Maharashtra
Tel : (022) 2385 6339 / 2386 9976, Fax : (022) 2386 9976
Email : niralimumbai@pragationline.com

DISTRIBUTION BRANCHES

NAGPUR **JALGAON**
Pratibha Book Distributors *Nirali Prakashan*
Above Maratha Mandir, Shop No. 3, First Floor, 34, V. V. Golani Market, Navi Peth, Jalgaon 425001,
Rani Jhanshi Square, Sitabuldi, Nagpur 440012, Maharashtra, Tel : (0257) 222 0395
Maharashtra, Tel : (0712) 254 7129 Mob : 94234 91860

BENGALURU **KOLHAPUR**
Pragati Book House *Nirali Prakashan*
House No. 1, Sanjeevappa Lane, Avenue Road Cross, New Mahadvar Road,
Opp. Rice Church, Bengaluru – 560002. Kedar Plaza, 1st Floor Opp. IDBI Bank
Tel : (080) 64513344, 64513355, Kolhapur 416 012, Maharashtra. Mob : 9855046155
Mob : 9880582331, 9845021552
Email:bharatsavla@yahoo.com

CHENNAI
Pragati Books
9/1, Montieth Road, Behind Taas Mahal, Egmore,
Chennai 600008 Tamil Nadu, Tel : (044) 6518 3535,
Mob : 94440 01782 / 98450 21552 / 98805 82331, Email : bharatsavla@yahoo.com

RETAIL OUTLETS
PUNE

Pragati Book Centre *Pragati Book Centre*
157, Budhwar Peth, Opp. Ratan Talkies, 676/B, Budhwar Peth, Opp. Jogeshwari Mandir,
Pune 411002, Maharashtra Pune 411002, Maharashtra
Tel : (020) 2445 8887 / 6602 2707, Fax : (020) 2445 8887 Tel : (020) 6601 7784 / 6602 0855
Pragati Book Centre *PBC Book Sellers & Stationers*
Amber Chamber, 28/A, Budhwar Peth, 152, Budhwar Peth, Pune 411002, Maharashtra
Appa Balwant Chowk, Pune : 411002, Maharashtra, Tel : (020) 2445 2254 / 6609 2463
Tel : (020) 20240335 / 66281669
Email : pbcpune@pragationline.com

MUMBAI
Pragati Book Corner
Indira Niwas, 111 - A, Bhavani Shankar Road, Dadar (W), Mumbai 400028, Maharashtra
Tel : (022) 2422 3526 / 6662 5254, Email : pbcmumbai@pragationline.com

PREFACE

The book is written mainly for the second year students of Mechanical and Automation Engineering course of Shivaji University, Kolhapur for the subject **"Thermal Science"**. It is written as per the new revised syllabus (2014) of Shivaji University, Kolhapur.

New text book is written, taking in to account all the new features that have been introduced. All the entrants to the engineering field will definitely find this book, complete in all respect. Students will find the subject matter presentation quite lucid. There are large number of illustrative examples and well graded exercises.

Salient features of this book are :

- **Written strictly according to revised syllabus of Shivaji University.**
- **Adequate emphasis on both Theory and Problems.**
- **Unnecessary Theory is avoided.**

Our sincere hope is that the material presented in the book will be useful in understanding the subject as well as for attempting examination questions.

We take this opportunity to express our thanks to **Shri. Dineshbhai Furia** and **Shri. Jignesh Furia** and **Shri. M.P. Munde** for publishing this book in time.

We are also take this opportunity to express our thank all the staff members of Nirali Prakashan namely Mrs. Anita Kulkarni, Mrs. Ulka Chavan, Mrs. Sarika Wagh also Miss Sarika Shinde and Miss Rani Zinjade for their tremendous dedication and hard work in bringing out this book in an excellent form.

We are also thankful to **Mr. Virdhaval Shinde**, Branch Manager, Kolhapur Office and **Mr. Ashok Nanaware**, Branch Manager, Sangli District for their valuable help and efforts for promotion of my book.

Our special thanks to our family members, students and all those who directly or indirectly supported me in this project.

Any suggestions and feedback shall be appreciated and acknowledged.

August 2014   **Author**

Pune

SYLLABUS

SECTION - I

Unit I : Review of Laws of Thermodynamics (3)
Zeroth law, first law & Second law of thermodynamics, Equivalence & Corrolories of Second Law, Numerical treatment on second law.

Unit II : Entropy & Availability (6)
(A) Entropy : Clausius inequality, entropy as a property of system, entropy of pure substance. T-S and h-s planes, entropy change in a reversible and irreversible processes, increase of entropy principle, calculation of entropy changes of gases and vapours, Statement of third law of thermodynamics.
(B) Availability : Available and unavailable energy: availability of a closed and open system, availability of work and heat reservoirs, and simple numericals.

Unit III : Properties of Pure Substances and Vapour Power Cycles (7)
Properties of steam, use of steam table and Mollier chart, Deviation of real gases from ideal gases, Equations of state- Vander Waal, Beattie-Bridgemen, Virial & Diterici's equations, P-V-T surfaces & triple point of water.(Descriptive treatment). Carnot cycle using steam, limitations of Carnot cycle. Rankine cycle, representation on T-s and h-s planes, thermal efficiency, specific steam consumption. Work ratio, effect of steam supply pressure and temperature, condenser pressure on the performance. (Numerical Treatment)

Unit IV : Steam Condensers (4)
Functions, elements of condensing plant, types of steam condensers, surface and jet condensers, comparison, vacuum efficiency, condenser efficiency, loss of vacuum, sources of air leakages, methods of leak detection, air extraction methods, estimation of cooling water required, capacity of air extraction pump, air ejectors.

SECTION - II

Unit V : Steam Nozzles (5)
Functions, shapes, critical pressure ratio, maximum discharge condition, effect of faction, design of throat and exit areas, nozzle efficiency, velocity coefficient, coefficient of discharge, supersaturated flow, degree of under-cooling and degree of super saturation, effects of super saturation.

Unit VI : Steam Turbines (15)
Principles of operation, classification, impulse and reaction steam turbine, compounding of steam turbines. Flow through impulse turbine blades, velocity diagrams, work done, efficiencies, end thrust, blade friction, influence of ratio of blade speed to steam speed on efficiency of single and multistage turbines and its condition curve and reheat factors. Flow through impulse reaction blades, velocity diagram, and degree of reaction, parson's reaction turbine, and backpressure and pass out turbine. Reheat regenerative steam power cycles. Governing of steam turbines. losses in steam turbines, performance of steam turbines. Function of diaphragm, glands, turbine troubles like erosion, corrosion, vibration, fouling etc.

CONTENTS

SECTION - I

1. Review of Laws of Thermodynamics — 1.1 – 1.110

2. Entropy and Availability — 2.1 – 2.66

3. Properties of Pure Substance and Vapour Power Cycles — 3.1 – 3.60

4. Steam Condensers — 4.1 – 4.62

SECTION - II

5. Steam Nozzles — 5.1 – 5.36

6. Steam Turbines — 6.1 – 6.38

Unit - I
REVIEW OF LAWS OF THERMODYNAMICS

1.1 INTRODUCTION

Thermodynamics is a science that deals with matter, energy and interactions between matter and energy.

The subject of thermodynamics is based essentially on three main concepts, these are

- **Energy**, is an idea central to the development of all branches of science and engineering. A fundamental postulate of thermodynamics is that matter has energy (which can be in several forms) and energy is conserved.
- **Thermodynamic Equilibrium**; a state which every isolated system with no internal constraints eventually attains.
- **Entropy**; which determines whether a specified type of the change can occur or not.

1.2 SCOPE OF THERMODYNAMICS

Every engineering activity involves an interaction between energy and matter, thus it is hard to imagine an area which does not relate to thermodynamics in some respect. Therefore, a good understanding of thermodynamic principles has been an essential part of engineering education.

One does not need to go very far to see some application areas of thermodynamics. These areas are where one lives. Many household utensiles and appliances are designed, by using thermodynamic principles. For Problem, electric heaters, LPG stove, heating and air conditioning systems, the refrigerator, pressure cooker, water heater, shower, electric iron. On large scale, thermodynamics plays a major part in the design and analysis of automotive engines, rockets, jet engines, and conventional power plants (thermal power plants) and also nuclear power plants. At this stage, it is essential to mention that human body is an interesting application area of thermodynamics.

Under thermodynamics, we study the working and performance of (i) Conventional or nuclear power plant, (ii) Compression Ignition (C.I.) and Spark Ignition (S.I.) engines, (iii) Gas turbines, (iv) Steam turbines, (v) Refrigerators, (vi) Air conditioners, (vii) Air compressors, (viii) Refrigerant compressors, (ix) Pumps, etc.

1.3 BASIC DEFINITIONS

1.3.1 Working Substance

In heat engine, a fluid is used to receive heat, expand and produce work output. In refrigerators and heat pumps, a fluid is used to receive heat at a low temperature and reject at higher temperature. Such a fluid with essential properties is known as a working substance. A working substance absorbs heat and rejects heat. Working substance does work or work is done on it. It is compressed or expanded, heated or cooled so that the desired energy transfer is achieved.

Problems of working substances are: air in an air compressor, water in hydraulic turbines, air and fuel mixture in gas turbines and I. C. engines, steam in a steam power plant, carbon dioxide or water in nuclear power plant.

Pure Substance

This has a homogeneous and invariable chemical composition, even if the substance changes its phase from solid to liquid or liquid to vapour.

Water is a pure substance; the chemical composition (formula) of H_2O will not change, even if it undergoes phase change from ice to water and water to vapour.

1.3.2 System

Thermodynamic system or simply a system, is defined as a quantity of matter or a region in space chosen for study. The region outside the system is called as *surroundings*. The real or imaginary surface that separates the system from its surroundings is called the *boundary*. These are illustrated in Fig. 1.1.

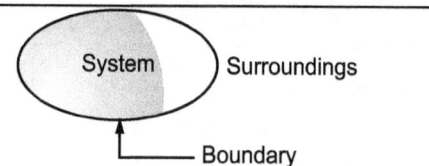

Fig. 1.1: System, surroundings and boundary

The boundary of a system can be fixed or movable.

Classification of Systems:

- System may be classified as closed, open and isolated.

(a) Closed System (Non-flow system):

It consists of fixed amount of mass and no mass can cross its boundary. That is, no mass can enter or leave a closed system as shown in Fig. 1.2. But energy, in the form of heat or work can cross the boundary and the volume of a closed system does not have to be fixed. It consists of fixed mass while volume changes. Boundaries of such system are real and moving. For Problem, pressure cooker, stirling cryogenerator.

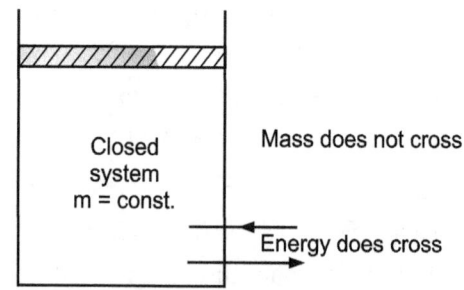

Fig. 1.2 : Mass cannot cross the boundaries of a closed system but energy can

(b) Open System or Control Volume (Flow system):

The system which can exchange both mass as well as energy with the surroundings is called as open or flow system. It consists of fixed volume while mass enters and leaves the system. Boundaries of such system are fixed and may be imaginary.

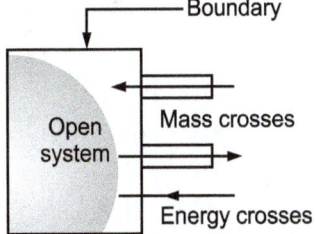

Fig. 1.3: Both mass and energy can cross the boundaries of a system

As an Problem of open system, consider the water heater as shown in Fig. 1.4.

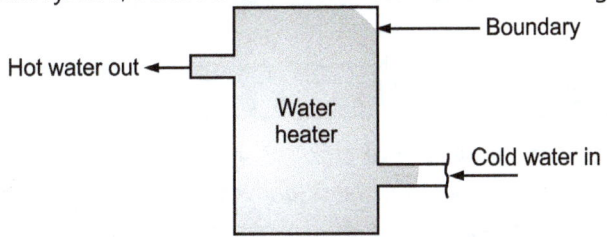

Fig. 1.4: An open system with one inlet and one exit

For Problem, air compressor, turbines, nozzles, etc.

(c) Isolated System:

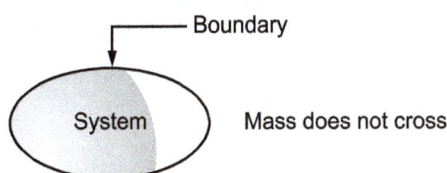

Energy does not cross

Fig. 1.5: Isolated system

This is one in which there is no interaction between the system and the surroundings. No transfer of mass and energy across the boundary.

For Problem, thermos flask, cryogenic gas container.

(ii) System can also be classified as homogeneous and heterogeneous.

(a) Homogeneous system:

In this working substance is present a single phase. e.g. air, water, crude oil.

(b) Heterogeneous system:

In this working substance is present in more than one phases. e.g. fog, mixture water and ice.

Control Volume and Control Surface:
If the volume of system under study remains constant and has a fixed position, then this volume is called as a control volume. The control volume is bounded by a control surface.

Fig. 1.6 shows a control volume bounded by a control surface. Both mass and energy entering and leaving the system are shown in the figure. Control volume is same as open system. The volume may change in open system, but it remains constant in control volume.

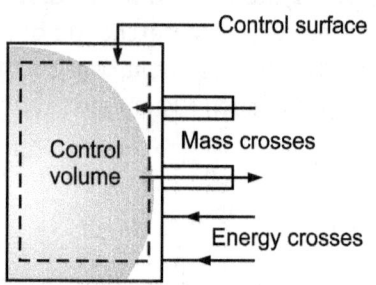

Fig. 1.6: Control volume

1.4 DIMENSIONS AND UNITS

In this book the International System of Units or System International d' Units (SI) is used. The units are divided into base units and derived units. The following table will give information about their names and symbols.

Base Units :

Quantity	Unit Name	Unit Symbol
Mass	Kilogram	kg
Length	Meter	m
Time	Second	s
Temperature	Kelvin	K
Amount of Matter	Mole	mol.

Derived Units (I) :

Quantity	Unit Name	Unit Symbol
Area	Square meter	m^2
Volume	Cubic meter	m^3
Velocity	Meter per second	m/s
Acceleration	Meter per second	m/s^2
Density	Kilogram per cubic meter	kg/m^3
Specific Volume	Cubic meter per kilogram	m^3/kg

Derived Units (II) :

Quantity	Name	Symbol	Expression in terms of other units	Expression in terms of base units
Force	Newton	N	–	kg·m/s²
Pressure	Pascal	Pa	N/m²	kg/ms²
energy, work, heat	Joule	J	N.m	kg·m²/s²
Power	Watt	W	J/s	kg·m²/s²

1.4.1 Common multiples of SI Units

The most common multiples and submultiples used in SI units can be summarised as follows:

Multiplication factor	Prefix	Symbol
10^6	Mega	M
10^3	Kilo	k
10^{-3}	Milli	m
10^{-6}	Micro	μ
10^{-9}	Nano	n
10^{-12}	Pico	p

1.4.2 Some More Units

1. **Volume:** The unit of volume is cubic meter (m³). The unit litre is also commonly used and 1 litre equals 10^{-3} m³. The basic unit of m³ however should be used in technical work.

2. **Mass:** The basic unit of mass is kilogram (kg). For large masses 1 tonne or 1 Megagram (10^3 kg) is used. For small masses 1 milligram (10^{-6} kg) is used.

   The term weight should not be used in place of mass. Weight is force while mass is quantity of matter.

3. **Force:** The unit of force is Newton (N) and it is defined as the force which will accelerate one kg of mass with an acceleration of one meter per second.

   Newton's 2nd law gives us the relation

   F α m × a where F is force, m is mass, and a is acceleration.

   or $\qquad F = \dfrac{ma}{g_c}$ where g_c is constant of proportionality $\qquad$ ... (1.1)

As one Newton produces acceleration of 1m/s² in 1 kg of mass we have

$$1 \text{ Newton} = \frac{1}{g_c} \times 1 \text{ kg} \times 1 \text{ m/s}^2$$

$$\therefore \quad g_c = 1$$

when $g_c = 1$ the system is said to be coherent or consistent and the product of units of mass and acceleration becomes the unit of force.

If the mass is allowed to fall freely under the action of standard gravitational force it is accelerated at the rate of 9.806 m/s² (9.81 m/s²) and we have

$$\text{Force} = 1 \text{ kg} \times 9.81 \text{ m/s}^2 = 9.81 \text{ N} \quad \ldots (1.2)$$

It follows that the weight of 1 kg mass equals 9.81 Newtons.

4. **Density:** Density ρ is defined as mass (not weight) per unit volume. Its units are kilogram per cubic metre (kg/m³). Density of water is 1000 kg/m³ or 1 tonne/m³. The reciprocal of density is called specific volume and is defined as volume occupied by unit mass of a substance. Its units are cubic metre per kilogram (m³/kg)

$$v = m^3/kg \text{ and } v = \frac{1}{\rho} \quad \ldots (1.3)$$

5. **Specific weight:** It is defined as the force of gravity on unit volume (not unit mass). It is denoted by γ and its units are Newton per cubic meter (N/m³).

$$\gamma = \frac{\text{force of gravity}}{\text{volume}} = \frac{m \cdot g}{g_c V} = \frac{rg}{g_c} \quad \ldots (1.4)$$

Where g is local acceleration due to gravity. At earth's surface $g = g_c$ and $\gamma = \rho$.

Also
$$\frac{g}{g} = \frac{r}{g_c}$$

6. **Pressure:** It is defined as force per unit area. Its units are Newton per square meter (N/m²). This unit is also called as *Pascal* (P_a).

$$\therefore \quad P_a = \frac{N}{m^2} \text{ or } 1 \text{ Pascal} = \frac{1 \text{ Newton}}{1 \text{ meter}^2} \quad \ldots (1.5)$$

Pascal is a small unit and kilo pascal (1 kN/m²) and Megapascal (1 MN/m² = 10⁶ N/m²) may be used.

Also $\quad 1 \text{ MN/m}^2 = 1 \text{ N/mm}^2$

Most common unit of pressure is 1 bar which is equal to 10^5 P_a.

$$\therefore \quad 1 \text{ bar} = 10^5 \text{ N/m}^2 = 10^5 P_a = 100 \text{ kP}_a \quad \ldots (1.6)$$

The pressure exerted by the atmosphere is known as atmospheric pressure and is denoted by 1 atm. In various units the values of 1 atmospheric pressure are given below :

$$1 \text{ atm} = 760 \text{ mm. of Hg} = 10.33 \text{ meter of } H_2O = 101325 \text{ N/m}^2$$

= 1.01325 bar = 1.033 kgf/cm² ... (1.7)

Another useful unit of pressure is,

1 tor = 1 mm of Hg = 133.32 N/m² = 133.32 Pa ... (1.8)

1.5 WAYS OF PRESSURE MEASUREMENT

Pressure and its Measurements:

Pressure is the force exerted by a fluid on unit area. In thermodynamics, pressure is measured in kgf/cm² in MKS and N/m² in S.I. system.

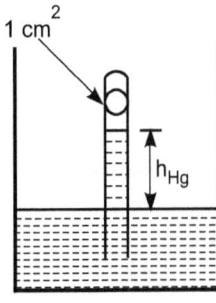

Fig. 1.7

(a) Atmospheric Pressure : The atmosphere, surrounding the earth, exerts a pressure on its surface equal to the weight of air over a unit surface area of the earth. This pressure of the atmosphere is measured with the help of barometer. The height of the mercury in the barometer at sea level and 0°C is equivalent to 760 mm of Hg. This pressure is known as physical or barometric atmospheric pressure(atm).

The average or standard pressure of the atmosphere on earth's surface is equivalent to the pressure exerted by a mercury column of 76 cm.

Considering the barometric tube of 1 m² cross-sectional area as shown in Fig. 1.7, the pressure exerted by the mercury column

$$= \text{Area} \times h_{Hg} \times \text{Weight of mercury per cm}^3$$

$$= 1 \times \frac{76}{100} \times 13600 \times 9.81 \text{ as } h_{Hg} = 76 \text{ cm at standard}$$

condition and ρ (density of mercury is 13600 kg/m³)

$$= 1.01325 \times 10^5 \text{ N/m}^2$$

∴ 1 atm = 1.01325×10^5 N/m² = 101.325 kN/m²

This is also known as physical atmosphere.

The height of the mercury column (h_{Hg}) varies with the attitude above or below sea level. This also changes with the change in atmospheric temperatures.

1 bar pressure is defined as equivalent to 10^5 N/m² = 10^5 Pascals as 1 Pascal = 1 N/m².

∴ 1 atm = 1.01325×10^5 N/m² = 1.01325 bar

(b) Vacuum : When the pressure exerted by the working substance in a vessel is less than atmospheric pressure, then it is said that vacuum exists in the vessel. The instrument used for measuring the pressure in the vessel below atmosphere is known as vacuum gauge. A vessel having no pressure within it is said to be under perfect vacuum.

(c) Gauge Pressure:

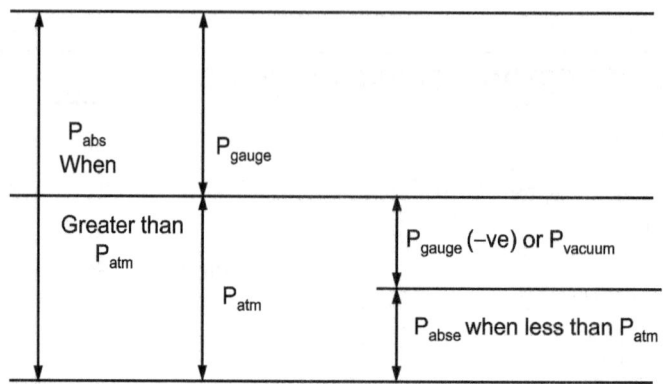

Fig. 1.8: Relation between absolute and gauge pressure

The pressure of atmosphere acts both on the container and the gauge which measures pressure inside the container.

The gauge thus measures pressure on and above atmospheric pressure.

If we wish to find the real pressure or absolute pressure we have to add the atmospheric pressure to the gauge pressure.

This can be written as

$$\text{Absolute Pressure} = \text{Atmospheric Pressure} \pm \text{Gauge Pressure}$$

or

$$P_{abs} = P_{atm} \pm P_{gauge} \quad \ldots (1.9)$$

The negative sign is used when the absolute pressure is less than the atmospheric pressure. Fig. 1.8 gives an idea of this relation.

1.5.1 Devices for Measurement of Pressure

Pressure is measured by means of instruments known as pressure gauges. A gauge used for measuring the pressure above atmosphere is known as pressure gauge. A gauge used for measuring the pressure below the atmospheric pressure is known as vacuum gauge.

(a) Manometer :

A manometer is a U-tube filled with mercury, water or some suitable liquid and is used for measuring pressures, above or below atmosphere. When the pressure is considerably large (say 10-30 cm of Hg), mercury is used in the manometer. If the pressure is low (1-2 cm Hg) water is used in the manometer to improve the accuracy of measurement.

The Fig. 1.9 shows the use of manometer to measure pressure above or below atmospheric pressures.

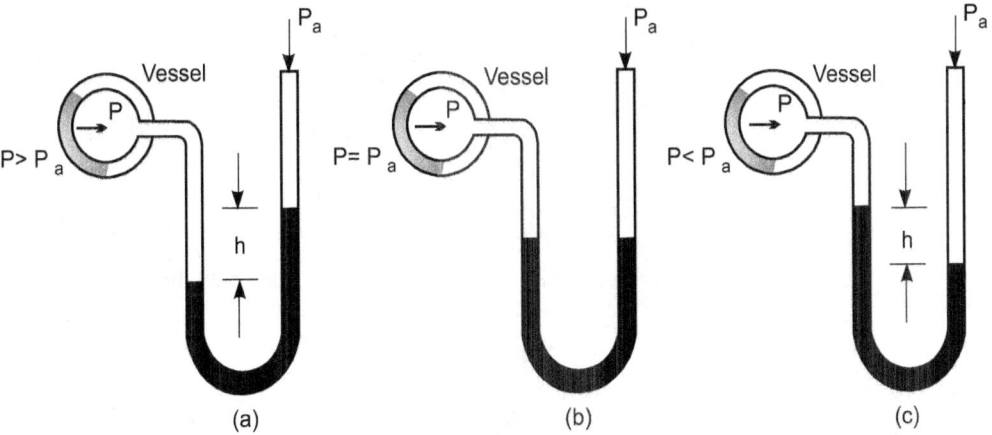

Fig. 1.9: U-tube manometer

When the pressure in the vessel is above atmospheric pressure as shown in Fig. 1.9 (b), the pressure above atmosphere is equivalent to h cm of Hg. When the pressure in the vessel is below atmospheric pressure as shown in Fig. 1.9 (c), the pressure below atmosphere is equivalent to h cm of Hg.

The actual pressure in the vessel is given by,

$$P_{actual} = P_a \pm \text{pressure due to h cm of Hg} \qquad \ldots (1.10)$$

positive sign is used when the pressure is above atmosphere and negative sign is used when the pressure is below atmosphere. The unit of pressure in S.I. units is Pascal (N/m²) which is very small. Instead of this, the common units such as bar, kPa or MPa are used.

∴ 1 bar = 10^5 Pa

100 kPa = 0.1 MPa

(b) Pressure Gauge :

Whenever the pressure is considerably high (2 bar and above), the instrument used for measuring the pressure is known as pressure gauge.

The pressure of steam in a boiler or the pressure of air coming out of a compressor is measured with the help of pressure gauge. The pressure gauge indicates the difference between the pressure inside the vessel (boiler, or receiver) and the pressure of the atmosphere. The pressure measured by the pressure gauge is known as gauge pressure. The absolute pressure is calculated by adding the atmospheric pressure to the gauge reading.

∴ $P_{absolute} = P_{gauge} + P_{atmosphere}$

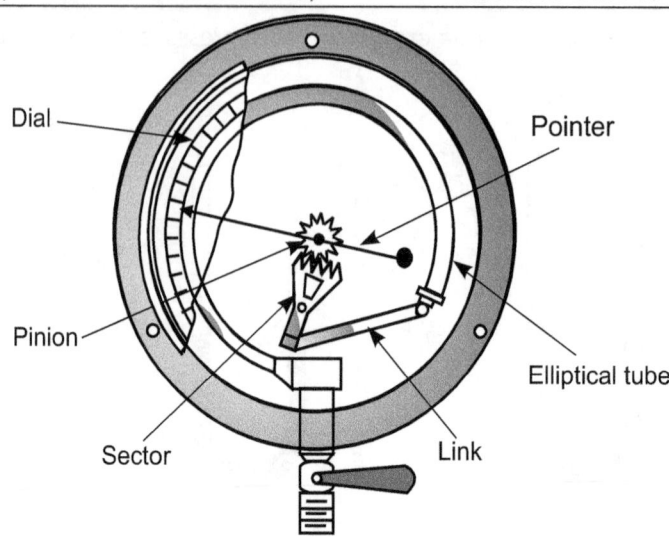

Fig. 1.10: Bourdon pressure gauge

The common type of pressure gauge used is Bourdon type pressure gauge which is shown in Fig. 1.10. The working of the gauge is rather simple. As the pressure inside the tube increases, the tube tends to straighten and causes the rotation of the indicator through the sector gear and the pinion.

In S.I. system, the unit of pressure is N/m^2 or kN/m^2. The pressure of N/m^2 is also known as pascal. The larger unit used is bar which is equivalent to 10^5 N/m^2 very nearly equal to atmospheric pressure.

1.6 TEMPERAURE

Temperature:

Temperature is a property of the system or of a body which distinguishes a hot body from a cold body. A hot body A is said to have a higher temperature than a cold body B. Thus the temperature is a thermal state of a body. The temperature of a body is proportional to the stored molecular energy i.e. the average molecular kinetic energy of the molecules in a system. A particular molecule does not have a temperature. It has energy. The gas as a system has temperature.

1.6.1 Zeroth Law of Thermodynamics

When a body is brought into contact with another body which is at a different temperature, heat is transferred from the body at higher temperature to the body at lower temperature until both bodies attain the same temperature (Fig. 1.11). At that instant (point), the heat transfer stops, and the two bodies are said to have reached **thermal equilibrium**. *The equality of temperature is the only requirement for thermal equilibrium.*

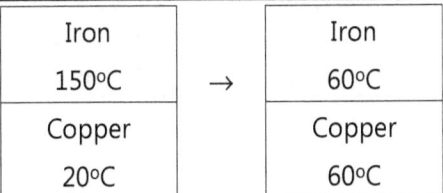

Fig. 1.11: Two bodies reaching thermal equilibrium after being brought into contact

The two bodies are said to be in thermal equilibrium if they attain same (equal) temperature.

Zeroth Law of Thermodynamics:

When a body 'A' is in thermal equilibrium with a body 'B' and also body 'A' is in thermal equilibrium with body 'C' separately, then bodies B and C will be in thermal equilibrium with each other. (Fig. 1.12).

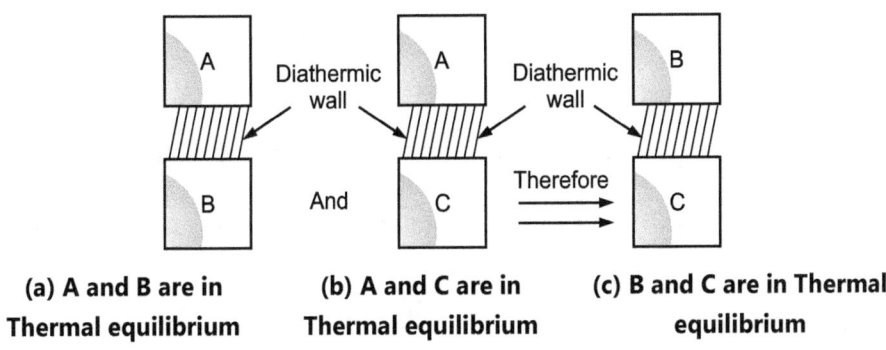

(a) A and B are in Thermal equilibrium
(b) A and C are in Thermal equilibrium
(c) B and C are in Thermal equilibrium

Fig. 1.12: Zeroth law of thermodynamics

Diathermic wall is one which allows heat transfer in both directions, but impermeable to electrical, magnetic and other types of work interactions and isolated from the surroundings. In general, energy exchange occurs as heat between them.

Zeroth law of thermodynamics is the base for temperature measurement.

1.6.2 Thermometers

There are many measurable physical properties that vary as the temperature of a body changes. Any of these properties, which is named as thermometric property, can be used to construct a thermometer.

For Problem, a very common thermometer consists of a small amount of mercury in an evacuated capillary tube. The change in the length of mercury column is used to indicate the change in temperature. The thermometric property used here is length. Other thermometric properties used, alongwith the type of thermometer they suggest, are given as follows.

Thermometer	Thermometric Substance	Thermometric property
1. Constant Volume gas thermomter	Gas	Pressure
2. Constant Pressure gas thermometer	Gas	Volume
3. Electrical Resistance thermometer	Wire	Resistance
4. Thermocouple	Wire	Electrical potential
5. Optical thermometer	Wire	Brightness
6. Mercury in Glass Thermometer	Mercury	Length

1.6.3 The Principle of Measurement

Let x be the value of any thermometric property as given in above table and θ be the temperature corresponding to x.

The value of temperature is proportional to the values of thermometric properties and we have

$$\theta_1 = ax_1$$

and $\theta_2 = ax_2$ ... where a is a constant of proportionality

Dividing we get $\dfrac{\theta_1}{\theta_2} = \dfrac{x_1}{x_2}$ or the ratio of temperatures is equal to the ratio of the values of the properties such as volumes, pressures, resistances etc.

To construct a scale we need a reference point. The international reference point is taken as a tripple point of water which is a temperature at which all the three phases of water i.e. liquid, ice and vapour exist in equilibrium. This point has been given an arbitrary value of 273.16 K where K stands for "degrees Kelvin". The pressure at this point is 0.006108 bar. The equation now becomes,

$$273.16 = ax_t$$

where x_t is the value of property at t = 273.16 K i.e. temperature of tripple point. If θ is any temperature and x is value of property at that temperature, we have,

$$\theta = ax = \dfrac{273.16}{x_t} \cdot x$$

$$\theta = 273.16 \dfrac{x}{x_t} \qquad \ldots (1.11)$$

Thus for any given value of 'x', the temperature θ can be found out. The tripple point of water is known as standard fixed point of thermometry. It is universal constant like a gas constant. With equation (1.11) we can construct a scale and calibrate it to give us direct temperature reading for change in the value of thermometric property x.

1.6.4 Constant Volume Gas Thermometer

It consists of a small bulb A in which a small amount of gas is collected. It is connected to a manometer C with the help of a capillary tube B. The two legs of manometer are connected by a flexible tube D.

The other leg of the mercury manometer is open to the atmosphere and can be moved vertically to adjust the mercury level, so that mercury just touches lip P of the capillary. This adjustment is carried out for each measurement, to ensure that volume of gas remains constant. As volume of gas is constant, change in temperature of gas is proportional to the change in pressure of the gas.

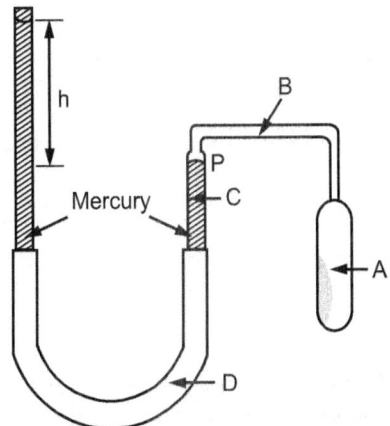

Fig. 1.13 : Constant volume gas thermometer

The change in pressure of the gas is measured by manometer which indicates change in temperature.

1.6.5 Scale of Temperature

To measure inequality of temperature, the thermometers are used. To construct a thermometer, two arbitrary reference points are chosen. They are known as fixed points or reference points. They are so chosen that they are easily reproducible.

For Problem, to construct a mercury–in–glass thermometer, a mixture of ice and water at a pressure of one atmosphere is taken. This system is known as ice point and denoted by θ_{ice}. To get another point, a system of water boiling at a pressure of one atmosphere is taken. This is known as steam point and denoted by θ_{steam}.

When mercury–in–glass thermometer comes in contact with θ_{ice}, the position of mercury column is noted and marked by a scratch on the glass. Similarly the position of mercury column is marked when the thermometer is kept in contact with θ_{steam}.

(a) Celsius Scale

When θ_{ice} is marked as zero and θ_{steam} is marked as 100 with 100 equal subdivisions, we get a Celsius scale. One division on this scale is known as one degree Celsius or one degree Kelvin and is denoted by 0°C or K.

(b) Fahrenheit Scale:

If ice point is given value as 32 and steam point as 212 with 180 equal subdivisions, we get a Fahrenheit scale. One division for this scale is known as one degree Fahrenheit or one degree Rankine and is denoted by °F or R.

The relation between Celsius and Fahrenheit scales is

$$t_c = \frac{5}{9}(t_f - 32) \quad \text{or} \quad t_f = \frac{9}{5} t_c + 32$$

The fraction $\frac{9}{5}$ is $\frac{180}{100}$. Thus if Celsius scale shows 60°, then the corresponding value on Fahrenheit scales will be

$$= \frac{9}{5} \times 60 + 32 = 140°F$$

Extrapolation:

The scale so far is defined between ice point and steam point. The graduation of scale, however, can be extended below ice point and above steam point. This is known as extrapolation. Thus, if mercury rises 40 divisions above steam point on Celsius thermometer, its temperature would be 140°C.

Mercury freezes at $-38.9°C$ and therefore another liquids e.g. alcohol is used to measure low temperature. Alcohol thermometer can be used upto $-110°C$. At high temperatures, glass is not suitable. So electric resistance thermometer is used. It can measure the temperature upto 1000°C.

Difficulty in Using Different Thermometers:

Two different thermometers show different readings when used to measure the temperature of the same system; even though they are graduated by using same fixed reference points. Thus, if a mercury thermometer shows a temperature of 60°C of a certain system, the alcohol thermometer may show the reading of 59.5°C when used for the same system. But both the thermometers will agree at ice and steam points. As the liquid in the thermometer, material of the thermometer, values of fixed points, number of graduations etc. are chosen arbitrarily, it is difficult to say which thermometer is correct and which is wrong. So one thermometer should be decided as correct and used as a standard.

(c) International Practical Temperature Scale (IPTS–68)

To decide the standard of measurement, so that everyone should use the same standard, International Temperature Scale was adopted in 1927 by the Seventh General Conference on

Weights and Measures. This was revised in 1948, 1960 and 1968. It is now known as International Practical Temperature Scale (IPTS – 68).

The IPTS – 68 gives:

(a) The values of temperatures of easily reproducible equilibrium states or fixed points such as boiling points, melting points or triple points of some pure substances.

(b) The standard type of thermometers to be used in between these fixed points.

(c) The formulae to be used to interpolate the temperatures between these fixed points.

The following table gives a list of such fixed points.

No.	Fixed points	Temperature in °C
1	Triple point of hydrogen	– 259.34
2	Boiling point of neon	–246.048
3	Triple point of oxygen	–218.789
4	Triple point of water	0.01
5	Boiling point of water	100
6	Melting point of zinc	419.58
7	Melting point of silver	969.93
8	Melting point of gold	1064.43

The standard instruments used are as follows :

1. From 13.81 K to 630.74°C   – Platinum resistance thermometer
2. From 630.74°C to 1064.43°C   – Thermocouple of Platinum and alloy of platinum – rhodium (90–10)
3. Above 1064.43°C   – Temperatures are calculated by Planck's Law of radiation.

1.6.6 Celsius, Rankine and Fahrenheit Scales

(a) Celsius Scale :

The *Celsius temperature scale* (also called the centigrade scale) uses the unit degree Celsius (°C), which has the same magnitude as the Kelvin. Thus, temperature *differences* are identical on both sales. However, the zero point on the Celsius scale is shifted to 273.15 K, as shown by the following relationship between the Celsius temperature and the Kelvin temperature.

$$T\ (°C) = T\ (K) - 273.15 \qquad \ldots (1.12)$$

From this it can be seen that on the Celsius scale the triple point of water is 0.01°C and that 0 K corresponds to – 273.15°C.

The Celsius scale is defined so that the temperature at the *ice point*, 273.15 K, is 0.00°C, and the temperature at the *steam point*, 373.15 K, is 100.00°C. Accordingly, there are 100 Celsius degrees in this interval of 100 kelvins, a correspondence that is contrived through the selection of 273.16 K as the triple point temperature.

Observe that since the temperatures at the ice and steam points are experimental values subject to revisions in light of more precise determinations, the only Celsius temperature that is fixed *by definition* is that at the triple point of water.

(b) Rankine scale:

Two other temperature scales are in common use in engineering in the United States. By definition, the *Rankine scale*, the unit of which is the degree Rankine (°R), is proportional to the Kelvin temperature according to

$$T (°R) = 1.8\, T (K) \qquad (1.13)$$

As evidenced by equation (1.11), the Rankine scale is also an absolute thermodynamic scale with an absolute zero that coincides with the absolute zero of the Kelvin scale. In thermodynamic relationships, temperature is always in terms of the Kelvin of Rankine scale unless specifically stated otherwise.

(c) Fahrenheit scale :

A degree of the same size as that on the Rankine scale is used in the *Fahrenheit scale*, but the zero point is shifted according to the relation

$$T (°F) = T (°R) - 459.67 \qquad \ldots (1.14)$$

Substituting equations (1.12) and (1.13) into equation (1.14), it follows that

$$T (°F) = 1.8\, T (°C) + 32 \qquad \ldots (1.15)$$

This equation shows that the Fahrenheit temperature of the ice point (0°C) is 32°F and that of the steam point (100°C) is 212°F. The 100 Celsius of Kelvin degrees between the ice point and steam point correspond to 180 Fahrenheit or Rankine degrees, as shown in Fig. 1.14, where the Kelvin, Celsius, Rankine and Fahrenheit scales are compared.

When making engineering calculations, it is common to round off the last numbers in equations (1.12) and (1.14) to 273 and 460, respectively. This is frequently done in subsequent sections of the text.

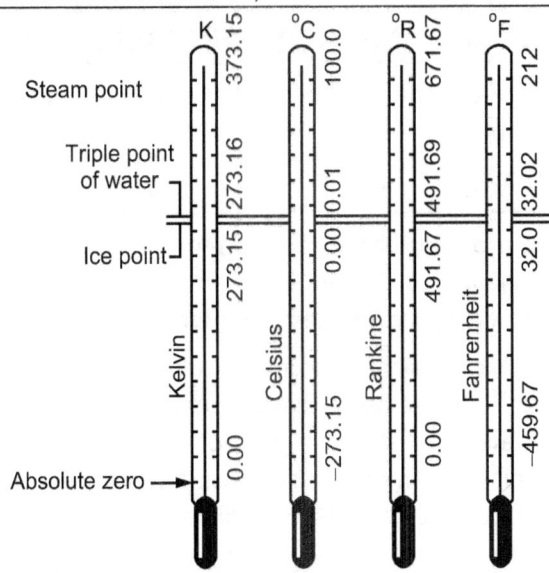

Fig. 1.14: Comparison of temperature scales

Summary of Temperature Scales

No.	Name of the scale	Remarks
1.	Celsius Temperature Scale	These scales are used for day to day ordinary temperature measurements. These scales take ice point and steam point as reference points. The readings depend upon the nature of working substance.
2.	Fahrenheit Temperature Scale	— " —
3.	International Practical Temperature Scale	This scale gives different standard reference points. It also gives the type of thermometer to be used for different ranges and gives formula to be used for these thermometers. This scale is also dependent on the nature of working substance.
4.	Thermodynamic Temperature Scale or Kelvin Temperature Scale or Absolute Temperature Scale.	This scale is independent of the nature of the working substance. It is based on efficiency expression of Carnot Engine viz. $$\frac{Q_H}{Q_L} = \frac{T_H}{T_L}$$
5.	Ideal gas Temperature Scale	This scale is given by gas thermometers. It is numerically identical with Thermodynamic Temperature Scale.

1.7 MACROSCOPIC AND MICROSCOPIC VIEWS

There are two points of view from which the behaviour of matter can be studied: the macroscopic and microscopic.

1.7.1 Macroscopic View

In this analysis, the system or equipment is considered as a whole. It considers the whole effect of matter without taking into account the events occurring at the molecular level. The branch which takes this view is termed as classical thermodynamics.

Macroscopic thermodynamics is only concerned with the effects of the action of many molecules and these effects can be perceived by human senses. For Problem, Macroscopic quantity, pressure is the average rate of change of momentum due to all the molecular collisions occurring per unit area. The effect of pressure can be felt. Similarly, temperature of a gas is due to average value of translational kinetic energies of millions of individual molecules. This can also be sensed.

1.7.2 Microscopic View

From the microscopic point of view, matter is composed of myriads of molecules. If it is a gas, each molecule at a given instant has a certain position, velocity and energy and for each molecule, these change vary frequently as a result of collisions. The behaviour of the gas molecule is described by summing up the behaviour of each molecule. Such a study is made in microscopic or statistical thermodynamics.

To find the behaviour of a system, statistical methods are used. The properties like velocity, momentum, kinetic energy which describe the molecule cannot be easily measured with required accuracy. They cannot be felt by our senses. The analysis of behaviour of a system is same by both the methods and the results are also compatible. Only macroscopic study i.e. classical approach to thermodynamics is adopted in this book.

1.8 TERMODYNAMIC EQUILIBRIUM

- Thermodynamics deals with equilibrium states.
- Equilibrium means state of balance.
- Therefore, in an equilibrium state, there is no unbalanced potential (or driving force) within the system or between system and surroundings).
- A system which is in thermodynamic equilibrium, does not undergo any spontaneous change.

When a system is isolated from its surroundings, it reaches a state of thermodynamic equilibrium. The system is said to be in **thermodynamic equilibrium** state if it is in mechanical, chemical and thermal equilibrium.

Mechanical Equilibrium: In the absence of any unbalanced force within the system itself and also between the system and surroundings, the system is said to be in **mechanical equilibrium**.

Chemical Equilibrium: If there is no spontaneous chemical reaction or transfer of matter from one part of the system to another, such as diffusion, then the system is said to be in **chemical equilibrium**.

Thermal Equilibrium: When a system existing in chemical and mechanical equilibrium is separated from its surrounding by a diathermic wall (**diathermic wall** means which allows heat to flow) and if there is no spontaneous change in any property of the system, the system is said to be in a state of **thermal equilibrium**. Such a system exists with equality of temperature.

1.9 THERMODYNAMIC SYSTEM DESCRIPTION

1.9.1 Properties

Any measurable characteristic of a system is called a property. Some familiar Problems are pressure P, temperature T, volume V, and mass m. Other properties are viscosity, thermal conductivity, modulus of elasticity, electric resistivity and even velocity and elevation.

Not all properties are independent, however, some are defined in terms of other ones. For Problem, density is defined as mass per unit volume.

$$\rho = \frac{m}{V} \ (kg/m^3)$$

Properties are considered to be either intensive or extensive.

Intensive and Extensive Properties:

Intensive properties are those which are independent of the mass (size) of a system. For Problem, temperature, pressure and density.

Extensive properties vary directly with mass (or size) of the system. For Problem, mass, volume, and total energy.

An easy way to determine whether a property is intensive or extensive is to divide the system into two equal parts as shown in Fig. 1.15.

Each part will have the same value of intensive properties as the original system, but extensive properties are half the original.

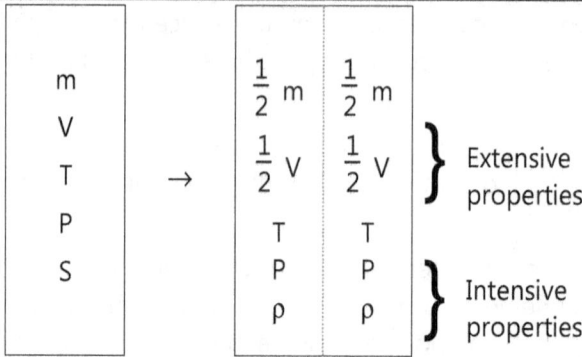

Fig. 1.15: Extensive and intensive properties

1.9.2 State

It is the condition of a system. This condition or state of a system is described by the thermodynamic properties, such as pressure, temperature and volume.

The state of a pure substance can be defined by any two independent properties.

Thermodynamics deals with equilibrium states. The word equilibrium implies a state of balance. In an equilibrium state, there are no unbalanced potentials (or driving forces) within the system. A system which is in equilibrium, experiences no spontaneous changes.

1.9.3 Processes

Any change that a system undergoes from one equilibrium state to another is called a **process** and the series of states through which a system passes during a process is called the path of the process. (Fig. 1.16). To describe a process completely, one should specify the initial and final states of the process, as well as the path it follows and the interactions with the surroundings. The system changes its state from one state to another, by energy transfer across the boundaries.

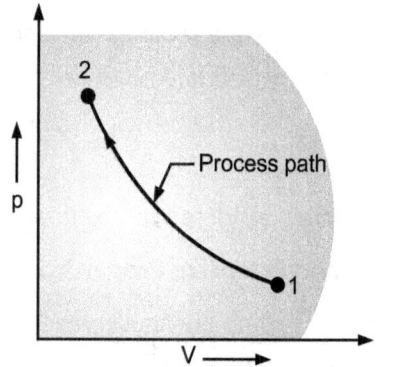

Fig. 1.16: Process between states 1 and 2

The values of the properties at the beginning and at the end of a process are different.

If the value of one of the properties is kept constant, the process is known by the property which is kept constant.

The various processes are as listed below:

(a) **Constant pressure or Isobaric process:** The pressure is maintained constant during the process.

(b) **Constant volume or Isochoric process:** The volume is kept constant during the process.

(c) **Constant temperature or Isothermal process:** Temperature is kept constant during the process.

(d) **Constant entropy or Isentropic process:** The entropy remains constant during the process. This is also known as reversible adiabatic process.

1.9.4 Cycle or Cyclic Process

A **thermodynamic cycle** or simply cycle is defined as a series of state changes such that the final state is identical with the initial state. It can also be defined as if the number of processes in sequence bring the system back to its initial state, then the system is said to execute a cycle or cyclic process.

The cyclic process plays an important role in the study of thermodynamics. Because, a net effect of a cyclic process may be conversion of heat into work or maintaining a system at lower temperature than surroundings (refrigerator) by means of work input.

Cyclic processes are classified as closed cycles or open cycles. In **closed cyclic** process, the same working substance is used again and again and only heat and work transfer take place between system and surroundings. The steam power plant and refrigeration system work on a closed cycle. In an **open cycle**, the working fluid once used during the cyclic process is thrown out and new mass of working fluid is taken in during the next cyclic process. Internal combustion engines and gas turbines work on an open cycle.

Different ideal closed cyclic processes are shown in Fig. 1.17.

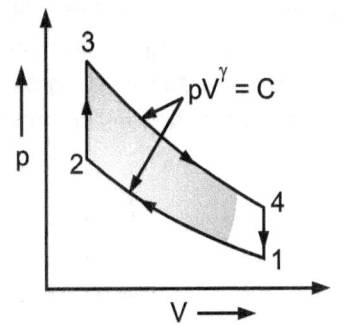
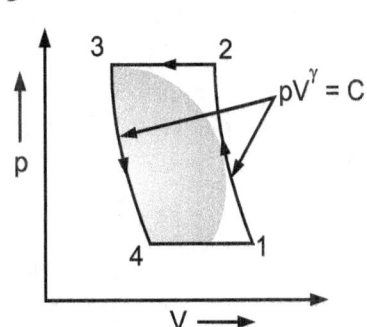

(a) Otto cycle (power generation)　　(b) Reversed Joule cycle (Refrigeration)

Fig. 1.17: Otto and Joule cycles

The cyclic process shown in Fig. 1.17 (a) is used for power generation and Fig. 1.17 (b) shows a refrigeration cycle.

1.9.5 Reversible, Quasistatic and Irreversible Process

When a process proceeds in such a manner that the system remains infinitesimally close to an equilibrium state at all times, it is called a quasi - static or quasi - equilibrium process.

Quasi means **'almost'. Infinite slowness** (dead slow) is the characteristic feature of a quasi - static process.

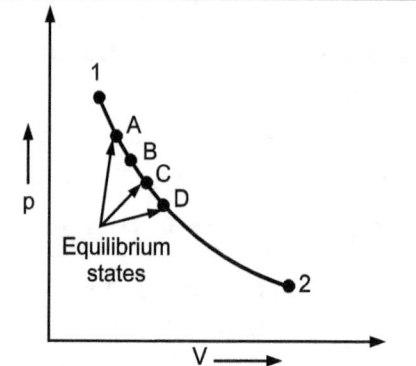

Fig. 1.18: Quasi-static process

Consider a process wherein the involved energy transfers are extremely small, i.e. infinitesimal in magnitude (Refer Fig. 1.18). Starting from state 1, a new equilibrium state 'A' very close to state 1 will be reached due to a very small energy exchange. If any process consists of such a large number of equilibrium states, say A, B, C, D .... as in the figure, it may be represented by a continuous curve joining states 1 to 2. Such a process should occur extremely slowly, through a succession of equilibrium states. It is therefore, called a **quasi-static process**. All the states in quasi-static process are equilibrium states. If the process is carried out in the reverse direction, it should reach the same equilibrium states at the same time by evolving the same amount of energy exchange. Therefore, *quasi-static* process is a *reversible process*.

A process which is not a quasi-static process, is known as an **irreversible process**. For an irreversible process, only end states are in equilibrium state. The other states are non-equilibrium states. The values of properties at intermediate non-equilibrium states are not known. Therefore, irreversible process cannot be shown on thermodynamic plane. (P - V plane, P - T plane etc.). Therefore, it is shown as a dotted curve on thermodynamic plane. (See Fig. 1.19).

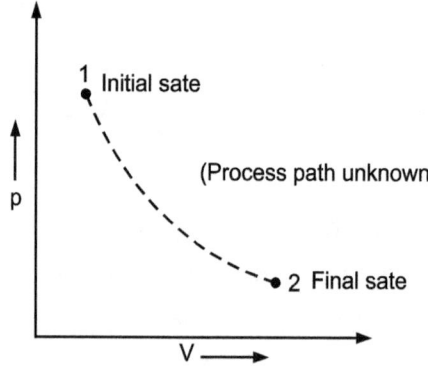

Fig. 1.19: Irreversible process

1.9.6 Point Function

Any point on x - y plane can be defined by x and y co-ordinates. Similarly, thermodynamic planes (such as P - V, P - T and T - s) can be formed by any two variables. On such planes, any two properties are sufficient to define a state.

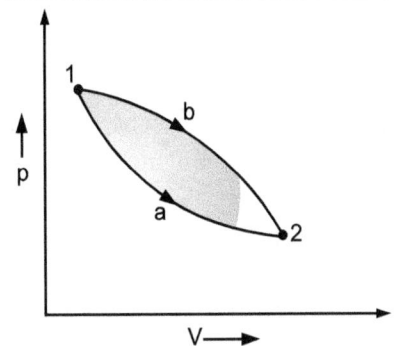

Fig. 1.20: Point function

Consider a P - V plane as shown in Fig. 1.20 and any point 1 defined by the pressure P_1 and volume V_1. Also, let P_2 and V_2 define a state point 2 on P - V diagram. The state point 2 is reached from state point 1 by two ways: (i) through 1 - a - 2 and (ii) through 1 - b - 2. It is clear that the values of P_2 and V_2 are same at the end of two processes. Therefore, the change in the values of pressure P and volume V are not dependent on the path followed but only dependent on end state.

Two properties define a state. Therefore, all the properties are state or point functions. The characteristics such as pressure, temperature, volume, internal energy and entropy are state functions and are properties of a system. The property which is not a state or point function, then it is not a property. Problems are heat, work, etc.

Let ϕ is any property and $d\phi$ is its differential. As property is a point function, we can write $\int_{1}^{2} d\phi = \phi_2 - \phi_1$. This change depends only on end states. Therefore, $d\phi$ is an **exact differential**.

A characteristic of a system which has an exact differential is a property of the system and otherwise it is a non-property.

Therefore, we can have the following points: (i) A property is defined by a point on any thermodynamic plane. (ii) The change in thermodynamic property depends on only end states and not on the path. (iii) The properties are exact differentials.

1.9.7 Path Function

Heat and work are path functions.

The amount of heat transferred when a system changes from a state 1 to state 2 depends on the intermediate states through which the system passes i.e. its path. Therefore, dQ is an inexact differential.

$$\int_1^2 dQ = Q_{1-2} \text{ i.e. } \int_1^2 dQ \neq Q_2 - Q_1$$

Heat is represented by an area under the curve on Temperature-entropy (or T – s) diagram. T - s diagrams for three-processes are illustrated in Fig. 1.21.

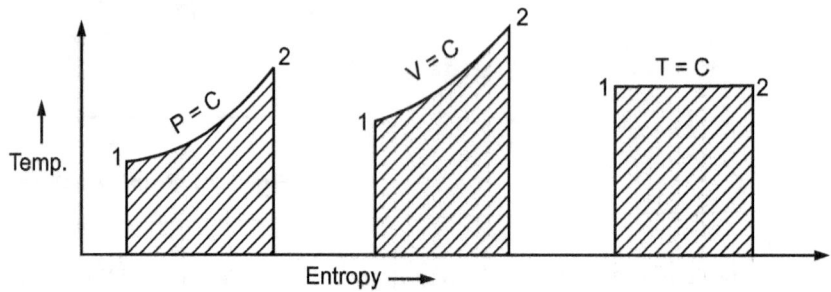

Fig. 1.21: Heat transfer depends on path. Q_{1-2} is different for different paths

Work is represented by an area under the pressure - volume (or P - V) diagram. Therefore, work cannot be represented by a point on P - V plot.

The P - V diagrams for three processes are illustrated in Fig. 1.22.

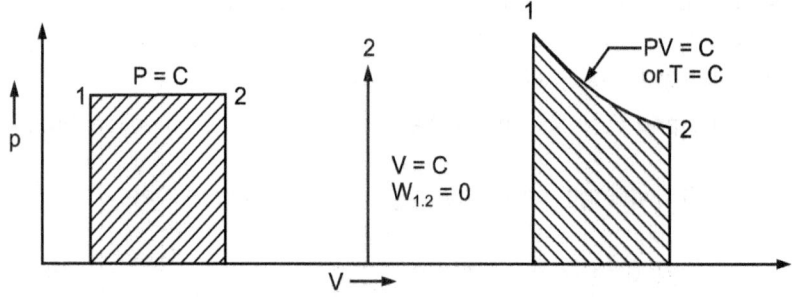

Fig. 1.22: Work depends on path. Its value is different for different paths

$$\int_1^2 dW \neq W_2 - W_1 \text{ or } \int_1^2 dW = W_{1-2}$$

A little consideration shows that, the quantities heat and work are different for different processes. Hence heat and work are path functions. Their differentials are **inexact** differentials.

1.10 ENERGY AND ITS FORMS

There are many forms of energy. Energy is realised when it is moving from one place to another or it may be stored in the system.

We will discuss the following forms of energy. Potential Energy, Kinetic Energy, Work Energy and Heat Energy.

1.10.1 Potential Energy (P.E.)

Potential energy of a system is energy stored in the system due to its position in the gravitational force field.

There should be a reference datum from which P.E. is measured. Let Z be the distance of mass m from the reference datum. Let force F acts on the mass m and raise the system through distance Z, then,

$$d(P.E.) = F\, dZ = mg\, dZ \qquad \ldots (1.16)$$

$$\int_1^2 d(P.E.) = \int_1^2 F\, dZ = m \int_1^2 g\, dZ \qquad \ldots (1.17)$$

The limits are from initial to final position. If distance from 1 to 2 is not great then g is constant. The equation becomes,

$$(P.E.)_2 - (P.E.)_1 = mg\,(Z_2 - Z_1) \text{ N.m. or joule} \qquad \ldots (1.18)$$

So potential energy increases as the height is increased.

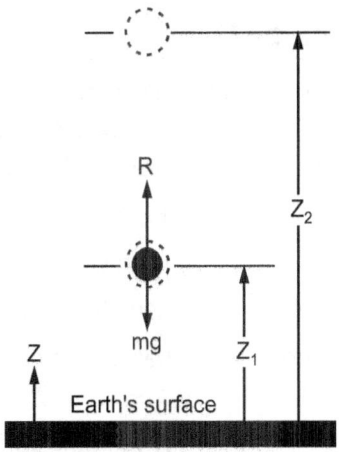

Fig. 1.23: Illustration used to introduce the potential energy concept

1.10.2 Kinetic Energy (K.E.)

It is related to the motion or horizontal motion where P.E. does not change. If mass m moves through distance dx, the work done is F dx and K.E. is defined as work done in moving the system.

$$\therefore \quad d(K.E.) = F\,dx$$

but $F\,dx = m.a.\,dx = m\dfrac{dC}{dt}\,dx$ where C is velocity and a is acceleration.

$$\therefore \quad F\,dx = m\,dC\,\dfrac{dx}{dt}$$

$$= m.C.dC \text{ as } \dfrac{dx}{dt} = C = \text{velocity}$$

$$d(K.E.) = F\,dx = mC\,dC$$

and $\displaystyle\int d(K.E.) = \int F\,dx$

$$= \int_{C_1}^{C_2} mC\,dC = \dfrac{m}{2}(C_2^2 - C_1^2) \text{ N-m or J}$$

$$\therefore \quad \text{Change in K.E.} = \dfrac{m}{2}(C_2^2 - C_1^2) \text{ N-m or J}$$

The kinetic energy of the fluid is zero when its velocity is zero.

1.10.3 Internal Energy (IE or U)

Internal energy is associated with the molecular structure of the substance. This is stored energy and it is stored in the molecular structure by five modes. Consider a simple diatomic molecule (molecule with 2 atoms). The modes are as follows. [See Fig. 1.24].

(1) Translational K.E. — due to motion of translation of molecules.

(2) Vibrational K.E. — due to vibratory motion of atoms.

(3) Rotational energy of 1st kind — when atoms rotate as a pair.

(4) Rotational energy of 2nd kind — when atoms rotate around their own centres of mass.

(5) Energy of attraction — between the adjacent molecules.

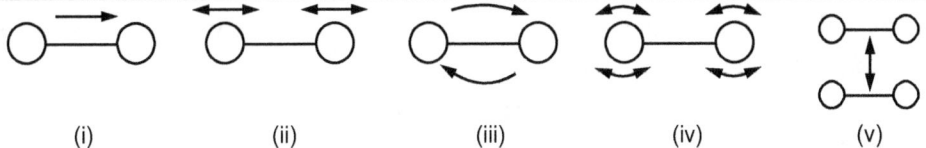

Fig. 1.24 : Modes of kinetic energy in diatomic molecule
(i) translation (ii) vibration (iii) and (iv) rotation (v) attraction

Some other energies like electron spin and electron attraction forces also contribute to internal energy.

The symbol for specific internal energy is 'u' and for total internal energy is U.

$$u = \text{Specific internal energy} = J/kg$$
$$U = m \times u = \text{Total internal energy} = J.$$

There is no absolute value of internal energy and we calculate the change in internal energy between two states of the system, or from a chosen reference point where the value of internal energy is assumed to be zero.

The various forms of energy are given in *Table 1.2*.

Table 1.2

	Form of Energy	Energy indicated by
1.	Potential energy	elevation
2.	Kinetic energy	velocity
3.	Internal energy	
	(a) kinetic	motion of molecules
	(b) rotational	rotation of molecules
	(c) vibrational	vibrations of molecules
	(d) attraction	attraction of molecules
4.	Heat	Heat flows from one place to another because of a temperature difference.
5.	Work	Change of system boundaries as a result of pressure difference or volume difference etc.

1.10.4 Heat

Heat is defined as the form of energy that is transferred across a boundary by virtue of temperature difference.

Heat is an interaction which may occur between two systems, when they are brought into communication.

The concept of heat is related with the temperature difference between the two systems or between the system and surroundings.

Heat is not stored in the system, it is the **energy in transit**. It is not a property of the system, and it is a path function. It is represented by an inexact differential $\int \delta Q = Q_{1-2}$.

Comments:

(1) Heat is not that which inevitably causes temperature rise. For Problem, boiling of water at 100°C to convert into steam.

(2) Heat is not that which is always present when temperature rise occurs. For Problem, (a) A compression of gas in an adiabatically insulated cylinder, (b) Conversion of water into vapour at 100°C.

Heat should not be confused with temperature.

Sign Convention for Heat:

The heat supplied to a system is considered as positive while the heat rejected by the system is considered as negative.

1.10.5 Work

In mechanics, work is defined as the product of force and distance, while the direction of application of force on the body is in the direction of motion.

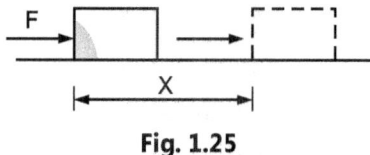

Fig. 1.25

$W = F \cdot X$ (Nm), where F = force, N; X = distance in metres.

Work is one of the basic modes of energy transfer. In thermodynamics, work transfer occurs between the system and surroundings. **Work is said to be done by a system, if the sole effect external to the system can be reduced to the raising of a weight.**

Thus in thermodynamics,

(i) Work is either done on a system or it is done by the system.

(ii) The weight may not be raised actually, but the net effect of work can be converted to raise the weight.

Let us consider an Problem of a battery driving a motor (Fig. 1.26). The motor is driving a fan. If we limit the system boundary for battery and motor as shown, then work is done by the system (battery and motor) on the surroundings (fan). It means work crosses the boundary.

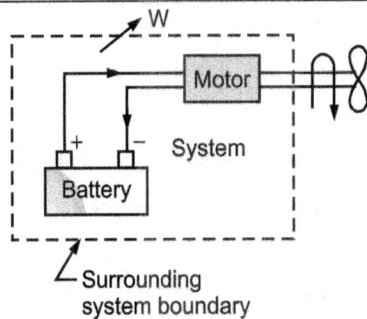

Fig. 1.26: Battery - motor system driving a fan

Now, replace a fan with a pulley and weight as shown in Fig. 1.27.

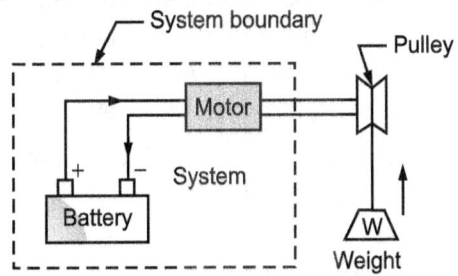

Fig. 1.27: Work transfer from a system

The weight may be raised with the pulley and motor. It means total effect external to the system is to raise the load.

If work is done by a system, then it is considered as positive and when work is done on a system, it is taken as negative (Fig. 1.28).

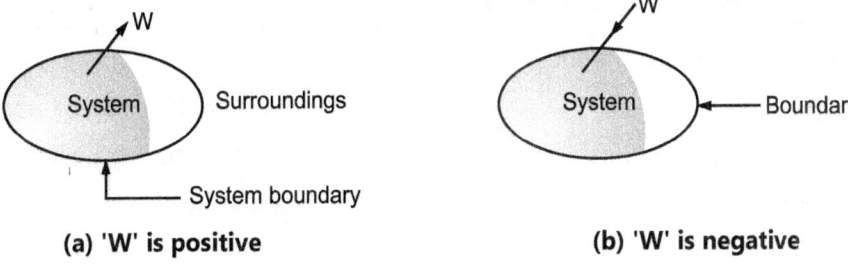

(a) 'W' is positive

(b) 'W' is negative

Fig. 1.28: Sign conventions for work

Comments:

- Work is energy in transit. It appears only when it crosses the boundary.
- It is a path function and not a property of the system.
- The work is an inexact differential i.e. $\int dW \neq W_2 - W_1$.

(a) Similarities Between Heat and Work

- Both are boundary phenomena and in both cases energy should cross the system boundary.
- Both are transient phenomena and exist whenever a system executes a process.
- Both are path functions and therefore form the inexact differentials. Hence they are not thermodynamic properties.

(b) Difference between Heat and Work

- If a system is in a stable equilibrium state, then work interaction between the system and the surroundings cannot take place whereas there is no such restriction for the heat interaction. This is clear from the Problem of a gas contained in a rigid container at high pressure and temperature. The rigidity of the container provides an upper limit to the volume of the system. In this case, no work interaction will occur. But due to temperature difference between the system and surroundings, heat interaction occurs.
- For heat interaction between the system and the surroundings, the temperature potential difference should exist between them, but no temperature difference is required for work interaction.

(c) Sign Convention for Heat and Work

The heat supplied to a system is considered as positive while the heat rejected by the system is considered as negative.

The work done by a system is considered as positive while the work done on the system is considered as negative.

1.10.6 Different Forms of Work

(a) PdV work or displacement work.   (b) Shaft work
(c) Flow work   (d) Paddle wheel work or stirring work
(e) Electrical work   (f) Work done in stretching a wire
(g) Magnetization work   (h) Surface tension work
(i) Free expansion work

(a) PdV Work or displacement work:

Consider a cylinder and piston arrangement as shown in Fig. 1.29.

$\therefore \quad \delta W = $ Force × distance moved

$\therefore \quad \delta W = $ Pressure × area of piston × δx

$\qquad = P (A \cdot \delta x) = P dV$

Total work done for the expansion of system from state point 1 to state point 2 is

$$W = \int_1^2 PdV \qquad \ldots (1.19)$$

= Area under the curve

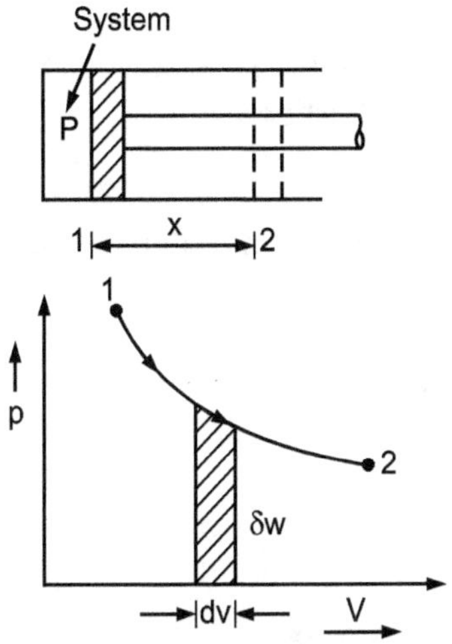

As the piston moves from position 1 to position 2, work is done by the system on the piston i.e. work is obtained from the system.

The work done by the system to move the piston through a small distance δx is say δW.

Fig. 1.29: P-v diagram

Thus we can say PdV work is a path function. The above equation (1.19) is valid only when:
- The piston has very slow movement so that change in pressure is uniform throughout, i.e. it must be a quasi-static process.
- It should be frictionless process.
- System is closed.
- The boundary of the system moves so that work can be transferred.

The above equation (1.2) can be solved if the exact relation between P and V is known and the process must be **non-flow process**.

(b) Shaft work:

A rotating shaft can raise a weight, if a pulley is fixed to its end. (See Fig. 1.30).

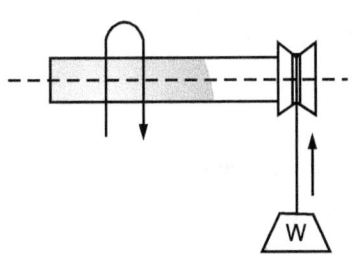

Fig. 1.30: Shaft work

The work done is given by

$$\delta W = T \delta \theta$$

where, T = torque, in N-m

$\delta \theta$ = angle of rotation.

If the shaft rotate at N-rpm, then rate of work (Power) is

$$= \frac{2 \pi NT}{60} \text{ N-m/s or watt}$$

(c) Flow work (Flow energy):

It is the energy associated with the flowing fluid. The flow work represents the amount of work that must be done to push a unit mass into or out of the system boundary.

Mathematically, work done per unit mass = p dv, Joule ... (1.20)

where p is the pressure, N/m², normal to the boundary, and v = specific volume of fluid, m³/kg which crosses the boundary. It is explained in detail in further text.

(d) Paddle wheel work or stirring work:

Consider a fluid (system) in a container alongwith a paddle wheel mounted at the end of a shaft and pulley and weight arrangement as shown in Fig. 1.31.

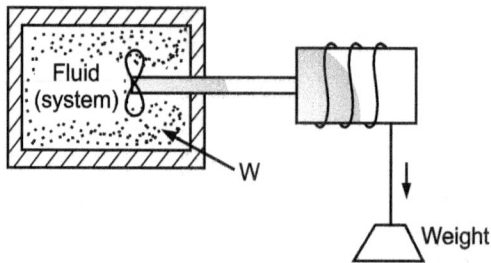

Fig. 1.31: Paddle wheel work

As the weight is lowered, the paddle wheel rotates, doing the work on the system. Due to this, temperature of the fluid increases and hence internal energy of the fluid increases.

Boundary of the system does not move, hence there is no change in the volume.

$$\therefore \quad \int p\,dv = 0 \text{ but } \delta W \neq 0$$

(e) Electrical work:

Consider a resistor as a system as shown in Fig. 1.32. As the current passes through the resistor, heat is generated. If the resistor is replaced by a motor, motor can drive a pulley and pulley can raise a weight.

The rate of work transfer = I · V ... (1.21)

where I = current in amperes, V = potential difference in volts.

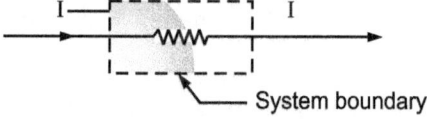

Fig. 1.32: Electrical work

(f) Work done in stretching a wire:

If L is the length of wire which is subjected to a tension 'T', it will change its length to L + dL, the small quantity of work done is

$$dW = -T \cdot dL$$

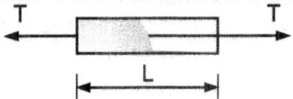

Fig. 1.33: Work doe in stretching a wire

Negative sign is due to the work done on the wire (system).

For a finite change of length from L_i to L_f

$$W_{i-f} = \int_{L_i}^{L_f} -T \cdot dL \qquad \ldots (1.22)$$

(g) Magnetization work:

The work done per unit volume on a magnetic material through which the magnetic and magnetization fields are uniform is

$$dW = -H \cdot dI$$

$$W_{1-2} = -\int_{I_1}^{I_2} H \cdot dI \qquad \ldots (1.23)$$

where H is field strength and I is the component of magnetization field in the direction of field. Negative sign is on account of work done on the system.

(h) Surface tension work:

The work done on the homogeneous liquid film in changing its surface area by an infinitesimal amount dA is

$$dW = \sigma \, dA \text{ Or } W_{1-2} = \int_{A_1}^{A_2} \sigma \cdot dA \qquad \ldots (1.24)$$

where σ is the surface tension in N/m.

(i) Free expansion work:

The expansion of gas against vacuum is called as free or unstrained expansion. The gas expands in a rigid vacuum container, hence no work is done and hence $dW = 0$ although $pdv \neq 0$.

Total Work done by a System:

Different forms of work transfer may occur simultaneously during a process. But the net or total work done by the system would be equal to the algebraic sum of these as given below:

$$W_{total} = W_{displacement} + W_{flow} + W_{electrical} + \ldots \qquad \ldots (1.25)$$

SOLVED PROBLEMS

Problem 1.1:

Convert the following readings of pressure in terms of kPa when the barometer reading is 76 cm of Hg.

(a) 80 cm of Hg, (b) 50 cm of Hg vacuum, (c) 1.5 m of H_2O and (d) 3.5 bar.

Take ρ_{Hg} = 13596 kg/m³ and g = 9.806.

Solution:

Pressure equivalent to 76 cm of Hg

$$= \rho g h$$

$$= 13596 \times 9.806 \times \frac{76}{100} = 101325 \text{ N/m}^2 = 101325 \text{ pa}$$

(a) 80 cm of Hg $= \frac{80}{76} \times \frac{101325}{1000}$ = **106.66 kPa** ... Ans.

(b) 50 cm of vacuum = 76 – 50 = 26 cm of Hg pressure

$$= \frac{26}{76} \times \frac{101325}{100} = \textbf{34.66 kPa} \quad \text{... Ans.}$$

(c) Pressure due to 1.5 m of water

$$= \rho g H = 1000 \times 9.806 \times 1.5 = 14709 \text{ Pa} \approx \textbf{14.71 kPa} \quad \text{... Ans.}$$

(d) 3.5 bar $= 3.5 \times 10^5$ Pa $= \frac{3.5 \times 10^5}{1000}$ = **350 kPa** ... Ans.

Note : 1 atm = 101325 N/m² = 1.01325 bar ... Ans.

Problem 1.2:

A pipe of 10 cm diameter is carrying a steam. The pressure of steam in the pipe is measured with the help of U-tube manometer containing mercury. The level of Hg in open arm is 10 cm above the level of arm connected to the pipe. Some of the steam in the pipe is condensed in the manometer arm connected to the pipe whose height is 4 cm. The barometer reads 75 cm of Hg. Find the absolute pressure of steam flowing through the pipe. Take ρ_{Hg} = 13600 kg/m³.

Solution

The configuration of the system is shown in Fig. 1.34.

Now balancing the pressure at the axis X-X, we can write,

$$P_{steam} + P_{condensed\ water} = P_{Hg} + P_{atm}$$

$$\therefore \quad P_{steam} + \rho_{H2O}\ g \cdot H_{H2O} = \rho_{Hg} \cdot H_{Hg} + \rho_{Hg} \cdot gH_{Hg}'$$

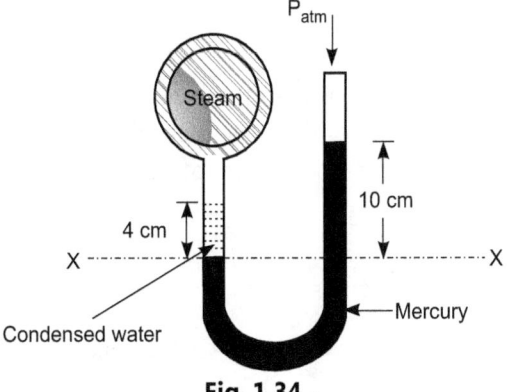

Fig. 1.34

where H_{Hg}' is the mercury head which represents barometer head and H_{Hg} is the mercury head in the U-tube as shown in figure.

$$\therefore P_{steam} = g [\rho_{Hg}(H_{Hg} + H_{Hg}') - \rho_{H2O} \cdot H_{H2O}]$$

$$= 9.81 \left[13600 \left(\frac{10 + 75}{100} \right) - 1000 \times \frac{4}{100} \right]$$

$$= 9.81 \times 1000 [13.6 \times 0.85 - 0.04] = 9810 \times 11.52$$

$$= 113010 \text{ N/m}^2 = 113010 \text{ Pa} = \textbf{1.13 bar} \text{ (absolute As 1 bar} = 10^5 \text{ bar)}$$

Problem 1.3:

The flow of air through a pipe is measured with the help of an orifice meter. The manometer used for measuring the head loss due to orifice contains a liquid of 0.85 specific gravity. The head loss measured is 9.2 cm, find the head loss of air passing through the orifice in kPa.

Solution: The configuration of the system is shown in Fig. 1.35.

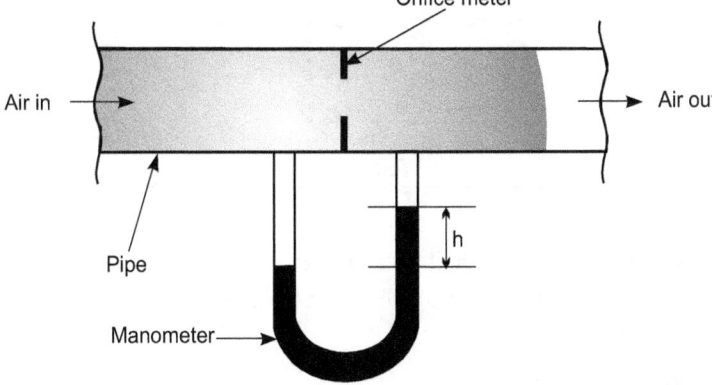

Fig. 1.35

The pressure head carrying the air flow through the orifice meter is given by

$$\Delta p = \rho g h = (0.85 \times 1000) \times 9.81 \times \left(\frac{9.2}{100} \right)$$

$$= 767.14 \text{ pa} = \textbf{0.767 kPa} \qquad \textbf{Ans.}$$

Problem 1.4:

A U tube manometer is connected to a gas pipe. The level of the liquid in the manometer arm open to atmosphere is 17 cm lower than the level of the liquid in the arm connected to the gas pipe. The liquid in the manometer has specific gravity of 0.8. Find the absolute pressure of the gas if the manometer reads 76 cm of Hg.

Solution:

From the Fig. 1.30, we have,

$$P_{gas} + P_{liquid} = P_{atmosphere}$$

$$P_{liquid} = \rho \times g \times h = 0.8 \times 1000 \times 9.81 \times \frac{17}{100}$$

$$= 1334.16 \text{ N/m}^2$$

$$= 0.0133416 \text{ bar}$$

$$P_{atmosphere} = 760 \text{ mm of Hg}$$

$$= 1.01325 \text{ bar}$$

$$P_{gas} = P_{atm} - P_{liquid}$$

$$= 1.01325 - 0.103341$$

$$= \mathbf{0.999909 \text{ bar}} \quad \text{... Ans.}$$

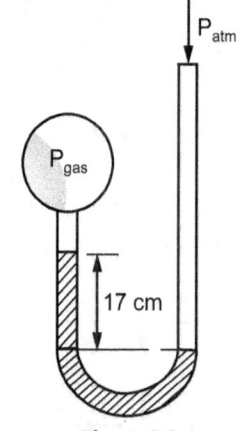

Fig. 1.36

Problem 1.5 :

A vertical composite liquid column with its upper end exposed to atmospheric pressure comprises 45 cm of Hg. (sp. gr. = 13.6); 65 cm of water and 80 cm of oil. (sp. gr. = 0.8) Calculate pressure in bar

(i) at the bottom of the column,

(ii) at the interface of oil and water,

(iii) at the interface of water and Hg.

Assume atmospheric pressure = *100 kPa*

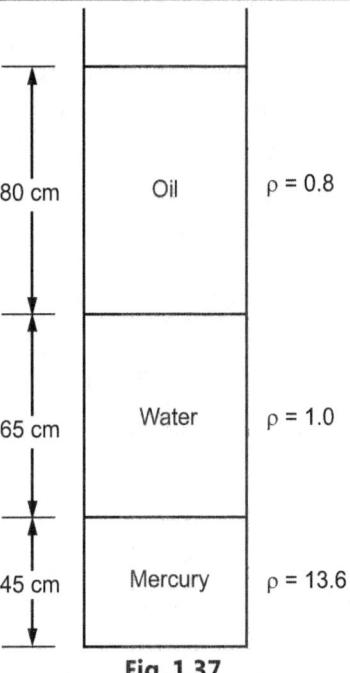

Fig. 1.37

Solution:

Pressure due to column of Hg = $\rho g h$

$$= \frac{13.6 \times 1000 \times 9.81}{10^5} \times \frac{45}{100}$$

$$= 0.600372 \text{ bar}$$

Pressure due to column of H_2O = $\frac{10^3 \times 9.81}{10^5} \times \frac{65}{100}$

$$= 0.063765 \text{ bar}$$

Pressure due to column of oil = $\frac{0.8 \times 10^3 \times 9.81}{10^5} \times \frac{80}{100}$

$$= 0.62784 \text{ bar}$$

∴ Pressure at the bottom of the column

$$= 1 + 0.062784 + 0.063765 + 0.600372$$

$$= \mathbf{1.726921 \text{ bar}} \quad \ldots \text{Ans.}$$

Pressure at the interface of oil and water

$$= 1 + 0.062784 = \mathbf{1.062784 \text{ bar}} \ldots \text{Ans.}$$

Pressure at the interface of water and mercury

$$= 1.0 + 0.062784 + 0.063765$$

$$= \mathbf{1.126549 \text{ bar}} \quad \ldots \text{Ans.}$$

Problem 1.6:

Both a bourdon gauge and a manometer are attached to a gas tank. If the reading on the pressure gauge is 80 kPa, determine the distance between the two fluid levels of the manometer if the fluid is

(i) mercury having specific gravity of 13.6

(ii) water.

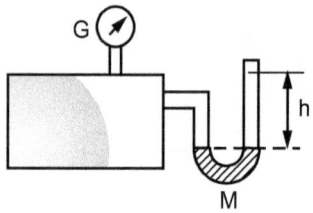

Fig. 1.38

Solution: The arrangement is shown in the figure. Since the bourdon gauge 'G' and manometer will indicate the same value, the pressure shown by manometer will also be equal to 80 kPa. However, pressure in manometer = $\rho g h$, where ρ is density, g is gravitational acceleration and h is height of the liquid column.

Therefore, $P_{gauge} = (\rho \times g \times h)$ Pa

(i) When the fluid is mercury, we have,

$$1000 \times 80 = (13.6 \times 1000 \times 9.8 \times h) \text{ Pa}.$$

∴ $h = 0.59962$ m ... Ans.

(ii) When the fluid is water, we have,

$$80 \times 10^3 = 1000 \times 9.81 \times h$$

∴ $h = 8.1549$ m ... Ans.

Problem 1.7:

The basic barometer can be used to measure the height of a building. If the barometer readings at top and bottom of a building are 730 and 755 mm of Hg respectively, determine the height of the building. Assume an average air density of 1.18 kg/m³.

Solution: Let the height of the building be 'h' meters.

Pressure at B = Pressure at A + Pressure of air column of height h

∴ $P_B - P_A$ = Pressure of air column of height h

∴ $P_B - P_A = \rho_{air} \times g \times h$

∴ $(0.755 - 0.730) \times 13600 \times 9.81 = 1.18 \times 9.81 \times h$

∴ h (Height of building) = **288.14 meters** ... Ans.

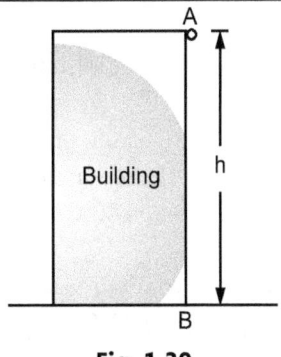

Fig. 1.39

Problem 1.8:

A temperature scale of certain thermometer is given by the relation t = a ln P + b, where a and b are constants and P is the thermometric property of the fluid in the thermometer. If at the ice point and steam point, the thermometric properties are found to be 1.5 and 7.5 respectively, what will be the temperature corresponding to the thermometric property of 3.5 on Celsius scale?

Solution :

On Celsius scale, ice point

0°C and steam point = 100°C

∴ From given condition we have,

$$0 = a \ln 1.5 + b \quad \ldots (1)$$
$$100 = a \ln 7.5 + b \quad \ldots (2)$$

i.e. $\quad 0 = a (0.405) + b \quad \ldots (3)$

and $\quad 100 = a (2.015) + b \quad \ldots (4)$

Subtracting (3) from (4), we get,

$$100 = 1.61 \, a$$

∴ $\quad a = 62.112$

Substituting in (3), we get,

$$b = -0.405 \, a = -0.405 \,(62.112)]$$
$$= -25.155$$

∴ For P = 3.5, the value of temperature is given by,

$$t = (62.112) \ln (3.5) - 25.155]$$

∴ $\quad t = (62.112)(1.253) - 25.155$

∴ $\quad \mathbf{t = 52.671°C} \quad \ldots \textbf{Ans.}$

Problem 1.9:
A thermocouple with test junction at t°C on gas thermometer scale and reference junction at ice point gives the e.m.f. as,

$$\varepsilon = 0.20\,t - 5 \times 10^{-4}\,t^2 \text{ mV}.$$

The millivoltmeter is calibrated at ice and steam points. What will be reading on this thermometer where the gas thermometer reads 60°C?

Solution:

At ice point, when $t = 0°C$, $\varepsilon = 0$ mV
At steam point, when $t = 100°C$,
$$\varepsilon = 0.20 \times 100 - 5 \times 10^{-4} \times (100)^2$$
∴ $\varepsilon = 15$ mV

At 60°C,
$$\varepsilon = 0.20 \times 60 - 5 \times 10^{-4} \times (60)^2 = 10.2 \text{ mV}$$

∴ When the gas thermometer reads 60°C, the thermocouple will read,
$$t = \frac{100 \times 10.2}{15} = 68°C \qquad \text{... Ans.}$$

Problem 1.10:
A gas at pressure of 1500 kPa is expanded in a cylinder - piston arrangement. The piston has a diameter of 10 cm. The expansion curve is a straight line. At the end of expansion, the pressure of the gas is 120 kPa. Find the work done by the gas on the piston if stroke length is 0.25 m.

Solution:

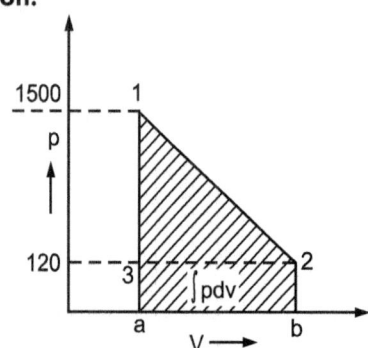

Fig. 1.40

$$W = \int_1^2 P\,dV$$
$$= \text{Area under the curve}$$

∴ $V_b - V_a = \dfrac{\pi}{4} d^2 \cdot L = \dfrac{\pi}{4}(0.1)^2 \times 0.25 = 1.96 \times 10^{-3} \text{ m}^3$

∴ $W = \text{Area } 1-2-3 + \text{Area } a-b-2-3$

$$= \frac{1}{2} \times (1500 - 120) \times V_s + 120 \times V_s$$

$$= \left[\frac{1}{2}(1500 - 120) + 120\right] \times 1.96 \times 10^{-3} = 1.355 \text{ kN-m ... Ans.}$$

1.11 FIRST LAW OF THERMODYNAMICS

Heat and work, the forms of energy which are discussed in the earlier unit, are related by the first law of thermodynamics. This is a law of conservation of energy which states that 'energy can neither be created nor be destroyed'. This law cannot be proved mathematically, but no exception has been observed.

1.11.1 First Law of Thermodynamics and Joule's Experiment

Before defining the first law of thermodynamics, it is better to discuss some experimental results on which it is based. Such an experiment was carried out by a scientist J. P. Joule, during the period 1840-1849. In one of the experiment, he used the apparatus similar to that shown in Fig. 1.41.

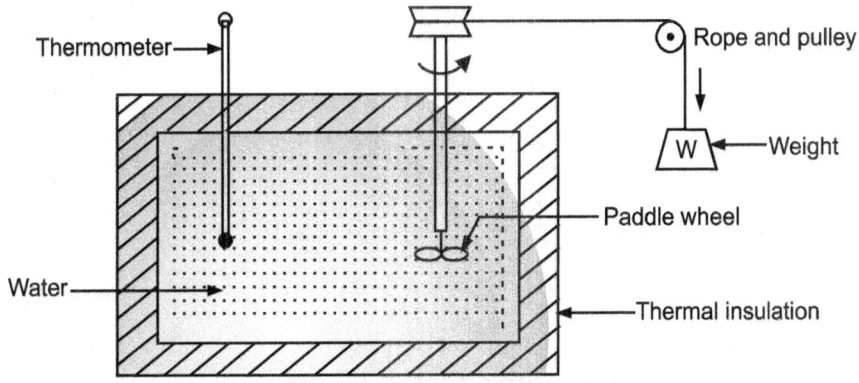

Fig. 1.41: Joule's Experiment

It consists of a closed container insulated from outside, filled with certain amount of water, having thermometer and a paddle wheel. The temperature of water is measured before and after the work is done on it through a paddle wheel, which rotates due to the weight moving down. The rise in the temperature of water is always proportional to the work done on it due to the potential energy lost by the weight. Let W_{1-2} is the work done on the water (system), t_1 = initial temperature of water, t_2 = temperature of water after the work is done ($t_2 > t_1$). This process is as shown in Fig. 1.42.

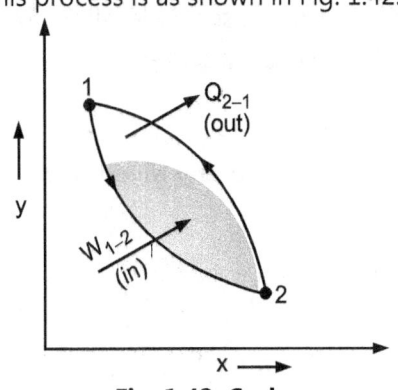

Fig. 1.42: Cycle

Now, assume the insulation is removed, therefore heat transfer takes place from the system to the surroundings. Therefore, its temperature reaches to the original temperature t_2. The amount of heat Q_{2-1} is transferred to the surroundings. Thus, a system completes a cycle, with definite amount of work W_{1-2} input to the system and followed by Q_{2-1}, amount of heat dissipated from the system.

Joule had conducted this experiment number of times for different weights moving through different distances. Each time he measured the temperature rise of the system.

He found that Q_{1-2} is proportional to W_{1-2}. ($Q_{1-2} \propto W_{1-2}$). This constant of proportionality is known as **'Joule's equivalent or the mechanical equivalent of heat'**.

In SI units, work is measured in N-m and heat in joules (J) and the relation is
1 N-m = 1 joule and hence Joule's constant is unity.

If the cycle shown in Fig. 1.42 involves many more heat and work transfers, the same conclusion will be found. Expressed mathematically,

$$(\Sigma W)_{cycle} = J (\Sigma Q)_{cycle} \qquad \ldots (1.26)$$

It can be written as $\oint \delta W = J \oint \delta Q$

As $J = 1$, $\qquad \oint \delta W = \oint \delta Q \qquad \ldots (1.27)$

where the symbol $\oint$ denotes the cyclic integral for the closed path. This is the first law applied to a closed system undergoing a cyclic process.

1.11.2 Other Statements of First Law of Thermodynamics

Principle of Energy Conservation:

According to this concept, energy can neither be created nor be destroyed. This implies that the sum of the energies of a system at the microscopic and macroscopic levels is fixed, unless there is an interaction with the surroundings, involving an energy exchange.

This can be simply stated as

"The total energy of an isolated system, measured with respect to any given frame of reference remains constant." Mathematically, for an isolated system,

$$E \text{ (total)} = U + K.E. + P.E. + \text{Chemical energy} + \ldots\ldots$$
$$= \text{Constant}$$

1.12 FIRST LAW APPLIED TO A CLOSED SYSTEM UNDERGOING A CHANGE OF STATE

The expression $(\Sigma W)_{cycle} = (\Sigma Q)_{cycle}$ applies only to a system undergoing a cyclic process. But in practice, a system may undergo a *non-cyclic* process which produces a change of state in the system.

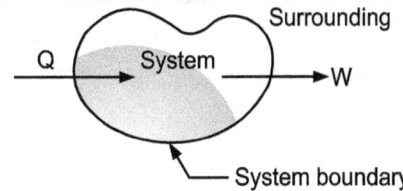

Fig. 1.43: A system interacting with the surroundings which involves work and heat transfer

Let us consider a system interacting with surroundings which involves work and heat transfer (Fig. 1.43). If Q is the amount of heat transferred to the system and W is the work obtained from it, then Q – W is the energy stored in the system. This stored energy in the system is not a heat or work but referred as internal energy or simply energy of the system.
$\Delta E = Q - W$, where ΔE is the increase in internal energy of the system.

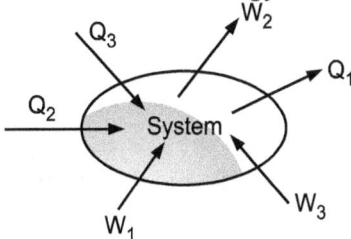

Fig. 1.44: System interacting with the surroundings involving more energy transfers

If more energy transfers are involved in the process, as shown in Fig. 1.44, the first law gives

$(Q_2 + Q_3 - Q_1) = \Delta E + (W_2 + W_1 - W_3)$ ... (1.28)

Energy is conserved in this operation also.

1.13 INTERNAL ENERGY

Let a system undergoes a cyclic process as shown in Fig. 1.45. Consider this system changes its state from state 1 to state 2 following the path A. Apply first law to this process.

$Q_A = \Delta E_A + W_A$ ... (1.29)

The system returns from state 2 to state 1 along the path B.

$\therefore Q_B = \Delta E_B + W_B$ ... (1.30)

These two processes form a cycle, for which,

$(\Sigma W)_{cycle} = (\Sigma Q)_{cycle}$

$\therefore W_A + W_B = Q_A + Q_B$

$\therefore Q_A - W_A = W_B - Q_B$ ... (1.31)

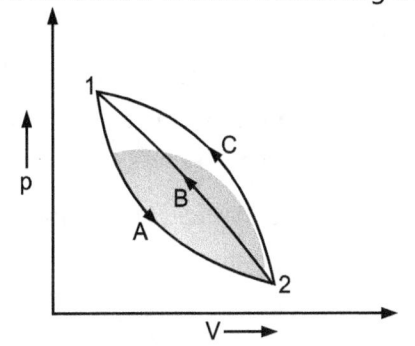

Fig. 1.45: Energy - a property of a system

From equations (1.29), (1.30) and (1.31), it results,
$$\Delta E_A = -\Delta E_B \qquad \ldots (1.32)$$
Similarly, if we consider the cycle as 1 – A – 2 – C – 1, then,
$$\Delta E_A = -\Delta E_C \qquad \ldots (1.33)$$
Comparison of the equations (1.31) and (1.32) will lead to,
$$\Delta E_B = \Delta E_C \qquad \ldots (1.34)$$

Hence, the change in energy between the states 1 and 2 is same for the paths B and C. It means the internal energy is independent of the path of the process. It is fixed for a particular state of the system. Therefore, one can conclude that internal energy is a point function and property of the system.

We have, $\delta Q - \delta W = dE$

The total energy change, $\delta E = \delta U + \delta KE + \delta PE$

where, $\delta KE \rightarrow$ change in K.E.

$\delta PE \rightarrow$ change in P.E.

$\delta U \rightarrow$ change in internal energy

If there is no change in K.E. and P.E., then
$$\delta PE = \delta KE = 0,$$

hence, $\delta Q - \delta W = \delta U \qquad \ldots (1.35)$

As $(\delta Q - \delta W)$ is independent of path and depends only on end states, the internal energy $U = \int (\delta Q - \delta W)$ is also independent of path and therefore, a property of the system.

1.14 STEADY FLOW PROCESS

A steady flow process is said to exist when the working substance flows in and out of the control volume and the properties of the working substance at any section of flow do not vary with time.

A steady flow process must satisfy the following conditions:

(i) The rates of work and heat transferred across the control surface do not change with time.

(ii) The mass flow rates at entrance and exit sections of the control volume are equal and do not change with time. Naturally, the mass within the control volume does not change with time and there is no change in energy within the system.

(iii) The state of the working substance at any section within the control volume or at entrance or exit sections does not change with respect to time.

1.15 FLOW WORK

Unlike closed systems, control volumes involve mass flow across their boundaries, and some work is required to push the mass into or out of the control volume. This work is known as the flow work or flow energy and is necessary for maintaining a continuous flow through a control volume (open system). To obtain a relation for flow work, consider a volume 'V' of the fluid element shown in Fig. 1.46. The fluid immediately upstream will force this fluid element to enter the control volume, thus it can be regarded as an imaginary piston. The fluid element can be chosen to be sufficiently small.

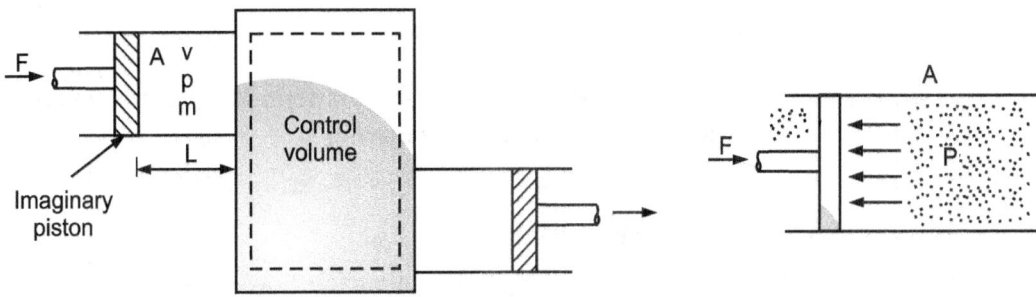

Fig. 1.46: Schematic for flow work

Fig.1.47: The force applied on a fluid by a piston is equal to the force applied on the piston by a fluid

If the fluid pressure is P and cross-sectional area of the fluid element is A, (Fig. 1.47), the force applied on the fluid element by the imaginary piston is $F = P \cdot A$.

To push the entire fluid element into the control volume, this force must act through a distance L. Thus the work done in pushing the fluid element across the boundary (i.e. the flow work) is

$$W_{flow} = F \cdot L = P \cdot A \cdot L = PV, \, kJ \qquad \ldots (1.36)$$

The flow work per unit mass is obtained by dividing both sides of this equation by the mass of the fluid element.

$$W_{flow} = PV_s \, (kJ/kg) \qquad \ldots (1.37)$$

where V_s = Specific volume of fluid, m^3/kg

The total energy of the flowing fluid

The total energy of the flowing fluid is

$$= PV_s + (U + KE + PE)$$

But, $\quad U + PV_s =$ enthalpy h

∴ Total energy of flowing fluid per unit mass

$$= h + KE + PE \qquad \ldots (1.38)$$

$$= h + \frac{V^2}{2} + gZ \qquad \ldots (1.39)$$

1.16 CONVERSION OF MASS AND CONTINUITY EQUATION

By the conservation of mass, for steady flow, the mass flow rate entering the control volume must be equal to the mass flow rate leaving the control volume. (Volume flow rate at entry and exit of control volume may be different).

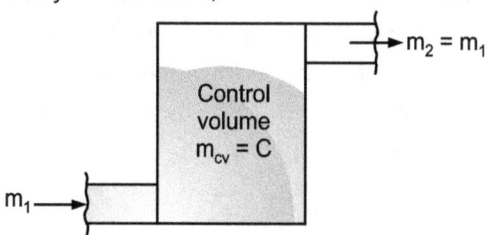

Fig.1.48: During a steady flow process, the amount of mass entering the control volume equals the amount of mass leaving

See Fig. 1.48.

Conservation of Mass and Continuity Equation :

The principle/law of conservation of mass for a general steady flow system with multiple inlets and outlets may be expressed in the rate form as

$$\begin{pmatrix} \text{Total mass entering} \\ \text{the control volume per unit time} \end{pmatrix} = \begin{pmatrix} \text{Total mass leaving the} \\ \text{control volume per unit time} \end{pmatrix}$$

or $\quad \sum m_i = \sum m_e$

where the subscripts i and e refer to inlet and outlet respectively.

For a single-stream steady flow system,

$$m_i = m_e$$

or $\quad \boxed{\rho_1 A_1 V_1 = \rho_2 A_2 V_2} \qquad \ldots (1.40)$

ρ_2 = density of fluid at exit
V_1 = velocity of fluid at entrance
V_2 = velocity of fluid at exit
A_1 = cross-section of stream at entry
A_2 = cross-section of stream at exit

The equation (1.40) is called as continuity equation.

1.17 FIRST LAW APPLIED TO A STEADY FLOW PROCESS

A steady flow system is shown in Fig. 1.49, where one stream of fluid enters the control volume at section 1 – 1 and other stream of the fluid leaves the control volume at section 1.12.

The properties at any location within the control volume are steady with time.

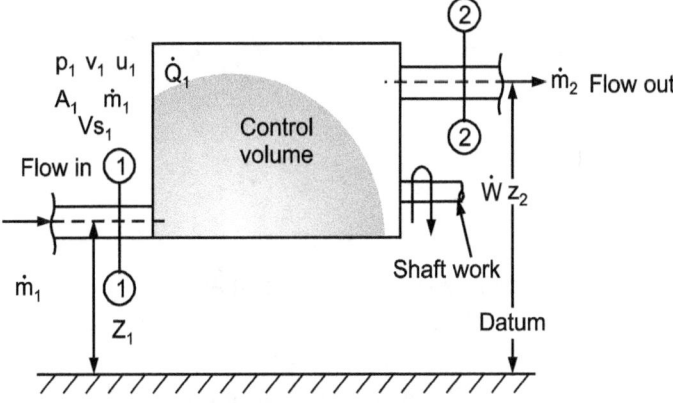

Fig. 1.49: Steady flow process

The following quantities are expressed with reference to Fig. 1.49.

A_1, A_2 — cross section of stream, m²

m_1, m_2 — mass flow rate, kg/s

P_1, P_2 — absolute pressure, N/m²

V_{s1}, V_{s2} — specific volume, m³/kg

u_1, u_2 — specific internal energy, J/kg

v_1, v_2 — velocity of fluid, m/s

z_1, z_2 — elevation above an arbitrary datum, m

Q — net rate of heat flow into control volume, J/s

W — net rate of work transfer through control volume, J/s

Subscripts 1 and 2 refer to the inlet and outlet sections.

The sum of energy quantities entering into the system

$$= Q + m_1 \left(u_1 + \frac{v_1^2}{2} + gz_1 + PV_{s1} \right) \quad \ldots (1.41)$$

$$= Q + m_1 \left(h_1 + \frac{v_1^2}{2} + gz_1 \right) \quad \ldots (1.42)$$

The sum of energy quantities leaving the control volume

$$= W + m_2 \left(h_2 + \frac{v_2^2}{2} + gz_2 \right) \quad \ldots (1.43)$$

The change in energy ΔE of the control volume (system) is zero for **steady state conditions**.

Apply first law, i.e. the total energy entering the control volume is equal to the total energy leaving the control volume plus ΔE.

For steady flow, $m_1 = m_2 = m$ and $\Delta E = 0$.

$$\therefore \quad Q + m\left(h_1 + \frac{V_1^2}{2} + gz_1\right) = W + m\left(h_2 + \frac{V_2^2}{2} + gz_2\right) \text{ J/s}$$

$$\therefore \quad Q - W = m\left(h_2 + \frac{V_2^2}{2} + gz_2\right) - m\left(h_1 + \frac{V_1^2}{2} + gz_1\right) \text{ J/s} \quad \ldots(1.44)$$

In words,

$$\begin{pmatrix} \text{Total energy} \\ \text{crossing boundary} \\ \text{as heat-work} \\ \text{per unit time} \end{pmatrix} = \begin{pmatrix} \text{Total energy} \\ \text{transported out} \\ \text{of CV with mass} \\ \text{per unit time} \end{pmatrix} - \begin{pmatrix} \text{Total energy} \\ \text{transported into} \\ \text{CV with mass} \\ \text{per unit time} \end{pmatrix} \quad \ldots(1.45)$$

It can be expressed as

$$Q - W = m\left[(h_2 - h_1) + \left(\frac{V_2^2 - V_1^2}{2000}\right) + \frac{g(z_2 - z_1)}{1000}\right] \text{ kW} \quad \ldots(1.46)$$

$$Q - W = m\,(\Delta h + \Delta KE + \Delta PE) \text{ kW} \quad \ldots(1.47)$$

Dividing these equations by m, we obtain the "steady flow energy equation (SFEE)" on a unit mass basis as

$$q = Q/m, \qquad w = W/m \text{ kJ/kg}$$

$$q - w = h_2 - h_1 + \frac{V_2^2 - V_1^2}{2000} + g\frac{(z_2 - z_1)}{1000} \text{ kJ/kg} \quad \ldots(1.48)$$

1.19 APPLICATION OF STEADY FLOW ENERGY EQUATION DIFFERENT DEVCIES

(a) Nozzle and Diffuser:

A nozzle is a device used to accelerate the fluid flow while the diffuser is a device used to convert the kinetic energy of a flowing fluid into pressure head.

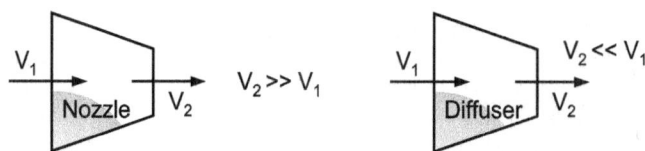

Fig. 1.50: Nozzle and Diffuser

$Q = 0$, The rate of heat transfer between the fluid and surroundings is very small and neglected.

$W = 0$, As there is no shaft work available from these or even work is not supplied.

ΔPE ≈ 0, The fluid usually experiences no change of elevation.

The SFEE equation reduces to

$$0 = h_2 - h_1 + \frac{v_2^2 - v_1^2}{2000}$$

Usually v_1 is very small ($v_1 << v_2$) for nozzle,

$$\therefore v_2 = \sqrt{2000(h_1 - h_2)} \text{ m/s}$$

Here $(h_1 - h_2)$ is in J/kg.

(b) Turbine and Compressor:

Turbines are prime-movers which generate power, whereas compressors and pumps require power input.

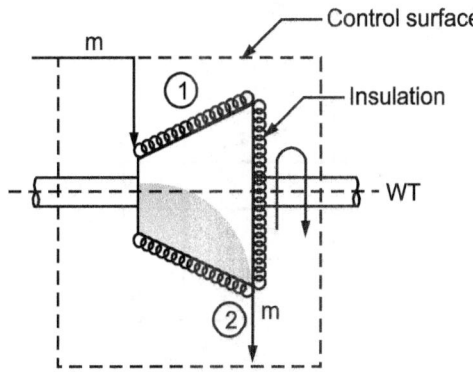

Fig. 1.51: Flow through a turbine

As the turbine is insulated, no heat exchange takes place, therefore, Q = 0. The flow velocities are often small in steam turbines, and K.E. term can be neglected. Also for steam turbines, ΔPE = 0.

$\therefore$ SFEE then becomes $h_1 = h_2 + W$
or $W = h_1 - h_2$ kJ/kg
  $= m(h_1 - h_2)$ kW

where m = mass flow rate in kg/s.

Similarly, for an adiabatic pump or compressor, the SFEE is,

$$W = (h_2 - h_1) \cdot m \text{ kW}$$

where 'h_1' and 'h_2' are in kJ/kg.

(c) Throttling Valves:

Throttling valves are a kind of flow restricting devices that cause a significant pressure drop in the fluid. Some familiar examples are ordinary adjustable valves, capillary tubes and porous plugs. Unlike turbines, they produce a pressure drop without involving any work. The pressure drop in the fluid is often accompanied by a large drop in temperature and for that reason throttling devices are commonly used in refrigeration and air conditioning applications.

Throttling devices are very small in size, therefore flow through them is adiabatic (Q = 0). No work is involved, hence W = 0. Change in potential energy, $\Delta PE \approx 0$, Increase in KE of the fluid is insignificant, $\Delta KE = 0$.

$$\therefore \quad Q - W = \Delta h + \Delta KE + \Delta PE$$
$$0 = \Delta h + 0 + 0$$
$$\therefore \quad 0 = \Delta h$$
i.e. $\quad h_1 = h_2 \text{ kJ/kg} \quad \ldots (1.49)$

i.e. enthalpy values at the inlet and exit of a throttling valve are same.

(d) Heat Exchanger:

Heat exchanger is a device, where two moving fluid streams exchange heat without mixing. The simplest form of a heat exchanger is a double tube (also called tube and shell) heat exchanger shown in Fig. 1.52.

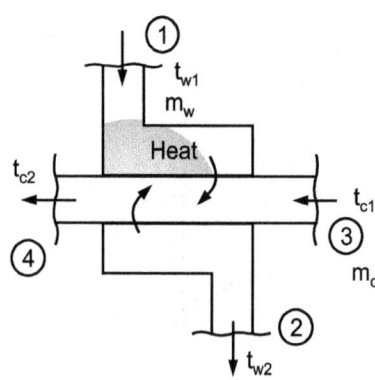

Fig. 1.52

$W = 0, \Delta PE = 0, \Delta KE = 0$

$$m_w h_1 + m_c h_3 = m_w h_2 + m_c h_4$$
$$\therefore \quad m_w (h_1 - h_2) = m_c (h_4 - h_3) \quad \ldots (1.50)$$

c = cold fluid, w = water (hot fluid)

1.18.1 Work Done in a Reversible Steady Flow Process

Refer Fig. 1.53.

We know that SFEE is

$$Q + \left(h_1 + \frac{v_1^2}{2000} + \frac{gz_1}{1000}\right) = W + \left(h_2 + \frac{v_2^2}{2000} + \frac{gz_2}{1000}\right)$$

$$\therefore \quad Q - W = \Delta h + \Delta PE + \Delta KE \text{ kJ/kg}$$

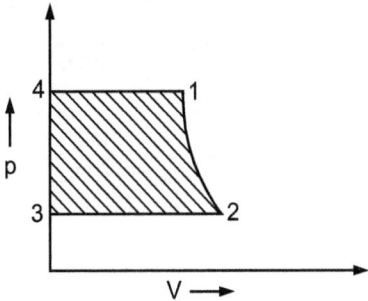

Fig. 1.53: Meaning of $-\int VdP$

In the differential form,

$$\delta q = \delta W + dh + dPE + dKE$$

From first law, $\delta q = \delta W + dU$

and $\delta W = P\, dV$ for a reversible work

$$\delta q = PdV + dU$$

Enthalpy, $h = U + PV$

$$dh = dU + PdV + VdP$$

Substituting values of δq and dh from equations (II) and (III) in equation (I),

$$PdV + dU = \delta W + dU + PdV + VdP + dPE + dKE$$

$$\therefore \quad -\int VdP = \int \delta W + \Delta PE + \Delta KE$$

which is to say that, in a reversible steady flow process, $-\int VdP$ equals the shaft work 'W' plus changes in KE and PE.

(a) If ΔPE is negligible,

$$-\int V\, dP = W + \Delta KE$$

(b) If ΔKE is negligible,

$$-\int V\, dP = W + \Delta PE$$

(c) If ΔKE and ΔPE both are negligible, then

$$-\int V\, dP = W_{shaft}$$

i.e. in a reversible steady flow process, $-\int V\, dP$ equals shaft work 'W' when changes in kinetic energy and potential energy are neglected.

1.19 SIGNIFICANCE OF $\int_1^2 PDV$ IN CASE OF STEDY FLOW PROCESS

Refer Fig. 1.54.

The SFEE is

$$Q + \left(h_1 + \frac{v_1^2}{2} + gz_1\right) = W + \left(h_2 + \frac{v_2^2}{2} + gz_2\right)$$

$$\therefore \quad Q + \left(U_1 + P_1V_1 + \frac{v_1^2}{2000} + \frac{gz_1}{1000}\right) = W + \left(U_2 + P_2V_2 + \frac{v_2^2}{2000} + \frac{gz_2}{1000}\right) \text{ kJ/kg}$$

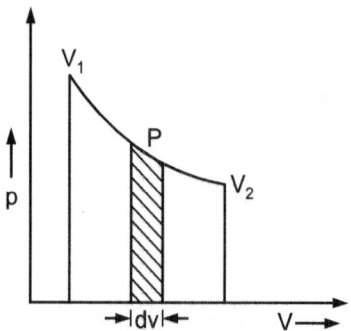

Fig. 1.54

$$Q = \Delta U + \Delta(PV) + \Delta KE + \Delta PE + W$$

In differential form, $\quad \delta Q = dU + d(PV) + d(KE) + d(PE) + \delta W$

For any reversible process,

$$\delta Q = dU + PdV$$

$\therefore \quad dU + PdV = dU + d(PV) + d(KE) + d(PE) + \delta W$

$\therefore \quad PdV = d(PV) + d(KE) + d(PE) + \delta W$

Integrating

$$\therefore \quad \int_1^2 PdV = \Delta PV + \Delta KE + \Delta PE + W$$

$\int_1^2 PdV$ for a steady flow process is sum of change in flow work plus change in kinetic energy, plus change in potential energy and shaft work.

Note: For **non-flow** reversible process, $\int_1^2 P\,dV$ is the area under the curve and it represents shaft work when the pressure changes from P_1 to P_2 and volume from V_1 to V_2.

$$\int_1^2 P\,dv = W_{1-2}$$

1.20 PERPETUAL MOTION MACHINE OF FIRST KIND, PMM - I

First law states that energy can neither be created nor be destroyed but only gets transformed from one form to another.

A device which violates the first law of thermodynamics is called as perpetual motion machine of first kind.

A device which continuously produces work without consuming any energy, is known as perpetual motion machine of first kind. This is illustrated in Fig. 1.55. PMM - I is against first law, hence PMM - I is impossible.

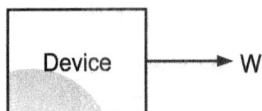

Fig. 1.55: PMM - I

The converse of PMM - I is, there can be no machine which would continuously consume work without some other form of energy appearing simultaneously (Fig. 1.56).

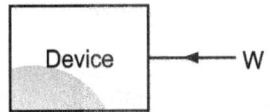

Fig. 1.56: Converse of PMM - I

This is also not possible.

SOLVED PROBLEMS

Problem 1.11:

In a cylinder - piston arrangement, the pressure is inversely proportional to the square of volume. The initial pressure in the cylinder is 20 bar and initial volume is 0.1 m³. The volume is increased so that final pressure reduces to 2 bar. Find the work done in kJ.

Solution: Given: $P_1 = 20 \times 10^5$ N/m² or Pa

$P_2 = 2 \times 10^5$ N/m² or Pa

$$P \propto \frac{1}{V^2} \quad \text{and} \quad V_1 = 0.1 \text{ m}^3$$

$$\text{Work done} = \int_1^2 P\, dV$$

$$P = \frac{C}{V^2} \quad \therefore \text{Work done} = \int_1^2 \frac{C}{V^2} \cdot dV$$

$$\text{Work done} = C \int_1^2 \frac{dV}{V^2} = C \left[\frac{V_2^{-1} - V_1^{-1}}{-1} \right] = C \left[\frac{1}{V_1} - \frac{1}{V_2} \right]$$

$$C = PV^2 = P_1 V_1^2 = 20 \times 10^5 \times (0.1)^2 = 20{,}000$$

$$\therefore \quad W = 20{,}000 \left[\frac{1}{V_1} - \frac{1}{V_2} \right]$$

$$P_2 V_2^2 = C$$

$$\therefore \quad V_2 = \sqrt{\frac{C}{P_2}} = \sqrt{\frac{20000}{2 \times 10^5}} = 0.31 \text{ m}^3$$

$$\therefore \quad W = 20{,}000 \left[\frac{1}{0.1} - \frac{1}{0.31} \right] = 135.4 \times 10^3 \text{ N-m}$$

$$= 135.4 \text{ kJ} \quad \text{... Ans.}$$

Problem 1.12:

The volume of a sample of a gas is 0.04 m³ and at a pressure of 10 bar. If the final volume of gas is 0.1 m³ after the following processes were carried out, evaluate the work done in each process.

    (i) Constant pressure process
    (ii) PV = constant

Solution: The work done in each case is calculated by the formula $\int P\, dV$.

(i) Constant pressure process:

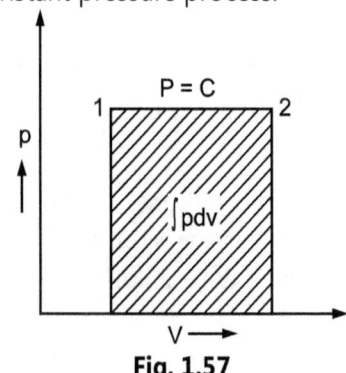

Fig. 1.57

$$P_1 = 10 \times 10^5 \text{ N/m}^2, \quad P_2 = P_1$$
$$V_1 = 0.04 \text{ m}^3, \quad V_2 = 0.1 \text{ m}^3$$

$$W = \int_1^2 P\, dV = P(V_2 - V_1)$$

$$= 10 \times 10^5 [0.1 - 0.04]$$
$$= 60{,}000 \text{ J} = 60 \text{ kJ} \quad \text{... Ans.}$$

(ii) PV = Constant for isothermal process:

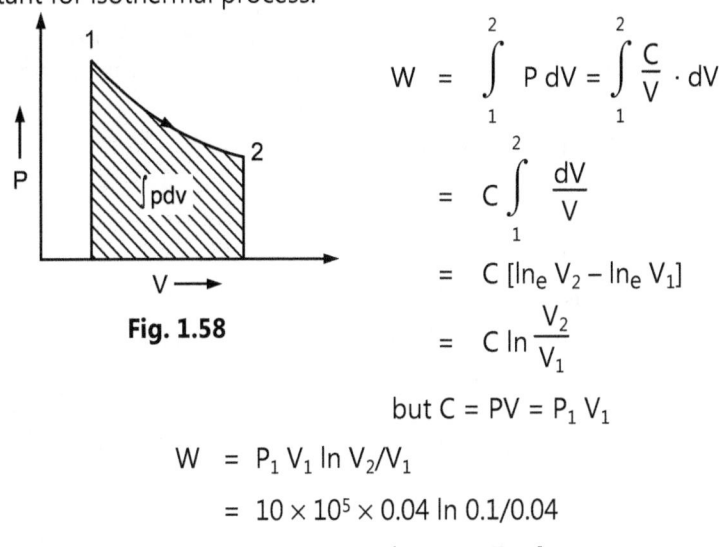

Fig. 1.58

$$W = \int_1^2 P\,dV = \int_1^2 \frac{C}{V} \cdot dV$$

$$= C \int_1^2 \frac{dV}{V}$$

$$= C[\ln_e V_2 - \ln_e V_1]$$

$$= C \ln \frac{V_2}{V_1}$$

but $C = PV = P_1 V_1$

$$\therefore W = P_1 V_1 \ln V_2/V_1$$

$$= 10 \times 10^5 \times 0.04 \ln 0.1/0.04$$

$$= 36652.6 \text{ joule} = \mathbf{36.651\ kJ} \qquad \text{... Ans.}$$

Problem 1.13:

A system of gas in a cylinder-piston arrangement expands according to $\left(P + \dfrac{a}{V^2}\right)(V - b) = mRT$, where a, b and R are constants. Obtain the expression for the work done by the system on the piston for the expansion process.

Solution: The work done is

$$W = \int_1^2 P\,dV$$

Given relation is, $\left(P + \dfrac{a}{V^2}\right)(V - b) = mRT$

$$\therefore P = \frac{mRT}{V - b} - \frac{a}{V^2}$$

$$\therefore W = \int_1^2 \left(\frac{mRT}{V - b} - \frac{a}{V^2}\right) dV$$

$$= mRT \ln\left(\frac{V_2 - b}{V_1 - b}\right) + \frac{a}{V_2} - \frac{a}{V_1} \qquad \text{... Ans.}$$

Problem 1.14:

A refrigerator is loaded with food and the door of the refrigerator is closed. During a certain period, the machine required 1 kWh energy and internal energy of the system drops by 6000 kJ. Find the net heat transferred to or from the system.

Solution:
$$1 \text{ kWh} = 3600 \text{ kJ}$$
$$Q = \Delta U + W$$

Internal energy drops,

i.e.
$$\Delta U = -6000 \text{ kJ}$$
$$W = -3600 \text{ kJ}$$

∴
$$Q = -6000 + (-3600)$$
$$= -9600 \text{ kJ (Heat rejected)} \quad \text{... Ans.}$$

Problem 1.15:

A system undergoes a frictionless non-flow process according to the law

$$P = \frac{4.5}{V} + 2$$

where P is in bar and V in m³/kg. During the process, volume changes from 0.12 m³/kg to 0.04 m³/kg and temperature increases by 133°C. The internal energy of the fluid varies as $dU = C_v \cdot dT$, where $C_v = 0.71$ kJ/kg °C. Find out the heat transfer and its direction for fluid of mass 10 kg.

Solution: Given,

$$P = \frac{4.5}{V} + 2, \; V_1 = 0.12 \text{ m}^3/\text{kg}, \; V_2 = 0.04 \text{ m}^3/\text{kg}, \; (\Delta T)_{increase} = 133°C$$

$$C_v = 0.71 \text{ kJ/kg °C}, \; m = 10 \text{ kg}$$

$$dU = C_v \, dT$$

Work done in a frictionless non-flow reversible process

$$= \int_1^2 P \, dV = 10^5 \int_1^2 \left(\frac{4.5}{V} + 2\right) dV \text{ joule/kg}$$

$$= 10^5 \left[4.5 \ln_e V_2/V_1 + 2 (V_2 - V_1)\right]_{0.12}^{0.04}$$

$$= 10^5 \left[4.5 \ln_e \frac{0.04}{0.12} + 2 (0.04 - 0.12)\right] \text{ joule/kg}$$

$$= -510375 \text{ joule/kg} = -510.375 \text{ kJ/kg}$$

$$\Delta U = \int C_v dT = C_v \cdot \Delta T = 0.71 \times 133 = 94.43 \text{ kJ/kg}$$

$$q = \Delta U + W = 94.43 - 510.375 = -415.94 \text{ kJ/kg}$$
$$Q = m \cdot q = 10 \times (-415.94) \text{ kJ} = -4159.4 \text{ kJ} \quad \text{... Ans.}$$

Problem 1.16:

A closed system undergoes a thermodynamic cycle. There are four processes AB, BC, CD and DA in the cycle. The heat transfer and work transfer in kW for each process are given below:

Process	Heat transfer, kW	Work, kW
AB	Nil	− 366.67
BC	300	Nil
CD	− 66.67	+ 500
DA	− 33.33	+ 66.667

Show that the data is consistent with the first law of thermodynamics and determine:
(a) Net rate of work output in kW
(b) Efficiency of the cycle.
(c) Change in internal energy of each process.

Solution: For cyclic process,

$$\oint \delta Q = \oint \delta W$$

For the cycle, $\oint \delta Q = 0 + 300 - 66.67 - 33.33 = 200$ kW

$$\oint W = -366.67 + 0 + 500 + 66.67 = 200 \text{ kW}$$

∴ $\oint \delta Q = \oint \delta W$, the data is consistent with first law of thermodynamics

(a) Net rate of work/sec. = **200 kW** ... **Ans.**

(b) Efficiency of cycle = $\dfrac{\text{Net work output}}{\text{Heat supplied}} = \dfrac{200}{300} = $ **66.67%** ... **Ans.**

(c) According to first law,

$$\delta Q = \delta U + \delta W$$
$$\delta U = \delta Q - \delta W$$

Hence for all processes, change in internal energy can be calculated.

Process	δQ	δW	$\delta U = \delta Q - \delta W$
AB	Nil	− 366.67	= 0 − (− 366.67) = 366.67
BC	300	Nil	= 300 − 0 = 300 kW
CD	− 66.67	+ 500	= − 66.67 − 500 = − 566.67 kW
DA	− 33.33	+ 66.67	= − 33.33 − 66.67 = − 100 kW

Problem 1.17:

Steady flow process is applied to nozzle. Steam enters a horizontal steam nozzle at a pressure of 10 bar. The pressure of steam at the exit of the nozzle is 1 bar. The internal energy of the steam decreases by 250 kJ/kg and the specific volume increases from 0.2 m³/kg to 2.7 m³/kg as the steam flows through the nozzle. Find the exit velocity of steam if its inlet velocity is 900 m/min. Heat transferred from the nozzle is negligible.

Solution: Steady flow energy equation

$$Q + \left(u_1 + P_1 V_{s1} + \frac{V_1^2}{2} + gz_1\right) = W + \left(u_2 + P_2 V_{s2} + \frac{V_2^2}{2} + gz_2\right)$$

$gz_1 = gz_2$ horizontal

No work is transferred ∴ W = 0. Also, Q = 0.

$$u_1 + P_1 V_{s1} + \frac{V_1^2}{2} = u_2 + P_2 V_{s2} + \frac{V_2^2}{2}$$

$$\frac{V_2^2}{2} = (u_1 - u_2) + (P_1 V_{s1} - P_2 V_{s2}) + \frac{V_1^2}{2}$$

$$= 250 \times 10^3 + 10^5 (10 \times 0.2 - 1 \times 2.7) + \frac{15^2}{2}$$

$$= 250{,}000 + 30{,}000 + 112.5$$

$$\frac{V_2^2}{2} = 280112.5$$

∴ V_2 = **748.5 m/s**   ... Ans.

Problem 1.18:

A nozzle is used for increasing the velocity of a steam. The enthalpy and velocity of the steam entering the nozzle are 2750 kJ/kg and 50 m/s respectively. The enthalpy at the exit of nozzle is 2600 kJ/kg. The heat losses from this horizontal nozzle are negligible.

   (i)   Find the velocity at exit from the nozzle.
   (ii) If the inlet area is 0.1 m² and specific volume at inlet is 0.18 m³/kg, find the mass flow rate.
   (iii) If the specific volume at the outlet is 0.498 m³/kg, find the area at the exit of the nozzle.

Solution: Given : h_1 = 2750 kJ/kg, v_1 = 50 m/s, h_2 = 2600 kJ/kg

(i) Steady flow energy equation is

$$Q + \left(h_1 + \frac{V_1^2}{2} + gz_1\right) = W + \left(h_2 + \frac{V_2^2}{2} + gz_2\right)$$

Q = 0, W = 0, ΔPE = 0

$$\therefore \quad h_1 + \frac{V_1^2}{2} = h_2 + \frac{V_2^2}{2}$$

$$\therefore \quad 2750 + \frac{50^2}{2000} = 2600 + \frac{V_2^2}{2000}$$

$$\therefore \quad V_2 = 550 \text{ m/s}$$

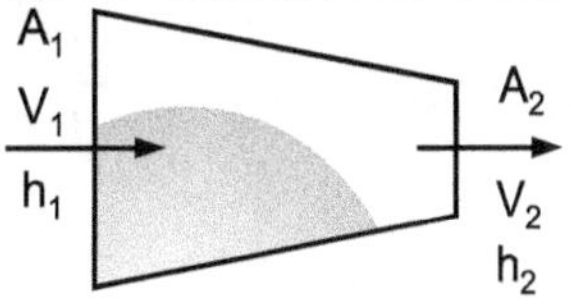

Fig. 1.59

(ii) For nozzle,

$$\text{Mass flow rate (at inlet)} = \frac{\text{(Inlet area)} \cdot \text{(Inlet velocity)}}{\text{Specific volume at inlet}}$$

$$= \frac{(0.1) \times 50}{0.18} = 27.7 \text{ kg/s} \quad \text{... Ans.}$$

(iii) For nozzle, Mass flow rate at inlet = Mass flow rate at outlet

$$27.7 = \frac{A_2 \times V_2}{\text{Specific volume at exit}}$$

$$27.7 = \frac{A_2 \times 550}{0.498}$$

$$\therefore \quad A_2 = \mathbf{0.025 \text{ m}^2} \quad \text{... Ans.}$$

Problem 1.19:

Air at 100 kPa and 280 K is compressed steadily to 600 kPa and 400 K. The mass flow rate of the air is 0.02 kg/s and a heat loss of 16 kJ/kg occurs during the process. Assuming the changes in kinetic and potential energies are negligible, determine the necessary power input to the compressor.

Assume enthalpy of air at inlet and exit as 280.13 kJ/kg and 400.98 kJ/kg respectively.

Solution: Steady flow energy equation is

$$q + \left(h_1 + \frac{V_1^2}{2} + gz_1\right) = w + \left(h_2 + \frac{V_2^2}{2} + gz_2\right)$$

$$q - w = \Delta h + \Delta PE + \Delta KE$$

$$\therefore \quad q - w = \Delta h + 0 + 0$$

$$\therefore \quad q - w = h_2 - h_1$$

$$\therefore \quad -16 - w = (400.98 - 280.13)$$

$$w = -136.85 \text{ kJ/kg}$$

This is the work done on the air per unit mass. The power input to the compressor is determined by multiplying this value by the mass flow rate.

$$W = m \cdot w = (-136.85) \times (0.02) = \mathbf{-2.74 \text{ kW}} \quad \text{Ans.}$$

Problem 1.20:

A water turbine receives water through a nozzle at the rate of 36000 kg/min. The head of water from the centre of the turbine is 300 m and discharge 5 m below the centre line of turbine. The velocity of water at outlet is 8 m/s. Neglecting the initial velocity of water, find the power output of the turbine.

Solution: Given: $m_w = \dfrac{3600}{60}$ kg/s = 600 kg/s, $v_1 = 0$, $v_2 = 8$ m/s

SFEE is,

$$Q + \left(h_1 + \dfrac{v_1^2}{2} + gz_1\right) = W + \left(h_2 + \dfrac{v_2^2}{2} + gz_2\right)$$

$h_1 = h_2 = 0$, $Q = 0$, $v_1 = 0$, $z_2 = 0$

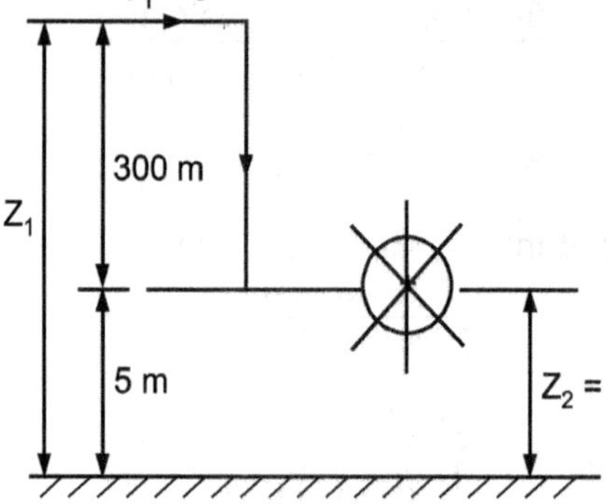

Fig. 1.60

∴ $\quad W = gz_1 - \dfrac{v_2^2}{2}$ J/kg

$\quad\quad\quad = 9.81 \times (305) - \dfrac{8^2}{2} = 2960$ J/kg

Power output $= 2960 \times m_w = \dfrac{2960 \times 600}{1000} = $ **1776 kW** ... **Ans.**

Problem 1.21:
In a steady flow machine, 405 kW of work is done by the machine. The flow of fluid is 3 kg/s. The specific volume of the fluid, pressure and velocity at inlet are 0.37 m³/kg, 6 bar and 16 m/s respectively. The inlet is 32 m above the floor and discharge pipe is at the level of floor. The discharge conditions are 0.62 m²/kg, 1 bar and 270 m/s respectively. The total heat loss between the inlet and discharge is 9 kJ/kg of the fluid. Find the change in specific internal energy.

Solution: Refer Fig. 1.61.

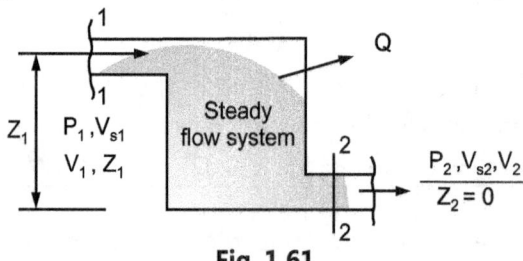

Fig. 1.61

Given: W = 405/3 = 135 kJ/kg

m = 3 kg/s $\quad\quad\quad z_1 = 32$ m

$V_{s1} = 0.37 \text{ m}^3/\text{kg}$ \quad\quad $V_{s2} = 0.62 \text{ m}^3/\text{kg}$
$P_1 = 6 \text{ bar}$ \quad\quad $P_2 = 1 \text{ bar}$
$V_1 = 16 \text{ m/s}$ \quad\quad $V_2 = 270 \text{ m/s}, z_2 = 0$
$Q = 9 \text{ kJ/kg}$ \quad\quad $u_2 - u_1 = ?$

Using SFEE

$$Q + \left(u_1 + P_1 V_{s1} + \frac{V_1^2}{2} + gz_1\right) = W + \left(u_2 + P_2 V_{s2} + \frac{V_2^2}{2} + gz_2\right)$$

$-9 + (u_1 + 6 \times 10^5 \times 0.37 + \frac{16^2}{2} + 9.81 \times 32)$

$= 135 + (u_2 + 1 \times 10^5 \times 0.62 + \frac{270^2}{2} + 9.81 \times 0)$

∴ \quad\quad $u_2 - u_1 = -20 \text{ kJ/kg}$

∴ \quad\quad Total $\Delta U = -20 \times m = -20 \times 3 = -60 \text{ kJ/s} = \mathbf{-60 \text{ kW}}$ \quad ... **Ans.**

Problem 1.22:

Air flows steadily at the rate of 0.5 kg/s, through an air compressor entering at 7 m/s velocity, 100 kPa and 0.95 m³/kg and leaving at 5 m/s, 700 kPa and 0.19 m³/kg respectively. The internal energy of the air leaving is 90 kJ/kg greater than that of air entering. Cooling water in the compressor jacket absorbs heat from the air at the rate of 58 kW.

(a) Compute the rate of shaft work input to the compressor in kW.
(b) Find the ratio of inlet and outlet pipe diameter.

Solution:

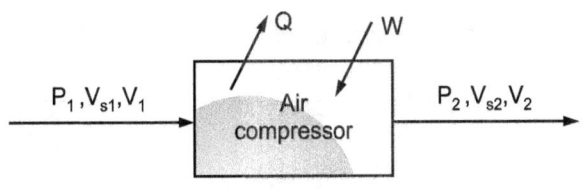

Fig. 1.62

Given: m = 0.5 kg/s
$V_1 = 7 \text{ m/s}$ \quad\quad $V_2 = 5 \text{ m/s}$
$V_{s1} = 0.95 \text{ m}^3/\text{kg}$ \quad\quad $V_{s2} = 0.19 \text{ m}^3/\text{kg}$
$P_1 = 100 \times 10^3 \text{ N/m}^2$ \quad\quad $P_2 = 700 \times 10^3 \text{ N/m}^2$
$u_2 - u_1 = 90 \text{ kJ/kg}$ \quad\quad $Q = -5.8 \text{ kW}$

$Q = \frac{-58}{m} = \frac{-58}{0.5} = -116 \text{ kJ/kg}$

$$Q + \left(u_1 + P_1 V_{s1} + \frac{V_1^2}{2} + gz_1\right) = W + \left(u_2 + P_2 V_{s2} + \frac{V_2^2}{2} + gz_2\right)$$

(a) $W = \left[(u_1 - u_2) + P_1 V_{s1} - P_2 V_{s2} + \dfrac{V_1^2}{2} - \dfrac{V_2^2}{2}\right] + Q$

$= \left[-90 \times 10^3 + 100 \times 10^3 \times 0.95 - 700 \times 10^3 \times 0.19 + \dfrac{7^2}{2} - \dfrac{5^2}{2}\right] - 116$ J/kg

$= [-90 + 95 - 133 + 0.012 - 116]$ kJ/kg

$= -223.98$ kJ/kg

Mass flow rate is m = 0.5 kg/s

Net work done/s = W × m = $-223.98 \times 0.5 = -112$ kW ... **Ans.**

(b) $m \times V_{s1} = A_1 v_1$ ∴ $A_1 = \dfrac{m \cdot V_{s1}}{v_1} = \dfrac{0.5 \times 0.95}{7} = 0.0678$ m²

$A_2 = \dfrac{m \cdot V_{s2}}{v_2} = \dfrac{0.5 \times 0.19}{5} = 0.019$ m²

$\dfrac{A_1}{A_2} = \dfrac{\frac{\pi}{4} \cdot d_1^2}{\frac{\pi}{4} \cdot d_2^2} = \dfrac{0.0678}{0.019} = 3.568$

∴ $\dfrac{d_1^2}{d_2^2} = 3.568$

∴ $\dfrac{d_1}{d_2} = \dfrac{\text{inlet pipe diameter}}{\text{outlet pipe diameter}} = 2.889$ ... **Ans.**

Problem 1.23:
The following data is given for an air compressor :
(i) Rate of air flow 5 kg/s

	Inlet	Outlet
Pressure	80 kPa	600 kPa
Sp. volume	0.65 m³/kg	0.12
Sp. internal energy	40 kJ/kg	140 kJ/kg
Velocity	6 m/s	4 m/s

Heat rejected to cooling water is 50 kW.

Find: (i) Power required to drive the compressor in kW.

(ii) Ratio of inlet pipe diameter to outlet pipe diameter.

Solution: $\Delta PE = 0$, $Q = \dfrac{50}{5} = 10$ kJ/kg

The SFEE is

THERMAL SCIENCE (S.E. MECH. & AUTO. SEM. III SU)   REVIEW OF LAWS OF THERMODYNAMICS

$$Q + \left(u_1 + P_1 V_{S1} + \frac{v_1^2}{2} + gz_1\right) = W + \left(u_2 + P_2 V_{S2} + \frac{v_2^2}{2} + gz_2\right) \text{ J/kg}$$

$$Q + \left(u_1 + P_1 V_{S1} + \frac{v_1^2}{2}\right) = W + \left(u_2 + P_2 V_{S2} + \frac{v_2^2}{2}\right)$$

$$10 + \left(40 + 80 \times 0.65 + \frac{6^2}{2} \times 10^{-3}\right)$$

$$= W + \left(140 + 600 \times 0.12 + \frac{4^2}{2} \times 10^{-3}\right) \text{ kJ/kg}$$

∴ $W = -129.99 \text{ kJ/kg}$ ... Ans.

For determining the ratio of diameters, use continuity equation.

$$\dot{m} = \frac{A_1 v_1}{V_{S1}} = \frac{A_2 v_2}{V_{S2}}$$

∴ $$\frac{A_1}{A_2} = \frac{V_{S1}}{V_{S2}} \times \frac{v_2}{v_1}$$

$$= \frac{0.65}{0.12} \times \frac{4}{6} = 3.611$$

∴ $$\frac{d_1}{d_2} = \sqrt{\frac{A_1}{A_2}} = \sqrt{3.611} = 2.9$$ ... Ans.

Problem 1.24:

Air flows in a compressor at a rate of 0.7 kg/sec. The air enters at 5 m/sec velocity, 100 kPa pressure, 0.85 m³/kg, volume leaving at 3 m/sec, 700 kPa and 0.17 m³/kg. The internal energy of the air leaving is 80 kJ/kg greater than that of air entering. Cooling water in the compressor jacket absorb heat from air at the rate of 60 kW.

(a) Determine the rate of shaft work input to the air in kW.
(b) Find the ratio of inlet pipe diameter to outlet pipe diameter.

Solution:

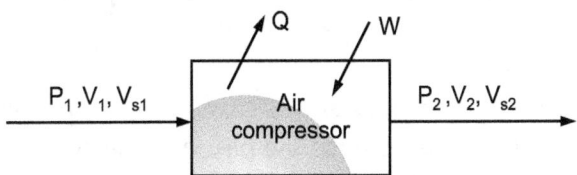

Fig. 1.63: Block diagram of a compressor

Given: $m = 0.7 \text{ kg/sec.}$
$v_1 = 5 \text{ m/sec}, v_2 = 3 \text{ m/sec}$

$v_{s_1} = 0.85 \text{ m}^3/\text{kg}, \ v_{s_2} = 0.17 \text{ m}^3/\text{kg}$

$P_1 = 100 \times 10^3 \text{ N/m}^2, \ P_2 = 700 \times 10^3 \text{ N/m}^2$

$u_2 - u_1 = 80 \text{ kJ/kg}, \ Q = \dfrac{-60}{0.7} = -85.7 \text{ kJ/kg}$

(a) Shaft work: Steady flow energy equation:

$$Q + \left(u_1 + P_1 v_{s_1} + \frac{v_1^2}{2} + gz_1\right) = W + \left(u_2 + P_2 v_{s_2} + \frac{v_2^2}{2} + gz_2\right)$$

$\therefore \quad W = \left[(u_1 - u_2) + P_1 v_{s_1} - P_2 v_{s_2} + \dfrac{v_1^2}{2} - \dfrac{v_2^2}{2}\right] + Q$

$= \left[-80 \times 10^3 + 100 \times 10^3 \times 0.85 - 700 \times 10^3 \times 0.17 + \dfrac{5^2}{2} - \dfrac{3^2}{2}\right] - 85.7$

$= -80 + 85 - 119 - 0.008 - 85.7$

$= -199.7 \text{ kJ/kg}$

Mass flow rate of air $= 0.7$ kg/sec.

Net work $= m \times W = 0.7 \times (-199.7) = \mathbf{-139.8 \text{ kW}}$ ... **Ans.**

(b) Ratio of inlet to outlet pipe diameter

$= m v_{s_1} = A_1 v_1$

$\therefore \quad A_1 = \dfrac{m \cdot v_{s_1}}{v_1} = \dfrac{0.7 \times 0.85}{5} = 0.119 \text{ m}^2$

Similarly, $\quad A_2 = \dfrac{m \cdot v_{s_2}}{v_2} = \dfrac{0.7 \times 0.17}{3} = 0.0396$

$\therefore \quad \dfrac{A_1}{A_2} = \dfrac{\frac{\pi}{4} \cdot d_1^2}{\frac{\pi}{4} \cdot d_2^2} = \dfrac{0.119}{0.0396} = 3$

$\therefore \quad \dfrac{d_1}{d_2} = \dfrac{\text{Inlet pipe diameter}}{\text{Outlet pipe diameter}} = 2.732$ ... **Ans.**

Problem 1.25:

1 kg of fluid contained in a cylinder receives 150 kJ of work by paddle wheel together with 50 kJ in the form of heat. At the same time, the piston in the cylinder moves in such a way that pressure remains constant at 200 kN/m² and fluid expands from 2m³ to 5 m³. Estimate the change in internal energy and change in enthalpy.

Solution:

$P = \text{constant} = 200 \text{ kN/m}^2$

$V_1 = 2 \text{ m}^3, \ V_2 = 5 \text{ m}^3$

W = 150 kJ done on the gas.

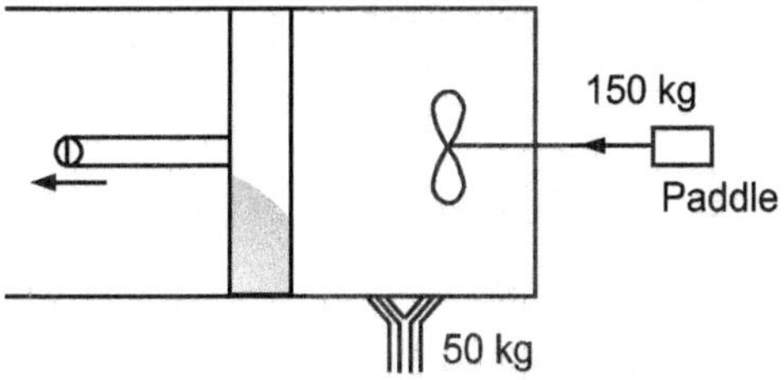

150 kg
Paddle

50 kg

Fig. 1.64

$$Q = \Delta U + W$$

Change in internal energy,

$$\Delta U = Q - W = 50 - 150 = -\textbf{100 kJ} \quad \text{... Ans.}$$

Change in enthalpy, $\Delta H = \Delta U + d(Pv)$

$$= \Delta U + P \cdot dv$$

$\therefore \quad P\,dv = P(v_2 - v_1)$

$$= 200 \times 10^3 (5 - 2) = 600 \times 10^3 \text{ Nm} = 600 \text{ kJ}$$

$\therefore \quad \Delta H = \Delta U + P\,dv$

$$= -100 + 600 = +\textbf{500 kJ} \quad \text{... Ans.}$$

Positive sign indicates that the enthalpy increases.

Problem 1.26:

In a particular non-flow system, a certain amount of working substance undergoes a frictionless process according to the law

$$P = \left(\frac{5}{v} + 3\right)$$

where P is in bar and v is in m³. During the process, volume changes from $v_1 = 0.12$ m³ to $v_2 = 0.04$ m³. The system rejects 93 kJ of heat during the process. Determine the change in internal energy and the change in enthalpy.

Solution: Given: Initial volume, $v_1 = 0.12$ m³

Final volume, $v_2 = 0.04$ m³.

It is a compression process.

$$\text{Work done, } W = \int_1^2 P\,dv = \int_1^2 \left(\frac{5}{v} + 3\right) dv \cdot 10^5$$

$$= [5 \log v + 3v]_1^2 \times 10^5$$

$$= \left[5 \log \frac{v_2}{v_1} + 3(v_2 - v_1)\right] \times 10^5$$

$$= -5.73 \times 10^5 \text{ joule}$$
$$= -573 \text{ kJ, work is done on the gas.}$$

Now, $\quad Q = \Delta U + W$

where $\quad \Delta U$ = change in internal energy
$$= Q - W$$
$$= -93 \text{ kJ} - (-573) \text{ kJ} = \mathbf{480 \text{ kJ}} \quad \text{... Ans.}$$

$\Delta H = dU + d(Pv) = dU + P\,dv$
$$= 480 - 573 = \mathbf{-93 \text{ kJ}} \quad \text{... Ans.}$$

Problem 1.27:

Air at 100 kPa and 280 K is compressed steadily to 600 kPa and 400 K. The mass flow rate of air is 0.02 kg/s and heat loss 16 kJ/kg occurs during the process. Assuming changes in kinetic and potential energies to be negligible, determine the necessary power input to the compressor. Assume enthalpy of air at inlet and exit at 280.13 kJ/kg and 400.98 kJ/kg respectively.

Solution: Given:

$P_1 = 100$ kPa $\qquad \dot{m}_{air} = 0.02$ kg/s

$T_1 = 280$ K $\qquad Q = -16$ kJ/kg

$P_2 = 600$ kPa $\qquad h_1 = 280.13$ kJ/kg

$T_2 = 400$ K $\qquad h_2 = 400.98$ kJ/kg

The steady flow energy equation is

$$q + \left(h_1 + \frac{v_1^2}{2} + gz_1\right) = w + \left(h_2 + \frac{v_2^2}{2} + gz_2\right)$$

Change in K.E. and P.E. are negligible.

$\therefore \qquad q - w = \Delta h$

$\qquad w = q - \Delta h$
$$= -16 - (400.98 - 280.13)$$
$$= -136.85 \text{ kJ/kg}$$

Power input, $W = m \cdot w$
$$= 0.02 \frac{\text{kg}}{\text{s}} \times (-136.85) \frac{\text{kJ}}{\text{kg}} = \mathbf{-2.737 \text{ kW}} \quad \text{... Ans.}$$

Problem 1.28:

A cylinder fitted with frictionless piston containing gas at a pressure 200×10^3 N/m² executes the cycle by undergoing the following processes :

(i) 1200 N-m of stirring work is done on gas by paddle wheel and cylinder is well insulated. As a result, volume increases by 0.0028 m³.

(ii) With the insulation removed and paddle wheel stationary, heat transfer from the gas restores the gas to its initial state. Evaluate :

(a) net work done by gas during process (i)

(b) net work done and heat transfer by gas in process (i)

(c) increase in energy of gas in processes (i) and (ii)

(d) the increase in energy of gas for combined processes (i) and (ii).

Solution: (a) Work done by the gas on the piston

$$= P \cdot dv = 200 \times 10^3 \text{ N/m}^2 \times (0.0028 \text{ m}^3) = 560 \text{ N-m}$$

The work supplied to the gas by paddle = 1200 N-m.

∴ The difference between 1200 N-m and 560 N-m is stored in the gas in the form of internal energy.

∴ Increase in internal energy = 1200 – 560 = **640 N-m.** ... **Ans.**

(b) Net work done in process (i) = **560 N-m.**

Since the cylinder is well insulated, the rate of heat transfer is zero. ... **Ans.**

(c) In process (i), internal energy increases by 640 N-m. In process (ii), the insulation is removed, it means heat transfer from gas to the surroundings takes place. It means internal energy decreases by 640 N-m, so that the gas returns to the original state. ... **Ans.**

(d) The gas undergoes a cyclic process because it expands from initial state due to addition of work by paddle wheel. The gas returns to the initial state as the internal energy decreases by the same amount. Therefore, the net change in internal energy in the combined processes (i) and (ii) is zero.

Problem 1.29:

A gas turbine receives gases at 7.2 bar and 850°C and velocity of 160 m/s. The gases come out of turbine at 2.15 bar and 450°C and a velocity of 250 m/s. Find out the work output from the gas turbine in kW/kg. The process may be assumed as adiabatic.

Take C_p = 2.04 kJ/kg-°C for gas.

Solution: The general energy equation on the basis of 1 kg flow can be written as

$$\left(\frac{V_1^2}{2} + gZ_1 + h_1\right) \pm Q \pm W = \left[\frac{V_2^2}{2} + gZ_2 + h_2\right]$$

For the gas turbine, $Z_1 = Z_2$, $Q = 0$

(as the flow is adiabatic (given)

Gas turbine is work developing system.

$$\therefore \quad \left(\frac{V_1^2}{2} + h_1\right) - W = \left(\frac{V_2^2}{2} + h_2\right)$$

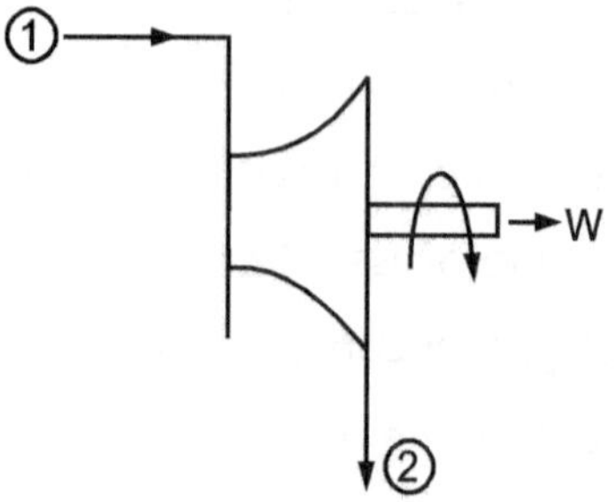

Fig. 1.65

$$\therefore \quad W = \frac{V_1^2 - V_2^2}{2} + (h_1 - h_2) = \frac{V_1^2 - V_2^2}{2} + C_p (T_1 - T_2)$$

$$= \left[\frac{(160)^2 - (250)^2}{2}\right] + 2.04 \times 10^3 \times (850 - 450) \text{ joules}$$

$$= (-18450 + 416 \times 10^3) \text{ joules} = -18.45 + 416$$

$$= 397.55 \text{ kJ/kg}$$ ... **Ans.**

Problem 1.30 :

The internal energy of a system is given by,

$$U = (100 + 50\,T + 0.04\,T^2) \text{ joules}$$

and heat transfer Q is given by

$$Q = (4000 + 16\,T) \text{ joules, where T is in K.}$$

If the temperature of the system changes from 300 K to 500 K, find the work transfer and its direction.

Solution: $U = 100 + 50\,T + 0.04\,T^2$

$$\therefore \quad \frac{dU}{dT} = 50 + 0.08\,T$$

$$\therefore \quad dU = (50 + 0.08\,T)\,dT$$

$$Q = 4000 + 16\,T$$

$$\therefore \quad \frac{dQ}{dT} = 2.6$$

$$\therefore \quad dQ = 16\,dT$$

As per first law of thermodynamics,

$$dQ = dW + dU$$

$$\therefore \quad dW = dQ - dU = (16\,dT) - (50 + 0.08\,T)\,dT$$

$$= (16 - 50 - 0.08\ T)\ dT = -(34 + 0.08\ T)\ dT$$

$$\therefore\quad W = -\int_{T_1}^{T_2} (34 + 0.08\ T)\ dT$$

$$= \int_{T_2}^{T_1} (34 + 0.08\ T)\ dT$$

$$= 34\ (T_1 - T_2) + 0.08\left(\frac{T_1^2 - T_2^2}{2}\right)$$

$$= 34\ (300 - 500) + 0.04\ [(300)^2 - (500)^2]$$

$$= -6800 - 6400 = -13200\ J = \mathbf{-13.2\ kJ} \qquad \text{... Ans.}$$

The negative sign indicates that the work is done on the system.

Problem 1.31:

A steam turbine receives steam at 15 bar and velocity of 300 m/s. The internal energy at inlet is 2000 kJ/kg and specific volume is 0.15 m³/kg. The steam leaves the turbine at 130 kPa with a velocity of 200 m/s, internal energy of 1500 kJ/kg and specific volume of 2.2 m³/kg. If inlet condition is 3 m above the discharge, find out the power output of the turbine if the steam flow rate is 300 kJ/min. Heat lost to the surrounding is 50 kJ/kg.

Solution: The generalised flow energy equation on the basis of 1 kg mass is given by,

$$\left(\frac{V_1^2}{2} + Z_1 g + p_1 v_{s1} + u_1\right) \pm Q \pm W = \left(\frac{V_2^2}{2} + Z_2 g + p_2 v_{s2} + u_2\right)$$

As it is work developing system, it can be written as

$$\left(\frac{V_1^2}{2} + Z_1 g + p_1 v_{s1} + u_1\right) - Q - W = \left(\frac{V_2^2}{2} + Z_2 g + p_2 v_{s2} + u_2\right)$$

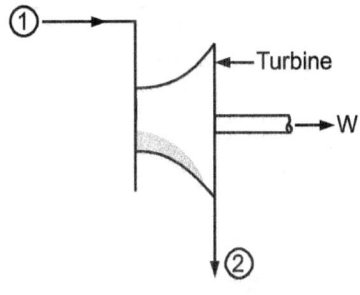

Fig. 1.66

$$\therefore \quad W = \frac{V_1^2 - V_2^2}{2} + g(Z_1 - Z_2) + (p_1 v_{s1} - p_2 v_{s2}) + (u_1 - u_2) - Q$$

$$= \frac{(300)^2 - (200)^2}{2} + 9.81 \times (3) + 10^5 \times (15 \times 0.15 - 2.3 \times 2.2)$$

$$+ 10^3 \times (2000 - 1500) - 50 \times 10^3$$

$$= 2.5 \times 10^4 + 29.43 + 10^5 \times (2.25 - 2.56) + 10^3 \times 500 - 50 \times 10^3$$

$$= 10^3 \times [25 + 0.0294 + 69 + 500 - 50] \text{ joules} = 544.03 \text{ kJ/kg} \quad \text{... Ans.}$$

As steam flow (m) = 300 kg/min = 5 kg/sec

$$\therefore \quad P = m \cdot W = 5 \times 544.03 = \mathbf{2720 \text{ kW}} \quad \text{... Ans.}$$

Problem 1.32:
A closed system executes a process in which it develops 8000 kJ of work by receiving 1500 kJ of heat. What is the change in internal energy? The system then is brought to original state with the rejection of 800 J of heat. What is the work done during the second process?

Solution: The first process is represented by 1-a-2 and second process is represented by 2-b-1 on p-v diagram as shown in Fig. 1.67.

Consider the process 1-a-2.

$$Q_{1a2} = +1500 \text{ kJ}, \quad W = 1000 \text{ kJ}$$

$$\therefore \quad Q_{1a2} = W_{1a2} + U_2 - U_1$$

$$\therefore \quad \Delta U = U_2 - U_1$$

$$= Q_{1a2} - W_{1a2}$$

$$= 1500 - 1000 = 500 \text{ kJ}$$

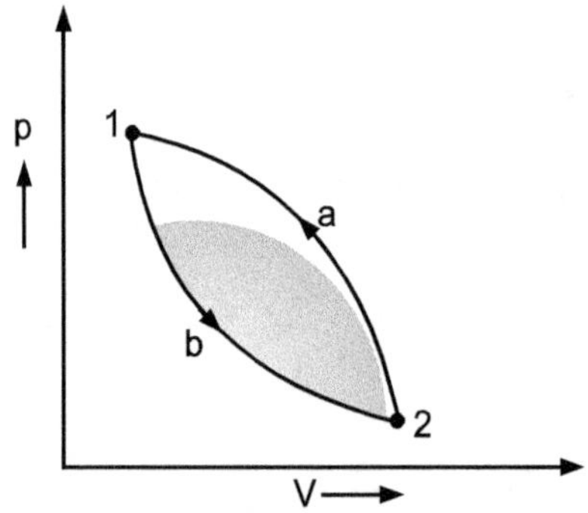

Fig. 1.67

For closed cycle,

$$\oint dQ = \oint dW$$

$$\therefore \quad Q_{1a2} + Q_{2b1} = W_{1a2} + W_{2b1}$$

$$\therefore \quad 1500 - 800 = 1000 + W_{2b1}$$

$$\therefore \quad W_{2b1} = \mathbf{-300 \text{ kJ}} \quad \text{... Ans.}$$

The negative sign indicates that the work is done on the system.

Problem 1.33:

A turbine operates under steady flow conditions with the following inlet and outlet conditions of the working fluid.

Property	Inlet	Outlet
Pressure (kPa)	1177	19.6
Specific volume (m³/kg)	0.218	7.79
Velocity (m/s)	35	100
Internal energy (kJ/kg)	2792.7	2456.5
Elevation (m)	3	0.0

Heat lost to the surrounding is 25 kJ/min. If the rate of steam flow through the turbine is 240 kg/min, what is the power output of the turbine?

Solution: The general flow energy equation considering mass flow rate m kg/sec can be written as

$$m\left[\frac{V_1^2}{2} + Z_1 g + u_1 + p_1 v_{s1}\right] - Q - W = m\left[\frac{V_2^2}{2} + Z_2 g + u_2 + p_2 v_{s2}\right]$$

where m is mass flow in kg/sec and Q and W are also on second basis.

where Q is heat rejected in J/sec = $\frac{25 \times 1000}{60}$ = 416.6 J/s

and W is the work developed in J/sec = watts

and m is mass of working fluid passing through the turbine = $\frac{240}{60}$ = 4 kg/sec

$$\therefore \quad W = m\left[\frac{V_1^2 - V_2^2}{2} + g(Z_1 - Z_2) + (u_1 - u_2) + (p_1 v_{s1} - p_2 v_{s2})\right] - Q$$

Substituting the given values in proper units,

$$W = 4\left[\frac{(35)^2 - (100)^2}{2} + 9.81(3-0) + 10^3(2792.7 - 2456.5) + (0.1177 \times 0.218 - 19.6 \times 7.79) \times 10^3\right] - 416.6$$

$$\therefore \quad W = 4 \times [-4387.5 + 29.43 + 10^3 \times 336.2 + 10^3 \times 103.9] - 416.6$$

$$= 4 \times 10^3 [-4.38 + 0.029 + 336.2 + 103.9] - 416.6$$

$$= 4 \times 10^3 [435.8] - 416.6$$

$$= \textbf{1742.6 kWz} \qquad \qquad \text{... Ans.}$$

1.21 LIMITATIONS OF FIRST LAW OF THERMODYNAMICS

- First law of thermodynamics tells that energy can be transformed from one form to another, but it does not tell how much energy can be transformed from one form to another. It means it is not quantitative law.
- Energy of an isolated system remains constant, as stated by first law. But it does not give information regarding whether a system which undergoes a process or not.
- Let us consider the following examples. Let a room is heated by an electric resistor (Fig. 1.68).

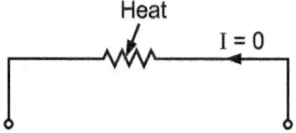

Fig. 1.68: Transferring heat to the wire will not generate electricity

Again the first law dictates that the amount of electrical energy supplied to the resistance wire be equal to the amount of energy transformed to the room air as heat. Now, attempt to reverse this process. If the same amount of heat supplied to the resistance wire will not generate electric energy, still it will not violate first law.

Again consider a paddle - wheel mechanism that is operated by the fall of mass. (Fig. 1.69).

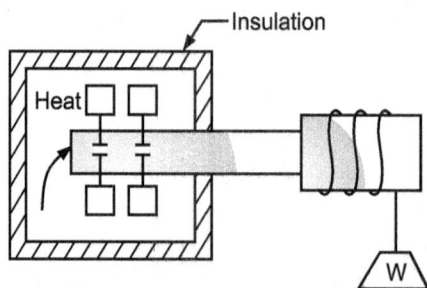

Fig. 1.69: Transferring heat to paddle wheel does not cause it to rotate

As the weight falls, paddle wheel rotates, stirring the fluid. Therefore, fluid gets heated. Now, attempt to reverse the process. That is transferring heat from the fluid to the paddle wheel, does not make the paddle wheel to rotate in reverse direction raising the weight from lower level to higher level. Still it will not violate the first law. It is clear from above, that processes proceed naturally in a **certain** direction and not in the reverse direction. The first law places no restriction on the direction of a process; but satisfying the first law does not ensure that process will actually occur.

These limitations of first law make necessary to study second law of thermodynamics.

1.22 THE SECOND LAW OF THERMODYNAMICS

1.22.1 Thermal Energy Reservoirs

A hypothetical body with a large thermal capacity (mass × specific heat) that can supply or absorb finite amount of heat energy without undergoing a change in temperature is termed as **thermal energy reservoir**. In practice, large bodies of water such as oceans, lakes and rivers as well as the atmospheric air are considered as thermal reservoirs.

A reservoir that supplies energy in the form of heat is called a **source** and one that absorbs energy in the form of heat is called a **sink**.

1.22.2 Heat Engine or Carnot Engine

Work can easily be converted into other forms of energy, but converting other forms of energy into work is not that easy. A device used to convert heat energy to work is known as **heat engine**.

Heat engines differ considerably from one another, but all are characterised by the following (Fig. 1.70).

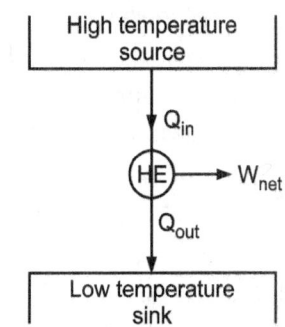

Fig. 1.70: Part of the heat received by a heat engine is converted to work while the rest is rejected)

(1) They receive heat from a high temperature source (solar energy, oil furnace, nuclear reactor, etc.)
(2) They convert part of this heat to work (usually in the form of a rotating shaft).
(3) They reject the remaining waste heat to a low temperature sink (the atmosphere, rivers, oceans etc.)
(4) They operate on a cycle.

Heat engines and other cyclic devices usually involve a fluid to and from which heat is transferred while undergoing a cycle. This fluid is called a working substance.

A steam power plant is best example of heat engine, which operates on thermodynamic cycle.

The work developing devices such as Internal combustion type (gas turbines and car engines) are also heat engines but they operate on mechanical cycle.

Let, Q_{in} = amount of heat supplied to heat engine, kJ

Q_{out} = amount of heat rejected to heat engine, kJ

The net work output, $W_{net} = Q_{in} - Q_{out}$ kJ

Thermal Efficiency:

Q_{out} is never zero. Therefore, W_{net} of heat engine is always less than Q_{in}.

∴ Thermal efficiency = $\dfrac{\text{net work output}}{\text{total heat input}}$

$$\eta_{th} = \dfrac{W_{net}}{Q_{in}} = \dfrac{Q_{in} - Q_{out}}{Q_{in}}$$

$$= 1 - \dfrac{Q_{out}}{Q_{in}} \qquad \ldots (1.51)$$

1.22.3 Refrigerator

A device which transfers heat from a low temperature body (medium) to a high temperature one is called as a **refrigerator**.

A refrigerator is a cyclic device which uses refrigerant as a working fluid. The most frequently used refrigeration is a vapour - compression refrigeration cycle.

A refrigerator is shown schematically in Fig. 1.71. Here Q_L is the amount of heat removed from the refrigerated space at temperature T_L, Q_H is the amount of heat rejected to the warm environment at temperature T_H and W_{net} is the net work input to the refrigerator.

The efficiency of a refrigerator is expressed in terms of the **coefficient of performance** (COP), denoted by COP_R.

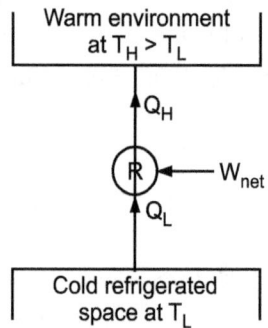

Fig. 1.71: Schematic of refrigerator

Coefficient of Performance:

The objective of a refrigerator is to remove heat (Q_L) from the refrigerated space. To accomplish this, it requires W_{net} work as input. Therefore, COP of a refrigerator is

$$COP_R = \dfrac{\text{desired effect}}{\text{required input}} = \dfrac{Q_L}{W_{net}} \qquad \ldots (1.52)$$

but, $\quad W_{net} = Q_H - Q_L$

∴ $\quad COP_R = \dfrac{Q_L}{Q_H - Q_L} = \dfrac{1}{(Q_H/Q_L) - 1} \qquad \ldots (1.53)$

COP may be greater than unity also.

1.22.4 Heat Pump (HP)

Another device that transfers heat from a low temperature space to a high temperature one is the heat pump. (Fig. 1.72). The objective of a heat pump is to maintain a heated space at high temperature.

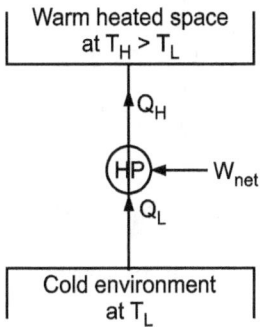

Fig. 1.72: Schematic of heat pump

The measure of performance of a heat pump is also expressed in terms of the coefficient of performance (COP_{HP}), defined as

$$COP_{HP} = \frac{\text{desired output}}{\text{required input}} = \frac{Q_H}{W_{net}} \quad \ldots (1.54)$$

$$= \frac{Q_H}{Q_H - Q_L} = \frac{1}{1 - \frac{Q_L}{Q_H}} \quad \ldots (1.55)$$

A comparison of equations (1.54) and (1.55) reveals that

$$COP_{HP} = COP_R + 1$$

1.22.5 The Second Law of Thermodynamics

In the last section, it is discussed that heat engine must reject some heat to a low temperature reservoir to complete the cycle, i.e. no heat engine can convert all the heat it receives to useful work. This limitation on the thermal efficiency of heat engine forms the basis for the *Kelvin-Planck statement*.

(a) Kelvin - Planck - Statement:

"It is impossible to construct a device that operates on a cycle and produces no effect other than withdrawal energy as heat from a single reservoir and converting all of it into work".

Simply, it can also be stated as "It is impossible for any device that operates on a cycle to receive heat from a single reservoir and produce an equivalent amount of work."

It can also be stated as "No engine can have thermal efficiency of 100 percent" (Fig. 1.73).

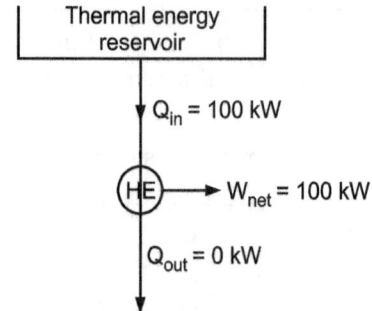

Fig. 1.73: A heat engine that violates Kelvin-Planck statement of second law (PMM - II)

A device that violates the second law of thermodynamics is called a perpetual motion machine of the second kind (PMM - II).

PMM - II is practically impossible.

(b) Clausius - Statement (Second Law of Thermodynamics)

"It is impossible to construct a device that operates in a cycle and produces no effect other than the transfer of heat from a low temperature body to a higher temperature body without external aid".

It simply states that a refrigerator will not operate unless its compressor is driven by an external power (electric motor). It means a device requires external energy to transfer heat from a low temperature body to a higher temperature body.

A device that violates Clausius statement is shown in Fig. 1.74.

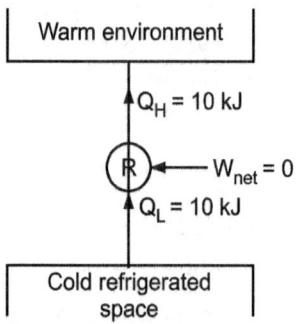

Fig. 1.74: A refrigerator that violates the Clausius statement of the second law (PMM - II)

1.22.6 Equivalence of Kelvin-Planck and Clausius Statements

- Kelvin-Planck statement tells that any heat engine will not convert the thermal energy of heat source completely into useful work. It means that a heat engine does not have 100 percent efficiency.

- Clausius statement tells that it will not be possible to transfer heat from a body at lower temperature to a body at higher temperature without external aid (energy input).

- From above paragraphs, one feels that the two statements are totally different and have no way interlinked. But conceptually the two statements of second law of thermodynamics are equivalent in all respect and can be proved here.

- The proof is not in the form of mathematical steps but violation of one statement implies the violation of the second and vice-versa.

(a) Consider a cyclic heat pump 'P' shown in Fig. 1.75 which transfers heat from a low temperature reservoir (T_2) to a high temperature reservoir (T_1) with no other effect i.e. with no expenditure of work, violating Clausius statement.

Let us assume a heat engine 'E' working between the same thermal reservoirs producing net work (W_{net}) in a thermodynamic cycle. Assume that the rate of working of the heat engine is such that it draws an amount of heat Q_1 from the reservoir equal to that discharged by the heat pump (P). It means there is no need of high temperature reservoir and the heat Q_1 discharged by the heat pump (P) is directly fed to the heat engine. So one concludes that heat pump 'P' and the heat engine 'E' working together constitute a heat engine operating in cycles and producing net work while exchanging heat only with one body at a single fixed temperature. This violates the Kelvin-Planck statement.

(b) Let us consider a perpetual motion machine of second kind (PMM-II) 'E' which produces net work in a cycle by exchanging heat with only one thermal energy reservoir (at T_1) and thus violates the Kelvin-Planck statement (See Fig. 1.76).

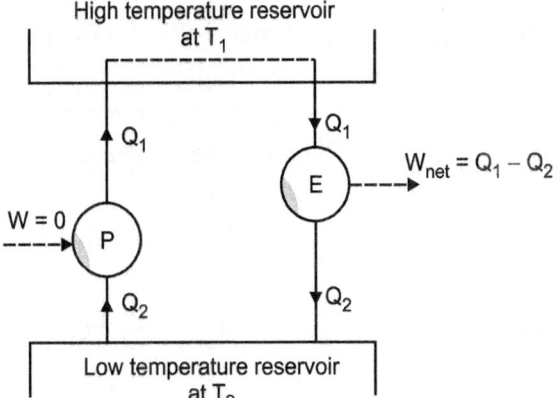

Fig. 1.75: Violation of Clausius statement   **Fig. 1.76: Violation of Kelvin-Planck statement**

Now, consider a cyclic heat pump (P) extracting heat Q_2 from a low temperature reservoir at T_2 and discharging heat to the high temperature reservoir at T_1 with the expenditure of work 'W' equal to that of the PMM-II delivers to a complete cycle. So E and P together constitute a heat pump working in cycles and producing the sole effect of transferring heat from a body at low temperature to a body at high temperature, thus violating the Clausius statement.

1.23 CONCEPT OF REVERSIBILITY AND IRREVERSIBILITY

1. A reversible process is carried out infinitely slowly with an infinitesimal gradient, so that every state passed through by the system is an equilibrium state.
2. Any natural process carried out with a finite gradient is an irreversible process. A reversible process consists of a succession of equilibrium states. So it is an idealized hypothetical process. It is said to be an asymptote to reality. All spontaneous processes are irreversible.
3. Time has an important effect on reversibility. If the time allowed for a process to occur is infinitely large, even though the gradient is finite, the process becomes reversible. However, if this time allowed is reduced to a finite value, the finite gradient makes the process irreversible.

1.23.1 Causes of Irreversibility

The irreversibility of a process may be due to either lack of equilibrium during the process or involvement of dissipative effects.

(a) Irreversibility Due to Lack of Equilibrium

When there is no thermodynamic equilibrium (mechanical, thermal or chemical) between the system and its surroundings, or between two systems, or two parts of the same system, causes a continuous change which is irreversible. The following are few specific examples in this regard:

Heat Transfer through a Finite Temperature Difference: To transfer a finite amount of heat through an infinitesimal temperature difference would require an infinite amount of time, or infinite area. All actual heat transfer processes are through a finite temperature difference and are, therefore, irreversible, and greater the temperature difference, the greater is the irreversibility.

We can demonstrate by the second law that heat transfer through a finite temperature difference is irreversible.

- Let us assume that a source at T_A and a sink at T_B ($T_A > T_B$) are available, and let Q_{A-B} be the amount of heat flowing from A and B (See Fig. 1.77).
- Let us assume engine operating between A and B, taking heat Q_1 from A and discharging heat Q_2 to B.

- Let the heat transfer process be reversed, and Q_{B-A} be the heat flowing from B to A (See Fig. 1.78) and let the rate of working of the engine be such that

$$Q_2 = Q_{B-A}$$

Then the sink B may be eliminated. The net result is that E produces net work W in a cycle by exchanging heat only with A, thus violating the Kelvin-Plank statement. So the heat transfer process Q_{A-B} is irreversible, and Q_{B-A} is not possible.

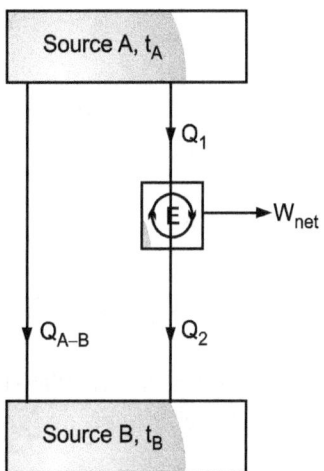
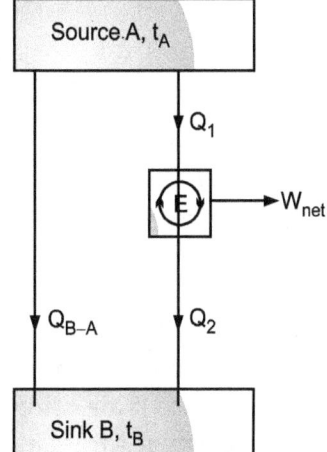

Fig. 1.77: Heat transfer through a finite temperature difference

Fig. 1.78: Heat transfer through a finite temperature difference is irreversible

Lack of pressure: Equilibrium within the Interior of the System or between the System and the Surroundings: When there exists a difference in pressures between the system and the surroundings, or within the system itself, then both the system and its surroundings, will undergo a change of state. For example, let any system is at a pressure p_1 greater than the surrounding. In this case, a process occurs wherein the system pressure reduces to surrounding pressure resulting into the mechanical equilibrium. The reverse of this process is not possible spontaneously without producing any other effect.

Free Expansion: Let us consider an insulated container (See Fig. 1.79) which is divided into two compartments A and B by a thin diaphragm. Compartment A contains a mass of gas, while compartment B is completely evacuated. If a hole is made in the diaphragm, the gas in A will expand into B until the pressures in A and B compartments become equal. This is known as free or unrestrained expansion. We can demonstrate by the second law, that the process of free expansion is irreversible.

- To prove this, assume that free expansion is reversible, and that the gas in B returns into compartment A with an increase in pressure, and compartment B becomes evacuated as before (See Fig. 1.80).
- There is no other effect. Let us install an engine (a machine, not a cyclic heat engine) between A and B, and permit the gas to expand through the engine from A to B.

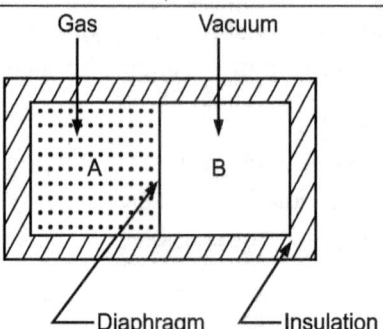

Fig. 1.79: Free expansion

- The engine develops a work output W at the expense of the internal energy of the gas. The internal energy of the gas (system) in B can be resorted to its initial value by heat transfer Q (=W) from a source.
- Now, by the use of the reverse free expansion, the system can be resorted to the initial state of high pressure in A and vacuum in B.
- The net result is a cycle, in which we observe that net work output W is accomplished by exchanging heat with a single reservoir.
- This violates the Kelvin-Planck statement. Hence, free expansion is irreversible. The same argument will hold if the compartment B is not in vacuum but at a pressure lower than that in compartment A (case b).

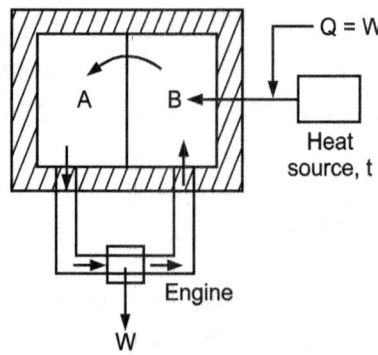

Fig. 1.80: Second law demonstrates that free expansion is irreversible

(b) Irreversibility due to Dissipative Effects

The transformation of work into molecular internal energy either of the system or of the reservoir takes place through the agency of such phenomena as friction, viscosity, inelasticity, electrical resistance, and magnetic hysteresis. These effects are known as dissipative effects, and work is said to be dissipated. The irreversibility of a process may be due to the dissipative effects in which work is done without producing an equivalent increase in the kinetic or potential energy of any system.

Friction: Friction is always present when two moving surfaces are in contact. Friction may be reduced by suitable lubrication, but it can never be completely eliminated. If this were possible, a movable device could be kept in continual motion without violating either of the two laws of thermodynamics. The continual motion of a movable device in the complete absence of friction is known as perpetual motion of the third kind.

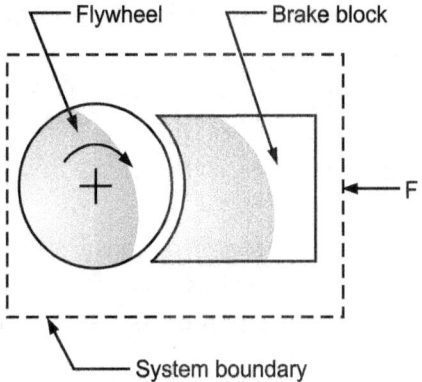

Fig. 1.81 : Reversibility due to friction

- That friction makes a process irreversible can be demonstrated by the second law. Let us consider a system consisting of a flywheel and a brake block (See Fig. 1.81).
- The flywheel was rotating with a certain rpm, and it was brought to rest by applying the friction brake.
- The distance moved by the brake block is very small, so work transfer is very nearly equal to zero.
- If the braking process occurs very rapidly, there is little heat transfer. Using suffix 2 after braking and suffix 1 before braking, and applying the first law, we have

$$Q_{1-2} = E_2 - E_1 + W_{1-2}$$
$$0 = E_2 - E_1 + 0$$
∴ $$E_2 = E_1 \qquad \ldots (1.56)$$

The energy of the system (isolated) remains constant. Since the energy may exist in the forms of kinetic, potential, and molecular internal energy, we have,

$$U_2 + \frac{mV_2^2}{2} + mZ_{2g} = U_1 + \frac{mV_1^2}{2} + mZ_{1g}$$

Since the wheel is brought to rest, $V_2 = 0$, and there is no change in P.E.

$$U_1 = U_1 + \frac{mV_1^2}{2} \qquad \ldots (1.57)$$

Therefore, the molecular internal energy of the system (i.e., of the brake and the wheel) increases by absorption if the K.E. of the wheel. The reverse process, i.e., the conversion of this increase in molecular internal energy into K.E. within the system to cause the wheel to rotate is not possible to prove it by the second law, let us assume that it is possible, and imagine the following cycle with three processes:

Process A: Let initially the wheel and the brake are at high temperature as a result of the absorption of the K.E. of the wheel, and the flywheel is at rest. Let the flywheel now start rotating at a particular rpm at the expense of the internal energy of the wheel and brake, the temperature of which will then decrease.

Process B: Let the flywheel be brought to rest by using its K.E. in raising weights, with no change in temperature.

Process C: Now, let heat be supplied from a source to the flywheel and the weights, with no change in temperature.

Therefore, the processes A, B, and C together constitute a cycle producing work by exchanging heat with a single reservoir. This violates the Kelvin-Planck statement, and it will become a PMM2. So the braking process, i.e., the transformation of K.E. into molecular internal energy, is irreversible.

Paddle-Wheel Work Transfer:

- Consider an insulated tank with a fluid (system) in it. Work may be transferred into a system by means of a paddle wheel (See Fig. 1.82) whiich is also known as stirring work. Here work transferred is dissipated adiabatically into an increase in the molecular internal energy of the system.

- To prove the irreversibility of the process, let us assume that the same amount of work is delivered by the system at the expense of its molecular internal energy, and the temperature of the system goes down (See Fig. 1.83).

- The system is brought back to its initial state by heat transfer from a source. These two processes together constitute a cycle in which there is work output and the system exchanges heat with a single reservoir.

- It becomes a PMM2, and hence the dissipation of stirring work to internal energy is irreversible.

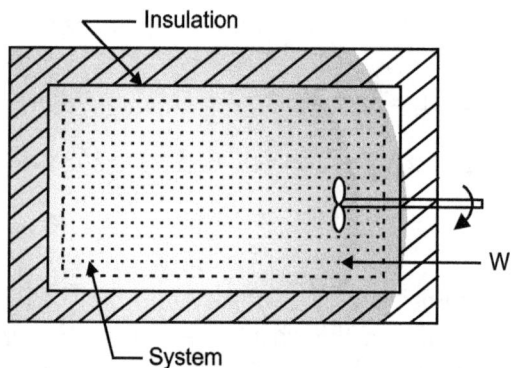

Fig. 1.82: Adiabatic work transfer

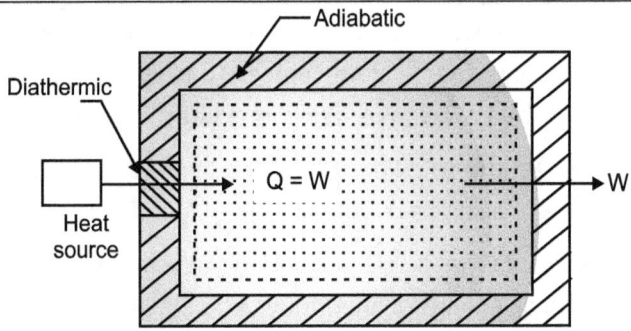

Fig. 1.83: Irreversibility due to dissipation of stirring work into internal energy

Transfer of Electricity through a Resistor: The flow of electric current through a wire represents work transfer, because the current can drive a motor which can raise a weight. Taking the wire/ the resistor as the system (See Fig. 1.84) and the first law as,

$$Q_{1-2} = U_2 - U_1 + W_{1-2}$$

Here both W_{1-2} and Q_{1-2} are negative.

$$W_{1-2} = U_2 - U_1 + Q_{1-2} \qquad \ldots (1.58)$$

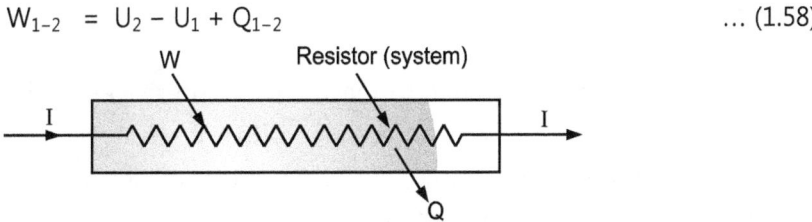

Fig. 1.84: Irreversibility due to dissipation of electrical work into internal energy

A part of the work transfer is stored as an increase in the internal energy of the wire (to give an increase in its temperature), and the remainder leaves the system as heat. At steady state, the internal energy and hence the temperature of the resistor become constant with respect to time and

$$W_{1-2} = Q_{1-2} \qquad \ldots (1.59)$$

The reverse process, i.e. the conversion of heat Q_{1-2} into electrical work W_{1-2} of the same magnitude is not possible. Let us assume that this is possible. Then heat Q_{1-2} will be absorbed and equal work W_{1-2} will be delivered. But this will become a PMM2. So the dissipation of electrical work into internal energy or heat is irreversible.

1.23.2 Conditions for Reversibility

- A natural process is irreversible because the conditions for mechanical, thermal and chemical equilibrium are not satisfied, and the dissipative effects, in which work is transformed into an increase in internal energy, are present.

- For a process to be reversible, it must not possess these features. If a process is performed quasistatically, the system passes through states of thermodynamic equilibrium, which may be traversed as well in one direction or in the opposite direction.
- *If there are no dissipative effects, all the work done by the system during the performance of a process in one direction can be returned to the system during the reverse process.*
- A process will be reversible when it is performed in such a way that the system is at all times infinitesimally near a state of thermodynamic equilibrium and in the absence of dissipative effect of any form. Reversible processes are, therefore, purely ideal, limiting cases of actual processes.

1.23.3 Types of Irreversibility

A process becomes irreversible if it occurs due to a finite potential gradient like the gradient in temperature or pressure, or if there is dissipative effect like friction, in which work is transformed into internal energy increase of the system. Two types of irreversibility can be distinguished:

(a) Internal irreversibility

(b) External irreversibility

The internal irreversibility is caused by the internal dissipative effects like friction, turbulence, electrical resistance, magnetic hysteresis, etc. within the system. The external irreversibility refers to the irreversibility occurring at the system boundary like heat interaction with the surroundings due to finite temperature gradient.

Sometimes, it is useful to make other distinctions. If the irreversibility of a process is due to the dissipation of work into the increase in internal energy of a system, or due to a finite pressure gradient, it is called mechanical irreversibility. If the process occurs in account of a finite temperature gradient, it is thermal irreversibility, and if it is due to a finite concentration gradient or a chemical reaction, it is called chemical irreversibility.

A heat engine cycle in which there is a temperature difference (i) between the source and the working fluid during heat supply, and (ii) between the working fluid and the sink during heat rejection, exhibits external thermal irreversibility. If the real source and sink are not considered and hypothetical reversible processes for heat supply and heat rejection are assumed, the cycle can be reversible. With the inclusion of the actual source and sink, however, the cycle becomes externally irreversible.

1.24 CARNOT CYCLE (REVERSIBLE CYCLE)

It is also called as **reversible cycle** because all the processes are reversible one. It works between two different temperature reservoirs. It consists of two reversible adiabatic and two reversible isothermal processes.

Carnot engine working between two thermal reservoirs is shown in Fig. 1.85.

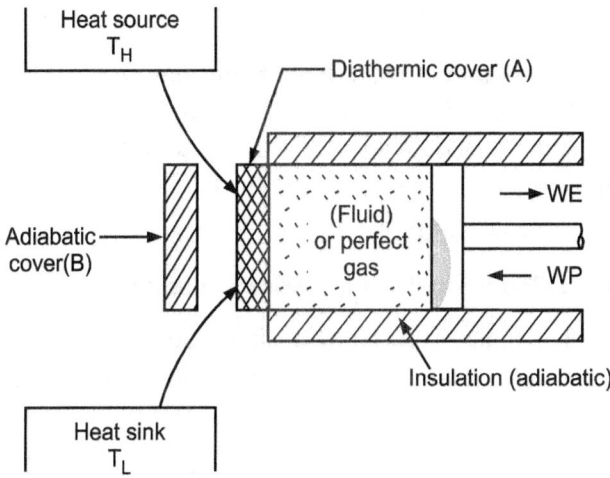

Fig. 1.85: Carnot heat engine

The assumptions made for describing the working of the Carnot engine are as follows:
- The piston moving in a cylinder does not develop any friction during motion.
- The walls of piston and cylinder are considered as perfect insulators of heat.
- The cylinder head is so arranged that it can be a perfect heat conductor or perfect heat insulator.
- The transfer of heat does not affect the temperature of source or sink.
- Working medium is a perfect gas and has constant specific heat.
- Compression and expansion are reversible.

Carnot cycle is represented on p-V plane [Fig. 1.86 (a)] and on T-s plane [Fig. 1.86 (b)].

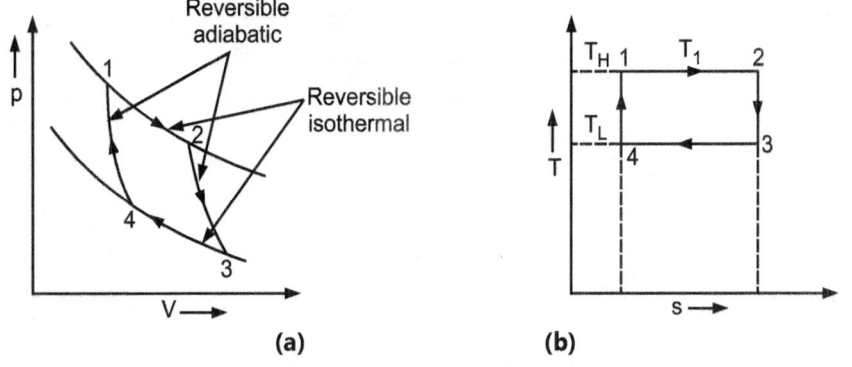

(a)   (b)

Fig. 1.86: p-V and T-s diagrams

Process 1 - 2 : Reversible Isothermal Expansion process:

The hot body at temperature T_H is brought in contact with working fluid (diathermic cover A is in contact with cylinder head), so that heat is transferred isothermally.

∴ According to the first law of thermodynamics,

$$Q_{1-2} = \Delta U + W_{1-2} \qquad (\because \Delta U = 0)$$

∴
$$Q_{1-2} = W_{1-2} = m \cdot R \cdot T_H \ln\left(\frac{V_2}{V_1}\right)$$

$$= T_1(s_2 - s_1) \text{ kJ}$$

Process 2 - 3: Reversible Adiabatic (Isentropic) Expansion process :

In this process, diathermic cover 'A' is assumed to be replaced by the adiabatic cover 'B'. No heat transfer occurs. Work W_E is obtained from the system; at the cost of internal energy. Therefore, temperature decreases from T_H to T_L (T_2 to T_3).

∴
$$Q_{2-3} = 0$$

Process 3 - 4: Reversible Isothermal Compression process :

Again adiabatic cover 'B' is replaced by cover 'A'. It is assumed that the fluid is brought into contact with low temperature sink (T_L). The heat is rejected isothermally from the fluid to sink.

$$Q_{3-4} = W_{3-4} = -mRT_L \cdot \ln\left(\frac{V_4}{V_3}\right)$$

$$= mRT_L \ln\left(\frac{V_3}{V_4}\right) = T_3(s_3 - s_4) \text{ kJ}$$

Process 4 – 1: Reversible Adiabatic (Isentropic) Compression process :

This compression process is continued till the fluid reaches initial state at point 3. The work is done on the fluid in this process and therefore internal energy increases. So temperature increases from T_L to T_H.

$$\text{Thermal efficiency} = \frac{\text{Heat supplied} - \text{Heat rejected}}{\text{Heat supplied}}$$

$$= \frac{mRT_H \ln\left(\frac{V_2}{V_1}\right) - mRT_L \ln\left(\frac{V_3}{V_4}\right)}{mRT_H \ln\left(\frac{V_2}{V_1}\right)}$$

$$\frac{V_3}{V_2} = \frac{V_4}{V_1} \quad \text{or} \quad \frac{V_2}{V_1} = \frac{V_3}{V_4}$$

$$\eta_{th} = \frac{T_H - T_L}{T_H} \quad \text{or} \quad \frac{T_1 - T_3}{T_1} \qquad \ldots (1.60)$$

$$= 1 - \frac{T_L}{T_H}$$

If T_L is constant (i.e. the temperature of heat sink such as atmosphere, lake water etc.) and source temperature T_H increases, the thermal efficiency of the cycle increases.

The relative work outputs of various piston engine cycles are given by mean effective pressure (mep or p_m). The **mean effective pressure** is defined as the constant pressure producing the same net work output while causing the piston to move through the same swept volume as in the actual cycle (See Fig. 1.86).

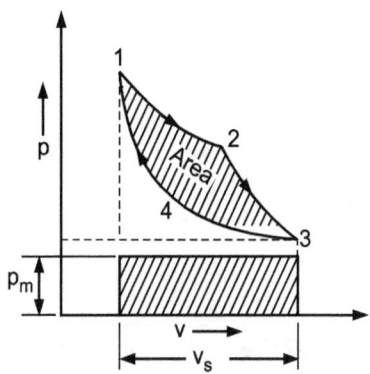

Fig. 1.86: Mean effective pressure

Let
- p_m = mean effective pressure, N/m²
- V_s = swept volume, m³
- W = net work output per cycle, N-m

Then, $p_m = \dfrac{\text{Work done per cycle}}{\text{Stroke volume}}$

$$= \frac{W}{V_s} = \frac{\int p dV}{V_s} \quad \ldots (1.61)$$

∴ $p_m = \dfrac{\text{Area of indicator diagram}}{\text{Stroke volume}}$

1.25 CARNOT'S THEOREM

"It states that of all engines operating between a given constant temperature source and a given constant temperature sink, none has a higher efficiency than a reversible engine".

Proof:

Two cyclic heat engines HE_A and HE_B operating between the same source and sink, of which HE_B is reversible.

HE_A and HE_B are the two engines operating between the given source at temperature T_1 and the given sink at temperature T_2 as shown in Fig. 1.87.

Let HE_A be any heat engine and HE_B be any reversible heat engine. We have to prove that efficiency of HE_B is more than that of HE_A. Let us assume that $\eta_A > \eta_B$.

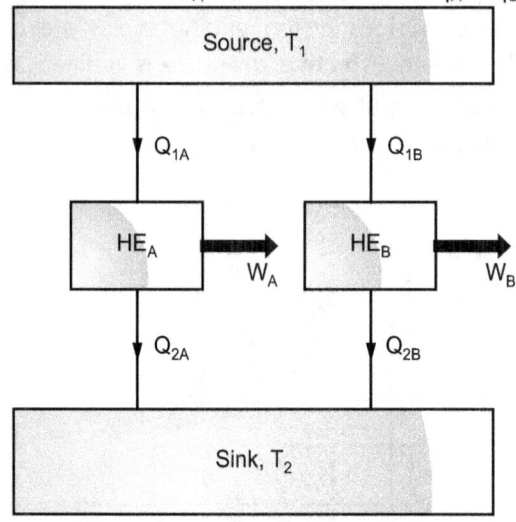

Fig. 1.87: Two cyclic heat engines

Let the rates of working of the engines be such that as shown in Fig. 1.87.

$$Q_{1A} = Q_{1B} = Q_1$$
$$\eta_A > \eta_B$$
$$\frac{W_A}{Q_{1A}} = \frac{W_B}{Q_{1B}}$$
$$W_A > W_B$$

Now, let HE_B be reversed.

Since HE_B is a reversible heat engine, the magnitudes of heat and work transfer quantities will remain the same, but their directions will be reversed, as shown in Fig. 1.88.

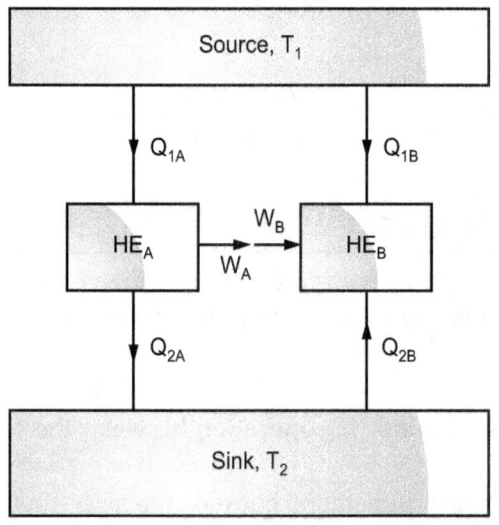

Fig. 1.88: Reversible heat engine is reversed

Now, if both the engine that is 'A' and 'reversed B' are combined together as shown in Fig. 1.89.

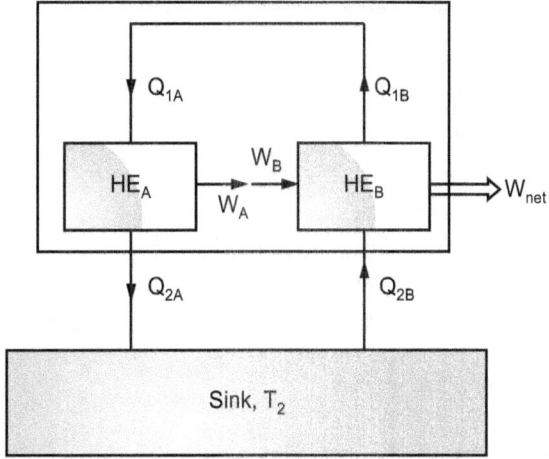

Fig. 1.89: Combined heat engine and heat pump

Thus, this combined heat engine is producing net work, $W_{net} = W_A - W_B$, by exchanging heat with a single reservoir. However it is not possible because it is thus violating Kelvine- Planck Statement of Second law of thermodynamics.

Therefore the assumption that efficiency of *irreversible heat engine is more than that of reversible heat engine is wrong.*

Therefore the efficiency of *irreversible heat engine can not be more than that of reversible heat engine.*

In other word, the efficiency of irreversible heat engine is always less than that of reversible heat engine.

Corollary1

1.26 DEFINITION OF THERMODYNAMIC TEMPERATURE

The efficiency of the engine is the work divided by the heat introduced to the system or

$$\eta = \frac{w_{cy}}{q_H} = \frac{q_H - q_C}{q_H} = 1 - \frac{q_C}{q_H} \qquad \ldots (1.62)$$

where w_{cy} is the work done per cycle. Thus, the efficiency depends only on q_C/q_H.

Because all reversible engines operating between the same heat reservoirs are equally efficient, any reversible heat engine operating between temperatures T_1 and T_2 must have the same efficiency, meaning, the efficiency is the function of the temperatures only:

$$\frac{q_C}{q_H} = f(T_H, T_C) \qquad \ldots (1.63)$$

In addition, a reversible heat engine operating between temperatures T_1 and T_3 must have the same efficiency as one consisting of two cycles, one between T_1 and another (intermediate) temperature T_2, and the second between T_2 and T_3. This can only be the case if

$$f(T_1, T_3) = \frac{q_3}{q_1} = \frac{q_2 q_3}{q_1 q_2} = f(T_1, T_2) f(T_2, T_3)$$

Specializing to the case that T is a fixed reference temperature: the temperature of the triple point of water. Then for any T^2 and T_3,

Therefore, if thermodynamic temperature is defined by

$$T = 273.16 \cdot f(T_1, T)$$

then the function f, viewed as a function of thermodynamic temperature, is

$$f(T_2, T_3) = \frac{T_3}{T_2}$$

and the reference temperature T_1 has the value 273.16. (Of course any reference temperature and any positive numerical value could be used—the choice here corresponds to the Kelvin scale.)

It follows immediately that

$$\frac{q_C}{q_H} = f(T_H, T_C) = \frac{T_C}{T_H} \qquad \ldots (1.64)$$

Substituting Equation (1.63) back into Equation (1.64) gives a relationship for the efficiency in terms of temperature.

$$\eta = 1 - \frac{q_C}{q_H} = 1 - \frac{T_C}{T_H}$$

1.26.1 Definition of Absolute Temperature Scale

In discussing the matter of temperature in Chapter 1, we pointed out that the zeroth law of thermodynamics provides a basis for temperature measurement, but that a temperature scale must be defined in terms of a particular thermometer substance and device. A temperature scale that is independent on any particular substance, which might be called an absolute temperature scale, would be most desirable. In the last paragraph, we noted that the efficiency of a Carnot cycle is independent of the working substance and depends only on the temperature. This fact provides the basis for such an absolute temperature scale, which we call the thermodynamic scale.

The concept of this temperature scale may be developed with the help of Fig. 1.90, which shows three reservoirs and three engines that operate on the Carnot cycle. T_1 is the highest temperature, T_3 is the lowest temperature, and T_2 is an intermediate temperature, and the engines operate the various reservoirs as indicated. Q_1 is the same for both A and C and since we are dealing with reversible cycles, Q_3 is the same for B and C.

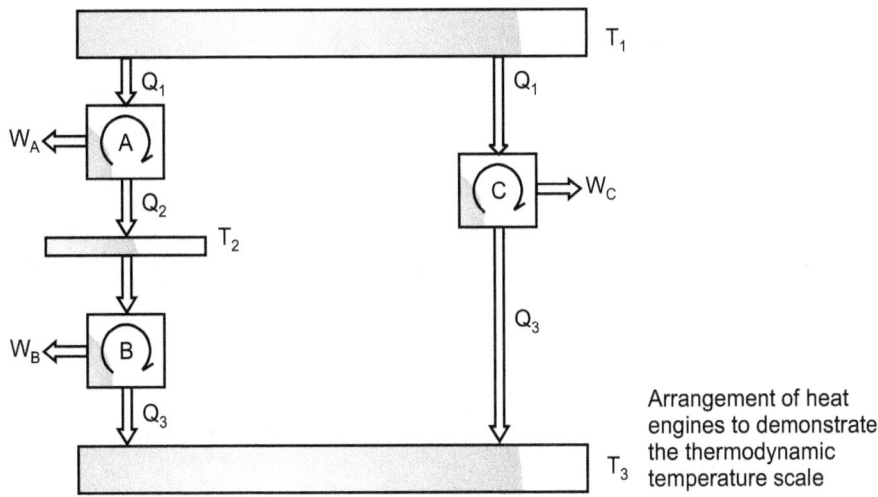

Arrangement of heat engines to demonstrate the thermodynamic temperature scale

Fig. 1.90: Arrangement of heat engines to demonstrate the thermodynamic temperature scale

Since the efficiency of a Carnot cycle is a function only of the temperature, we can write,

$$\eta_{thermal} = 1 - \frac{Q_L}{Q_H} = 1 - \Psi(T_L, T_H)$$

where, Ψ designates a functional relation.

Let us apply this functional relation to the three Carnot cycles of Fig. 1.90.

$$\frac{Q_1}{Q_2} = \Psi(T_1, T_2)$$

$$\frac{Q_2}{Q_3} = \Psi(T_2, T_3)$$

$$\frac{Q_1}{Q_3} = \Psi(T_1, T_3)$$

Since

$$\frac{Q_1}{Q_3} = \frac{Q_1 Q_2}{Q_2 Q_3}$$

it follows that

$$\Psi(T_1, T_3) = \Psi(T_1, T_2) \times \Psi(T_2, T_3)$$

Note that the left side is a function of T_1 and T_3 (and not T_2) and therefore the right side of this equation must also be a function of T_1 and T_3 (and not of T_2). From this fact, we can conclude that the form of the function Ψ must be such that,

$$\Psi(T_1, T_2) = \frac{f(T_1)}{f(T_2)}$$

$$\Psi(T_2, T_3) = \frac{f(T_2)}{f(T_3)}$$

for in this way $f(T_3)$ will cancel from the product of $\Psi(T_1, T_3)$. Therefore, we conclude that,

$$\frac{Q_1}{Q_3} = \Psi(T_1, T_3) = \frac{f(T_1)}{f(T_3)}$$

In general terms,

$$\frac{Q_H}{Q_L} = \frac{f(T_H)}{f(T_L)}$$

Now, three are several functional relations that will satisfy this equation. For the thermodynamic scale of temperature, which was originally proposed by Lord Kelvin, the selected relation is,

$$\frac{Q_H}{Q_L} = \frac{(T_H)}{(T_L)}$$

With absolute temperature so defined, the efficiency of a Carnot cycle may be expressed in terms of the absolute temperature.

$$\eta_{thermal} = 1 - \frac{Q_L}{Q_H} = 1 - \frac{T_L}{T_H}$$

This means that if the thermal efficiency of a Carnot Cycle operating between two given constant-temperature reservoirs is known, the ratio of the two absolute temperatures is also known.

Suppose, we had a heat engine operating on the Carnot cycle that received heat at the temperature of the steam and rejected heat at the temperature of the ice point. (Because a Carnot cycle involves only reversible processes, it is impossible to construct such a heat engine and perform the proposed experiment. However, we can follow the reasoning as a "thought experiment" and gain additional understanding of the thermodynamic temperature scale). If the efficiency of such an engine could be measured, we would find it to be 26.80%. Therefore, from equation

$$\eta_{th} = 1 - \frac{T_L}{T_H} = 1 - \frac{T_{ice\ point}}{T_{steam\ point}} = 0.2680$$

$$\frac{T_{ice\ point}}{T_{steam\ point}} = 0.7320$$

This gives us one equation concerning the two unknowns T_H and T_L. The second equation comes from an arbitrary decision regarding the magnitude of the degree on the thermodynamic temperature scale. If we wish to have the magnitude of the degree on the absolute scale correspond to the magnitude of the degree on the Celsius scale, we can write,

$$T_{steam\ point} - T_{ice\ point} = 100$$

Solving these two equations simultaneously, we find

$$T_{steam\ point} = 373.15\ K,$$

$$T_{ice\ point} = 273.15\ K$$

It follows that,

$$T(°C) + 273.15 = T(K)$$

The absolute scale related to the Fahrenheit scale is the Rankine scale, designated by R. On both these scales there are 180 degrees between the ice point and the steam point. Therefore, for a Carnot cycle heat engine operating between the steam point and the ice point, we would have the two relations.

$$T_{steam\ point} - T_{ice\ point} = 180$$

$$\frac{T_{ice\ point}}{T_{steam\ point}} = 0.7320$$

Solving these two equations simultaneously, we find

$$T_{steam\ point} = 671.67\ R,$$

$$T_{ice\ point} = 491.67\ R$$

1.27 ENTROPY

Entropy is a useful property and serves as a valuable tool in the second law analysis of engineering devices. Entropy is not a common word as energy is. But with continued use, our understanding of entropy will deepen and we will grow in understanding entropy. In the following paragraphs, it has been tried out to introduce the entropy to the reader.

Entropy can be defined as a measure of molecular disorder or molecular randomness. Let us discuss the entropy of a fluid which could exist in three different phases. A common fluid water exists in vapour, liquid and solid phase depending upon the temperature at a fixed pressure. In vapour state, the molecular distance is more as compared with liquid and solid state. It means the molecules in vapour phase have more freedom to move in any direction, it means the molecules arranged in most disorderly manner. Hence, the entropy of a system (fluid) in vapour state is more as compared with its liquid state. Similarly, the water molecules are more systematically/orderly organised in the solid state than liquid. Therefore, the entropy of liquid water is always more compared to that it in solid state. This discussion is equally applicable to all the systems which could be in different phases. This is as shown in Fig. 1.91.

Molecules in the gas phase possess a considerable amount of kinetic energy. However, no matter how large their kinetic energy are, the gas molecules will not rotate a paddle wheel inserted into the container and produce work. This is so because the gas molecules and the energy they carry with them are disorganised. Probably the number of molecules which try to rotate the paddle wheel in one direction is equally opposed by the remaining gas molecules, resulting in no rotation of the paddle wheel. Hence, one cannot extract useful work directly from disorganised energy (See Fig. 1.91 (a)).

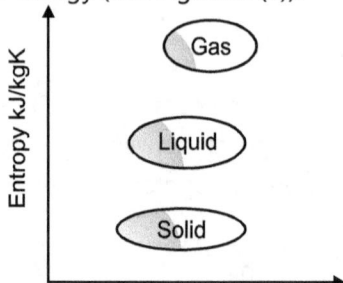

Fig. 1.91: The entropy (molecular disorder) of a substance increases as it changes its phase to liquid or gas

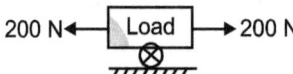

Fig. 1.91 (a): The disorganised energy does not create useful effect
(equal and opposite forces applied to a load will not move it)

Now, consider a rotating shaft as shown in Fig. 1.92. Here all the molecules of shaft are organised and rotate in one direction. Hence, one can extract useful work from the organised molecules as exist in the form of solid shaft. The rotation of the shaft can be utilised to raise or lower the load. Being an organised form of energy, work is free of disorder or randomness and thus free of entropy. There is no transfer of entropy associated with energy transfer as work.

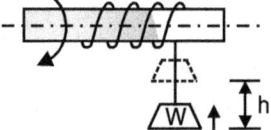

Fig. 1.92: Weight can be raised or lowered by a rotating shaft which does not create any disorder (entropy)

Let us consider one more example in which heat is transferred from a hot body to a cold body as shown in Fig. 1.92.

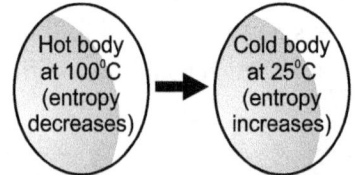

Fig. 1.93: During a heat transfer process, the net disorder (entropy) increases

Heat, a disorganized energy, and disorganization (entropy) will result with heat. As a result, the entropy of the hot body will decrease while the entropy and disorder of the cold body increase. As per second law, the increase in entropy of cold body be greater than the decrease in entropy of the hot body, and thus the net entropy of the combined system (cold body and hot body) increases. It means the combined system is at a state of greater disorder at the end state.

"Steel has got a great strength and looses all when red hot". You may be surprised at this stage to read the sentence. Let us apply entropy concept to our life style. When a person is angry it means the body organs are in the most disordered state. Therefore, when an angry person will perform badly or he does unwanted/not useful task, which may lead to any type of destruction. Therefore, every person should try to keep entropy of his body to a minimum level to do the constructive job.

1.28 LAW FOR TWO ADIABATIC PATH

Two reversible adiabatic lines never intersect each other on a thermodynamic plane.
Proof:
Let us assume the contradictory statement.

Let us assume that two adiabatic curves intersect, as shown in Fig. 1.94 at point 'a' and an isotherm intersect these curves at 'b' and 'c'.

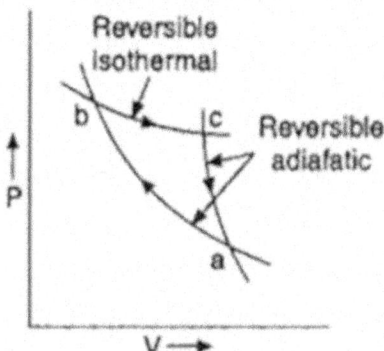

Fig. 1.94: Law for adiabatic path

A cycle is thus formed for which the heat is supplied during isothermal process and no heat is rejected because other two processes are adiabatic.

That means this cycle is performing net work by exchanging heat with a single reservoir during isothermal process.

This is violation of Kelvine -Planck statement of the Second Law of Thermodynamics.

The cycle represents a PMM 2, Since a PMM-2 is not possible to be designed our assumptions are wrong. **Hence, two adiabatic lines should never intersect on P-V plane.**

1.29 CLAUSIUS INEQUALITY

An important inequality that has major consequences in thermodynamics is the Clausius inequality, which is expressed as,

$$\oint \frac{\delta Q}{T} \leq 0$$

The cyclic integral of $\frac{\delta Q}{\delta T}$ is always less than or equal to zero. This inequality is valid for all cycles, reversible or irreversible. The $\oint$ is used to indicate that integration is to be carried out over the entire cycle.

The validity of the Clausius inequality can be illustrated with the help of two heat engines, one reversible and the other irreversible both operating between the same temperature limits of T_H and T_L.

Here T_H represents the temperature of high-temperature reservoir while T_L is that of low-temperature reservoir as shown in Fig. 1.95.

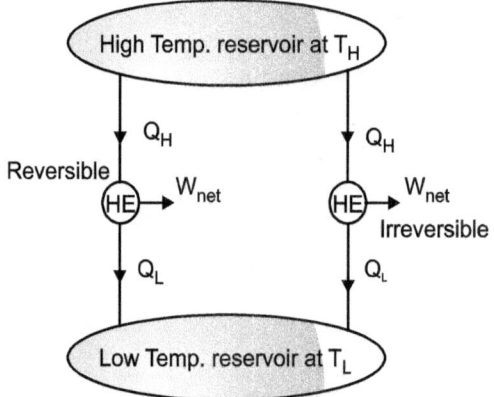

Fig. 1.95: A reversible and irreversible heat engine operating between the same temperature limits (same reservoir)

Here Q_H and Q_L are the rate of heat transfer taking place at constant temperatures T_H and T_L respectively.

(A) For reversible heat engine, the cyclic integral of $\frac{\delta Q}{T}$ becomes,

$$\oint \left(\frac{\delta Q}{T}\right)_{rev} = \int \frac{\delta Q_H}{T_H} - \int \frac{\delta Q_L}{T_L}$$

$$= \frac{1}{T_H} \oint \delta Q_H - \frac{1}{T_L} \oint \delta Q_L$$

$$= \frac{Q_H}{T_H} - \frac{Q_L}{T_L} = 0$$

Since, $\frac{Q_H}{T_H} = \frac{Q_L}{T_L}$ for reversible cycle, thus, for a reversible heat engine cycle,

$$\oint \left(\frac{\delta Q}{T}\right)_{rev} = 0 \qquad \ldots (1.65)$$

Equation (1.65) is developed for totally reversible heat engine, but is equally valid for heat engines that are only internally reversible. In such a situation, T_H and T_L can be considered as the temperature of the working fluid at locations heat is received and rejected respectively. Therefore, the above equation (1.65) can be written as,

$$\oint \left(\frac{\delta Q}{T}\right)_{int\ rev} = 0 \qquad \ldots (1.66)$$

(B) Now, consider the irreversible heat engine operating between the same thermal reservoirs (temperature limits) as the reversible one and receive the same amount of heat Q_H during a cyclic operation. But as per the Carnot principle, the irreversible heat engine will deliver less net work and which rejects more waste heat. Therefore,

$$Q_{L,\ irrev} > Q_L$$
$$Q_{L,\ irrev} = Q_L + Q_{diff}$$

where, Q_{diff} is a positive quantity.

Carrying out the cyclic integral of $\frac{\delta Q}{T}$ for this irreversible heat engines results,

$$\oint \left(\frac{\delta Q}{T}\right)_{irrev} = \frac{Q_H}{T_H} - \frac{Q_{L,\ irrev}}{T_L}$$

$$= \frac{Q_H}{T_H} - \frac{Q_L}{T_L} - \frac{Q_{diff}}{T_L}$$

$$= -\frac{Q_{diff}}{T_L} < 0$$

∴ For an irreversible heat engine cycle,

$$\oint \left(\frac{\delta Q}{T}\right)_{irrev} < 0$$

The Clausius inequality is obtained by combining the equations for irreversible and reversible engines.

$$\oint \frac{\delta Q}{T} \leq 0$$

This equation is valid for totally or just internally reversible cycles. Equality sign is for reversible engine while inequality sign is for irreversible engine.

1.30 ENTROPY AS A PROPERTY

The Clausius inequality discussed in Section 1.11 forms the definition of new property called entropy.

Consider a cycle that consists of two internally reversible processes, A and B, as shown in Fig. 1.96. Applying equation (1.28) to this internally reversible cycle, we obtain

$$\oint \left(\frac{\delta Q}{T}\right)_{int\,rev} = \int_1^2 \left(\frac{\delta Q}{T}\right)_A + \int_2^1 \left(\frac{\delta Q}{T}\right)_B = 0$$

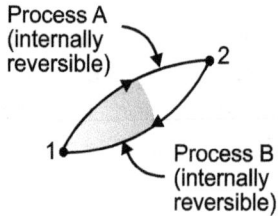

Fig. 1.96: Reversible cyclic processes between two end states

Reversing the limits of the last integral and changing its sign,

$$\int_1^2 \left(\frac{\delta Q}{T}\right)_A - \int_1^2 \left(\frac{\delta Q}{T}\right)_B = 0$$

$$\int_1^2 \left(\frac{\delta Q}{T}\right)_A = \int_1^2 \left(\frac{\delta Q}{T}\right)_B$$

Since A and B are any two internally reversible process paths between states 1 and 2, the value of this integral depends on the end states only and not on the path followed. Therefore, it must represent the change of a property. This property is called **entropy**. It is designated by s and is defined as,

$$ds = \left(\frac{\delta Q}{T}\right)_{int\,rev} \quad (kJ/K) \qquad \ldots (1.67)$$

Entropy is an extensive property of a system and sometimes is referred to as total entropy. Entropy per unit mass, designated s, is an intensive property and has the unit kJ/(kg·K). The term entropy is generally used to refer to both total entropy and entropy per unit mass.

The entropy change of a system during a process can be determined by integrating above equation between the initial and the final states:

$$\Delta s = s_2 - s_1 = \int_1^2 \left(\frac{\delta Q}{T}\right)_{int\,rev} \quad (kJ/K) \qquad \ldots (1.68)$$

1.31 PRINCIPLE OF INCREASE OF ENTROPY

Consider a cycle that consists of two processes, one internally reversible and the other irreversible as shown in Fig. 1.97.

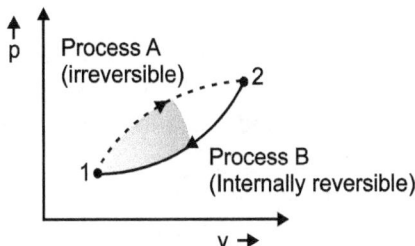

Fig. 1.97: A cycle composed of a reversible and an irreversible process

Clausius inequality tells that the cyclic integral of $\dfrac{\delta Q}{T}$ for the irreversible cycle is less than zero, i.e.

$$\oint \left(\frac{\delta Q}{T}\right)_{irrev} < 0$$

or $\displaystyle\int_{1,A}^{2}\left(\frac{\delta Q}{T}\right)_{irrev} + \int_{2,B}^{1}\left(\frac{\delta Q}{T}\right)_{int,\,rev} < 0$

The second term in the above equation represents entropy change $s_1 - s_2$. Thus,

$$\int_{1,A}^{2}\left(\frac{\delta Q}{T}\right)_{irrev} + (s_1 - s_2) < 0$$

This can be rearranged as,

$$\Delta s = (s_2 - s_1) > \int_{1,A}^{2}\left(\frac{\delta Q}{T}\right)_{irrev} \qquad \ldots (1.69)$$

From equation (1.69) one can say "the entropy change of a closed system during an irreversible process is greater than the integral of $\dfrac{\delta Q}{T}$ evaluated for that process".

In general, the relation between the change of entropy of a closed system and the integral of $\dfrac{\delta Q}{T}$ can be expressed as,

$$\Delta s \geq \int_1^2 \frac{\delta Q}{T} \qquad \ldots (1.70)$$

or in the differential form,

$$ds \geq \frac{\delta Q}{T} \qquad \ldots (1.71)$$

Here the equality sign holds for a totally or just internally reversible process and the inequality for an irreversible process. δQ represents a differential amount of actual heat transfer between the system and surroundings and 'T' is the absolute temperature at the boundary.

Let us now consider an isolated system. It is known that in an isolated system, matter, work and heat cannot cross the boundary of the system. Hence, according to the first law of thermodynamics, the internal energy of the system remains constant.

For isolated system, $\delta Q = 0$, from equation (2.9), we get,

$$(ds)_{isolated} \geq 0 \qquad \ldots (1.72)$$

Equation (1.72) tells that the entropy of an isolated system either increases or remains constant. This is a corollary of second law of thermodynamics. It explains the principle of increase in entropy.

1.32 CHANGE IN ENTROPY OF THE UNIVERSE

The entropy of an isolated system either increases or remains constant i.e.

$$(ds)_{isolated} \geq 0$$

Let us consider a system at temperature T and a surrounding at temperature T_o within a single boundary as shown in Fig. 1.98, where it forms an isolated system.

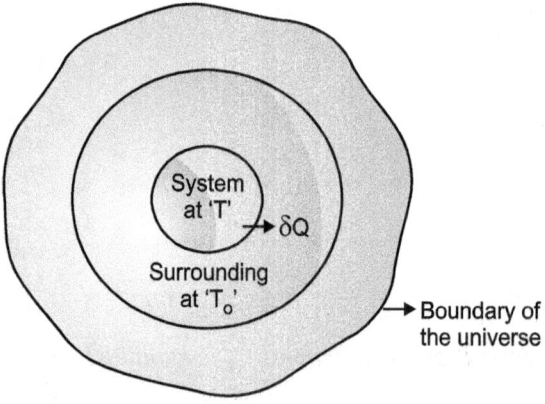

Fig. 1.98: A combination of a system and surrounding to form an universe

The combination of the system and the surroundings within a single boundary is sometimes called the universe. Let us apply principle of increase of entropy to the universe.

$$(ds)_{universe} \geq 0$$

$$\therefore (ds)_{universe} = (ds)_{system} + (ds)_{surroundings}$$

Let δQ be the quantity of heat transferred from the system at temperature 'T' to the surrounding at temperature 'T_o'.

$$(ds)_{system} \geq -\frac{\delta Q}{T}$$

(−ve sign indicates that heat is rejected from system).

Similarly, since an amount of heat δQ is received by the surroundings, for a reversible process,

$$(ds)_{surroundings} = \frac{\delta Q}{T_o}$$

Hence, the total change in entropy for the combined system

$$(ds)_{system} + (ds)_{surroundings} \geq -\frac{\delta Q}{T} + \frac{\delta Q}{T_o}$$

$$(ds)_{universe} \geq dQ\left(-\frac{1}{T} + \frac{1}{T_o}\right)$$

The same result can also be obtained for the open system. Therefore, for both closed and open system, one can write

$$(ds)_{universe} \geq 0 \qquad \ldots (1.73)$$

The above equation (1.73) states that the process involving heat interaction between the system and surroundings takes place only if the net entropy of the combined system increases or in the limit remains constant. Since all the real processes are irreversible, the entropy increases continuously.

SOLVED PROBLEMS

Problem 1.34:

A Carnot engine which rejects heat to a cooling pond at 27°C has an efficiency of 30 percent. If the cooling pond receives 837.2 kJ/min, what is the power developed by the cycle? Find the temperature of the source.

Solution: $T_L = 27 + 273 = 300$ K

$\eta_{th} = 30\%$, $Q_L = 837.2$ kJ/min = 139.5 kW

$$\eta_{carnot} = \frac{T_H - T_L}{T_H}$$

$$0.3 = \frac{T_H - (300)}{T_H}$$

∴ $T_H = $ **428.5 K**

For reversible engine,

$$\frac{Q_L}{Q_H} = \frac{T_L}{T_H}$$

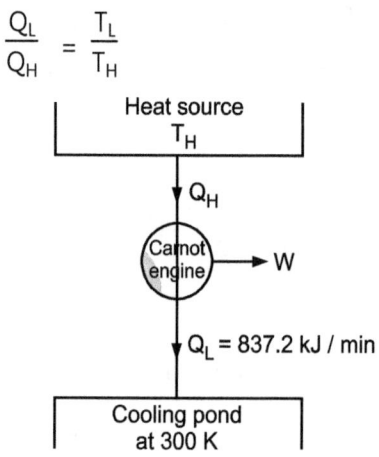

Fig. 1.99: Heat engine

$$Q_H = \frac{Q_L}{T_L} \cdot T_H$$

$$= \frac{837.2 \times 428.5}{300} = \textbf{1196 kJ/min.}$$

Power developed, $W = Q_H - Q_L$

$= 1196 - 837.2 = 358.6$ kJ/min = **5.97 kW** ... **Ans.**

Problem 1.35:

The working substance in a Carnot engine is 0.05 kg of air. The maximum cycle temperature is 900 K and maximum pressure is 8.5 MPa. The heat added per cycle is 5 kJ. Determine the maximum cylinder volume if the minimum temperature during the cycle is 300 K.

Solution: Given : m = 0.05 kg, T_H = 900 K

Maximum pressure = $p_1 = 8.5 \times 10^6$ N/m²

The maximum temperature and pressure corresponds to a point 1 on p-V diagram (See Fig. 1.97) and maximum volume at state 3.

We apply gas equation to find the volume V_3.

$$p_1 V_1 = mRT_1 \qquad \therefore V_1 = \frac{mRT_1}{p_1} = \frac{0.05 \times 0.287 \times 900}{8.5 \times 10^3} = 3.52 \times 10^{-3} \text{ m}^3$$

Heat supplied, $Q = p_1 V_1 \ln V_2/V_1$

$$5 \times 10^3 = 8.5 \times 10^6 \times 3.52 \times 10^{-3} \ln \frac{V_2}{V_1}$$

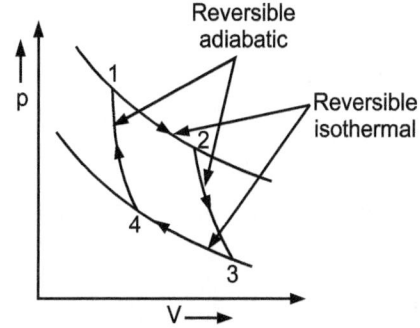

Fig. 1.100: Carnot cycle

$\therefore \qquad \log \dfrac{V_2}{V_1} = 0.387 \qquad \therefore \dfrac{V_2}{V_1} = 3.4727$

$\therefore \qquad V_2 = 3.52 \times 10^{-3} \times 3.4727 = 2.23 \times 10^{-3}$ m³

But $\qquad \dfrac{V_3}{V_2} = \left(\dfrac{T_2}{T_3}\right)^{1/\gamma - 1}$

$\therefore \qquad V_3 = V_2 \left(\dfrac{T_2}{T_3}\right)^{1/\gamma - 1} = 2.23 \times 10^{-3} \left(\dfrac{900}{300}\right)^{1/1.4 - 1}$

$\qquad = 0.0347$ m³

$\therefore$ Maximum cylinder volume = **0.0347 m³** ... **Ans.**

Problem 1.36:

A heat engine operates between two thermal reservoirs which are at 900 K and 300 K. The heat engine receives 500 kJ heat from the source and rejects 300 kJ to heat sink at 300 K. Determine if this heat engine violates the second law of thermodynamics on the basis of (a) Clausius inequality and (b) the Carnot principle.

Solution: Refer Fig. 1.101.

(a) The cyclic integral of $\dfrac{\delta Q}{T}$ for the heat-engine cycle under consideration is,

$$\oint \frac{\delta Q}{T} = \frac{Q_H}{T_H} - \frac{Q_L}{T_L} = \frac{500 \text{ kJ}}{900 \text{ K}} - \frac{300 \text{ kJ}}{300 \text{ K}}$$

$$= -0.444 \text{ kJ/kg} \qquad \text{... Ans.}$$

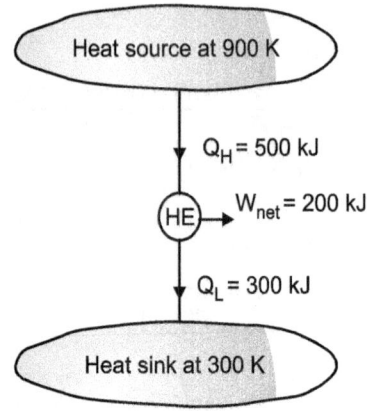

Fig. 1.101

The value is negative, this satisfies the Clausius inequality and the second law of thermodynamics.

(b) To check Carnot principle,

$$\eta_{th} = 1 - \frac{Q_L}{Q_H} = 1 - \frac{300}{500} = 0.4 \qquad \text{... Ans.}$$

$$\eta_{th\ rev} = 1 - \frac{T_L}{T_H} = 1 - \frac{300}{900} = 0.66 \qquad \text{... Ans.}$$

The efficiency of reversible engine (0.66) is higher than the efficiency of actual heat engine (0.4) i.e. $\eta_{th} < \eta_{th\ rev}$. The cycle that violates the Clausius inequality will also violate the Carnot principle.

Problem 1.37:

In a heat exchanger, water flows through a tube which is surrounded by air. Water at 80°C and 1 bar pressure rejects 600 kJ heat to the air at 300 K. Assume the heat exchanger is insulated (water rejects heat to air only). Air flows through shell-side of the heat exchanger. Determine (a) the entropy change of the water, (b) the entropy change of air during the process and (c) whether this process is reversible, irreversible or impossible.

Solution: (a) The temperature of flowing water is 80°C. Therefore, the entropy change of water during internally reversible, isothermal process (since temperature of water at 80°C will not change) can be found.

$$\Delta s_{water} = \frac{Q_{water}}{T_{water}} = \frac{-600 \text{ kJ}}{(80 + 273) \text{ K}} = -3.69 \text{ kJ/K} \qquad \text{... Ans.}$$

Q_{water} is negative, since heat is rejected.

(b) The entropy change of air

Q_{air} = +600 kJ as it receives.

$$\Delta s_{air} = \frac{Q_{air}}{T_{air}} = \frac{600 \text{ kJ}}{300 \text{ K}} = \mathbf{2.0 \text{ kJ/K}} \qquad \text{... Ans.}$$

(c) The total change of entropy for this process

$$\Delta s_{Total} = \Delta s_{water} + \Delta s_{air}$$

$$= -3.69 + 2.0 = \mathbf{0.31 \text{ kJ/K}} \qquad \text{... Ans.}$$

The total energy change of the whole process is positive. Hence, it is an irreversible process.

EXERCISE

1. What is thermodynamics?
2. How thermodynamics is studied?
3. Explain the difference between microscopic and macroscopic studies.
4. What is meant by pure substance?
5. Explain with suitable sketches, following thermodynamic systems : closed, open, isolated and adiabatic.
6. What do you understand by control volume and control surface?
7. What is thermodynamic property? Explain intensive and extensive properties.
8. What is meant by state, process and a cycle?
9. What is thermodynamic equilibrium?
10. What is a quasi-static process? Is it a reversible process?
11. Distinguish between reversible and irreversible processes.
12. What is point function and path function?
13. Discuss : 'Property is an exact differential'. Discuss property and non-property.
14. What is heat and work? What are the similarities in heat and work? Also differentiate heat and work.
15. What is displacement work?
16. What are the different forms of work?
17. What do you understand by equation of temperature?
18. Explain zeroth law of thermodynamics.

19. What is energy? What are the forms of energy?
20. What do you understand by internal energy?
21. What is the outcome of Joule's experiment?
22. Give different statements of first law of thermodynamics.
23. Prove that energy is a property of the system.
24. What is meant by steady flow process?
25. Explain the meaning of flow work.
26. Apply first law of thermodynamics to steady flow process.
27. Explain few examples of steady flow process with the assumptions.
28. What are the limitations of first law of thermodynamics?
29. What is the meaning of $-\int V\, dP$ in a steady flow process?
30. What is meant by perpetual motion machine of first kind?
31. A cycle comprises of three processes. The energy transfers in each process are tabulated below:

Process	Q (kJ)	W (kJ)	ΔU (kJ)
1 – 2	+ 50	+ 30	–
2 – 3	–	– 40	+ 30
3 – 1	–	–	–

If the cycle rejects 30 kJ of heat and if 10 such cycles are completed per minute, complete the table and find the power. State whether it is a power producing or power absorbing system.

(**Ans.** $\Delta U_{1-2} = +20$ kJ, $Q_{2-3} = -10$ kJ, $\Delta U_{3-1} = -50$ kJ, $Q_{3-1} = -70$ kJ, $W_{3-1} = -20$ kJ

Net power $= -5$ kW, Power absorbing system)

32. The power output of an adiabatic steam turbine is 5 MW and the inlet and exit conditions of steam are as under.

	Pressure	Temp.	Velocity	Elevation
Inlet	2 MPa	400° C	50 m/s	10 m
Exit	15 kPa	0.9 dry	180 m/s	6 m

Determine the work done / kg of steam and the mass flow rate in kg/s.

(**Ans.** W_s = 872.91 kJ/kg, $\dot{m}$ = 5.734 kg/s)

33. During a certain reversible process, volume changes from 0.5 m³ to 2.5 m³. The law of the process is P = (10 − 3 V), where 'P' is in bar and 'V' in m³. The internal energy of the air decreases by 150 kJ.

    Find:

    (i) ∫ PdV, Q and Δh and work transfer if it is a reversible non-flow process.

    (ii) ∫ PdV, − ∫ vdp, Q, Δh and work transfer if it is steady flow process with ΔP = 0 and ΔK = 0 kJ.

34. A centrifugal pump operates under steady flow conditions. It delivers 0.3 m³ of water per minute at 20°C. The suction pressure is 80 kPa, and the delivery pressure is 3 bar. Diameters of suction and delivery pipes are 15 cm and 10 cm respectively. The pump axis is 5 m above the sump level and is 15 m below the level in the overhead tank. Neglecting change of internal energy, calculate the power required to operate the pump. Given: g = 9.81 m/s², e_w = 1000 kg/m³. (**Ans.** w_s = − 2.1623 kW)

35. What do you understand by thermal reservoirs?

36. What is heat engine? Explain its working with block diagram. What is its thermal efficiency?

37. Define second law of thermodynamics.

    Explain: (i) Kelvin - Planck statement, (ii) Clausius statement

    Give suitable examples.

38. What is meant by perpetual motion machine of second kind?

39. What is refrigerator and heat pump? What is meant by COP?

40. What are the limitations of the First Law of Thermodynamics?

41. Prove the statement that "It is not possible to attain absolute zero K temperature."

42. Two heat pumps are connected in series between two heat reservoirs at T_1 and T_3. Heat pump 'A' transfers heat from a reservoir at 'T_3' and rejects heat to a intermediate reservoir at 'T_2' while the other heat pump 'B' transfers heat from reservoir at T_2 to the reservoir at 'T_1'. If $T_1 > T_2 > T_3$, show that (i) intermediate temperature 'T_2' is arithmetic mean of 'T_1' and 'T_3' when work input to both heat pumps is same, (ii) intermediate temperature 'T_2' is a geometric mean of 'T_1' and 'T_3' if both the heat pumps have same C.O.P.

43. An inventor claims to have developed a refrigerating machine which operates between −20°C and +30°C and consumes 1 kW power. The machine gives a refrigerating affect of 23.6 MJ/h. Verify the validity of his claim.

44. A domestic food freezer maintains a temperature of −15°C. The outdoor ambient is at 30°C. If the heat load on the freezer is 3.75 kW, what is the minimum power necessary to pump out this heat? If the actual C.O.P. of the freezer is half that of the ideal C.O.P., what is the actual power required?

        (**Ans.** Minimum power required = 0.305 kW, Actual power required = 0.61 kW)

45. A reversible heat pump is driven by a reversible heat engine. The heat rejected by the heat pump and by the heat engine is used to warm up a building. If the thermal efficiency of the heat engine is 27% and the C.O.P. of the heat pump is 4, find the ratio of heat supplied to building to the heat supplied to the heat engine.

        (**Ans.** Ratio = 2.08)

46. Prove that for a Carnot cycle,

$$\left.\frac{d\eta}{dT_2}\right|_{T_1=c} = \frac{-1}{T_1} \text{ and } \left.\frac{d\eta}{dT_1}\right|_{T_2=c} = \frac{T_2}{T_1^2}$$

and state which is a more effective way to increase the thermal efficiency of a Carnot cycle.

47. A reversible heat engine used for a satellite operates between a hot reservoir at T_1 and a radiating panel at T_2. The heat radiated from the panel is proportional to its area and T_4^2. For a given work output and a fixed temperature T_1, show that the area of the panel will be minimum when $\frac{T_1}{T_2} = \frac{4}{3}$.

48. Is it possible for the entropy of both a closed system and its surroundings to decrease during a process?

49. Define Clausius inequality and prove it.

50. Define entropy and show that it is a property of the system.

51. Give a physical explanation of entropy.

52. What do you understand by entropy principle?

53. Show that the entropy of an isolated system increases in all real process and is conserved in reversible process.

54. Show that the adiabatic mixing of two fluids is irreversible.

55. What causes an increase in entropy?

56. Why is the second law called a directional law of nature?

PROBLEMS FOR PRACTICE

1. A pump discharges into a tank of dimensions 4m × 4m × 4m. The flow rate of fluid is 400 litre/min. The density of fluid is 1.3 times that of water. Determine :
   (a) the flow rate in kg/sec.
   (b) the time to fill up the tank fully.
   Take ρ for water = 1000 kg/m³. **Ans.** (a) 8.667 kg/sec (b) 160 minutes

2. Estimate the height of water column supported by the standard atmosphere.

3. The pressure at the bottom of mountain is 101.3 kPa, while at top it is 81.3 kPa. If average density of air is 1.2 kg/m³, find the height of the mountain. **Ans.** 1698.947 m

4. 5 kg of water are heated from 20°C to 100°C. How much heat transfer is required?
   Take C_p for water = 4.18675 kJ/kg – K **Ans.** 1674.68 J.

5. A spring scale is used to measure force and determine mass of sample of rocks on moon's surface. The springs were calibrated for the earth's gravitational acceleration of 9.8 m/s². The scale reads 5.4 kg and Moon's gravitational attraction is 1.80 m/s².
   Determine sample mass. What would be the reading on beam balance scale?
   Ans. 29.4 kg; 29.4 kg.

6. To drill a hole in mild steel plate, power is supplied at the rate of 0.2 kW for 2 minutes. Determine the heat generated during the operation. **Ans.** 24 kJ.

7. Discuss the following systems. Show the boundaries. Tell whether the systems are open or closed. Show the directions of heat and work transfers.
   (1) A motor car battery
   (2) A pressure cooker
   (3) A tea kettle
   (4) An electric fan
   (5) A water pump
   (6) A scooter engine

8. Two liquids of different densities ρ_1 = 1500 kg/m³ and ρ_2 = 500 kg/m³ are poured together into a 100 litre tank so that tank is completely filled. The resulting density of the fluid is 800 kg/m³. Find the amounts of liquids and weight of the mixture. Local g = 9.675 m/s². **Ans.** m_1 = 45 kg; m_2 = 35 kg; W = 774 N.

9. At sea level the value of gravitational acceleration 'g' is 9.806 m/s². If 'g' decreases 0.003 m/s² per 1000 meters ascent, find the height in kilometers above sea level at a point for which value of 'g' = 9.616 m/s². **Ans.** 63.33 km

10. The following data is as shown in Fig. 1.102.

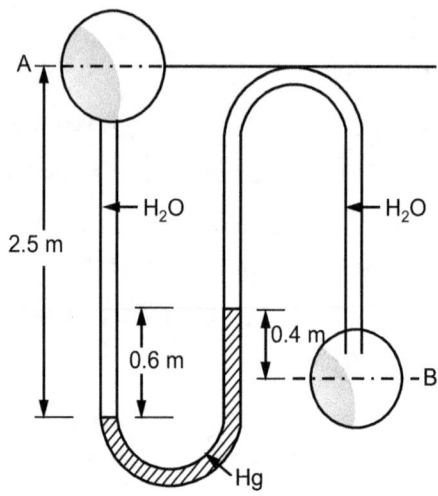

Fig. 1.102

Density of water = 1000 kg/m³

Density of mercury = 13590 kg/m³

Pressure at A = 400 kPa

g = 9.8 m/s². Find pressure at B.

Ans. 348.52 kPa

Unit - II

ENTROPY AND AVAILABILITY

(A) ENTROPY

2.0 INTRODUCTION

Entropy is a useful property and serves as a valuable tool in the second law analysis of engineering devices. Entropy is not a common word as energy is. But with continued use, our understanding of entropy will deepen and we will grow in understanding entropy. In the following paragraphs, it has been tried out to introduce the entropy to the reader.

Entropy can be defined as a measure of molecular disorder or molecular randomness. Let us discuss the entropy of a fluid which could exist in three different phases. A common fluid water exists in vapour, liquid and solid phase depending upon the temperature at a fixed pressure. In vapour state, the molecular distance is more as compared with liquid and solid state. It means the molecules in vapour phase have more freedom to move in any direction, it means the molecules arranged in most disorderly manner. Hence, the entropy of a system (fluid) in vapour state is more as compared with its liquid state. Similarly, the water molecules are more systematically/orderly organised in the solid state than liquid. Therefore, the entropy of liquid water is always more compared to that it in solid state. This discussion is equally applicable to all the systems which could be in different phases. This is as shown in Fig. 2.1.

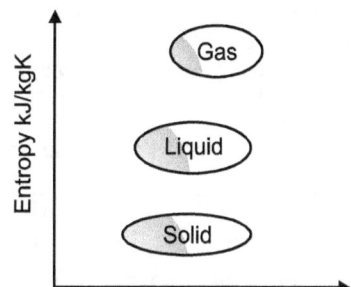

Fig. 2.1: The entropy (molecular disorder) of a substance increases as it changes its phase to liquid or gas

Molecules in the gas phase possess a considerable amount of kinetic energy. However, no matter how large their kinetic energy are, the gas molecules will not rotate a paddle wheel inserted into the container and produce work. This is so because the gas molecules and the energy they carry with them are disorganised. Probably the number of molecules which try to rotate the paddle wheel in one direction is equally opposed by the remaining gas molecules, resulting in no rotation of the paddle wheel. Hence, one cannot extract useful work directly from disorganised energy (See Fig. 2.2).

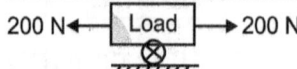

Fig. 2.2: The disorganised energy does not create useful effect (equal and opposite forces applied to a load will not move it)

Now, consider a rotating shaft as shown in Fig. 2.3. Here all the molecules of shaft are organised and rotate in one direction. Hence, one can extract useful work from the organised molecules as exist in the form of solid shaft. The rotation of the shaft can be utilised to raise or lower the load. Being an organised form of energy, work is free of disorder or randomness and thus free of entropy. There is no transfer of entropy associated with energy transfer as work.

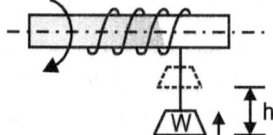

Fig. 2.3: Weight can be raised or lowered by a rotating shaft which does not create any disorder (entropy)

Let us consider one more example in which heat is transferred from a hot body to a cold body as shown in Fig. 2.4.

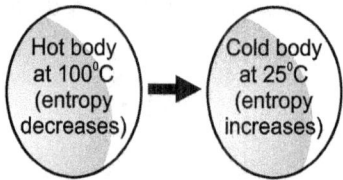

Fig. 2.4: During a heat transfer process, the net disorder (entropy) increases

Heat, a disorganized energy, and disorganization (entropy) will result with heat. As a result, the entropy of the hot body will decrease while the entropy and disorder of the cold body increase. As per second law, the increase in entropy of cold body be greater than the decrease in entropy of the hot body, and thus the net entropy of the combined system (cold body and hot body) increases. It means the combined system is at a state of greater disorder at the end state.

"Steel has got a great strength and looses all when red hot". You may be surprised at this stage to read the sentence. Let us apply entropy concept to our life style. When a person is angry it means the body organs are in the most disordered state. Therefore, when an angry person will perform badly or he does unwanted/not useful task, which may lead to any type of distruction. Therefore, every person should try to keep entropy of his body to a minimum level to do the constructive job.

2.1 CLAUSIUS INEQUALITY

An important inequality that has major consequences in thermodynamics is the Clausius inequality, which is expressed as,

$$\oint \frac{\delta Q}{T} \leq 0 \qquad \ldots (2.1)$$

The cyclic integral of $\frac{\delta Q}{\delta T}$ is always less than or equal to zero. This inequality is valid for all cycles, reversible or irreversible. The $\oint$ is used to indicate that integration is to be carried out over the entire cycle.

The validity of the Clausius inequality can be illustrated with the help of two heat engines, one reversible and the other irreversible both operating between the same temperature limits of T_H and T_L.

Here T_H represents the temperature of high-temperature reservoir while T_L is that of low-temperature reservoir as shown in Fig. 2.5.

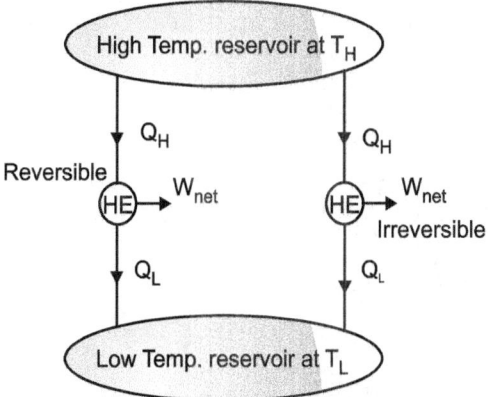

Fig. 2.5: A reversible and irreversible heat engine operating between the same temperature limits (same reservoir)

Here Q_H and Q_L are the rate of heat transfer taking place at constant temperatures T_H and T_L respectively.

(A) For reversible heat engine, the cyclic integral of $\frac{\delta Q}{T}$ becomes,

$$\oint \left(\frac{\delta Q}{T}\right)_{rev} = \int \frac{\delta Q_H}{T_H} - \int \frac{\delta Q_L}{T_L}$$

$$= \frac{1}{T_H} \int \delta Q_H - \frac{1}{T_L} \int \delta Q_L$$

$$= \frac{Q_H}{T_H} - \frac{Q_L}{T_L} = 0$$

Since, $\frac{Q_H}{T_H} = \frac{Q_L}{T_L}$ for reversible cycle, thus, for a reversible heat engine cycle,

$$\oint \left(\frac{\delta Q}{T}\right)_{rev} = 0 \qquad \ldots (2.2)$$

Equation (2.2) is developed for totally reversible heat engine, but is equally valid for heat engines that are only internally reversible. In such a situation, T_H and T_L can be considered as the temperature of the working fluid at locations heat is received and rejected respectively. Therefore, equation (2.2) can be written as,

$$\oint \left(\frac{\delta Q}{T}\right)_{int\ rev} = 0 \qquad \ldots (2.3)$$

(B) Now, consider the irreversible heat engine operating between the same thermal reservoirs (temperature limits) as the reversible one and receive the same amount of heat Q_H during a cyclic operation. But as per the Carnot principle, the irreversible heat engine will deliver less net work and which rejects more waste heat. Therefore,

$$Q_{L,\ irrev} > Q_L$$
$$Q_{L,\ irrev} = Q_L + Q_{diff}$$

where, Q_{diff} is a positive quantity.

Carrying out the cyclic integral of $\frac{\delta Q}{T}$ for this irreversible heat engines results,

$$\oint \left(\frac{\delta Q}{T}\right)_{irrev} = \frac{Q_H}{T_H} - \frac{Q_{L,\ irrev}}{T_L}$$

$$= \frac{Q_H}{T_H} - \frac{Q_L}{T_L} - \frac{Q_{diff}}{T_L}$$

$$= -\frac{Q_{diff}}{T_L} < 0$$

∴ For an irreversible heat engine cycle,

$$\oint \left(\frac{\delta Q}{T}\right)_{irrev} < 0 \qquad \ldots (2.4)$$

The Clausius inequality is obtained by combining the equations (2.3) and (2.4) as,

$$\oint \frac{\delta Q}{T} \leq 0 \qquad \ldots (2.5)$$

The equation (2.5) is valid for totally or just internally reversible cycles. Equality sign is for reversible engine while inequality sign is for irreversible engine.

2.2 ENTROPY AS A PROPERTY

The Clausius inequality discussed in Section 2.1 forms the definition of new property called entropy.

Consider a cycle that consists of two internally reversible processes, A and B, as shown in Fig. 2.6. Applying equation (2.3) to this internally reversible cycle, we obtain

$$\oint \left(\frac{\delta Q}{T}\right)_{int\,rev} = \int_1^2 \left(\frac{\delta Q}{T}\right)_A + \int_2^1 \left(\frac{\delta Q}{T}\right)_B = 0$$

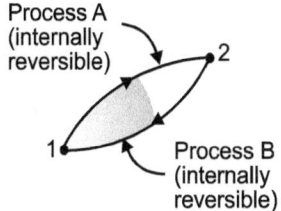

Fig. 2.6: Reversible cyclic processes between two end states

Reversing the limits of the last integral and changing its sign,

$$\int_1^2 \left(\frac{\delta Q}{T}\right)_A - \int_1^2 \left(\frac{\delta Q}{T}\right)_B = 0$$

$$\int_1^2 \left(\frac{\delta Q}{T}\right)_A = \int_1^2 \left(\frac{\delta Q}{T}\right)_B$$

Since A and B are any two internally reversible process paths between states 1 and 2, the value of this integral depends on the end states only and not on the path followed. Therefore, it must represent the change of a property. This property is called **entropy**. It is designated by s and is defined as,

$$ds = \left(\frac{\delta Q}{T}\right)_{int\,rev} \quad (kJ/K) \qquad \ldots (2.6\ a)$$

Entropy is an extensive property of a system and sometimes is referred to as total entropy. Entropy per unit mass, designated s, is an intensive property and has the unit kJ/(kg·K). The term entropy is generally used to refer to both total entropy and entropy per unit mass.

The entropy change of a system during a process can be determined by integrating equation (2.6 a) between the initial and the final states:

$$\Delta s = s_2 - s_1 = \int_1^2 \left(\frac{\delta Q}{T}\right)_{int\,rev} \quad (kJ/K) \qquad \ldots (2.6\ b)$$

2.3 PRINCIPLE OF INCREASE OF ENTROPY

Consider a cycle that consists of two processes, one internally reversible and the other irreversible as shown in Fig. 2.7.

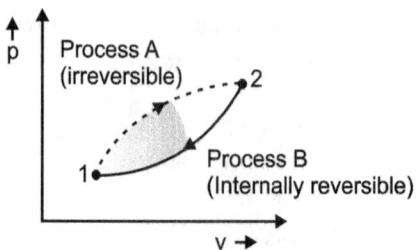

Fig. 2.7: A cycle composed of a reversible and an irreversible process

Clausius inequality tells that the cyclic integral of $\frac{\delta Q}{T}$ for the irreversible cycle is less than zero, i.e.

$$\oint \left(\frac{\delta Q}{T}\right)_{irrev} < 0$$

or

$$\int_{1,A}^{2} \left(\frac{\delta Q}{T}\right)_{irrev} + \int_{2,B}^{1} \left(\frac{\delta Q}{T}\right)_{int,\,rev} < 0$$

The second term in the above equation represents entropy change $s_1 - s_2$. Thus,

$$\int_{1,A}^{2} \left(\frac{\delta Q}{T}\right)_{irrev} + (s_1 - s_2) < 0$$

This can be rearranged as,

$$\Delta s = (s_2 - s_1) > \int_{1,A}^{2} \left(\frac{\delta Q}{T}\right)_{irrev} \qquad \ldots (2.7)$$

From equation (2.7) one can say "the entropy change of a closed system during an irreversible process is greater than the integral of $\frac{\delta Q}{T}$ evaluated for that process".

In general, the relation between the change of entropy of a closed system and the integral of $\frac{\delta Q}{T}$ can be expressed as,

$$\Delta s \geq \int_{1}^{2} \frac{\delta Q}{T} \qquad \ldots (2.8)$$

or in the differential form,

$$ds \geq \frac{\delta Q}{T} \qquad \ldots (2.9)$$

Here the equality sign holds for a totally or just internally reversible process and the inequality for an irreversible process. δQ represents a differential amount of actual heat transfer between the system and surroundings and 'T' is the absolute temperature at the boundary.

Let us now consider an isolated system. It is known that in an isolated system, matter, work and heat cannot cross the boundary of the system. Hence, according to the first law of thermodynamics, the internal energy of the system remains constant.

For isolated system, $\delta Q = 0$, from equation (2.9), we get,

$$(ds)_{isolated} \geq 0 \qquad \ldots (2.10)$$

Equation (2.10) tells that the entropy of an isolated system either increases or remains constant. This is a corollary of second law of thermodynamics. It explains the principle of increase in entropy.

2.4 CHANGE IN ENTROPY OF THE UNIVERSE

The entropy of an isolated system either increases or remains constant i.e.

$$(ds)_{isolated} \geq 0$$

Let us consider a system at temperature T and a surrounding at temperature T_o within a single boundary as shown in Fig. 2.8, where it forms an isolated system.

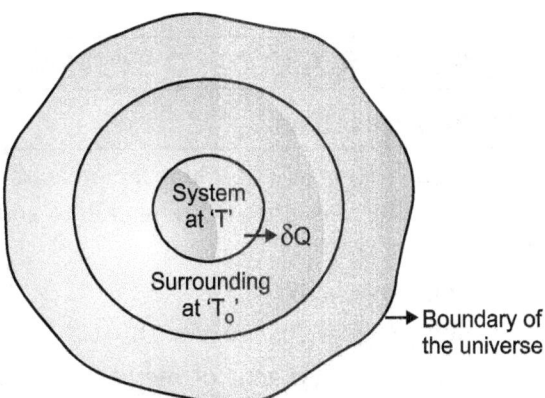

Fig. 2.8: A combination of a system and surrounding to form an universe

The combination of the system and the surroundings within a single boundary is sometimes called the universe. Let us apply principle of increase of entropy to the universe.

$$(ds)_{universe} \geq 0$$

∴ $$(ds)_{universe} = (ds)_{system} + (ds)_{surroundings}$$

Let δQ be the quantity of heat transferred from the system at temperature 'T' to the surrounding at temperature 'T_o'.

$$(ds)_{system} \geq -\frac{\delta Q}{T}$$

(–ve sign indicates that heat is rejected from system.)

Similarly, since an amount of heat δQ is received by the surroundings, for a reversible process,

$$(ds)_{surroundings} = \frac{\delta Q}{T_o}$$

Hence, the total change in entropy for the combined system

$$(ds)_{system} + (ds)_{surroundings} \geq -\frac{\delta Q}{T} + \frac{\delta Q}{T_o}$$

$$(ds)_{universe} \geq dQ\left(-\frac{1}{T} + \frac{1}{T_o}\right)$$

The same result can also be obtained for the open system. Therefore, for both closed and open system, one can write

$$(ds)_{universe} \geq 0 \qquad \ldots (2.11)$$

Equation (2.11) states that the process involving heat interaction between the system and surroundings takes place only if the net entropy of the combined system increases or in the limit remains constant. Since all the real processes are irreversible, the entropy increases continuously.

2.5 ENTROPY CHANGES FOR A CLOSED SYSTEM

2.5.1 Change of Entropy of a Gas

Let 1 kg of gas at a pressure p_1, volume V_1, absolute temperature T_1 and entropy s_1, be heated such that its final pressure, volume, absolute temperature and entropy are p_2, V_2, T_2 and s_2 respectively. According to first law,

$$dQ = du + dW$$

where, dQ = Small change of heat

du = Small change of internal energy and

dW = Small change of work done (pdV)

Now $\quad dQ = c_v dT + pdV$

Dividing both sides by T, we get

$$\frac{dQ}{T} = \frac{c_v dT}{T} + \frac{pdV}{T}$$

But $\quad \dfrac{dQ}{T} = ds$

and as
$$pV = RT$$
∴
$$\frac{p}{T} = \frac{R}{V}$$

Hence,
$$ds = \frac{c_v dT}{T} + R\frac{dV}{V}$$

Integrating both sides,
$$\int_{s_1}^{s_2} ds = c_v \int_{T_1}^{T_2} \frac{dT}{T} + R \int_{V_1}^{V_2} \frac{dV}{V}$$

or
$$(s_2 - s_1) = c_v \log_e \frac{T_2}{T_1} + R \log_e \frac{V_2}{V_1} \qquad \ldots (2.12)$$

This expression can also be obtained in the following way:
According to the gas equation, we have
$$\frac{p_1 V_1}{T_1} = \frac{p_2 V_2}{T_2}$$

or
$$\frac{T_2}{T_1} = \frac{p_2}{p_1} \times \frac{V_2}{V_1}$$

Substituting the value of $\frac{T_2}{T_1}$ in equation (2.12) we get,

$$s_2 - s_1 = c_v \log_e \frac{p_2}{p_1} \times \frac{V_2}{V_1} + R \log_e \frac{V_2}{V_1}$$

$$= c_v \log_e \frac{p_2}{p_1} + c_v \log_e \frac{V_2}{V_1} + R \log_e \frac{V_2}{V_1}$$

$$= c_v \log_e \frac{p_2}{p_1} + (c_v + R) \log_e \frac{V_2}{V_1}$$

$$= c_v \log_e \frac{p_2}{p_1} + c_p \log_e \frac{V_2}{V_1}$$

∴
$$s_2 - s_1 = c_v \log_e \frac{p_2}{p_1} + c_p \log_e \frac{V_2}{V_1} \qquad \ldots (2.13)$$

Again, from gas equation,
$$\frac{p_1 V_1}{T_1} = \frac{p_2 V_2}{T_2}$$

or
$$\frac{V_2}{V_1} = \frac{p_1}{p_2} \times \frac{T_2}{T_1}$$

Putting the value of $\frac{V_2}{V_1}$ in equation (2.12), we get,

$$(s_2 - s_1) = c_v \log_e \frac{T_2}{T_1} + R \log_e \frac{p_1}{p_2} \times \frac{T_2}{T_1}$$

$$= c_v \log_e \frac{T_2}{T_1} + R \log_e \frac{p_1}{p_2} + R \log_e \frac{T_2}{T_1}$$

$$= (c_v + R) \log_e \frac{T_2}{T_1} - R \log_e \frac{p_2}{p_1}$$

$$= c_p \log_e \frac{T_2}{T_1} - R \log_e \frac{p_2}{p_1}$$

$$\therefore \quad s_2 - s_1 = c_p \log_e \frac{T_2}{T_1} - R \log_e \frac{p_2}{p_1} \quad \ldots (2.14)$$

(a) Heating a Gas at Constant Volume

Refer Fig. 2.9. Let 1 kg of gas be heated at constant volume and let the change in entropy and absolute temperature be from s_1 to s_2 and T_1 to T_2 respectively.

Then
$$Q = c_v (T_2 - T_1)$$

Differentiating to find small increment of heat dQ corresponding to small rise in temperature dT,

$$dQ = c_v \, dT$$

Dividing both sides by T, we get

$$\frac{dQ}{T} = c_v \cdot \frac{dT}{T}$$

or
$$ds = c_v \cdot \frac{dT}{T}$$

Integrating both sides, we get

$$\int_{s_1}^{s_2} ds = c_v \int_{T_1}^{T_2} \frac{dT}{T}$$

or
$$s_2 - s_1 = c_v \log_e \frac{T_2}{T_1} \quad \ldots (2.15)$$

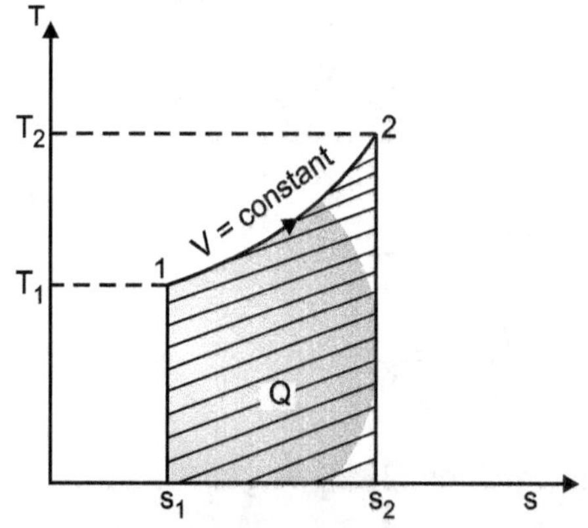

Fig. 2.9: Constant volume process on T-s diagram

(b) Heating a Gas at Constant Pressure

Refer Fig. 2.10. Let 1 kg of gas be heated at constant pressure, so that its absolute temperature changes from T_1 to T_2 and entropy s_1 to s_2.

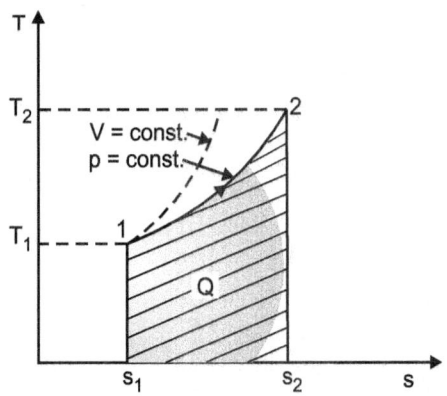

Fig. 2.10: T-s diagram: Constant pressure process

Then, $\quad Q = c_p (T_2 - T_1)$

Differentiating to find small increase in heat, dQ of this gas when the temperature rise is dT.

$$dQ = c_p \cdot dT$$

Dividing both sides by T, we get

$$dQ = dT$$

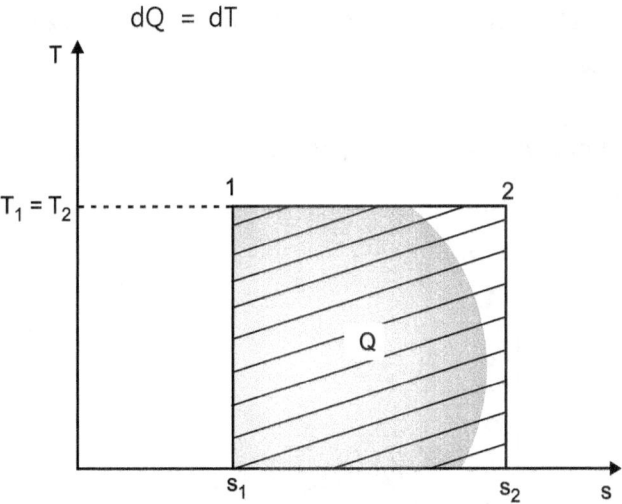

Fig. 2.11: T-s diagram: Isothermal process

$\therefore \qquad T(s_2 - s_1) = RT_1 \log_e \dfrac{V_2}{V_1}$

$\qquad\qquad s_2 - s_1 = R \log_e \dfrac{V_2}{V_1} \qquad\qquad [\because T_1 = T_2 = T] \ldots (2.16)$

(c) Adiabatic Process (Reversible)

During an adiabatic process as heat is neither supplied nor rejected,

$$dQ = 0$$
$$\frac{dQ}{dT} = 0$$
$$ds = 0 \qquad \ldots (2.17)$$

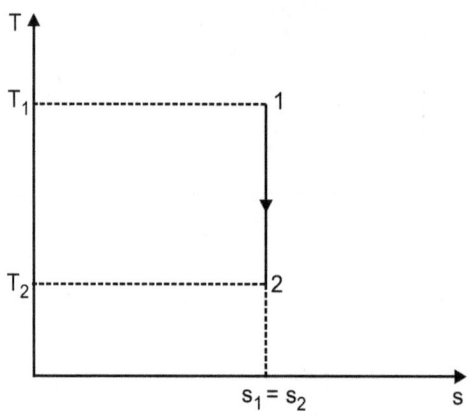

Fig. 2.12: T-s diagram: Adiabatic process

This shows that there is no change in entropy and hence it is known as isentropic process. Fig. 2.12 represents an adiabatic process. It is a vertical line (1-2) and therefore area under this line is nil; hence heat supplied or rejected and entropy change is zero.

(d) Polytropic Process

Refer Fig. 2.13.

The expression for 'entropy change' in polytropic process (pV^n = constant) can be obtained from equation (2.12).

i.e. $\quad s_2 - s_1 = c_v \log_e \frac{T_2}{T_1} + R \log_e \frac{V_2}{V_1}$

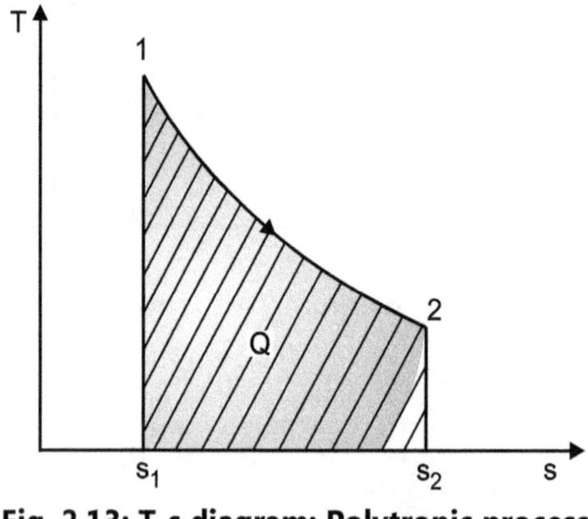

Fig. 2.13: T-s diagram: Polytropic process

Also $\quad p_1 V_1^n = p_2 V_2^n$

or $\quad \dfrac{p_1}{p_2} = \left(\dfrac{V_2}{V_1}\right)^n$ ... (i)

Again, as $\quad \dfrac{p_1 V_1}{T_1} = \dfrac{p_2 V_2}{T_2}$

or $\quad \dfrac{p_1}{p_2} = \dfrac{V_2}{V_1} \times \dfrac{T_1}{T_2}$ ... (ii)

From equations (i) and (ii), we get

$$\left(\dfrac{V_2}{V_1}\right)^n = \dfrac{V_2}{V_1} \times \dfrac{T_1}{T_2}$$

or $\quad \left(\dfrac{V_2}{V_1}\right)^{n-1} = \dfrac{T_1}{T_2}$

or $\quad \dfrac{V_2}{V_1} = \left(\dfrac{T_1}{T_2}\right)^{\frac{1}{n-1}}$

$$= c_v \log_e \dfrac{T_2}{T_1} - R\left(\dfrac{1}{n-1}\right) \log_e \dfrac{T_2}{T_1}$$

$$= c_v \log_e \dfrac{T_2}{T_1} - (c_p - c_v) \times \left(\dfrac{1}{n-1}\right) \log_e \dfrac{T_2}{T_1} \quad [\because R = c_p - c_v]$$

$$= c_v \log_e \dfrac{T_2}{T_1} - (\gamma \cdot c_v - c_v) \times \left(\dfrac{1}{n-1}\right) \log_e \dfrac{T_2}{T_1} \quad [\because c_p = \gamma \cdot c_v]$$

$$= c_v \left[1 - \left(\dfrac{\gamma-1}{n-1}\right)\right] \log_e \dfrac{T_2}{T_1} = c_v \left[\dfrac{(n-1)-(\gamma-1)}{(n-1)}\right] \log_e \dfrac{T_2}{T_1}$$

$$= c_v \left(\dfrac{n-1-\gamma+1}{n-1}\right) \log_e \dfrac{T_2}{T_1}$$

$$= c_v \left(\dfrac{n-\gamma}{n-1}\right) \log_e \dfrac{T_2}{T_1} \text{ per kg of gas}$$

$\therefore \quad s_2 - s_1 = c_v \left(\dfrac{n-\gamma}{n-1}\right) \log_e \dfrac{T_2}{T_1}$ per kg of gas ... (2.18)

(e) Approximation for Heat Absorbed

The curve AB shown in Fig. 2.14 is obtained by heating 1 kg of gas from initial state A to final state B. Let temperature during heating increase from T_1 to T_2. Then heat absorbed by the gas will be given by the area (shown shaded) under curve AB.

As the curve on T-s diagram which represents the heating of the gas, usually has very slight curvature, it can be assumed a straight line for a small temperature range. Then,

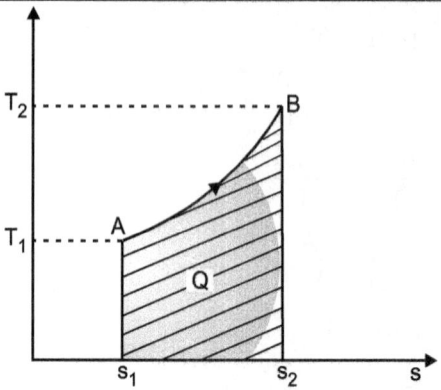

Fig. 2.14

Heat absorbed = Area under the curve AB

$$= (s_2 - s_1)\left(\frac{T_1 + T_2}{2}\right) \quad \ldots (2.19)$$

In other words, heat absorbed approximately equals the product of change of entropy and means absolute temperature.

Table 2.1: Summary of Formulae

Sr. No.	Process	Change of Entropy (per kg)
1.	General case	(i) $c_v \log_e \frac{T_2}{T_1} + R \log_e \frac{V_2}{V_1}$ (in terms of T and V) (ii) $c_v \log_e \frac{p_2}{p_1} + c_v \log_e \frac{V_2}{V_1}$ (in terms of p and V) (iii) $c_p \log_e \frac{T_2}{T_1} - R \log_e \frac{p_2}{p_1}$ (in terms of T and p)
2.	Constant volume	$c_v \log_e \frac{T_2}{T_1}$
3.	Constant pressure	$c_p \log_e \frac{T_2}{T_1}$
4.	Isothermal	$R \log_e \frac{V_2}{V_1}$
5.	Adiabatic	Zero
6.	Polytropic	$c_v \left(\frac{n - \gamma}{n - 1}\right) \log_e \frac{T_2}{T_1}$

2.5.2 Entropy Changes for an Open System

In an open system, as compared with closed system, there is additional change of entropy due to the mass crossing the boundaries of the system. *The net change of entropy of a system due to mass transport is equal to the difference between the product of the mass and its specific entropy at the inlet and at the outlet of the system.* Therefore, the total change of entropy of the system during a small interval is given by,

$$ds \geq \frac{dQ}{T_0} + \Sigma s_i \cdot dm_i - \Sigma s_o \cdot dm_o$$

where,
- T_0 = Temperature of the surroundings, in K
- s_i = Specific entropy at the inlet, J/kg·K
- s_o = Specific entropy at the outlet, J/kg·K
- dm_i = Mass entering the system, kg/sec
- dm_o = Mass leaving the system, kg/sec

(Subscripts i and o refer to inlet and outlet conditions.)

The above equation in general form can be written as,

$$ds \geq \frac{dQ}{T_0} + \Sigma s \cdot dm \qquad \ldots (2.20)$$

In equation (2.20), entropy flow into the system is considered positive and entropy outflow is considered negative. The equality sign is applicable to reversible process in which the heat interactions and mass transport to and from the system is accomplished reversibly. The inequality sign is applicable to irreversible processes.

If equation (2.20) is divided by dt, then it becomes a rate equation and is written as,

$$\frac{ds}{dt} \geq \frac{1}{T_0} \cdot \frac{dQ}{dt} + \Sigma s \cdot \frac{dm}{dt} \qquad \ldots (2.21)$$

In a steady-state, steady flow process, the rate of change of entropy of the system $\left(\frac{ds}{dt}\right)$ becomes zero.

∴
$$0 \geq \frac{1}{T_0}\frac{dQ}{dt} + \Sigma s \cdot \frac{dm}{dt}$$

or
$$\frac{1}{T_0} + \Sigma s \cdot \leq 0 \qquad \ldots (2.22)$$

where
$$= \frac{dQ}{dt} \quad \text{and}$$
$$= \frac{dm}{dt}$$

For adiabatic steady flow process,
$$= 0$$
$$\Sigma s \cdot \leq 0 \qquad \ldots (2.23)$$

If the process is reversible and adiabatic, then,
$$\Sigma s \cdot = 0 \qquad \ldots (2.24)$$

2.6 THE TDS RELATIONS

Earlier in this chapter, it is shown that the quantity $\left(\dfrac{\delta Q}{T}\right)_{int\ rev}$ corresponds to a differential change in property, called as entropy. The entropy change for various processes like constant volume process, constant pressure process, isothermal process etc. was evaluated and shown in the preceding sections. When the temperature varies during a process, we have a relation between δQ and T to perform this integration.

Finding such relations is the task done in this section.

The differential form of the conservation of energy equation for a closed stationary system having a simple compressible fluid for internally reversible process can be written as,

$$\delta Q = \delta w + \delta u$$

But
$$\delta Q = Tds$$
$$\delta w = pdV$$

Thus $Tds - pdv = du$

$$Tds = du + pdV \qquad \ldots (2.25)$$

or $\qquad Tds = du + pdV \qquad$ for unit mass $\ldots (2.26)$

This equation is known as first Tds or Gibb's equation.

The second Tds equation is obtained by eliminating du from equation (2.26) by using the definition of enthalpy ($h = u + pv$).

$$h = u + pV \rightarrow dh = du + pdV + Vdp$$

But $\qquad du + pdV = Tds$

$\therefore \qquad Tds = dh - Vdp \qquad \ldots (2.27)$

Equations (2.26 and 2.27) are extremely valuables as they relate entropy changes of a system to the changes in other properties.

2.7 ENTROPY CHANGE OF A PURE SUBSTANCE

The Tds relations developed in the previous section are not limited to a particular substance in a particular phase. These are valid for all pure substances at any phase or combination of phases. The use of these equations, however, depends on the availability of the property relations between T and du or dh and the p-V-T behaviour of the substance. The Tds relations for pure substance, in general are very complicated. Therefore, instead of using such complicated equations to find entropy, these are tabulated in exactly the same manner as other properties u, V and h. In steam tables, the entropy of a saturated liquid s_f at 0.01°C is assigned the value of zero. For refrigerant R_{22}, the zero value is assigned to saturated liquid at $-40°C$. The entropy values become $-ve$ at temperature below the reference value.

The entropy values of any pure substance are obtained just as any other property. It can be directly obtained in the compressed liquid and superheated regions. In the saturated mixture region, it is determined from,

$$s = s_f + x \, s_{fg} \qquad \ldots (2.28)$$

where, 'x' is the dryness fraction or quality of vapour and s_f and s_{fg} are listed in the property tables.

2.8 THE ENTROPY CHANGE OF SOLIDS AND LIQUIDS

The Tds equation is,

$$Tds = du + pdV \qquad \ldots (2.29)$$

or

$$ds = \frac{du}{T} + \frac{pdV}{T}$$

The solids and liquids are idealized as incompressible substances since their volumes remain essentially constant during a process.

Thus, change in volume, $dV = 0$ for solids and liquids.

Equation (2.29) reduces to

$$ds = \frac{du}{T} = c\frac{dT}{T} \qquad \ldots (2.30)$$

As $c_p = c_v = c$ for incompressible substances and $du = c \, dT$, the entropy change for a process is determined by integration.

$$s_2 - s_1 = \int_1^2 c(T) \frac{dT}{T} \text{ kJ/kg·K} \qquad \ldots (2.31)$$

The specific heat 'c' of liquids and solids depend on temperature. We need a relation for 'c' as a function of temperature to perform the integration. In many cases 'c' may be taken as average value.

∴

$$s_2 - s_1 = c_{av} \cdot \ln\left(\frac{T_2}{T_1}\right) \text{ kJ/kg·K} \qquad \ldots (2.32)$$

2.9 THIRD LAW OF THERMODYNAMICS

"Entropy of a pure substance at absolute zero temperature is zero."

At absolute zero temperature, the molecular movement stops completely, therefore, randomness becomes zero. Also pressure exerted by gas on walls of container becomes zero.

SOLVED PROBLEMS

Problem 2.1:

A heat engine operates between two thermal reservoirs which are at 900 K and 300 K. The heat engine receives 500 kJ heat from the source and rejects 300 kJ to heat sink at 300 K. Determine if this heat engine violates the second law of thermodynamics on the basis of (a) Clausius inequality and (b) the Carnot principle.

Solution: Refer Fig. 2.15.

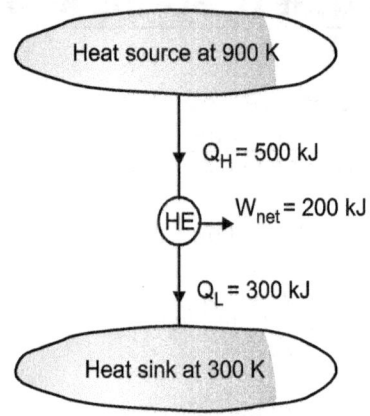

Fig. 2.15

(a) The cyclic integral of $\dfrac{\delta Q}{T}$ for the heat-engine cycle under consideration is,

$$\oint \frac{\delta Q}{T} = \frac{Q_H}{T_H} - \frac{Q_L}{T_L} = \frac{500 \text{ kJ}}{900 \text{ K}} - \frac{300 \text{ kJ}}{300 \text{ K}}$$

$$= -0.444 \text{ kJ/kg}$$

The value is negative, this satisfies the Clausius inequality and the second law of thermodynamics.

(b) To check Carnot principle,

$$\eta_{th} = 1 - \frac{Q_L}{Q_H} = 1 - \frac{300}{500} = 0.4$$

$$\eta_{th\,rev} = 1 - \frac{T_L}{T_H} = 1 - \frac{300}{900} = 0.66$$

The efficiency of reversible engine (0.66) is higher than the efficiency of actual heat engine (0.4) i.e. $\eta_{th} < \eta_{th\,rev}$. The cycle that violates the Clausius inequality will also violate the Carnot principle.

Problem 2.2:

In a heat exchanger, water flows through a tube which is surrounded by air. Water at 80°C and 1 bar pressure rejects 600 kJ heat to the air at 300 K. Assume the heat exchanger is insulated (water rejects heat to air only). Air flows through shell-side of the heat exchanger. Determine (a) the entropy change of the water, (b) the entropy change of air during the process and (c) whether this process is reversible, irreversible or impossible.

Solution: (a) The temperature of flowing water is 80°C. Therefore, the entropy change of water during internally reversible, isothermal process (since temperature of water at 80°C will not change) can be found.

$$\Delta s_{water} = \frac{Q_{water}}{T_{water}} = \frac{-600 \text{ kJ}}{(80 + 273) \text{ K}} = -1.69 \text{ kJ/K}$$

Q_{water} is negative, since heat is rejected.

(b) The entropy change of air

Q_{air} = +600 kJ as it receives.

$$\Delta s_{air} = \frac{Q_{air}}{T_{air}} = \frac{600 \text{ kJ}}{300 \text{ K}} = 2.0 \text{ kJ/K}$$

(c) The total change of entropy for this process

$$\Delta s_{Total} = \Delta s_{water} + \Delta s_{air}$$
$$= -1.69 + 2.0 = 0.31 \text{ kJ/K}$$

The total energy change of the whole process is positive. Hence, it is an irreversible process.

Problem 2.3:

A 100 kg iron casting at 600 K is put into a well having a large quantity of water at 285 K. Eventually, the iron casting attains thermal equilibrium with well water. The specific heat of cast iron is 0.5 kJ/kg·K. Determine (a) Entropy change of the cast iron block, (b) Entropy change of well water, (c) Total entropy change for this process.

Solution: (a) Cast iron block is treated as incompressible substance.

$$\Delta s_{iron} = m (s_2 - s_1) = m \cdot c_{av} \log\left(\frac{T_2}{T_1}\right)$$

$$= 100 \text{ kg} \times 0.5 \text{ kJ/kg·K} \ln\left(\frac{285}{600}\right)$$

$$= -37.2 \text{ kJ/K}$$

(b) The well water acts as a thermal reservoir which does not experience increase in temperature.

$$Q_{iron} = m \cdot c_{av} \cdot (T_2 - T_1)$$
$$= 100 \times 0.5 \times (285 - 600)$$
$$= -15750 \text{ kJ}$$
$$Q_{well} = -Q_{iron} = +15750 \text{ kJ}$$

$$\Delta S_{well} = \frac{Q_{well}}{T_{well}} = \frac{15750 \text{ kJ}}{285 \text{ K}} = 55.2 \text{ kJ/K}$$

(c) The total entropy change for the process is,

$$\Delta S_{total} = \Delta S_{iron} + \Delta S_{well}$$
$$= -37.2 + 55.0 = 18 \text{ kJ/K}$$

The total entropy change is positive, hence the process is irreversible.

Problem 2.4:

An iron cube at a temperature of 400°C is dropped into an insulated bath containing 10 kg water at 25°C. The water finally reaches a temperature of 50°C at steady state. Given that the specific heat of water is equal to 4186 J/kg·K. Find the entropy changes for the iron cube and the water. Is the process reversible? If so why?

Solution: Given: Temperature of iron cube = 400°C = 673 K
Temperature of water = 25°C = 298 K
Mass of water = 10 kg
Temperature of water and cube after equilibrium = 50°C = 323 K
Specific heat of water, c_{pw} = 4186 J/kg·K

Entropy changes for the iron cube and the water:

Now, Heat lost by iron cube = Heat gained by water

$$m_i c_{pi} (673 - 323) = m_w c_{pw} (323 - 298)$$
$$= 10 \times 4186 (323 - 298)$$

$$\therefore \quad m_i c_{pi} = \frac{10 \times 4186 (323 - 298)}{(623 - 323)} = 2990$$

where, m_i = Mass of iron, kg, and
c_{pi} = Specific heat of iron, J/kg·K

The iron cube rejects heat = Q_{iron}

The entropy of iron = $m_i c_{pi} \ln\left(\frac{T_2}{T_1}\right)$

(a) Entropy of iron at 673 K = $m_i c_{pi} \ln\left(\frac{T_2}{T_1}\right)$

$$= 2990 \ln\left(\frac{323}{673}\right) = \mathbf{-2195 \text{ J/K}}$$

Water receives heat (Q_w is positive).

(b) Entropy of water at 298 K = $m_w \cdot c_{pw} \ln\left(\frac{T_2}{T_1}\right)$

$$= 10 \times 4186 \ln\left(\frac{298}{273}\right) = 10 \times 4186 \ln\left(\frac{323}{298}\right) = \mathbf{3372 \text{ J/K}}$$

(c) The total entropy change for the process is,

$$\Delta s_{total} = \Delta s_{iron} + \Delta s_{water}$$
$$= -2195 + 3372$$
$$= 1177 \text{ J/K}$$

Net change in entropy $= 3372.24 - 2195$

Net change in entropy $= 3372.24 - 2195 = \mathbf{1177.24 \text{ J/K}}$

Since $\Delta s > 0$, hence, the process is **irreversible**.

Problem 2.5:

An ideal gas is heated from temperature T_1 to T_2 by keeping its volume constant. The gas is expanded back to its initial temperature according to the law pv^n = constant. If the entropy changes in the two processes are equal, find the value of n in terms of the adiabatic index γ.

Solution: Change in entropy during constant volume process

$$= m\, c_v \ln\left(\frac{T_2}{T_1}\right) \qquad \ldots (i)$$

Change in entropy during polytropic process (pv^n = constant)

$$= m\, c_v \left(\frac{\gamma - n}{n - 1}\right) \ln\left(\frac{T_2}{T_1}\right) \qquad \ldots (ii)$$

For the same entropy, equating (i) and (ii), we have

$$\frac{\gamma - n}{n - 1} = 1$$

or $\qquad (\gamma - n) = (n - 1)$ or $2n = \gamma + 1$

$\therefore \qquad n = \dfrac{\gamma + 1}{2}$

Problem 2.6:

1 kg of air has a volume of 56 litres and a temperature of 190°C. The air then receives heat at constant pressure until its temperature becomes 500°C. From this state the air rejects heat at constant volume until its pressure is reduced to 700 kN/m². Determine the change of entropy during each process stating whether it is on increase or decrease.

Take c_p = 1.006 kJ/kg·K and c_v = 0.717 kJ/kg·K

Solution: Given:

Mass of air = m = 1 kg.

Initial volume of air = V_1 = 56 litres

Initial temperature of air = T_1 = 190 + 273 = 463 K

Final temperature of air = T_2 = 500 + 273 = 773 K

Final pressure of air = p_3 = 700 kN/m²

Calculate: (i) Change of entropy during each process.

The given process is drawn in Fig. 2.16.

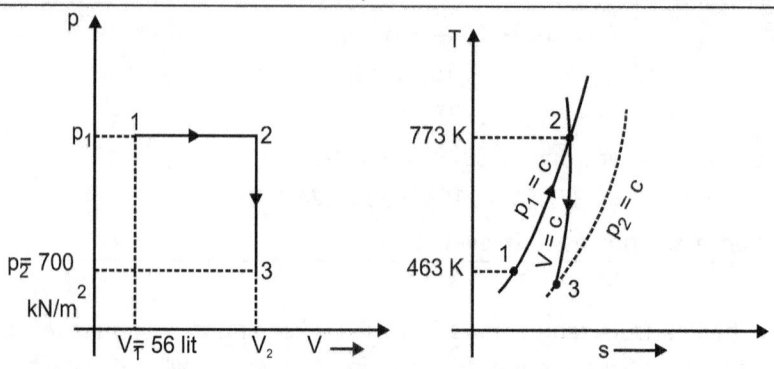

Fig. 2.16

For process 1-2 (Constant Pressure Process):

$$p_1 = p_2$$

By general gas equation,

$$\frac{p_1 V_1}{T_1} = \frac{p_2 V_2}{T_2}$$

$$\frac{V_1}{T_1} = \frac{V_2}{V_1}$$

$$V_2 = \frac{V_1}{T_1} \times T_2 = \frac{56 \times 10^{-3}}{463} \times 773$$

∴ $\quad V_2 = 0.09353 \text{ m}^3$

Using the equation of change of entropy,

$$s_2 - s_1 = mc_v \cdot \log_e \frac{T_2}{T_1} + mR \log \frac{V_2}{V_1}$$

$$= 1 \times 0.717 \log \frac{773}{463} + 1(1.006 - 0.717) \log \frac{0.09353}{0.056}$$

$$= 0.3675 + 0.48268$$

$$= \mathbf{0.85 \text{ kJ/kg·K (Increase)}}$$

Process 2-3 (Constant Volume): $V_2 = V_3$

From general gas equation,

$$p_2 V_2 = mRT_2$$

∴ $\quad p_2 = \frac{mRT_2}{V_2} = \frac{1 \times 0.289 \times 773}{0.09353}$

$$= 2388.51 \text{ kN/m}^2$$

and $\quad \dfrac{p_2 V_2}{T_2} = \dfrac{p_3 V_3}{T_3}$

$$\frac{p_2}{T_2} = \frac{p_3}{T_3} \qquad (\because V_2 = V_3)$$

$$\therefore \quad T_3 = \frac{p_3 T_2}{p_2} = \frac{700 \times 773}{2388.51}$$

$$T_3 = 226.54 \text{ K}$$

Using the equation of change of entropy,

$$s_3 - s_2 = mc_p \cdot \log_e \frac{T_3}{T_2} - mR \cdot \log_e \frac{p_3}{p_2}$$

$$= 1 \times 1.006 \log \frac{226.54}{773} - 1 \times 0.289 \log \frac{700}{2388.51}$$

$$= -1.23472 - (-0.3547)$$

$$= \mathbf{-0.88002 \text{ kJ/kg·K (Decrease)}}$$

Problem 2.7:

A mass 'm' kg of a gas at temperature T_1 K is isobarically and adiabatically mixed with an equal mass of same gas at temperature T_2 K ($T_1 > T_2$). Show that the change in entropy of the universe during the process is given by:

$$(\Delta s)_{uni} = 2m \cdot c_p \ln\left[\frac{T_1 + T_2}{2\sqrt{T_1 \cdot T_2}}\right]$$

Solution: Consider 'm' kg of gas at temperature T_1 in the compartment (A) and same mass i.e. 'm' kg of gas at temperature T_2 in another compartment (B). The gas from (A) and (B) is allowed to mix together as shown in Fig. 2.17.

The gases in compartment (A) and compartment (B) are allowed to mix together as shown in Fig. 2.17.

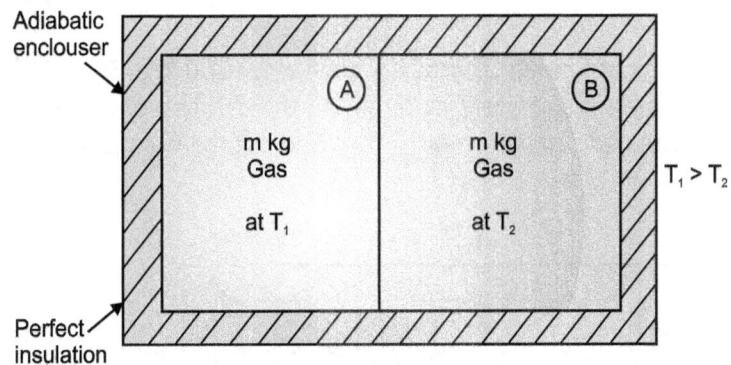

Fig. 2.17

Let the temperature of gas after mixing be T_3.

Heat given out by gas at T_1 = Heat lost by gas at T_2

$$\therefore \quad mc_p (T_1 - T_3) = mc_p (T_3 - T_2)$$

$$\therefore \quad T_3 = \frac{T_1 + T_2}{2} \quad \ldots (1)$$

(a) The change of entropy of gas in compartment (A) at constant pressure,

$$(\Delta s)_A = \int_{T_1}^{T_3} \frac{dQ}{T} = \int_{T_1}^{T_3} \frac{m \cdot c_p}{T} dT = mc_p \cdot \log_e \frac{T_3}{T_1} \qquad \ldots (2)$$

(b) The change of entropy of gas in compartment (B),

$$(\Delta s)_B = \int_{T_2}^{T_3} \frac{m \cdot c_p}{T} dT = mc_p \cdot \log_e \frac{T_3}{T_2} \qquad \ldots (3)$$

(c) The change of entropy of surroundings $(\Delta s)_{surr} = 0$ because it is an adiabatic process.

$$\therefore \quad (\Delta s)_{universe} = (\Delta s)_A + (\Delta s)_B + (\Delta s)_{surr}$$

$$= m \cdot c_p \cdot \log_e \frac{T_3}{T_1} + m \cdot c_p \cdot \log_e \frac{T_3}{T_2} + 0 \qquad \ldots (4)$$

Substituting value of T_3 from equation (1) in equation (4), we get,

$$(\Delta s)_{universe} = mc_p \left[\log_e \frac{T_1 + T_2}{2T_1} + \log_e \frac{T_1 + T_2}{2T_2} \right]$$

$$\therefore \quad (\Delta s)_{universe} = mc_p \left[\log_e \left(\frac{T_1 + T_2}{2T_1} \right) + \log_e \left(\frac{T_1 + T_2}{2T_2} \right) \right]$$

$$= mc_p \cdot \log_e \left[\frac{(T_1 + T_2)^2}{(2\sqrt{T_1 T_2})^2} \right] = mc_p \log_e \left[\frac{T_1 + T_2}{2\sqrt{T_1 T_2}} \right]^2$$

$$(\Delta s)_{universe} = 2 \cdot m \cdot c_p \log_e \left[\frac{T_1 + T_2}{2\sqrt{T_1 T_2}} \right] \qquad \ldots (5)$$

Hence proved.

Problem 2.8:

The two compartments of insulated air box contain air at 200 kPa, 300 K, 1 kg mass and at 150 kPa, 300 K, 1 kg mass respectively. By removing the partition of the compartment, prove that the entropy of isolated system increases. Also find out the change in entropy.

Solution:

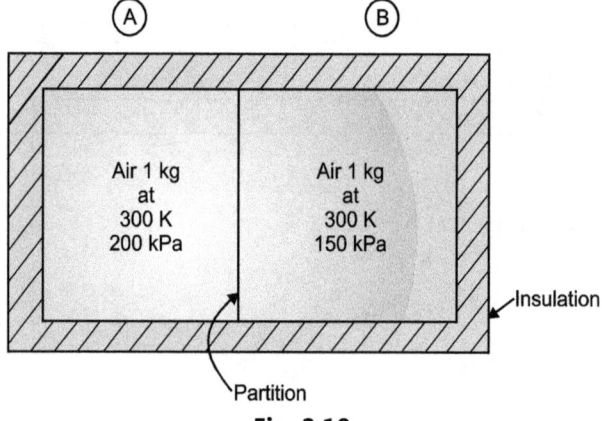

Fig. 2.18

Required:
(i) Proof of entropy of isolated system increases.
(ii) Change in entropy = Δs =?

Consider the volume of compartment (A) is V_A.
Apply ideal gas equation to the compartment 'A'

$$p_A V_A = m_A RT$$

$$\therefore \quad V_A = \frac{m_A RT}{p_A} = \frac{1 \times 287 \times 300}{200 \times 10^3} = 0.4305 \text{ m}^3$$

Similarly, for compartment B,

$$V_B = \frac{1 \times 287 \times 300}{150 \times 10^3} = 0.574 \text{ m}^3$$

The temperature in both compartments is same,

$$T_A = T_B = 300 \text{ K}$$

As the process is adiabatic mixing, the temperature reached after mixing is also 300 K.

The total mass of mixture = $m_A + m_B = 1 + 1 = 2$ kg

The total volume, $V = V_A + V_B$
$$= 0.4305 + 0.574$$
$$= 1.0045 \text{ m}^3$$

Now, using the characteristic gas equation,

$$pV = mRT$$

$$p = \frac{mRT}{V}$$

$$= \frac{2 \times 287 \times 300}{1.0045}$$

$$p = 171.43 \text{ kPa}$$

The partial pressure of air after mixing is given by,

$$p_{air(A)} = p \times \frac{n_{air}}{n} = p \times \frac{m_A}{M_A} \times \frac{M}{m}$$

$$= \left(171.43 \times \frac{1}{28.97}\right) \times \frac{28.97}{2} = 85.715 \text{ kPa}$$

and $\quad p_{air(B)} = 85.715$ kPa

Then, entropy change per kg is given by,

$$\Delta s =$$

$$(\Delta s)_{air(A)} = 0 - \frac{8314.4}{28.97} \log\left(\frac{85.715}{200}\right)$$

$$= 243.17 \text{ J/kg}$$

and $(\Delta s)_{air(B)} = 0 - \dfrac{8314.4}{28.97} \ln\left(\dfrac{85.715}{150}\right)$

$= 160.61$ J/kg

$= 0.161$ kJ/kg

Total change in entropy of the mixture

$(\Delta s)_{mix} = (\Delta s)_{air(A)} + (\Delta s)_{air(B)}$

$= 0.24317 + 0.161$

$= \mathbf{0.404}$ **kJ/kg**

The change in entropy of the mixture is 0.404 kJ/kg, which is a positive value. Hence, entropy of the total system always increases.

Problem 2.9:

1 kg of nitrogen at a temperature of 155°C occupies a volume of 0.3 m³. The gas undergoes constant pressure expansion to a volume of 0.4 m³. The gas is then expanded isothermally to a volume of 0.5 m³. Determine change of entropy for each process and total change of entropy. Represent the process on p-V and T-s diagrams. Take:

$$c_v = 0.743 \dfrac{kJ}{kg \cdot K}$$

and $$R = 0.297 \dfrac{kJ}{kg \cdot K}$$

Solution: Given data: m = 1 kg, T_1 = 155°C = 428 K, V_1 = 0.3 m³, V_2 = 0.4 m³, V_3 = 0.5 m³.

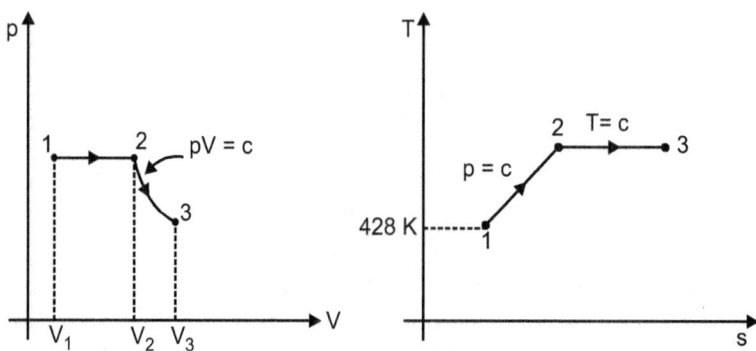

Fig. 2.19: p-V and T-s diagrams

At state point 1:

$p_1 V_1 = m R T_1$

∴ $p_1 = \dfrac{m R T_1}{V_1} = \dfrac{1 \times 297 \times 428}{0.3}$

∴ $p_1 = 4.2372$ bar

From general gas equation,

$$\frac{p_1 V_1}{T_1} = \frac{p_2 V_2}{T_2}$$

$$\therefore \quad T_2 = T_1 \cdot \frac{V_2}{V_1} \qquad (\because p_1 = p_2)$$

$$= 428 \times \frac{0.4}{0.3}$$

$$= 570.67 \text{ K}$$

Change in entropy for 1-2 process,

$$s_2 - s_1 = mR \log_e \frac{V_2}{V_1} + mc_v \log_e \frac{T_2}{T_1}$$

$$= 1 \times 0.297 \log_e \frac{0.4}{0.3} + 1 \times 0.743 \times \log_e \frac{570.67}{428}$$

$$= 0.08544 + 0.213752$$

$$= \mathbf{0.2992 \text{ kJ/kg}}$$

For process 2-3,

$$T_2 = T_3 = 570.67 \text{ K}$$

Change in entropy for 2-3 process,

$$s_3 - s_2 = mR \log_e \frac{V_3}{V_2} + mc_v \log_e \frac{T_3}{T_2}$$

$$= 1 \times 0.297 \log_e \frac{0.5}{0.4} + 1 \times 0.743 \times \log_e \frac{570.67}{570.67}$$

$$= \mathbf{0.06627 \text{ kJ/kg}}$$

Overall change in entropy,

$$s_3 - s_1 = (s_2 - s_1) + (s_3 - s_2)$$

$$= 0.2992 + 0.06627$$

$$= 0.36547 \text{ kJ/kg}$$

$\therefore \quad$ Total change of entropy $= \mathbf{0.36547 \text{ kJ/kg}}$

Problem 2.10:

1 kg of ice at −6°C is exposed to atmosphere which is at 30°C. The ice melts and comes into thermal equilibrium. Determine entropy increase of the universe. Take c_p of ice = 2009 kJ/kg·K and latent heat of fusion of ice = 333.3 kJ/kg.

Solution: Refer Fig. 2.20.

$$\text{Mass of ice} = m_1 = 1 \text{ kg}$$
$$\text{Temperature of ice} = -6 + 273 = 267 \text{ K}$$
$$\text{Temperature of atmosphere} = 30 + 273 = 303 \text{ K}$$

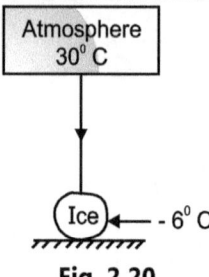

Fig. 2.20

Heat absorbed by ice from the atmosphere

= Heat absorbed in solid state + Latent heat + Heat absorbed in liquid phase

$= m_i \times c_{pi} \times \Delta t + L_i + m_w c_{pw} \Delta t$

$= 1 \times 2.09 \times [0 - (-6)] + 333.33 + 1 \times 4.187 \times (30 - 0)$

$= 12.54 + 333.33 + 125.61$

= **471.27 kJ**

Entropy change of the atmosphere

$$(\Delta s)_{atm} = -\frac{Q}{T} = -\frac{471.27}{303} = -1.5553 \text{ kJ/K}$$

(a) Entropy change of system (ice) as it gets heated from −6°C to 0°C,

(b) $$(\Delta s_I)_{system} = \int_{267}^{273} m_i c_{pi} \frac{dT}{T} = 1 \times 2.09 \times \log_e\left(\frac{273}{267}\right) = 0.04645 \text{ kJ/K}$$

(c) Entropy change of system as ice melts at 0°C to become water at 0°C,

$$(\Delta s_{II})_{system} = \frac{333.33}{273} = 1.2209 \text{ kJ/K}$$

(d) Entropy change of water as it gets heated from 0°C to 30°C,

$$(\Delta s_{III})_{system} = \int_{273}^{303} m_w c_{pw} \frac{dT}{T} = 1 \times 4.187 \times \log_e\left(\frac{303}{273}\right) = 0.4365 \text{ kJ/K}$$

Total entropy change of ice as it melts into water,

$(\Delta s)_{total} = \Delta s_I + \Delta s_{II} + \Delta s_{III}$

$= 0.04645 + 1.2209 + 0.4365 = 1.70385 \text{ kJ/K}$

The temperature-entropy diagram for the system as ice at −6°C converts to water at 30°C is shown in Fig. 2.21.

∴ Entropy increase of the universe,

$(\Delta s)_{universe} = (\Delta s)_{system} + (\Delta s)_{atm}$

$= 1.70385 + (-1.5553)$

= **0.14855 kJ/K**

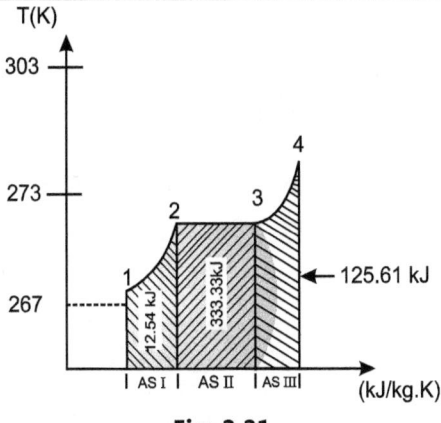

Fig. 2.21

Problem 2.11:
One kg of water at 300 K is first heated to 400 K by bringing it in contact with an intermediate heat reservoir at 400 K and then to 500 K as before. What will be the entropy change of the universe in this case?

Solution: Heating of water:

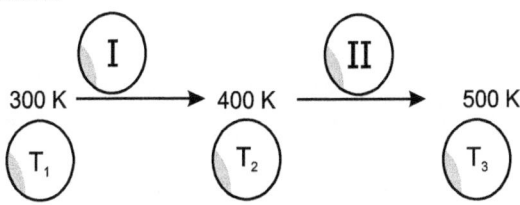

Fig. 2.22

Heat transfer in each reservoir (i.e. for I and II, it is same at $\Delta T = 100$ K)

$$Q = m_w \cdot c_{pw} \cdot \Delta T = 1 \times 4.1868 \times 100 = 418.7 \text{ kJ}$$

Entropy change of water, heat reservoir and universe,

$$(\Delta s)_{water} = m_w \cdot c_{pw} \cdot \left[\log_e \frac{T_2}{T_1} + \log_e \frac{T_3}{T_2} \right]$$

$$= 1 \times 4.1868 \left[\log_e \frac{400}{300} + \log_e \frac{500}{400} \right] = 2.1387 \text{ kJ/K}$$

$$(\Delta s)_{reservoir\ I} = \frac{-418.7}{400} = -1.04675 \text{ kJ/K}$$

$$(\Delta s)_{reservoir\ II} = \frac{-418.7}{500} = -0.8374 \text{ kJ/K}$$

Negative sign indicates that both reservoirs loss heat.

Then,
$$(\Delta s)_{universe} = (\Delta s)_{water} + (\Delta s)_{reservoir-I} + (\Delta s)_{reservoir-II}$$
$$= 2.1387 - 1.04675 - 0.8374$$
$$= \mathbf{0.25455 \text{ kJ/K}}$$

Problem 2.12:

At constant pressure 138 kPa, 5 kg of oxygen is cooled from 500 K to 300 K. The temperature of the surrounding is 277 K. Find the available part of heat removed and entropy increase of universe.

Solution: Given data: m = 5 kg, p_1 = 138 kPa, T_1 = 500 K, T_0 = 277 K, p_0 = 1 bar = 100 kPa.

Initial availability of O_2,

$$A_1 = (u_1 - u_0) + p_0 (V_1 - V_0) - T_0 (s_1 - s_0)$$

$$s_1 - s_0 = c_p \cdot \log_e \frac{T_1}{T_0} - R \log_e \frac{p_1}{p_0}$$

$$= 0.9169 \log_e \frac{500}{277} - 0.287 \log_e \frac{138}{100}$$

$$= 0.54151 - 0.09243 = 0.4491 \text{ kJ/kg·K}$$

$$\therefore A_1 = mc_v (T_1 - T_0) + mR\, p_0 \left[\frac{T_1}{p_1} - \frac{T_0}{p_0}\right] - mT_0 [0.4491]$$

$$= 5 \times 0.653 (500 - 277) + 5 \times 0.287 \times 100 \left[\frac{500}{138} - \frac{277}{100}\right]$$
$$- 5 \times 277 \times 0.4491$$

$$= 728.095 + 122.4325 - 622.00 = \mathbf{228.524 \text{ kJ}}$$

Final availability at T_2 = 300 K, T_0 = 277 K, $p_2 = p_1$ = 138 kPa, p_0 = 100 kPa

$$A_2 = mc_v (T_2 - T_0) + mR\, p_0 \left[\frac{T_2}{p_2} - \frac{T_0}{p_1}\right] - mT_0 (s_2 - s_0)$$

$$s_2 - s_0 = c_p \cdot \log_e (T_2/T_0) - R \log_e (p_2/p_0)$$

$$= 0.9169 \log_e \left(\frac{300}{277}\right) - 0.287 \log_e \left(\frac{138}{100}\right)$$

$$= -0.0193 \text{ kJ/kg·K}$$

$$A_2 = 5 \times 0.653 (300 - 277) + 5 \times 0.287 \times 100 \left[\frac{300}{138} - \frac{277}{100}\right]$$
$$- 5 \times 277 (-0.0193)$$

$$\therefore A_2 = 75.095 + (-85.54) + 26.7305 = 16.287 \text{ kJ}$$

Available part of heat removed = 16.287 − 228.524 = **−212.237 kJ**

Problem 2.13:

0.04 m³ of nitrogen contained in a cylinder behind a piston is initially at 1.05 bar and 15°C. The gas is compressed isothermally and reversibly until the pressure is 4.8 bar. Calculate: (i) Change of entropy, (ii) Heat flow, (iii) Work done.

Sketch the process on a p-V diagram and T-s diagram. Assume nitrogen to act as a perfect gas. Molecular weight of nitrogen = 28.

Solution: Given data:

$V_1 = 0.04 \text{ m}^3$
$p_1 = 1.05 \text{ bar} = 1.05 \times 10^5 \text{ N/m}^2$
$T_1 = 15°C = 15 + 273 = 288 \text{ K}$
$p_2 = 4.8 \text{ bar} = 4.8 \times 10^5 \text{ N/m}^2$
$T_2 = T_1 = 288 \text{ K}$

The process is shown on p-v and T-s diagrams as follows.

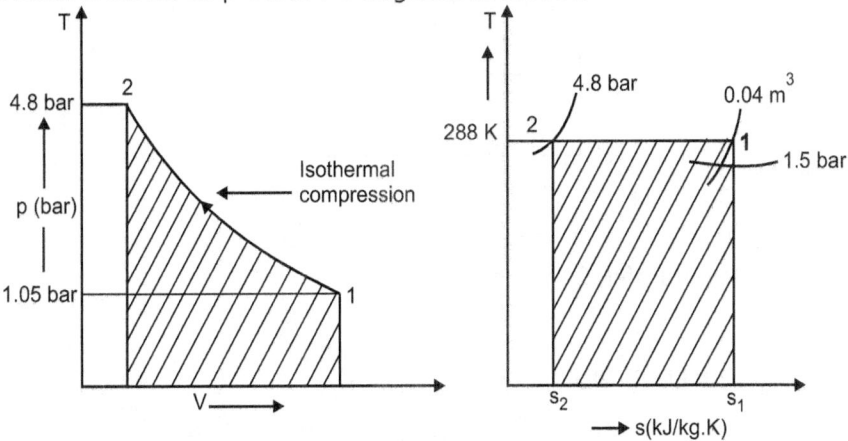

Fig. 2.23

Characteristic gas constant,

$$R = \frac{\text{Universal gas constant, R}_0}{\text{Molecular weight, M}} = \frac{8314}{28} = 297 \text{ N-m/kg·K}$$

Now, we have $p_1V_1 = mRT_1$

$$\therefore \quad m = \frac{p_1V_1}{RT_1} = \frac{1.05 \times 10^5 \times 0.04}{297 \times 288} = \mathbf{0.0491 \text{ kg}}$$

The Change of Entropy:

$$s_2 - s_1 = mR \ln \frac{p_1}{p_2} = 0.0491 \times \frac{297}{1000} \times \ln\left(\frac{1.05}{4.8}\right)$$
$$= \mathbf{-0.02216 \text{ kJ/K}}$$

Problem 2.14:

1 kg of air is allowed to expand reversibly in a cylinder behind a piston in such a way that the temperature remains constant at 260°C while the volume is doubled. The piston is then moved in, and heat is rejected by the air reversibly at constant pressure until the volume is the same as it was initially. Calculate the net heat flow and the overall change of entropy. Sketch the processes on a T-s diagram.

Solution: Given data:
$m = 1 \text{ kg}$
$T_1 = T_2 = 260$
$= 260 + 273$
$260 = 533 \text{ K}$
$V_1 = V_3$
$V_2 = 2V_1$

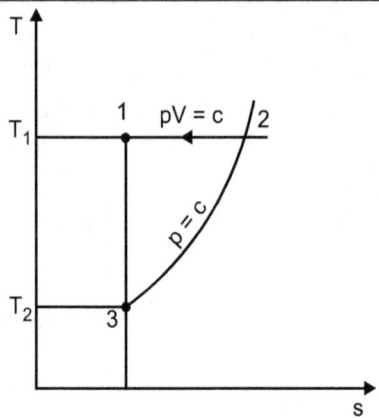

Fig. 2.24

For Process 1-2: $pV = c$

Heat transfer, $Q = mc(T_2 - T_1)$

$Q_{12} = 0$ kJ

Change in entropy $= \Delta s_{1-2} = mR \ln\left(\dfrac{V_2}{V_1}\right)$

For air, $c_p = 1.005$ kJ/kg·K, $c_v = 0.718$ kJ/kg + R = kJ/kg·K

$\Delta s_{1-2} = 1 \times 0.287 \times \ln\left(\dfrac{2V_1}{V_1}\right) = 0.1989$ kJ/K

For Process 2-3: $p = c$

$\dfrac{V_2}{T_2} = \dfrac{V_3}{T_3}$

Now, $V_2 = 2V_1$ and $V_3 = V_1$

$\dfrac{2V_1}{T_2} = \dfrac{V_1}{3}$

∴ $T_3 = \dfrac{T_2}{2} = \dfrac{533}{2} = 266.5$ K

∴ Heat transfer, $Q_{2-3} = m \cdot c_p (T_3 - T_2)$

$= 1 \times 1.005 \times (266.5 - 533) = -267.83$ kJ

$\Delta s_{2-3} = m \cdot c_v \cdot \ln\left(\dfrac{T_3}{T_2}\right) = 1 \times 0.718 \times \ln$

$\Delta s_{2-3} = -0.4976$ kJ/K

∴ Overall heat transfer $= Q_{1-2} + Q_{2-3}$

$\Delta Q = \mathbf{-267.83}$ **kJ (Heat is rejected)**

and overall entropy change $= \Delta s_{1-2} + \Delta s_{2-3}$

$= 0.1989 - 0.4976$

$\Delta s = \mathbf{-0.2987}$ **kJ/K (Entropy decreases)**

(B) AVAILABILITY

2.10 INTRODUCTION

It comes to our mind why an engineer has to understand the availability. The answer is to save energy, to consume energy in an optimal way, to reduce energy wastage etc. To achieve these, the engineers have to take a closer look at all the energy conversion devices (e.g. prime movers and energy consuming devices) and to develop new techniques to better utilize the existing limited resources. The first law of thermodynamics deals with conversion of energy from one form to another and tells that energy cannot be created or destroyed. It tells only the conversion of one form of energy to another however, it does not quantify the energy that changes from one form to another. First law is not a sufficient tool to quantify the process inefficiency or thermodynamic irreversibility which are inherently present in all real processes. For Problem, as per first law, throttling process is a constant enthalpy process. The energy content of the fluid before throttling and after throttling remains constant. Throttling is a real expansion process. The real process is always accompanied with process irreversibility. It is the limitation of first law that it could not quantify such process irreversibilities.

The second law of thermodynamics deals with the quality of energy. Second law is concerned with the degradation of energy during a process. It quantifies the process irreversibility and offers an opportunity to obtain maximum work output from a stream while bringing it from high temperature and pressure conditions to the reference temperature and pressure conditions. Therefore, at this stage, it becomes necessary to study available and unavailable energy of a system undergoing through a process.

2.11 AVAILABLE AND UNAVAILABLE ENERGY

'Available energy' is the maximum portion of the energy which could be converted into useful work and which reduces the system to a 'dead state'. The dead state is one at which the system reaches thermodynamic equilibrium with the surrounding.

When a system is at high pressure than atmospheric pressure, then there is an opportunity to obtain useful work while reducing it to ambient pressure through an expansion device. Similarly, any system which is at higher temperature than ambient temperature, then also there is an opportunity to obtain useful work while reducing its temperature to ambient temperature through a thermodynamic cycle.

Therefore, available energy can be further defined as "the theoretical maximum useful work that can be obtained from a system while changing its state (p_1 and T_1) to reference state (p_0 and T_0) through a reversible process".

To obtain a maximum useful work from a system, its state (p_1 and T_1) has to be reduced to reference state (p_0 and T_0) through a reversible process. However, in reality, the end state of the system will not be at reference state but little above that state. It means say the system reaches to a state (p_2 and T_2) which is in between the initial state (p_1 and T_1) and reference state (p_0 and T_0). Therefore, the actual work obtained is less than that of maximum possible work (available energy). The portion of the available energy which is not converted to useful work is known as **unavailable energy**.

2.12 AVAILABLE ENERGY REFERRED A CYCLE

The maximum work output obtainable from a certain heat input in a cyclic heat engine (reversible engine) is called the available energy (AE). The minimum energy that has to be rejected to the sink as per the second law is called the unavailable energy (UE) or the unavailable part of supplied energy.

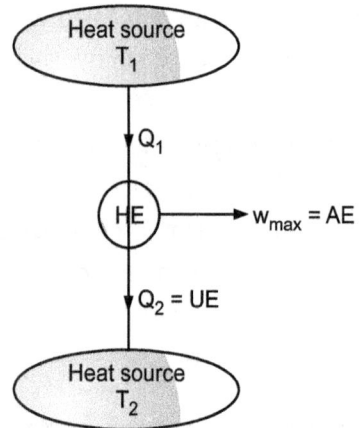

Fig. 2.25: Available and unavailable energy in a cycle

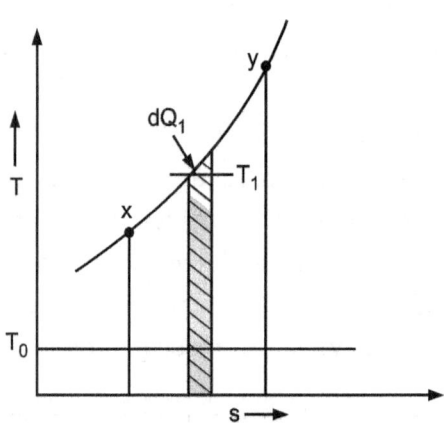

Fig. 2.26: Availability of energy

Let Q_1 be the heat energy supplied, which consists of two parts (AE and UE).

Therefore,
$$Q_1 = AE + UE \qquad \ldots (2.33)$$
$$W_{max} = AE = Q_1 - UE$$

For the heat engine working between T_1 and T_2,
$$\eta_{rev} = 1 - \frac{T_2}{T_1}$$

For a given source temperature T_1, η_{rev} will increase with decrease of sink temperature T_2. The lowest possible temperature at which heat rejection would take place is the temperature of the surroundings, T_0.

$$\eta_{max} = 1 - \frac{T_0}{T_1}$$

$$w_{max} = \left(1 - \frac{T_0}{T_1}\right) Q_1$$

Let us consider a process x-y, during which heat is supplied reversibly to a heat engine as shown in Fig. 2.26. Assuming an elementary cycle, dQ_1 is the heat supplied to a reversible heat engine at T_1, then

$$dw_{max} = \eta_{rev} \times dQ_1$$

$$= \left(\frac{T_1 - T_0}{T_1}\right) \cdot dQ_1$$

$$= dQ_1 - \frac{T_0}{T_1} dQ_1 = AE$$

The heat engine receiving heat for the whole process x-y and rejecting heat at T_0

$$\int_x^y dw_{max} = \int_x^y dQ_1 - \int_x^y \frac{T_0}{T_1} \cdot dQ_1$$

∴ $w_{max} = AE = Q_{xy} - T_0 (s_y - s_x)$ ... (2.34)

Unavailable energy, $UE = Q_{xy} - w_{max}$

$$= T_0 (s_y - s_x)$$

The unavailable energy is nothing but the product of the lowest temperature of heat sink (T_0) and the change of entropy of the system during the process, which is as shown in Fig. 2.27.

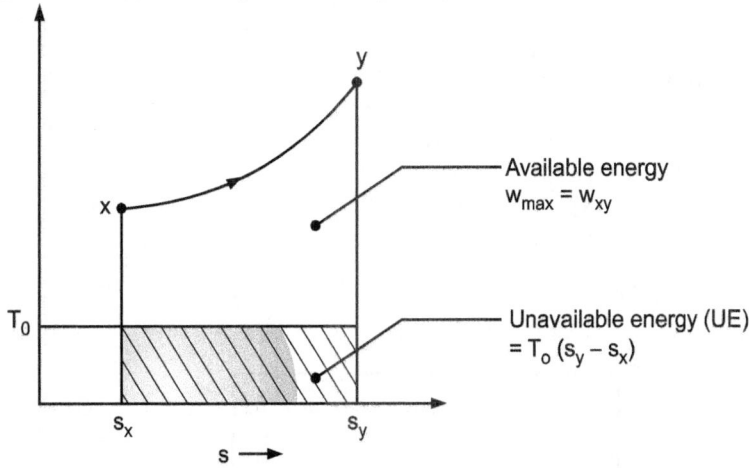

Fig. 2.27: Unavailable energy according to second law

The available energy is also known as **exergy** and the unavailable energy as **anergy**. It may please be note here that exergy and anergy are the correct words.

2.13 DECREASE IN AVAILABLE ENERGY IN A HEAT TRANSFER PROCESS THROUGH A FINITE TEMPERATURE DIFFERENCE

In order to transfer heat from one system to another, a finite temperature difference is needed. To achieve this, there is a decrease in the availability of energy. This can be shown as given below.

Consider a reversible heat engine (Carnot engine) operating between the temperature limits T_1 and T_0 as shown in Fig. 2.28.

$$\text{Heat supplied, } Q_1 = T \cdot \Delta s$$
$$\text{Heat rejected, } Q_2 = T_0 \cdot \Delta s$$
$$\text{Max. work done, } w = A.E = [T_1 - T_0] \Delta s$$

Assume heat Q_1 is transferred through a finite temperature difference (ΔT) from the source at T_1 to the engine absorbing heat at T_1', lower than T_1 (See Fig. 2.29). The availability of Q_1 as received by the engine at T_1' can be found by allowing the engine to operate reversibly in a cycle between T_1' and T_0 receiving Q_1 and rejecting Q_2'. Now, the heat supply Q_1 takes place at lower temperature.

The heat,	$Q_1 = T_1 \Delta s = T_1' \Delta s'$	
Since	$T_1 > T_1'$	
$\therefore$	$\Delta s' = \Delta s$	
The heat rejected,	$Q_2 = T_0 \Delta s$	
	$Q_2' = T_0 \Delta s'$	
$\therefore$	$\Delta s' > \Delta s$	
$\therefore$	$Q_2' > Q_2$	

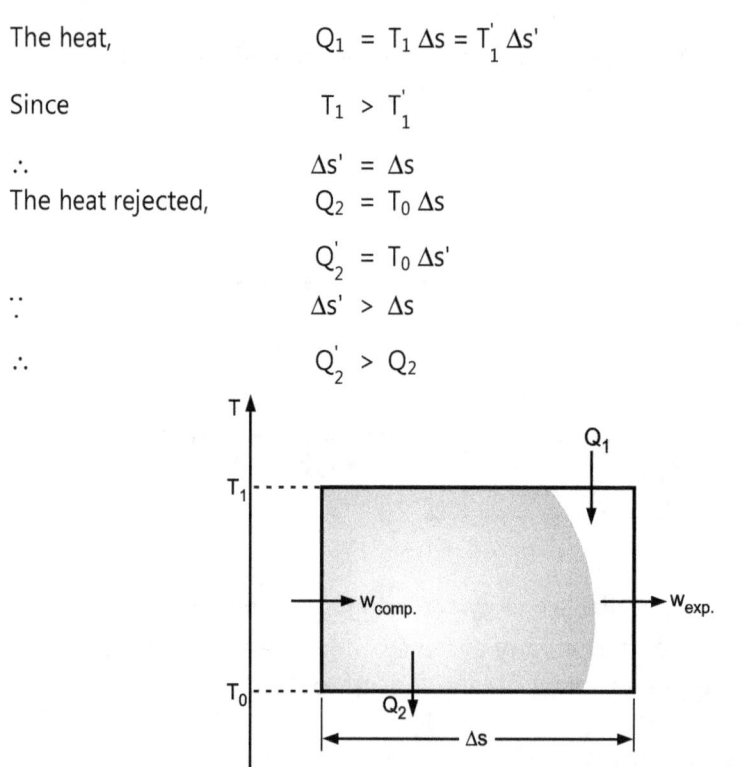

Fig. 2.28: Reversible (Carnot) engine on T-s diagram

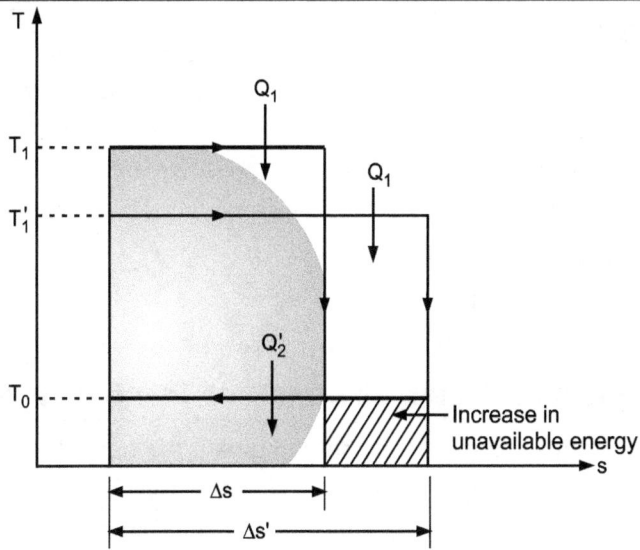

Fig. 2.29: Increase in unavailable energy due to heat transfer through a finite temperature difference

Now, work done in new cycle (with ΔT at source).

$$w' = Q_1 - Q_2' = T_1' \Delta s' - T_0 \Delta s'$$

and with no ΔT

$$w = Q_1 - Q_2 = T_1 \Delta s - T_0 \Delta s$$

$\therefore$ $\quad w' < w$, because $Q_2' > Q_2$

The loss of available energy due to irreversible heat transfer through finite temperature difference between the source and the working fluid during the heat addition process is given as,

$$w - w' = Q_2' - Q_2$$
$$= T_0 (\Delta s' - \Delta s)$$

i.e. decrease in available energy, A.E.

$$= T_0 (\Delta s' - \Delta s) \quad \ldots (2.35)$$

Hence, the decrease in AE is the product of the lowest feasible temperature of heat rejection (T_0) and the additional entropy change in the system while receiving heat irreversibly, compared to the case of reversible heat transfer from the same source. The greater is the temperature difference ($T_1 - T_1'$), the greater is the heat rejection Q_2' and the greater will be the unavailable part of the energy supplied which is shown in Fig. 2.29.

Energy is said to be degraded each time it flows through a finite temperature difference (ΔT). That is, why the second law of thermodynamics is sometimes called the law of degradation of energy.

2.14 AVAILABILITY OF HEAT

Consider a certain amount of heat δQ is withdrawn from a heat reservoir or from a system of finite size. Now, one has to understand the availability of heat δQ. To understand this one is required to find out the work that can be obtained when this heat δQ is supplied to a reversible cycle which will reject that heat at an environment temperature T_0.

The heat δQ will be available in two ways:

(i) Heat δQ is withdrawn at constant temperature.

(ii) Heat δQ is withdrawn not at constant temperature.

2.14.1 Heat δQ is withdrawn at Constant Temperature 'T'

Withdrawal of heat from a source at constant temperature is possible only when the source must be a thermal reservoir. Fig. 2.30 shows the Carnot cycle on T-s diagram, working between the temperature limits T and T_0. Here, it is assumed that heat is supplied to Carnot engine at constant temperature T and rejected to heat sink at T_0.

According to first law,

$$(\delta w_{rev})_{cycle} = (\delta Q)_{sup} - (\delta Q)_{rej}$$

or

$$(W_{cycle}) = \int_1^2 \delta Q - \int_4^3 T_0 \, ds$$

$$= Q - T_0(s_3 - s_4)$$

$$= T\Delta s - T_0 \Delta s$$

$\therefore$ Availability, $A = w_{rev} = Q - T_0 \Delta s$ ... (2.36)

Here, Δs represents change of entropy of fluid during unavailability of heat

$$= UA = Q - A = T_0 \cdot \Delta s \qquad \ldots (2.37)$$

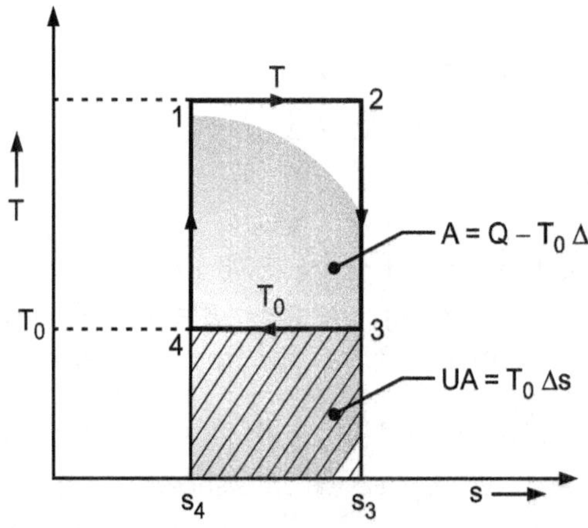

Fig. 2.30: Availability of heat

2.14.2 Heat δQ is withdrawn not at Constant Temperature (Available Energy from a finite Energy Source)

Assume a hot gas of mass m_g at temperature T. Let the gas be cooled at constant pressure from state 1 at T to state 3 at T_0 as shown in Fig. 2.31. The heat given up by the gas Q_1 be utilized in heating up reversibly a working fluid of mass m_{wf} from state 3 to state 1 along the same path so that ΔT between the gas and working fluid at any instant is zero and hence the entropy increase of the universe is also zero. The working fluid expands isentropically from state 1 to state 2. Further, it rejects heat Q_2 isothermally at T_0 to return to the initial state 3 to complete the heat engine cycle.

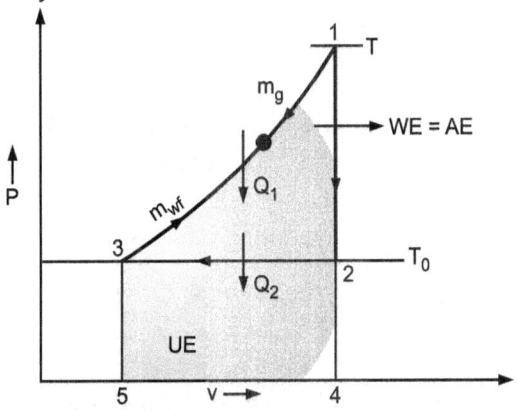

Fig. 2.31: Available energy of a finite energy source

$$Q_1 = m_g \cdot c_{pg}(T - T_0) = m_{wf} \cdot c_{pwf}(T - T_0)$$
$$= \text{Area } 14531$$

$$m_g \cdot c_{pg} = m_{wf} \cdot c_{pf}$$

$$\Delta s_{gas} = \int_T^{T_0} m_g \cdot c_{pg} \frac{dT}{T} = m_g \cdot c_{pg} \ln\left(\frac{T_0}{T}\right) \text{ negative}$$

$$\Delta s_{wf} = \int_{T_0}^{T} m_{wf} \cdot c_{pwf} \frac{dT}{T} = m_{wf} \cdot c_{pwf} \ln\left(\frac{T}{T_0}\right) \text{ positive}$$

$$\Delta s_{univ} = \Delta s_{gas} + \Delta s_{wf} = 0$$

$$Q_2 = T_0 \cdot \Delta s_{wf}$$
$$= T_0 \cdot m_{wf} \cdot c_{pwf} \cdot \ln\left(\frac{T}{T_0}\right) = \text{Area } 1231$$

Therefore, the available energy (availability) of a gas of mass m_g at temperature 'T' is given by,

$$AE = m_g \cdot c_{pg} \cdot \left[(T - T_0) - T_0 \cdot \ln\left(\frac{T}{T_0}\right)\right]$$

2.15 QUALITY OF ENERGY

Availability signifies the quality of energy. In order to demonstrate this consider the case of heat loss from a hot gas flowing through a pipeline as shown in Fig. 2.32. Due to heat loss to the surroundings, the temperature of the gas decreases continuously from inlet at A to the exit at B. Although the process is irreversible, but for the analysis consider a reversible isobaric path between the inlet and exit states of the gas as shown in Fig. 2.33. Now, consider an infinitesimal process on this irreversible isobaric process and for this change in entropy is given by,

$$ds = \frac{mc_p dT}{T}$$

or

$$\frac{dT}{ds} = \frac{T}{mc_p} \qquad \ldots (2.38)$$

where, m is the mass of gas flowing and c_p is the specific heat. The slope dT/ds depends on the gas temperature T. The decrement in T decreases the slope while increment in T will increase the slope.

Let the heat Q be lost to the surroundings during infinitesimal process as the temperature of the gas decreases from T_1' to T_1'', T_1 being the average of the two. Thus,

$$\text{Heat loss} = Q = mc_p (T_1' - T_1'') = T_1 \Delta s_1 \qquad \ldots (2.39)$$

Available energy loss with this heat at temperature T_1 is expressed as,

$$w_1 = A_1 = Q - T_0 \Delta s_1 \qquad \ldots (2.40)$$

During the process the gas temperature has reached T_2 ($T_2 < T_1$), assume that the same heat loss Q occurs as the gas temperature decreases from T_2' to T_2'', T_2 being the average temperature.

$$\text{Heat loss} = mc_p (T_2' - T_2'') = T_2 \Delta s_2 \qquad \ldots (2.41)$$

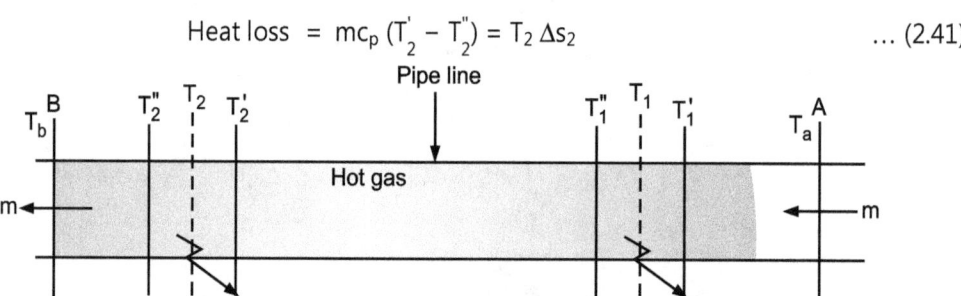

Fig. 2.32: Heat loss from a hot gas flowing through a pipe line

Thus, available energy lost with this heat loss at temperature T_2 is given by,

$$w_2 = A_2 = Q - T_0 \Delta s_2 \qquad \ldots (2.42)$$

From equations (2.39) and (2.40), we have $\Delta s_1 < \Delta s_2$ as $T_1 > T_2$

Thus, from equations (2.40) and (2.42), we have, $w_1 > w_2$ ... (2.43)

The loss of available energy is more, when heat loss occurs at a higher temperature T_1 than when the same heat loss occurs at a lower temperature T_2. Therefore, a loss of heat of 1 kJ at say 1200°C is more harmful than the same heat loss of 1 kJ at say 200°C. Adequate insulation must be provided for high temperature fluids (T >>> T_0) to prevent the heat loss. This may not be so important for low temperature fluids (T ~ T_0), since the loss of available energy such fluids would be low. Similarly, adequate insulation must be provided for very low temperature fluids (T << T_0) to prevent heat gain from surroundings.

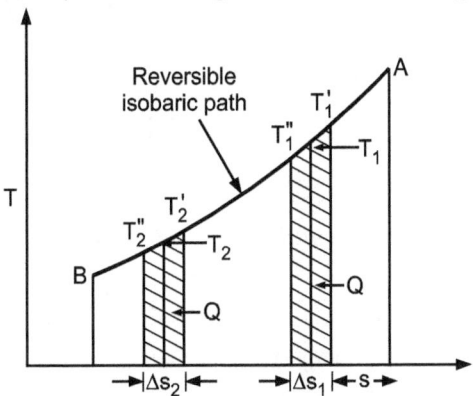

Fig. 2.33: Concept of energy quality

It is to be noted that the available energy or energy of a fluid at a higher temperature T_1 is more than at a lower temperature T_2 and decreases with temperature.

The above discussion tells that the second law affixes a quality of energy of a system at any state. Further, the quality of energy of gas at say 1200°C is much superior to that at, say 200°C, since the gas at 1500°C has the capacity doing more work than that the gas at 200°C, under the same environmental conditions. This clearly suggests that awareness of this energy quality as of energy quantity is essential for the efficient use of our precious energy resources and for energy conversion. Thus, a concept of energy or available energy provides a useful measure of this energy quality for better utilisation of energy sources.

2.16 AVAILABILITY IN A NON-FLOW (CLOSED) SYSTEM

Let us consider a system consisting of a fluid in a cylinder-piston arrangement as shown in Fig. 2.34. The fluid expands reversibly from initial condition of p_1 and T_1 to final atmospheric conditions of p_0 and T_0. Imagine also the system works in conjunction with a reversible heat engine which receives heat reversibly from the fluid in the cylinder such that the working substance of the heat engine follows the cycle 0-1-3-0 as shown in Fig. 2.35.

The cycle in Fig. 2.35 is possible only if an infinite number of reversible heat engines were arranged in parallel each operating on a Carnot cycle, each one receiving heat at a different constant temperature and each one rejecting heat at T_0.

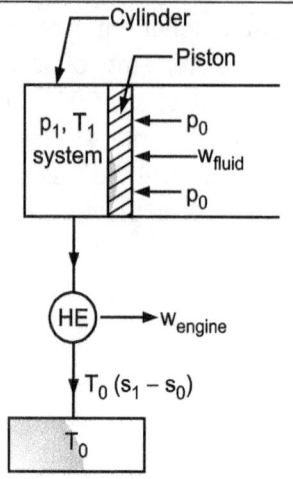
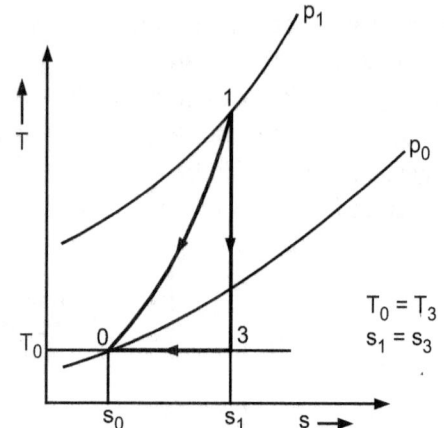

Fig. 2.34: Closed system conjunction with heat engine

Fig. 2.35: Imaginary engine

The work done by the engine is given as,

$$W_{engine} = \text{Heat supplied} - \text{Heat rejected}$$
$$= Q - T_0(s_1 - s_0) \qquad \ldots (i)$$

The heat supplied to the engine is equal to the heat rejected by the fluid in the cylinder. Therefore, we can write for the fluid in the cylinder undergoing the process from state 1 to state 0.

$$-Q = (u_0 - u_1) + W_{fluid}$$
$$W_{fluid} = (u_1 - u_0) - Q \qquad \ldots (ii)$$

Adding equations (i) and (ii), one gets

$$W_{fluid} + W_{engine} = [(u_1 - u_0) - Q] + [Q - T_0(s_1 - s_0)]$$
$$= (u_1 - u_0) - T_0(s_1 - s_0) \qquad \ldots (2.44)$$

The piston is pushed towards bds position by the fluid inside the cylinder, against the atmospheric pressure p_0. Therefore, the work done by the fluid on the piston is less than the total work done by the fluid.

Work done on atmosphere = $p_0(v_0 - v_1)$ ... (2.45)

Therefore, the maximum work available

$$W_{max} = (u_1 - u_0) - T_0(s_1 - s_0) - p_0(v_0 - v_1) \qquad \ldots (2.46)$$
$$W_{max} = (u_1 + p_0 v_1 - T_0 s_1) - (u_0 + p_0 v_0 - T_0 s_0) \qquad \ldots (2.47)$$
$$W_{max} = \alpha_1 - \alpha_2$$

The property, $\alpha = u + p_0 v - T_0 s$ (per unit mass) is called the **non-flow availability function (φ)**. The term $u + pv - Ts$ is called Gibb's function. This Gibb's function (G) does involve only properties of the system. The availability function involves the properties of the system and atmosphere.

2.17 AVAILABILITY IN STEADY FLOW SYSTEMS

Temperature remain constant at p_1 and T_1 through a device to atmospheric pressure of p_0. Let the reservoir be at a height Z_1 from the datum, which can be taken at exit from the device i.e. $Z_0 = 0$. For maximum work to be obtained from the device, the exit velocity, c_0, must be zero. It can be shown as for a reversible heat engine working between the limits would reject $T_0 (s_1 - s_0)$ units of heat, where T_0 is the atmospheric temperature. Thus,

$$w_{max} = \left(h_1 + \frac{c_1^2}{2} + Z_1 g\right) - h_0 - T_0 (s_1 - s_0)$$

In several thermodynamic systems, the kinetic and potential energy terms are negligible i.e.,

$$w_{max} = (h_1 - T_0 s_1) - (h_0 - T_0 s_0)$$
$$= b - b_0$$

The property, $b = h - T_0 s$ (per unit mass) is called the steady-flow availability function.
(In the equation $b = h - T_0 s$; the function 'b' (like the function 'a') is a composite property of a system and its environment; this is known as Keenan function.)

2.18 HELMOHLTZ AND GIBB'S FUNCTIONS

The work done in a non-flow reversible system (per unit mass) is given by,

$$w = Q - (u_0 - u_1)$$
$$= T \cdot ds - (u_0 - u_1)$$
$$= T (s_0 - s_1) - (u_0 - u_1)$$

i.e. $\quad w = (u_1 - Ts_1) - (u_0 - Ts_0)$ ... (2.48)

The term $(u - Ts)$ is known as Helmholtz function. This gives maximum possible output when the heat Q is transferred at constant temperature.
If work against atmosphere is equal to $p_0 (v_0 - v_1)$, then the maximum work available,

$$w_{max} = w - \text{Work against atmosphere}$$
$$= w - p_0 (v_0 - v_1)$$
$$= (u_1 - Ts_1) - (u_0 - Ts_0) - p_0 (v_0 - v_1)$$
$$= (u_1 + p_0 v_1 - Ts_1) - (u_0 + p_0 v_0 - Ts_0)$$
$$= (h_1 - Ts_1) - (h_0 - Ts_0)$$

i.e. $\quad w_{max} = g_1 - g_0$ ... (2.49)

where, $g = h - T \cdot s$ is known as Gibb's function or Free energy function.
The maximum possible available work when system changes from 1 to 2 is given below.

$$w_{max} = (g_1 - g_0) - (g_2 - g_0) = g_1 - g_2 \quad ... (2.50)$$

Similarly, for steady flow system, the maximum work available is,

$$w_{max} = (g_1 - g_2) + (KE_1 - KE_2) + (PE_1 - PE_2) \quad ... (2.51)$$

where, K.E. and P.E. represent the kinetic and potential energies.

It may be noted that Gibb's function $g = (h - Ts)$ is a property of the system where availability function $a = (u + p_0v - T_0s)$ is a composite property of the system and surroundings.

Again,
$$a = u + p_0v - T_0s$$
$$b = u + pv - T_0s$$
$$g = u + pv - Ts$$

When state 1 proceeds to dead state (zero state)
$$a = b = g$$

2.19 IRREVERSIBILITY

The actual work which a system does is always less than the idealized reversible work. The difference between the two is called the irreversibility of the process.

Thus, Irreversibility, $I = w_{max} - w$ ... (2.52)

This is also sometimes referred to as 'degradation' or 'dissipation'.

For a non-flow process between the equilibrium states, when the system exchanges heat only with environment, irreversibility (per unit mass),

$$i = [(u_1 - u_2) - T_0(s_1 - s_2)] - [(u_1 - u_2) + Q]$$
$$= T_0(s_2 - s_1) - Q$$
$$= T_0(\Delta s)_{system} + T_0(\Delta s)_{surr.}$$

i.e., $i = T_0[(\Delta s)_{system} + (\Delta s)_{surr.}]$ ... (2.53)

∴ $i \geq 0$

Similarly, for steady flow-process,

$$i = w_{max} - w \text{ (per unit mass)}$$
$$= \left[\left(b_1 + \frac{c_1^2}{2} + gZ_1\right) - \left(b_2 + \frac{c_2^2}{2} + gZ_2\right)\right]$$
$$- \left[\left(h_1 + \frac{c_1^2}{2} + gZ_1\right) - \left(h_2 + \frac{c_2^2}{2} + gZ_2\right) + Q\right]$$
$$= T_0(s_2 - s_1) - Q$$
$$= T_0(\Delta s)_{system} + T_0(\Delta s)_{surr.}$$

i.e. $i = T_0(\Delta s_{system} + \Delta s_{surr.})$

The same expression for irreversibility applies to both flow and non-flow processes.

The quantity $T_0(\Delta s_{system} + \Delta s_{surr.})$ represents (per unit mass) an increase in unavailable energy (or energy).

2.20 SECOND LAW EFFICIENCY OR EFFECTIVENESS

The first law efficiency is the ratio of output energy of a device to input energy of the device.

The first law is concerned only with the quantities of energy and disregards the forms in which the energy exists. Further, it does not also discriminate between the energies available at different temperatures.

The second law of efficiency (η_{II}) provides a means of assigning a quality index to energy through the concept of available energy or exergy. Improved energy resource utilisation can be realized by reducing unavailable energy within the system and or losses.

2.20.1 Effectiveness

The effectiveness of a cycle is defined as the ratio of increase in availability of the surroundings (due to work delivered by the cycle) to the decrease in availability of the surroundings (due to heat supplied to the cycle). Thus,

$$\eta_{II} = \varepsilon = \frac{|\text{Increase in availability of surrounding}|}{|\text{Decrease in availability of surroundings}|} \quad \ldots (2.54)$$

The algebraic sum of numerator and denominator of equation (2.54) represents the loss of available energy, $E_{x,\,loss}$ because of the irreversibility of cycle.

(a) Effectiveness of Power Cycle: The increase in the available energy of the surroundings in the case of power cycle is equal to the work delivered by the cycle and the decrease in the available energy of the surroundings is equal to the availability of heat supplied to the cycle. Thus,

$$\eta_{II} = (\varepsilon)_{\text{Power cycle}} = \frac{|\text{Work delivered by cycle}|}{|\text{Availability of heat supplied}|} = \frac{W_{\text{output}}}{(E_x)_{\text{fuel}}} \quad \ldots (2.55)$$

(b) Effectiveness of Steady Flow Process: The effectiveness of steady flow process is given by,

$$\eta_{II} = (\varepsilon)_{sf} = \frac{|\text{Increase in availability of surroundings}|}{|\text{Decrease in availability of the flow stream}|} \quad \ldots (2.56)$$

(c) Effectiveness of a Turbine: Fig. 2.36 shows the process path in a turbine on T-s diagram. Due to friction the entropy increases during the expansion process while due to heat losses entropy tends to decrease a little. The effectiveness of a turbine is given by,

$$\eta_{II} = (\varepsilon)_{\text{turbine}} = \left|\frac{w}{(\Delta a)_{sf}}\right| = \left|\frac{w}{a_{sf}}\right| \quad \ldots (2.57)$$

If changes in K.E. and P.E. are negligible, then the work delivered to the surroundings per unit mass is given by,

$$w = (h_1 - h_2) - q$$

Availability of a steady flow system,

$$a_{sf} = w_{\text{max}} = (h_1 - h_2) - T_0(s_1 - s_2)$$

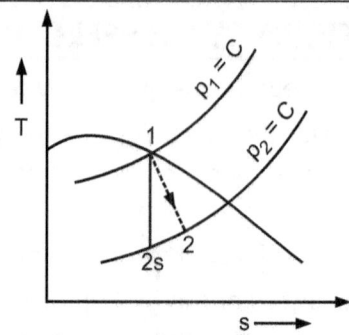

Fig. 2.36: Expansion through turbine

$$\eta_{II} = (\varepsilon)_{turbine} = \frac{h_1 - h_2 - q}{(h_1 - h_2) - T_0(s_1 - s_2)} \quad \ldots(2.58)$$

And, the loss of available energy,

$$I = a_{sf} - w = (h_1 - h_2) - T_0(s_1 - s_2) - (h_1 - h_2) + q$$

or
$$I = q - T_0(s_1 - s_2) \quad \ldots(2.59)$$

If the expansion process in the turbine is adiabatic, then $q = 0$, hence,

$$\eta_{II} = (\varepsilon)_{turbine} = \left| \frac{h_1 - h_2}{(h_1 - h_2) - T_0(s_1 - s_2)} \right| \quad \ldots(2.60)$$

and
$$I = T_0(s_2 - s_2) \quad \ldots(2.61)$$

(d) Effectiveness of Pump or Compressor: Since the work is supplied by the surroundings in the case of pump of compressor, there is an increase in available energy of the stream. The effectiveness of a pump or compressor is given by,

$$(\varepsilon)_{pump} = \left| \frac{\text{Increase in available energy of the flow stream}}{\text{Decrease in availability of surroundings}} \right|$$

or
$$\eta_{II} = (\varepsilon)_{pump} = \left| \frac{a_{sf}}{w} \right| \quad \ldots(2.62)$$

From First law, $w = q - \Delta h$. Taking sign convention of w in consideration,

$$(\Delta a)_{sf} = \Delta h - T_0 \Delta s \text{ if K.E. and P.E.} = 0$$

∴
$$\eta_{II} = (\varepsilon)_{pump} = \left| \frac{\Delta h - T_0 \Delta s}{q - \Delta h} \right| \quad \ldots(2.63)$$

And
$$I = w - a_{sf} = q + T_0 \Delta s$$

If the compression process is adiabatic, $\eta_{II} = (\varepsilon)_{pump} = \left| \frac{\Delta h - T_0 \Delta s}{-\Delta h} \right| \quad \ldots(2.64)$

and
$$I = T_0 \Delta s \text{ per unit mass} \quad \ldots(2.65)$$

2.21 DEAD STATE

If the state of the system (p_1, T_1) is different from the state of surroundings, then there exists a potential to obtain work while changing the state of the system to that of surroundings (See Fig. 2.37). However, as the system changes its state towards that of the surroundings, this opportunity of producing work diminishes and ceases to exist when the two are equilibrium with each other.

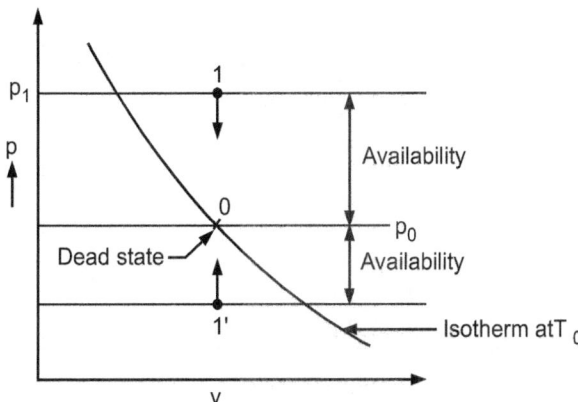

Fig. 2.37: Availability decreases as the state of the system approaches p_0 and T_0

The dead state is one at which the system is in thermodynamic equilibrium (mechanical, thermal and chemical equilibrium) with the surroundings. It means pressure and temperature of the system (p_1, T_1) and that of surroundings (p_0, T_0) are one and the same. Also, there is no chemical gradient as such so that a chemical reaction between system and surrounding occurs. All the spontaneous processes terminate at dead state.

2.22 CLASSIFICATION OF ENERGY

After studying the degradation of energy which says that the quality of heat energy depends upon its temperature at which it is available.

The sources of energy can be divided into two groups, viz. high grade energy and low grade energy. The high grade energy is fully convertible to useful work. Therefore, work and electrical energy are the two Problems of high grade energy.

Low grade energy are those which cannot be converted fully to useful work. These are heat or thermal energy, heat derived from nuclear fusion or fission and heat derived from combustion of fossil fuel.

SOLVED PROBLEMS

Problem 2.15:

A heat of 15000 kJ is withdrawn from a thermal reservoir at 225°C. The heat sink is at 15°C. Calculate the availability and unavailability.

Solution: The availability = $A = Q - T_0 \Delta s$.

Let the heat 15000 kJ is to be transferred reversibly to a cycle at constant temperature of 225°C. The increase in entropy

$$\Delta s = \frac{Q}{T} = \frac{15000}{(225 + 273)} = 30.1 \text{ kJ/K}$$

Availability, $A = Q - T_0 \Delta s$
$= 15000 - 288 \times 30.1$
$= \mathbf{6331.2 \text{ kJ}}$

Unavailable part of energy (heat)
$= T_0 \Delta s = 288 \times 30.1$
$= \mathbf{8668.8 \text{ kJ}}$

Problem 2.16:

Air initially at 10 bar and 500 K expands in a piston-cylinder arrangement to a final state of $p_2 = 1.5$ bar and $T_2 = 300$ K. Neglect the changes in PE and KE. Assume the environment at $T_0 = 288$ K and $p_0 = 1$ bar. Find the maximum work per kg of air due to its expansion. Also calculate the availability at the initial and final states and as a whole.

Solution: For a closed system (non-flow process)

$$W_{rev} = W_{max} = (u_1 - u_2) + p_0(V_1 - V_2) - T_0(s_1 - s_2)$$

$(u_1 - u_2) = c_v(T_1 - T_2) = 0.71 \text{ kJ/kg·K} (500 - 300) = 142 \text{ kJ/kg}$

$c_v = 0.71$ kJ/kg

$$p_0(V_1 - V_2) = p_0 \left(\frac{RT_1}{p_1} - \frac{RT_2}{p_2} \right) = 1 \times 10^5 \left(\frac{287 \times 500}{10 \times 10^5} - \frac{287 \times 300}{1.5 \times 10^5} \right)$$

$= 14350 - 57400 = -43050$ J/kg
$= -43.050$ kJ/kg

$$T_0(s_1 - s_2) = T_0 \left[R \ln \left(\frac{p_2}{p_1} \right) - c_p \ln \left(\frac{T_2}{T_1} \right) \right]$$

$$= 288 \left[287 \times \ln \left(\frac{1.5}{10} \right) - 1005 \ln \left(\frac{300}{500} \right) \right]$$

$= 288 [-544.47 + 513] = -8954$ J/kg
$= -8.954$ kJ/kg

$W_{max} = 142 - 43.0 - 8.954 = \mathbf{90.0 \text{ kJ/kg}}$

The availability at initial state, a_1,

$$= (u_1 - u_0) + p_0(V_1 - V_0) - T_0(s_1 - s_0)$$

$$= c_v(T_1 - T_0) + p_0 \cdot R \cdot \left(\frac{T_1}{p_1} - \frac{T_0}{p_0}\right) - T_0\left(c_p \ln\left(\frac{T_1}{T_0}\right) - R \ln\frac{p_1}{p_0}\right)$$

$$= 0.71(500 - 300) + 1 \times 0.287\left(\frac{500}{10} - \frac{288}{1}\right) -$$

$$288\left[1.005 \ln\frac{500}{300} - 0.287 \ln\left(\frac{10}{1}\right)\right]$$

$$= 142 - 68.3 - 288(1.617 - 0.66)$$

$$= 142 - 68.3 + 42.2 = 115.9 \text{ kJ/kg}$$

The availability at the final state, a_2

$$= (u_2 - u_0) + p_0(V_2 - V_0) - T_0(s_2 - s_0)$$

$$= c_v(T_2 - T_0) + p_0 R\left(\frac{T_2}{p_2} - \frac{T_0}{p_0}\right) - T_0\left(c_p \ln\frac{T_2}{T_0} - R \ln\frac{p_2}{p_0}\right)$$

$$= 0.71(300 - 288 + 1 \times 0.287)\left(\frac{300}{1} - \frac{288}{1}\right)$$

$$- 288\left(1.005 \ln\frac{300}{288} - 0.287 \ln\frac{1.5}{1}\right)$$

$$= 4.88 \text{ kJ/kg}$$

The availability as a whole, $a = W_{rev} = W_{max}$

$$= a_1 - a_2 = 115.9 - 4.88 = \mathbf{111.0 \text{ kJ/kg}}$$

Problem 2.17:

Find the availability of air during a non-flow process for the following different cases:
(a) $p = 10$ bar, $T = T_0$ (b) $p = p_0$, $T = 400$ K
(c) $p = 10$ bar, $T = 150$ K (d) $p = 0.5 p_0$, $T = T_0$

Solution: Availability for non-flow process, a_{nf}

$$a_{nf} = (u + p_0 V - T_0 s) - (u_0 + p_0 V_0 - T_0 s_0) \text{ kJ}$$

For unit mass

$$= (u - u_0) + p_0(V - V_0) - T_0(s - s_0)$$

(a)
$$a_{nf} = c_v(T - T_0) + p_0 R\left(\frac{T}{p} - \frac{T_0}{p_0}\right) - T_0\left(c_p \ln\frac{T}{T_0} - R \ln\frac{p}{p_0}\right)$$

Here, $p = 10$ bar and $T = T_0$.
The above formula reduces to,

$$a_{nf} = T_0\left[R \ln\left(\frac{p}{p_0}\right)\right] = 288\left[0.287 \ln\left(\frac{10}{1}\right)\right]$$

$$= \mathbf{190.3 \text{ kJ/kg}}$$

(b) $p = p_0$ and $T = 400$ K.

$$a_{nf} = c_v(T - T_0) + p_0 R\left(\frac{T}{p_0} - \frac{T_0}{p_0}\right) - T_0\left(c_p \ln\frac{T}{T_0} - R \ln\frac{p_0}{p_0}\right)$$

$$= c_v(T - T_0) + RT - RT_0 - T_0 \cdot c_p \cdot \ln\left(\frac{T}{T_0}\right)$$

$$= c_v (T - T_0) + R (T - T_0) - T_0 \cdot c_p \ln\left(\frac{T}{T_0}\right)$$

$$= 0.71 (400 - 288) + 0.287 (400 - 288) - 288 \times 1.005 \ln\left(\frac{400}{288}\right)$$

$$= 79.52 + 32.14 - 95.08 = \mathbf{16.57\ kJ/kg}$$

(c) $$a_{nf} = c_v (T - T_0) + \frac{p_0 RT}{p} - \frac{p_0 RT_0}{p_0} - T_0\left(c_p \ln\frac{T}{T_0} - R \ln\frac{p}{p_0}\right)$$

p = 10 bar, T = 150

$$= 0.71 (150 - 288) + \frac{0.287 \times 150}{10} - \frac{0.287 \times 288}{1}$$

$$- 288\left(1.005 \ln\frac{150}{288} - 0.287 \times \ln\frac{10}{1}\right)$$

$$= -97.98 + 4.30 - 82.65 + 39.5$$

$$= \mathbf{-136.75\ kJ/kg} \qquad \text{(negative because T is below °C)}$$

(d) p = 0.5 p$_0$, T = T$_0$ $\quad a_{nf} = c_v (T - T_0) + \frac{p_0 RT}{p} - RT_0 - T_0 (s - s_0)$

$$= c_v (T_0 - T_0) + p_0 R\left(\frac{T}{p} - \frac{T_0}{p_0}\right) - T_0\left(c_p \ln\frac{T}{T_0} - R \ln\frac{p}{p_0}\right)$$

$$= \frac{p_0 RT}{p} - RT_0 - T_0\left(0 - R \ln\frac{0.5\ p_0}{p_0}\right)$$

$$= RT_0 + (RT_0)(-0.693)$$

$$= (1 - 0.693)\ RT_0 = 0.3068\ RT_0$$

$$= 0.3068 \times 0.287 \times 288 = \mathbf{25.3\ kJ/kg}$$

Problem 2.18:

4 kg of water at 50°C is mixed with 6 kg of water at 80°C in a steady flow process. Determine (a) The temperature of resulting mixture. (b) Is the mixing process isentropic? (c) What is the unavailable energy with respect to the receiver at 50°C?

Solution: (a) From first law of thermodynamics,

$$m_1 h_1 + m_2 h_2 = m_3 h_3$$

Assuming specific heat of water constant,

$$m_1 \cdot c_p T_1 + m_2 c_p T_2 = m_3 c_p T_3$$

$$m_1 T_1 + m_2 T_2 = m_3 T_3$$

$$4\ T_1 + 6\ T_2 = 10\ T_3$$

$$4 \times 50 + 6 \times 80 = 10\ T_3$$

∴ $\quad \mathbf{T_3 = 68°C}$

(b) Increase in entropy due to mixing process is,

$$\Delta s = m_1 c_p \ln \frac{T_3}{T_1} + m_2 c_p \ln \frac{T_3}{T_2}$$

$$= 4 \times 4.186 \ln \frac{341}{323} + 6 \times 4.186 \ln \frac{341}{353}$$

$$= 0.9080 - 0.8686 = 0.0394 \text{ kJ/K}$$

(c) Unavailable energy $= T_0 \Delta s = 288 \times 0.0394 =$ **11.3 kJ**

Problem 2.19:

One kilogram of air at 1 bar pressure and temperature of 300 K is compressed to 8 bar, 370 K. Determine the irreversibility if the sink temperature is 293 K. Assume R = 297 J/kg·K, Q = 1.004 kJ/kg·K, c_v = 716 J/kg·K.

Solution: Irreversibility, $I = W_{max} - W_{act}$

     $- W_{max}$ = Change in internal energy $- T_0 \times$ Change in entropy

or $- W_{max} = (u_2 - u_1) - T_0 (s_2 - s_1) = W_{rev}$

or $- W_{max} = c_v (T_2 - T_1) - T_0 [c_p \ln (T_2/T_1) - R \ln (p_2/p_1)]$

     $= 0.716 (400 - 300) - 293 \times [1.005 \ln (400/300) - 0.287 \ln (8/1)]$

or $W_{max} = $ **−161.75 kJ/kg**

(negative sign indicates that work is done on the air)

The index of compression 'n' is given by,

$$\frac{T_2}{T_1} = \left(\frac{p_2}{p_1}\right)^{[(n-1)/n]}$$

or $\dfrac{n-1}{n} = \dfrac{\ln (T_2/T_1)}{\ln (p_2/p_1)} = \dfrac{\ln (370/300)}{\ln (6.8/1)} = 1$

or   n = **1.1606**

$$W_{actual} = \frac{mR(T_1 - T_2)}{n-1} = \frac{1 \times 0.287 (300 - 370)}{1.123 - 1}$$

$$= -178.7049 \text{ kJ/kg}$$

$I = W_{rev} - W_{act} = -149.53 - (-163.33) =$ **16.9549 kJ/kg**

Problem 2.20:

A system at 600 K receives 8200 kJ/min heat from a source of 1000 K. The temperature of atmosphere is 300 K. Assuming that the temperature of system and source remain constant during heat transfer, find out:

(i) The entropy produced during heat transfer.

(ii) The decrease in available energy after heat transfer.

Solution: Refer Fig. 2.38.

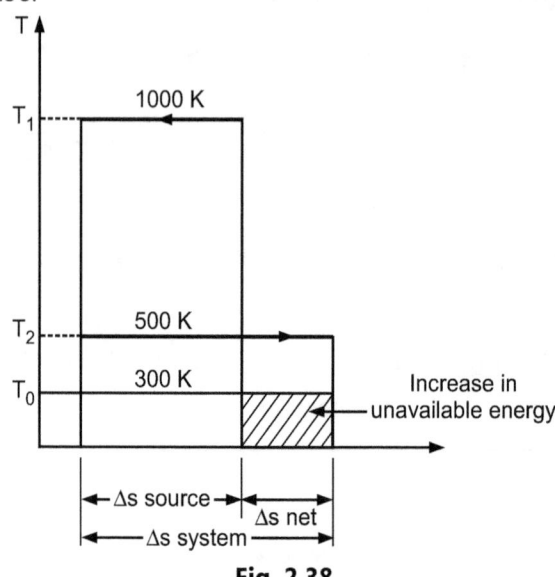

Fig. 2.38

Temperature of source, T_1 = 1000 K
Temperature of system, T_2 = 600 K
Temperature of atmosphere, T_0 = 300 K
Heat received by the system, Q = 8200 kJ/min

(i) Net Change of Entropy:

Change in entropy of the source during heat transfer

$$= \frac{-Q}{T_1} = \frac{-8200}{1000} = -8.2 \text{ kJ/min·K}$$

Change in entropy of the system during heat transfer

$$= \frac{Q}{T_2} = \frac{8200}{600} = 13.67 \text{ kJ/min·K}$$

The net change of entropy, Δs = −8.2 + 13.67 = 5.47 kJ/min·K

(ii) Decrease in Available Energy:

Available energy with source

$$= (1000 - 300) \times 8.2 = 5740 \text{ kJ}$$

Available energy with the system

$$= (600 - 300) \times 12.67 \text{ kJ} = 4101 \text{ kJ}$$

∴ Decrease in available energy = 5740 − 4101 = **1639 kJ**

Also, increase in available energy

$$= T_0 (s_2 - s_1) = T_0 \Delta s$$
$$= 300 \times 5.47 = \textbf{1641 kJ}$$

Problem 2.21:

10 kg of air at 550 K and 7.5 bar pressure is enclosed in a closed system. If the atmosphere temperature and pressure are 300 K and 1 bar respectively, determine:

(i) The availability if the system goes through the ideal work producing process.

(ii) The availability and effectiveness if the air is cooled at constant pressure to atmospheric temperature without bringing it to complete dead state. Take $c_v = 0.718$ kJ/kg·K; $c_p = 1.005$ kJ/kg·K.

Solution:

Mass of air, $m = 10$ kg
Temperature, $T_1 = 550$ K
Pressure, $p_1 = 7.5$ bar
Atmospheric pressure, $p_0 = 1$ bar
Atmospheric temperature, $T_0 = 300$ K
For air: $c_v = 0.718$ kJ/kg·K; $c_p = 1.005$ kJ/kg·K.

(i) Change in available energy (for bringing the system to dead state)

$$= m\left[(u_1 - u_0) - T_0 \Delta s\right]$$

Also,
$$\Delta s = c_v \log_e\left(\frac{T_1}{T_0}\right) + R \log_e \frac{V_1}{V_0}$$

Using the ideal gas equation,
$$\frac{p_1 V_1}{T_1} = \frac{p_0 V_0}{T_0}$$

∴
$$\frac{V_1}{V_0} = \frac{p_1}{p_0} \cdot \frac{T_0}{T_1} = \frac{7.5}{1} \times \frac{300}{550} = 4.0909$$

∴
$$\Delta s = 0.718 \log_e\left(\frac{550}{300}\right) + 0.287 \log_e\left(\frac{1}{4.0909}\right)$$

$$= 0.4352 + (-0.4043) = 0.3088 \text{ kJ/kg·K}$$

∴ Change in available energy
$$= m\left[(u_1 - u_0) - T_0 \Delta s\right] = m\left[c_v(T_1 - T_0) - T_0 \Delta s\right]$$
$$= 10\left[0.718(550 - 300) - 300 \times 0.3088\right] = 1702.36 \text{ kJ}$$

Loss of availability per unit mass during the process
$$= p_0(V_0 - V_1) \text{ per unit mass}$$

Total loss of availability $= p_0(V_0 - V_1)$

But,
$$V_1 = \frac{mRT_1}{p_1} = \frac{10 \times 287 \times 550}{7.5 \times 10^5} = 2.104 \text{ m}^3$$

$$\left[\because pV = mRT \text{ or } V = \frac{mRT}{p}\right]$$

and
$$V_0 = 4.0909 \times 2.104 = 8.60 \text{ m}^3$$

$$\therefore \quad \text{Loss of availability} = \frac{1 \times 10^5}{10^3} = (8.60 - 2.104) = \mathbf{649.6 \text{ kJ}}$$

(ii) Heat transferred during cooling (constant pressure) process

$$= m \cdot c_p (T_1 - T_0)$$
$$= 10 \times 1.005 \,(550 - 300) = 2512.5 \text{ kJ}$$

Change in entropy during cooling

$$\Delta s = mc_p \log_e \left(\frac{T_1}{T_0}\right)$$
$$= 10 \times 1.005 \times \log_e \left(\frac{550}{300}\right) = 6.09 \text{ kJ/K}$$

Unavailable energy $= T_0 \Delta s$
$$= 300 \times 6.09 = 1827.49 \text{ kJ}$$

Available energy $= 25125 - 1827.49 = \mathbf{685 \text{ kJ}}$

Effectiveness, $\varepsilon = \dfrac{\text{Available energy}}{\text{Change in available energy}}$

$$= \frac{685}{1702.36} = \mathbf{0.402}$$

Problem 2.22:

In a power station, the saturated steam is generated at 180°C by transferring the heat from hot gases in a steam boiler. Find the increase in total entropy of the combined system of gas and water and increase in unavailable energy due to irreversible heat transfer. The gases are cooled from 900°C to 450°C and all the heat from gases goes to water. Assume water enters the boiler at saturated condition and leaves as saturated steam.

Take: c_{pg} (for gas) = 1.0 kJ/kg·K, h_{fg} (latent heat of steam at 200°C) = 1940.7 kJ/kg.

Atmospheric temperature = 20°C.

Obtain the results on the basis of 1 kg of water.

Solution: Refer Fig. 2.39.

Temperature of saturation steam = 180 + 273 = 453 K
Initial temperature of gases = 900 + 273 = 1173 K
Final temperature of gases = 900 + 273 = 723 K
For gases: c_{pg} = 1 kJ/kg·K
Latent heat of steam at 200°C
saturation temperature, h_{fg} = 1940.7 kJ/kg
Atmospheric temperature = 20 + 273 = 293 K

Heat lost by gases = Heat gained by 1 kg saturated water when it is converted to steam at 200°C.

∴ $m_g c_{pg}(1173 - 723) = 1940.7$

[where, m_g = Mass of gases, c_{pg} = Specific heat of gas at constant pressure]

i.e. $m_g = \dfrac{1940.7}{1.0 \times (1173 - 723)} = 4.31$ kg

Change of entropy of m_g kg of gas,

$$(\Delta s)_g = m_g\, c_{pg} \log_e\left(\dfrac{723}{1173}\right)$$

$$= 3.88 \times 1.0 \times \log_e\left(\dfrac{723}{1173}\right)$$

$$= -1.877 \text{ kJ/K}$$

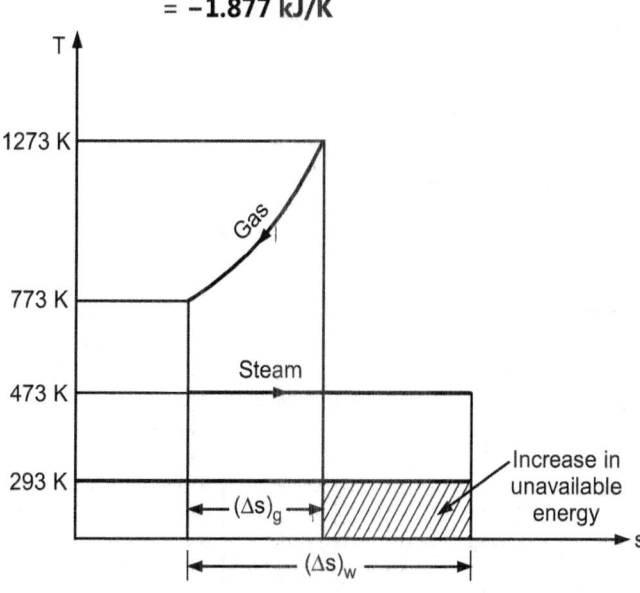

Fig. 2.39

Change of entropy of water (per kg) when it is converted into steam,

$$(\Delta s)_w = \dfrac{h_{fg}}{T_s} = \dfrac{1940.7}{180 + 273} = 4.28 \text{ kJ/kg·K}$$

Net change in entropy due to heat transfer

$$= -1.877 + 4.28$$

$$= \mathbf{2.40 \text{ kJ/K}}$$

Increase in unavailable energy due to heat transfer

$$= 293 \times 2.40 \text{ i.e. cross hatched area}$$

$$= \mathbf{705.28 \text{ kJ per kg of steam formed}}$$

Problem 2.23:

5 kg of gas (c_v = 705.28 kJ/kg·K) initially at 3.5 bar and 500 K receives 900 kJ of heat from an infinite source at 1100 K. If the surrounding temperature is 288 K, find the loss in available energy due to above heat transfer.

Solution: Refer Fig. 2.40.

$$\text{Mass of gas, } m_g = 5 \text{ kg}$$
$$\text{Initial pressure of gas} = 3.5 \text{ bar}$$
$$\text{Initial temperature, } T_1' = 500 \text{ K}$$
$$\text{Quantity of heat received by gas, } Q = 900 \text{ kJ}$$
$$\text{Specific heat of gas, } c_v = 0.81 \text{ kJ/kg·K}$$
$$\text{Surrounding temperature} = 288 \text{ K}$$
$$\text{Temperature of infinite source, } T_1 = 1100 \text{ K}$$

Heat received by the gas is given by,

$$Q = m_g\, c_v\, (T_2' - T_1')$$

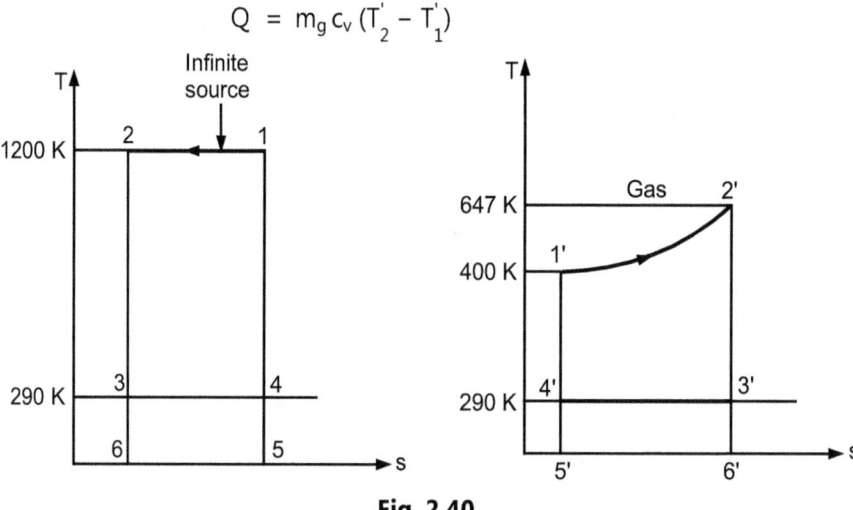

Fig. 2.40

$$900 = 5 \times 0.81\, (T_2' - 500)$$

$$\therefore \quad T_2' = \frac{900}{5 \times 0.81} + 500 = 722.22 \text{ K}$$

Available energy with the source

$$= \text{Area } 1\text{-}2\text{-}3\text{-}4\text{-}1$$
$$= (1100 - 288) \times \frac{900}{1100} = 664 \text{ kJ}$$

Change in entropy of the gas

$$= m_g c_v \log_e \left(\frac{T_2'}{T_1'}\right) = 5 \times 0.81 \times \log_e \left(\frac{722.22}{500}\right) = 1.49 \text{ kJ/K}$$

Unavailability of the gas = Area 3' - 4' - 5' - 6' - 3'
= 288 × 1.49 = 428.91 kJ
Available energy with the gas = 900 − 428.91 = 471.08 kJ
∴ Loss in available energy due to heat transfer
= 664 − 471.08 = **192.91 kJ**

Problem 2.24:

Calculate the unavailable energy in 60 kg of water at 60°C with respect to the surroundings at 288 K, the pressure of water being 1 atmosphere.

Solution: Refer Fig. 2.41.

Mass of water, m = 60 kg
Temperature of water, T_1 = 60 + 273 = 333 K
Temperature of surroundings, T_0 = 15 + 273 = 288 K
Pressure of water, p = 1 atm.

Assume the water is cooled at a constant pressure of 1 atm from 60°C to 6°C. The heat given up may be used as a source for a series of Carnot engines each using the surroundings as a sink. It is assumed that the amount of energy received by any engine is small relative to that in the source and temperature of the source does not change while heat is being exchanged with the engine.

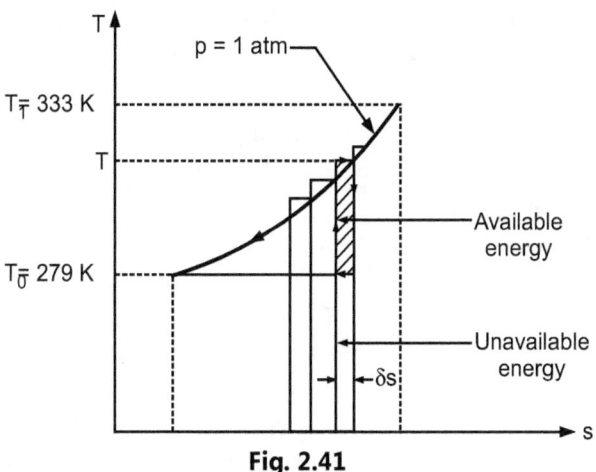

Fig. 2.41

Consider that the source temperature has fallen to T, at which level there operates a Carnot engine which takes in heat at this temperature and rejects heat T_0 = 279 K. If δs is the entropy change of water, the work obtained is,

$$\delta w = -m(T - T_0)\delta s$$

where, δs is negative.

$$\therefore \quad \delta w = -60(T - T_0)\frac{c_p \delta T}{T} = -60 c_p \left(1 - \frac{T_0}{T}\right)\delta T$$

With a large number of engines in the series, the total work (maximum) obtainable when the water is cooled from 333 K to 279 K would be,

$$w_{max} = \text{Available energy}$$

$$= -\lim \sum_{333}^{288} 60 c_p \left(1 - \frac{T_0}{T}\right)\delta T$$

$$= \int_{279}^{333} 60 c_p \left(1 - \frac{T_0}{T}\right) dT$$

$$= 60 c_p \left[(333 - 288) - 288 \log_e \left(\frac{333}{288}\right)\right]$$

$$= 60 \times 4.187 (45 - 41.81) = 801.39 \text{ kJ}$$

Also, $\quad Q_1 = 60 \times 4.187 \times (333 - 288) = 11304.9 \text{ kJ}$

$\therefore \quad$ Unavailable energy $= Q_1 - w_{max}$

$$= 11304.9 - 801.39 = \mathbf{10503.51 \text{ kJ}}$$

Problem 2.25:

10 kg of water is heated in an insulated tank by a churning process from 288 K to 340 K. If the surrounding temperature is 288 K, find the loss in availability for the process.

Solution: Mass of water, $m = 10$ kg
Temperature, $T_1 = 340$ K
Surrounding temperature, $T_0 = 288$ K
Specific heat of water, $c_p = 4.187$ kJ/kg·K

Loss in availability:

Work added during churning = Increase in enthalpy of the water
$$= 10 \times 4.187 \times (340 - 288) = 2177.24 \text{ kJ}$$

Now the energy in the water = 2177.24 kJ

The availability out of this energy is given by,

$$m[(u_1 - u_0) - T_0 \Delta s]$$

where, $\quad \Delta s = c_p \log_e \left(\frac{T_1}{T_0}\right)$

$\therefore \quad \Delta s = 4.187 \log_e \left(\frac{340}{288}\right) = 0.694$ kJ/kg·K

$\therefore \quad$ Available energy $= m[c_v(T_1 - T_0) - T_0 \Delta s]$
$$= 10[4.187(340 - 288) - 300 \times 0.694] = 95.24 \text{ kJ}$$

$\therefore \quad$ Loss in availability = $2177.24 - 95.24 = \mathbf{2082 \text{ kJ}}$

This shows that conversion of work into heat is highly irreversible process (since out of 2177.24 kJ of work energy supplied to increase the temperature, only 95.4 kJ will the available again for conversion into work).

Problem 2.26:

Calculate the decrease in available energy when 15 kg of water at 80°C mixes with 30 kg of water at 30°C, the pressure being taken as constant and the temperature of the surroundings being 288 K.
Take c_p of water as 4.18 kJ/kg·K.

Solution: Temperature of surrounding, $T_0 = 15 + 273 = 288$ K
Specific heat of water, $c_p = 4.18$ kJ/kg·K
The available energy of a system of mass, m specific heat c_p and at temperature T, is given by,

$$\text{Available energy, A.E.} = mc_p \int_{T_0}^{T} \left(1 - \frac{T_0}{T}\right) dT$$

Now, available energy of 15 kg of water at 80°C,

$$(A.E.)_{15\,kg} = 15 \times 4.18 \int_{15+273}^{80+273} \left(1 - \frac{288}{T}\right) dT$$

$$= 62.7 \left[(353 - 288) - 288 \ln(353/288)\right]$$

$$= 62.7 (65 - 68.61) = 400.65 \text{ kJ}$$

Available energy of 30 kg of water at 30°C,

$$(A.E.)_{30\,kg} = 30 \times 4.18 \int_{(15+273)}^{(30+273)} \left(1 - \frac{288}{T}\right) dT$$

$$= 30 \times 4.18 \left[(303 - 288) - 288 \log_e\left(\frac{288}{288}\right)\right]$$

$$= 125.4 (15 - 14.36) = 80.256 \text{ kJ}$$

Total available energy,

$$(A.E.)_{total} = (A.E.)_{20\,kg} + (A.E.)_{30\,kg} = 400.65 + 80.256 = 480.906 \text{ kJ}$$

If T°C is the final temperature after mixing, then,

$$15 \times 4.18 \times (80 - T) = 30 \times 4.18 \times (T - 30)$$

or $\quad 15(80 - T) = 30(T - 30) = \dfrac{15 \times 80 + 30 \times 30}{15 + 30} = 46.66°C$

Total mass after mixing = 15 + 30 = 45 kg
Available energy of 45 kg of water at 45.66°C

$$(A.E.)_{50\,kg} = 45 \times 4.18 \left[(319.66 - 288) - 288 \log_e\left(\frac{319.66}{288}\right)\right]$$

$$= 188.1 (31.66 - 30.03) = \mathbf{306.603}$$

∴ Decrease in available energy due to mixing

= Total energy before mixing − Total energy after mixing

= 480.906 − 306.603 = **174.306**.

Problem 2.27:

In an heat exchanger (parallel flow type) water enters at 50°C and leaves at 70°C while oil (specific gravity = 0.82, specific heat = 2.6 kJ/kg·K) enters at 250°C and leaves at 80°C. If the surrounding temperature is 27°C, determine the loss in availability on the basis of one kg of oil per second.

Solution: Refer Fig. 2.42.

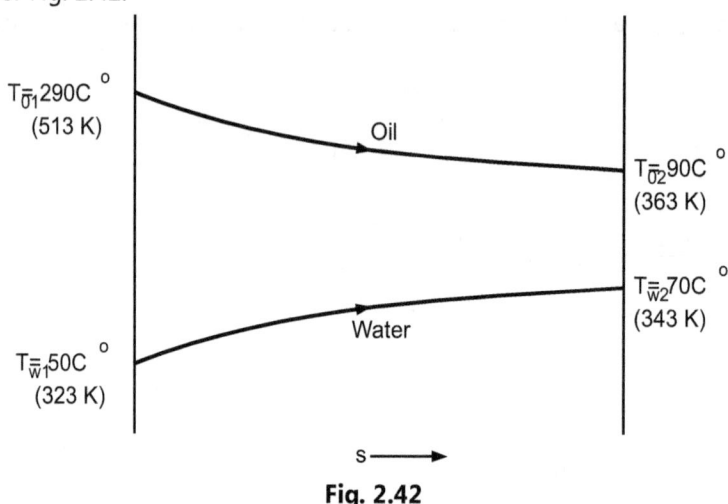

Fig. 2.42

$$\text{Inlet temperature of water, } T_{w1} = 50°C = 323 \text{ K}$$
$$\text{Outlet temperature of water, } T_{w2} = 70°C = 343 \text{ K}$$
$$\text{Inlet temperature of oil, } T_{o1} = 250 = 523 \text{ K}$$
$$\text{Outlet temperature of oil, } T_{o2} = 80 = 353 \text{ K}$$
$$\text{Specific gravity of oil} = 0.82$$
$$\text{Specific heat of oil} = 2.6 \text{ kJ/kg·K}$$
$$\text{Surrounding temperature, } T_0 = 27 + 273 = 300 \text{ K}$$

Loss in Availability:

Consider one kg of oil.

$$\text{Heat lost by oil} = \text{Heat gained by water}$$
$$m_o \times c_{po} \times (T_{o1} - T_{o2}) = m_w \times c_{pw} \times (T_{w2} - T_{w1})$$

where,
c_{po} = Specific heat of oil (2.6 kJ/kg·K)
c_{pw} = Specific heat of water (4.18 kJ/kg·K), and
m_o = Mass of oil (= 1 kg)
m_w = Mass of water (=?)

∴ $1 \times 2.6 \times (523 - 353) = m_w \times 4.18 \times (343 - 323)$

or $\quad 442 = 83.6\, m_w$ or $m_w =$ **5.288 kg**

Entropy change of water $= m_w\, c_{pw}\, \log_e \dfrac{T_{w2}}{T_{w1}} = 4.66 \times 4.18 \times \log_e \left(\dfrac{343}{323}\right) = 1.17$ kJ/K

$$= 5.288 \times 4.18 \times \ln\left(\dfrac{343}{323}\right) = 1.327 \text{ kJ/K}$$

Entropy change of oil $= m_o c_{po} \log_e \left(\dfrac{T_{o2}}{T_{o1}}\right) = 1 \times 2.6 \log_e \left(\dfrac{353}{523}\right) = -1.022$ kJ/K

Change in availability of water

$$= m_w\, [c_{pw}\, (T_{w2} - T_{w1})] - T_o\, (\Delta s)_w$$

$$= 5.28 \times [4.18\, (343 - 323)] - 300 \times 1.327 = \mathbf{43.308 \text{ kJ}}$$

+ve sign indicates an increase in availability.

Change in availability of oil $= m_o\, [c_{po}\, (T_{o2} - T_{o1})] - T_0\, (\Delta s)_0]$

$$= 1 \times [2.6\, (353 - 523) - 300 \times (-1.022)] = \mathbf{-135.41 \text{ kJ/K}}$$

(−ve sign indicates the loss).

Problem 2.28:

1 kg of ice at 0°C is mixed with 15 kg of water at 30°C. Assuming the surrounding temperature as 15°C, calculate the net increase in entropy and unavailable energy when the system reaches common temperature.

Given: Specific heat of water = 4.18 kJ/kg·K; Specific heat of ice = 2.1 kJ/kg·K and enthalpy of fusion of ice (latent heat) = 333.5 kJ/kg.

Solution:
$\quad$ Mass of ice, $m_{ice} = 1$ kg
$\quad$ Temperature of ice, $T_{ice} = 0 + 273 = 273$ K
$\quad$ Mass of water, $m_{water} = 15$ kg
$\quad$ Temperature of water, $T_{water} = 30 + 273 = 303$ K
$\quad$ Surrounding temperature, $T_0 = 15 + 273 = 288$ K
$\quad$ Specific heat of water = 4.18 kJ/kg·K
$\quad$ Specific heat of ice = 2.1 kJ/kg·K
$\quad$ Latent heat of ice = 333.5 kJ/kg

Let $T_c =$ Common temperature when heat flows between ice and water stops.

$\quad$ Heat lost by water = Heat gained by ice

i.e., $\quad 15 \times 4.18\, (303 - T_c) = 4.18\, (T_c - 273) + 333.5$

or $\quad 1899 - 62.8\, T_c = 4.18\, T_c - 1141.14 + 333.5$

or $\quad 66.88\, T_c = 20472.74$

∴ $\quad T_c = 306.11$ K or 33.11°C

Change of entropy of water $= 15 \times 4.18 \log_e \left(\dfrac{306.11}{300}\right) = \mathbf{+1.264 \text{ K}}$

Change of entropy of ice $= 1 \times 4.18 \log_e \left(\dfrac{306.11}{273}\right) + \dfrac{333.5}{273}$

$= 1.70$ kJ/K

Net change of entropy, $\Delta s = +1.264 + 1.7 = 2.964$

Hence, net increase in entropy = **2.964 kJ/K**

Increase in unavailable energy $= T_0 \Delta s = 288 \times 2.964 =$ **853 kJ**

Problem 2.29:

Calculate the decrease in available energy when 25 kg of water at 95°C mix with 35 kg of water at 35°C, the pressure being taken as constant and temperature of the surroundings being 15°C. Take c_p of water = 4.2 kJ/kg·K.

Solution: Mixing of Water:

25 kg and 95°C.

35 kg and 35°C.

To find temperature of the mixture, we equate enthalpies according to energy balance.

$m_1 \cdot c_p \cdot T_1 + m_2 \cdot c_p \cdot T_2 = m_3 \cdot c_p \cdot T_3$

∴ $25 \times c_p \times 95 + 35 \times c_p \times 35 = (35 + 25) c_p \cdot T_3$

∴ $T_3 = 60°C = 333$ K

Now, change in availability,

$\Sigma \Delta A = (A)_{25} + (A)_{35} - (A)_{60}$

Available energy of 25 kg water

$= (AE)_{25} = Q - T_0 \cdot \Delta S$

$= mc_p \left[(T_1 - T_0) - T_0 \log_e \dfrac{T_1}{T_0}\right]$

$= 25 \times 4.2 \times \left[(368 - 288) - 288 \log_e \dfrac{368}{288}\right] =$ **987.5 kJ**

Available energy of 35 kg water

$= (AE)_{35} = 35 \times 4.2 \times \left[(308 - 288) - 288 \log_e \dfrac{308}{288}\right] =$ **97.59 kJ**

Available energy of mixture

$= (AE)_{60} = 60 \times 4.2 \times \left[(333 - 288) - 288 \log_e \left(\dfrac{333}{288}\right)\right] =$ **803.27 kJ**

Decrease in availability $= (AE)_{25} + (AE)_{35} - (AE)_{60}$

$= 987.5 + 97.59 - 803.27 =$ **281.82 kJ**

Problem 2.30:

At constant pressure 138 kPa, 5 kg of oxygen is cooled from 500 K to 300 K. The temperature of the surrounding is 277°C. Find the available part of heat removed and entropy increase of universe.

Solution: Given Data: m = 5 kg, p_1 = 138 kPa, T_1 = 500 K, T_0 = 277 K, p_0 = 1 bar = 100 kPa.
Initial availability of O_2,

$$A_1 = (u_1 - u_0) + p_0(V_1 - V_0) - T_0(s_1 - s_0)$$

$$s_1 - s_0 = c_p \cdot \log_e \frac{T_1}{T_0} - R \log_e \frac{p_1}{p_0}$$

$$= 0.9169 \log_e \frac{500}{277} - 0.287 \log_e \frac{138}{100}$$

$$= 0.54151 - 0.09243 = 0.4491 \text{ kJ/kg·K}$$

$$\therefore \quad A_1 = mc_v(T_1 - T_0) + mR\, p_0 \left[\frac{T_1}{p_1} - \frac{T_0}{p_0}\right] - mT_0[0.4491]$$

$$= 5 \times 0.653(500 - 277) + 5 \times 0.287 \times 100 \left[\frac{500}{138} - \frac{277}{100}\right] - 5 \times 277 \times 0.4491$$

$$= 728.095 + 122.4325 - 622.00 = \textbf{228.524 kJ}$$

Final availability at T_2 = 300 K, T_0 = 277 K, $p_2 = p_1$ = 138 kPa, p_0 = 100 kPa

$$A_2 = mc_v(T_2 - T_0) + mR\, p_0 \left[\frac{T_2}{p_2} - \frac{T_0}{p_1}\right] - mT_0(s_2 - s_0)$$

$$s_2 - s_0 = c_p \cdot \log_e(T_2/T_0) - R \log_e(p_2/p_0)$$

$$= 0.9169 \log_e \left(\frac{300}{277}\right) - 0.287 \log_e \left(\frac{138}{100}\right) = -0.0193 \text{ kJ/kg·K}$$

$$A_2 = 5 \times 0.653(300 - 277) + 5 \times 0.287 \times 100 \left[\frac{300}{138} - \frac{277}{100}\right] - 5 \times 277(-0.0193)$$

$$\therefore \quad A_2 = 75.095 + (-85.54) + 26.7305 = 16.287 \text{ kJ}$$

Available part of heat removed = 16.287 − 228.524 = **−212.237 kJ**

Problem 2.31:

Two engines have same thermal efficiency as 30%. Their source temperatures are different as shown:

Temperature	Engine I	Engine II
Source	600 K	1000 K
Sink	300 K	300 K

Using second law efficiency, choose best performing engine.

Solution: Given Data:

$$\eta_{th} = 30\%$$

For I: T_H = 600 K; T_L = 300 K
For II: T_H = 1000 K; T_L = 300 K

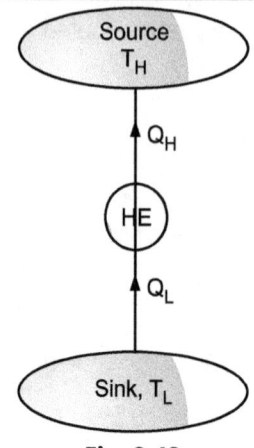

Fig. 2.43

According to second law,

$$\text{HE efficiency} = 1 - \frac{T_L}{T_H}$$

$$\text{For Engine I, } \eta = 1 - \frac{T_L}{T_H} = 1 - \frac{300}{600} = \textbf{0.5 or 50\%}$$

$$\text{For Engine II, } \eta = 1 - \frac{T_L}{T_H} = 1 - \frac{300}{1000} = \textbf{0.7 or 70\%}$$

Engine II is more efficient than engine I, according to second law.

Problem 2.32:

1 kg of air is contained in a rigid tank at 500 kPa and 700 K. The dead state is taken as 20°C and 100 kPa. Calculate the maximum useful work:
  (i) If the system were to change to dead state.
  (ii) When the air is cooled to 400 K in the tank.
(Take for air, c_p = 1.005 kJ/kg·K, R = 0.287 kJ/kg·K).

Solution: Given Data: p_1 = 500 kPa, T_1 = 700 K, p_0 = 100 kPa,
T_0 = 20°C = 50 + 273 = 293 K, c_p = 1.005 kJ/kg·K, R = 0.287 kJ/kg·K.

Now, $c_p - c_v = R$

∴ $c_v = c_p - R = 1.005 - 0.287 = 0.718$ kJ/kg·K

(i) If the System is Changed to Dead State:

$$A_1 = w_{max} = (u_1 - u_0) + p_0(V_1 - V_0) - T_0(s_1 - s_0)$$

$$= c_v(T_1 - T_0) + Rp_0\left(\frac{T_1}{p_1} - \frac{T_0}{p_0}\right) - T_0(s_1 - s_0)$$

Now,

$$s_1 - s_0 = c_p \cdot \log_e\left(\frac{T_1}{T_0}\right) - T\log_e\left(\frac{p_1}{p_0}\right)$$

$$= 1.005 \ln\left(\frac{700}{293}\right) - 0.287 \times \ln\left(\frac{500}{100}\right)$$

$$= \textbf{0.4133 kJ/kg·K}$$

$$\therefore \quad W_{max} = 0.178 \times (700 - 293) + 0.287 \times \left(\frac{p_0}{p_1} \times T_1 - T_0\right)$$

$$- 293 \times 0.4133$$

$$= 0.718 \times 407 + 0.287 \times \left(\frac{100}{500} \times 700 - 293\right) - 121.0969$$

$$= \mathbf{127.22 \ kJ/kg \cdot K}$$

(ii) When the System is Cooled to 400 K:

The availability in the final state,

$$A_2 = (u_2 - u_0) + p_0(V_2 - V_0) - T_0(s_2 - s_0)$$

$$= c_v(T_2 - T_0) + p_0 R \times \left(\frac{T_2}{p_2} - \frac{T_0}{p_0}\right) - T_0\left(c_p \ln \frac{T_2}{T_0} - R \ln \frac{p_2}{p_0}\right)$$

$$= c_v(T_2 - T_0) + p_0 R \times \left(\frac{T_2}{p_2} - \frac{T_0}{p_0}\right) - T_0(s_2 - s_0)$$

Now,

$$s_2 - s_0 = c_p \log_e\left(\frac{T_2}{T_0}\right) - R \log_e\left(\frac{p_2}{p_0}\right)$$

$$= 1.005 \ln\left(\frac{400}{293}\right) - 0.287 \times \ln\left(\frac{500}{100}\right)$$

$$= 0.3128 - 0.462 = \mathbf{-0.1492 \ kJ/kg}$$

$$\therefore \quad A_2 = c_v(T_2 - T_0) + R\left(\frac{p_0}{p_2} \times T_2 - T_0\right) - T_0 \times (s_2 - s_0)$$

$$= 0.718 \times (400 - 293) + 0.287 \times \left(\frac{100}{500} \times 400 - 293\right)$$

$$- 293 \times (-0.1492)$$

$$= 76.826 - 61.131 + 43.701 = \mathbf{59.396 \ kJ/kg}$$

The availability as a whole,

$$a = A_1 - A_2 = 127.22 - 59.396 = \mathbf{67.824 \ kJ/kg}$$

EXERCISE

1. Suppose you have to explain entropy production to a child, how will you explain it?
2. Think a process of a closed system for which the entropy of both the system and its surroundings increase.
3. Is it possible for the entropy of both a closed system and its surroundings to decrease during a process?
4. Discuss the transfer of entropy into or out of a closed system.
5. How will you calculate the entropy production in a nuclear reactor?
6. How will you calculate the entropy production during a storm?

7. All state of an adiabatic and internally reversible process of a closed system have the same entropy, but is a process between two states having same entropy necessarily adiabatic and internally reversible?
8. Define Clausius inequality and prove it.
9. Define entropy and show that it is a property of the system.
10. Give a physical explanation of entropy.
11. Why is the Carnot cycle on T-s plot a rectangle?
12. What do you understand by entropy principle?
13. Show that the entropy of an isolated system increases in all real process and is conserved in reversible process.
14. Why is the entropy increase of an isolated system a measure of the extent of irreversibility of the process undergone by the system?
15. State the summary given by Rudolf Clausius about first and second laws of thermodynamics.
16. Show that the transfer of heat through a finite temperature difference is irreversible.
17. Show that the adiabatic mixing of two fluids is irreversible.
18. What causes an increase in entropy?
19. Why is the second law called a directional law of nature?
20. Derive the expression for entropy generation (production) in a closed system.
21. Derive the expression for entropy generation in a open system (control volume).
22. What do you mean by absolute value of entropy?
23. Explain the concept of available and unavailable energy. When does the system become dead?
24. Define the term 'availability'.
25. Is the availability function same for a non-flow and a flow process?
26. Define availability function and find the relationship between availability function and change in availability.
27. How are the concepts of entropy and unavailable energy related to each other?
28. Derive an expression for availability in non-flow systems.
29. Derive an expression for availability in steady-flow systems.
30. Differentiate between availability function and Gibb's energy function.
31. Derive an expression for decrease in available energy when heat is transferred through a finite temperature difference.
32. Derive a general expression for irreversibility in (i) Non-flow process, (ii) Steady flow process.
33. What is the effectiveness of a system and how does it differ from efficiency?

Unit - III

PROPERTIES OF PURE SUBSTANCE AND VAPOUR POWER CYCLES

3.1 INTRODUCTION

Steam is a pure substance. A pure substance is defined as a homogeneous and chemically stable substance even though it undergoes a change of phase.

Steam is used in many engineering and chemical industries. It is used as a working substance for steam power plants and is used as a medium for heating in chemical, sugar and textile industries. Therefore, it is essential to study the properties of steam at different conditions.

Substances may exist in different phases. At atmospheric pressure and temperature conditions, copper is a solid, mercury is a liquid and nitrogen is a gas. Under different conditions, each may appear in different phase. So let us discuss the phase transformation of water at constant pressure.

3.2 PHASE TRANSFORMATION OF WATER AT CONSTANT PRESSURE

1. Assume 1 kg mass of ice at –20°C and 1 atm. pressure in a frictionless piston cylinder arrangement. Weight W is kept on the piston to maintain a pressure of 1 atm. on the ice.

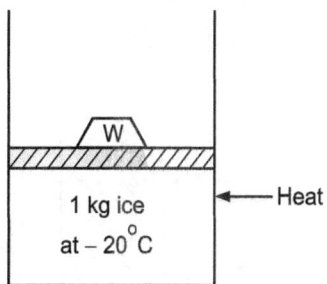

Fig. 3.1: At 1 atm. pressure and – 20°C, water exists in the solid phase

2. As we add heat, the temperature of ice will go on increasing till it reaches 0°C. At this stage, ice starts melting and there will be no rise in temperature till all the ice melts. (Process a – b in Fig. 3.7)

3. The addition of heat will be utilised to increase the temperature of water from 0°C to 100°C (Process c - d in Fig. 3.7).

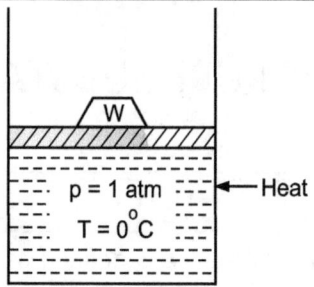

Fig. 3.2: At 1 atm. pressure and at 0°C, water exists in the liquid state (compressed liquid)

4. Now on further heating, water starts boiling and gets converted into vapour.

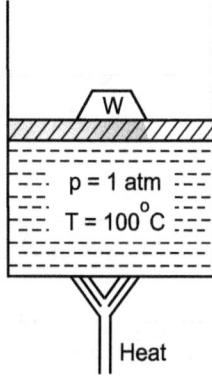

Fig. 3.3: At 1 atm. pressure and 100°C, water exists as a liquid which is ready to vaporise (saturated liquid)

5. Part of the water is evaporated. Therefore, there is a mixture of water and vapour.

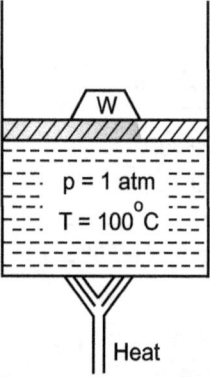

Fig. 3.4: As more heat is added, part of saturated liquid vaporizes (saturated liquid–vapour mixture)

6. See point 'd' in Fig. 3.7. The entire cylinder is filled with vapour. Any heat loss from this vapour will cause some of the vapour to condense.

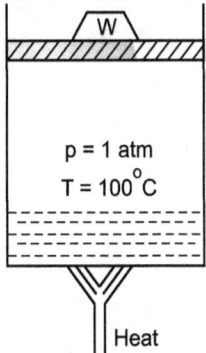

Fig. 3.5: At 1 atm. pressure, the temperature remains constant at 100°c until the last drop of liquid is vaporised (saturated vapour).

7. Further addition of heat will increase the temperature of steam. So, it is called as superheated steam.

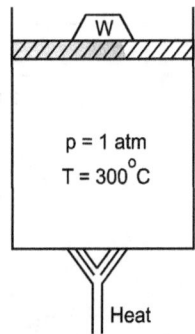

Fig. 3.6: As more heat is added, the temperature of the vapour starts rising (superheated vapour)

All the above steps are represented in Fig. 3.7.

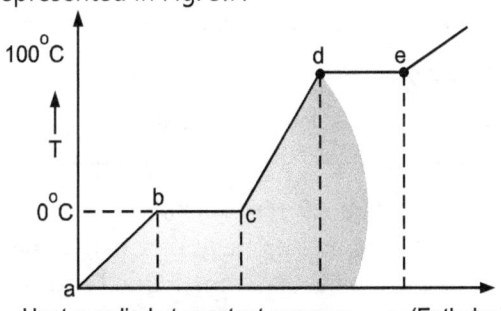

Fig. 3.7: Temperature - Heat supplied

In Fig. 3.7,   a – b → Sensible heating of ice
b – c → Melting of ice
c – d → Sensible heating of liquid
d – e → Saturated mixture of liquid and vapour

From point e – onwards, superheating of steam.

3.3 EFFECT OF PRESSURE ON BOILING POINT

The boiling temperature of water increases with increasing pressure. The 'Boiling Temperature' of water at a particular pressure is known as "saturation temperature" and corresponding pressure is known as 'saturation pressure.'

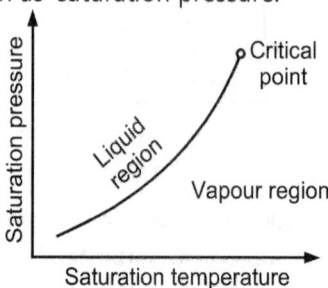

Fig. 3.8: Relation between saturation pressure and saturation temperature of water

3.4 CRITICAL STATE AND CRITICAL POINT

In (*Fig. 5.1*) we have studied heating of water at atmospheric pressure and have noted that line 'abcdef' is a constant pressure line.

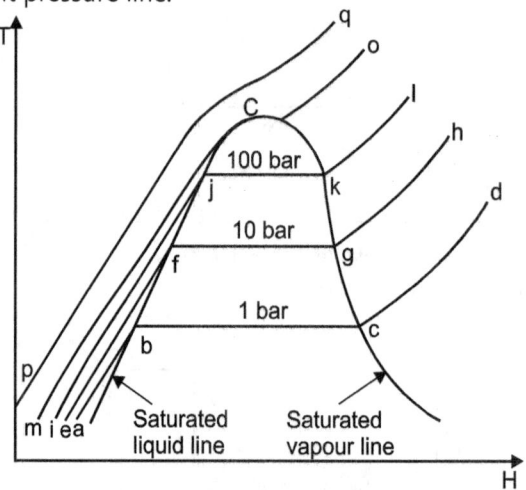

Fig. 3.9 : Critical Point

Fig. 3.9 shows some more such lines at a pressure of 1 bar, 10 bar, 100 bar, 221.2 bar and 300 bar. For simplicity we consider the heating from 0°C and above. i.e. heating of water only. From the Fig. 3.9 we note the following points.

- All the saturated liquid points b, f, j etc lie on a line. This line is known as saturated liquid line.
- All the points representing dry saturated steam condition such as c, g, k etc also lie on a line. This line is known as saturated vapour line.
- The saturated liquid line and saturated vapour line meet at point 'C'.

'C' is called the *critical point* for substance and the state of substance at point C is called the *critical state* of the substance.

3.4.1 Critical Point Parameters

Critical point of a pure substance is defined as a state point at which the latent heat is zero. It is the common point of saturated liquid line and saturated vapour line.

The pressure, temperature and specific volume at critical point are known as critical point parameters and are denoted by P_c, T_c and V_c respectively.

The values of parameters for water (steam) are P_c = 221.2 bar, T_c = 374.15°C and V_c = 0.00310 m³/kg.

3.4.2 Significance of Critical point

- Critical point is highest temperature below which the substance exists in a two phase system.
- Above the critical point, liquid-vapour two phase system does not exist. At and above the critical pressure and temperature, water suddenly and entirely flashes into steam without passing through liquid-vapour phase.
- Latent heat decreases as the pressure increases (Fig. 3.9). At critical point, the latent heat becomes zero. The saturated liquid line and saturated vapour line merge into each other to a point.
- It is observed that latent heat decreases with increase in pressure. In generation of steam in boilers, less latent heat will be required if boiler pressure is high and at critical pressure no latent heat will be needed to be supplied. So the boiler operating at critical pressure will be most economical in operation.

However as pressure increases, the boiler shell and other equipments have to be designed for higher pressures. This makes the boiler parts more thick and large in size. The weight and cost of boiler therefore increases. A compromise is made between the cost of manufacture and economical operation to decide optimum boiler pressure.

3.5 TRIPPLE POINT OF WATER

Let us consider heating of water at low pressures. With decrease in pressure, boiling point or saturation temperature of water decreases. If we go on lowering the pressure we come across a condition shown by line mnq (Fig. 3.10). At 'm' the substance is ice and at 'n' it is water. When water is heated, its temperature does not increase. It starts vapourising at the temperature T_p and continues to do so till at 'q' we get dry steam.

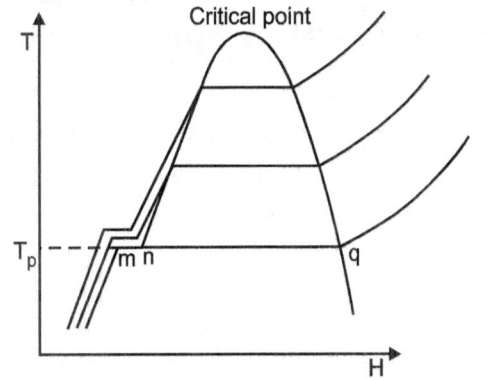

Fig. 3.10 : mnq-triple point line T_p-triple point temperature

Along the line mnq we get an equilibrium mixture of all the three phases viz. ice, water and steam. This is known as a triple point of water. The pressure and temperature at triple point for water are P = 0.006114 bar and T = 273.16 K or 0.01 °C. Below triple point pressure, there is no liquid phase for water and ice directly gets converted into steam. This is known as sublimation of ice.

3.6 PROPETY OF DIAGRAMS

3.6.1 p–v Diagram of Water

The p-v diagram of a pure substance is shown in Fig. 3.11.

From Fig. 3.11, it is clear that as the saturation temperature is increased, the volume of saturated liquid increases.

Volume of the saturated liquid is very small compared with the volume of saturated vapour. As the pressure goes on increasing, the volume of vapour goes on decreasing upto critical point.

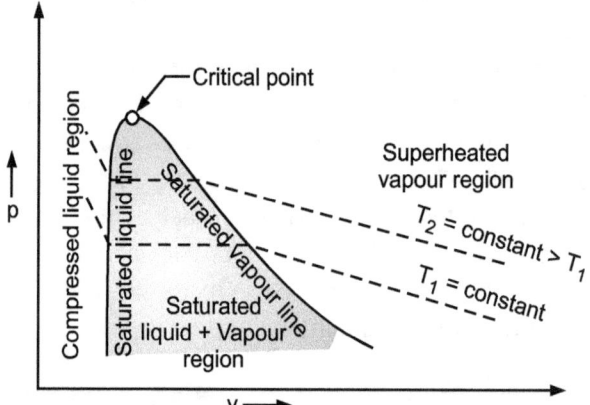

Fig. 3.11: p-v Diagram of a Pure Substance

3.6.2 Temperature Specific Volume Diagram of Water

The phase change diagram of water at 1 atm. pressure is described in Article 3.2.

The process is repeated for different pressures to draw T-v diagram as shown in Fig. 3.12.

From Fig. 3.12, we can draw the following conclusions:

1. Water starts boiling at a much higher temperature corresponding to higher pressures.
2. The specific volume of the saturated liquid is larger and the specific volume of saturated vapour is smaller than the corresponding values at 1 atm. pressure. It means, the horizontal line that connects the saturated liquid and saturated vapour states is much shorter.

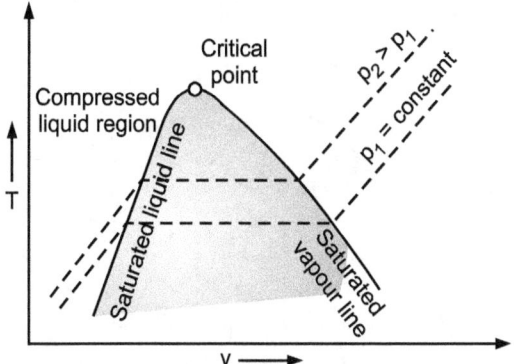

Fig. 3.12: T-v diagram for Pure Substance

3.6.3 Enthalpy – Entropy (h–s) Diagram of Water

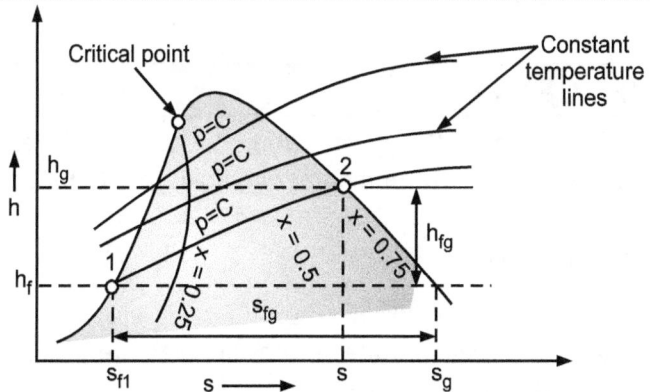

Fig. 3.13: Enthalpy-Entropy diagram of water (Mollier diagram)

Fig. 3.13 is the h-s or Mollier diagram indicating only the liquid and vapour phases. As the pressure increases, saturation temperature increases and also slope of the isobar increases. On this diagram, constant volume lines diverging in vapour region, is also shown. As the pressure increases, h_{fg} decreases and reduces to zero ($h_{fg} = 0$) at critical point.

3.6.4 T-s Diagram for Water

For reversible process, the change in entropy is given as:

$$ds = \frac{\partial Q}{T} = \int Tds = \int dQ$$

The area under the curve (T-s) for a process gives the heat transfer.

Fig. 3.14 shows T-s diagram for water. Constant pressure, constant specific volume and constant quality lines are also shown.

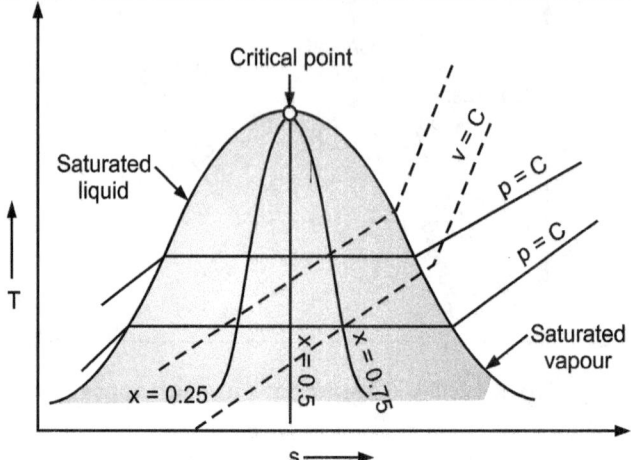

Fig. 3.14: Temperature-Entropy diagram for water

3.7 PROPERTIES OF STEAM

(a) Sensible Heat of Water or Enthalpy of Water: The quantity of heat absorbed by one kg of water to raise its temperature from the freezing point to the boiling point is known as sensible heat.

It is denoted by h_f and calculated as

$$h_f = c_p \Delta T \text{ for unit mass} \qquad \ldots (3.1)$$

where, c_p = Specific heat of water at constant pressure, kJ/kg·K

ΔT = Temperature rise, °C

h_f = Sensible heat, kJ/kg

The error resulted in the value of h_f, calculated by this formula increases as the temperature rises. Therefore, generally h_f is taken from Steam Table.

(b) Latent Heat (Enthalpy of Evaporation) (h_{fg}): It is the amount of heat required to convert one kg of water at a given saturated temperature T_s and pressure 'P' into steam at the same temperature and pressure conditions. This varies with pressure.

For given temperature or pressure, it can be obtained from steam table.

Example (i) Find the enthalpy of evaporation at 3.5 kPa pressure.

Ans. Referring the steam table based on pressure, h_{fg} = 1753.7 kJ/kg at 3.5 kPa.

(ii) Find enthalpy of evaporation at 150°C.

Ans. h_{fg} = 2114.3 kJ/kg at 150°C.

(c) Enthalpy or Total Heat: It is the amount of heat required to raise the temperature of one kg of water from freezing point to the boiling temperature, (corresponding to given pressure) and then to convert it into dry saturated steam at the same temperature and pressure.

It is denoted by h_g.

$$h_g = h_f + h_{fg} \quad \ldots (3.2)$$

where, h_f = Sensible heat, kJ/kg and
h_{fg} = Latent heat, kJ/kg

(d) Wet Steam: It is a homogeneous mixture of vapour and fine water particles. This exists in the steam space of boiler.

The quality of wet steam depends on the amount of water particles present in the mixture. The quality of wet steam is defined by the dryness fraction.

The dryness fraction (x) is expressed by the ratio of mass of dry vapour (steam) to the total mass of the mixture of water and steam.

$$\therefore \quad x = \frac{m_s}{m_w + m_s} \quad \ldots (3.3)$$

where, x = Dryness fraction or quality of steam
m_s = Mass of dry steam, kg
m_w = Mass of liquid water in the mixture, kg

If dryness fraction of wet steam (x) = 0.8, then one kg of steam contains 0.2 kg of water (moisture) and 0.8 kg of dry steam.

(i) Enthalpy of evaporation or Latent heat of 1 kg of wet steam

$$= x \cdot h_{fg} \text{ kJ/kg} \quad \ldots (3.4)$$

(ii) Total heat or enthalpy of one kg of wet steam is equal to the sum of the enthalpy of saturated water + enthalpy of evaporation i.e.

$$h_g = h_f + x h_{fg} \text{ kJ/kg} \quad \ldots (3.5)$$
$$= h_f + x (h_g - h_f)$$

(iii) Specific volume: Let us consider 1 kg of water heated at constant pressure (1.01325 bar). This heating process is shown in T-v diagram of Fig. 3.15.

Let point A be on the line 2–3 in vapour region having dryness fraction x. Therefore, each of mixture at 'A' contains x kg of vapour and (1 – x) kg of liquid water. At point 2, the water is at saturated liquid state completely (x = 0). At state point 3, the mixture is completely saturated steam (dry saturated state), therefore, x = 1.

If v_A is the specific volume at point A, then,

$$v_A = (1-x) v_f + x \cdot v_g \quad \ldots (3.6)$$

But $v_g = v_f + v_{fg}$

Put in equation (3.6) and simplify

$$V_A = v_f + x \cdot v_{fg} \text{ ...... m}^3/\text{kg} \qquad \text{... (3.7)}$$

This is the specific volume of wet steam having dryness fraction x.

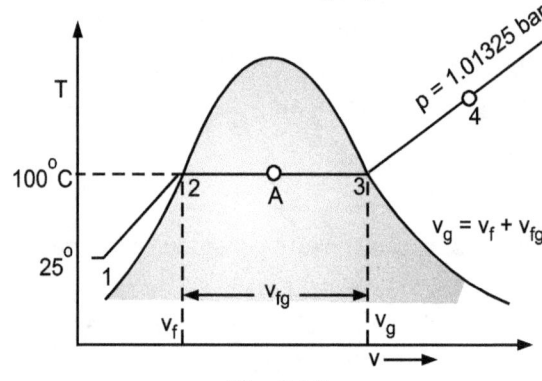

Fig. 3.15

(e) The specific volume of superheated steam at superheat temperature T_{sup} is calculated by using Charle's law.

$$\frac{V_g}{T_s} = \frac{V_{sup}}{T_{sup}}$$

$$\therefore \quad V_{sup} = \frac{V_g}{T_s} \cdot T_{sup} \qquad \text{... (3.8)}$$

where, V_g = Specific volume of dry saturated steam

T_s = Temperature of dry saturated steam, K

V_{sup} = Specific volume of superheated steam

(f) Superheated Steam: When steam is heated out of contact with water, it will result in increase of temperature. Superheating of the steam occurs at constant pressure. The amount of superheating is measured by the rise in temperature of the steam above its saturation temperature (t_s). Greater superheating of the steam will help to acquire the properties of perfect gas.

Enthalpy of superheat

$$= c_p (T_{sup} - T_{sat}) \text{ kJ/kg} \qquad \text{... (3.9)}$$

where, c_p = Mean specific heat of superheated steam at constant temperature

The term $(T_{sup} - T_{sat})$ is known as degree of superheat.

The value of c_p ranges from 2 kJ/kg·K to 2.5 kJ/kg·K

The enthalpy (total heat) of one kg of superheated steam (H_{sup}) is

$$h_{sup} = h_f + h_{fg} + c_p (T_{sup} - T_{sat}) \text{ kJ/kg} \qquad \text{... (3.10)}$$

$$= h_g + c_p (T_{sup} - T_{sat}) \qquad \text{... (3.11)}$$

(g) Internal Energy: We know that change in enthalpy is

$$dh = du + d(pv)$$
$$h_2 - h_1 = u_2 - u_1 + (p_2v_2 - p_1v_1) \text{ for unit mass}$$
$$\therefore \quad u_2 - u_1 = (h_2 - h_1) - (p_2v_2 - p_1v_1) \text{ for } m = 1 \qquad \ldots (3.12)$$

(i) For wet steam,

Let x_2 and x_1 be dryness fractions at conditions 2 and 1 respectively.

$$\therefore \quad h_2 = h_{f_2} + x_2 \cdot h_{fg_2}$$
and $\quad v_2 = x_2 v_{g2}$
$\quad h_1 = h_{f_1} + x_1 \cdot h_{fg_1}$
and $\quad v_1 = x_1 \cdot v_{g1}$

Then, change in internal energy,

$$(u_2 - u_1) = [(h_{f_2} + x_2 h_{fg_2}) - (h_{f_1} + x_1 h_{fg_1})]$$
$$- (p_2 \cdot x_2 \cdot v_{g_2} - p_1 x_1 \cdot v_{g_1}) \qquad \ldots (3.13)$$

(ii) Internal energy of superheated steam.

$$h_2 = h_{sup_2} = h_{g_2} + c_p(T_{sup_2} - T_{sat_1})$$

and $\quad v_2 = v_{sup_2} = \dfrac{V_{sat_2}}{T_{sat_2}} \times T_{sup_2}$

$$\therefore \quad u_2 - u_1 = (h_{sup_2} - h_1) - (p_2 v_{sup_2} - p_1 v_1) \qquad \ldots (3.14)$$

(h) Entropy (s): Entropy of a dry saturated steam can be obtained from steam table corresponding to a pressure or temperature of steam.

(i) Entropy of wet steam

$$s = (1-x) s_f + x \cdot s_g$$
or $\quad s = s_f + x \, s_{fg}$
$\quad = s_f + x(s_g - s_f)$
$\quad = s_f + x \, s_g \qquad \ldots (3.15)$

because xs_f is very small.

(ii) Entropy of superheated steam,

$$S_{sup} = s_g + \text{Entropy of superheat kJ/kg·K}$$

Entropy of superheat $= c_p \ln \dfrac{T_{sup}}{T_{sat}}$

$$\therefore \quad S_{sup} = s_g + c_p \ln \dfrac{T_{sup}}{T_{sat}} \qquad \text{kJ/kg·K for unit mass} \ldots (3.16)$$

3.8 STEAM TABLES

The properties of steam are given in the tabular form. These tables are known as steam tables. The generation of steam under different temperatures or pressures has been studied experimentally and various properties are measured under different conditions. To compute these properties different types of empirical relations and equations are used. These equations are very much complex and it is convenient to prepare a data in tabular form so that it can be readily used whenever required.

The steam tables are available for

- Saturated water and steam- on pressure basis.
- Saturated water and steam- on temperature basis.
- Superheated steam- on pressure basis for enthalpy, entropy and specific volume.

We will now study the structure of steam tables. We should note that the values given in the steam tables are computed for one kg of steam (or water) i.e. these are the values of specific properties.

We will study an extract of a steam table for saturated water and steam (on pressure basis). Please refer Table No. 3.1.

Table 3.1 : Extract of Steam Tables

For Saturated water and steam (on pressure basis)

Absolute Pressure in bar	Saturation temperature in °C	Specific volume in $\frac{m^3}{kg}$		Specific Enthalpy in kJ/kg			Specific Entropy in kJ/kg–K		
		Water	Steam	Water	Evaporation	Dry Steam	Water	Evaporation	Dry
(P)	(t)	(v_f)	(v_g)	(h_f)	(h_{fg})	(h_g)	(S_f)	(S_{fg})	(S)
10.00	179.88	0.0011274	0.19429	762.61	2013.6	2776.2	2.1382	4.4446	6.5828

For Saturated water and steam (on temperature basis)

Saturation temperature in °C	Absolute Pressure in bar	Specific volume in $\frac{m^3}{kg}$		Specific Enthalpy in kJ/kg			Specific Entropy in kJ/kg–K		
		Water	Steam	Water	Evaporation	Dry Steam	Water	Evaporation	Dry Steam
(t)	(P)	(v_f)	(v_g)	(h_f)	(h_{fg})	(h_g)	(S_f)	(S_{fg})	(S)
100	1.0133	0.00010437	1.6730	419.06	2256.9	2676.0	1.3069	6.0485	7.3554

The table contains ten columns and each column gives values of a particular property at different values of absolute pressure. The summary of the structure of the table can be given as follows.

Table 3.2

Column No.	Name of the property	Symbol	Unit
1.	Absolute pressure	P	bar
2.	Saturation temperature	t	°C
3.	Specific volume of saturated water	v_f	m³/kg
4.	Specific volume of dry saturated steam	v_g	m³/kg
5.	Specific enthalpy of saturated water	h_f	kJ/kg
6.	Specific enthalpy of evaporation	h_{fg}	kJ/kg
7.	Specific enthalpy of dry saturated steam	h_g	kJ/kg
8.	Specific entropy of saturated water	S_f	kJ/kg-K
9.	Specific entropy of evaporation	S_{fg}	kJ/kg-K
10.	Specific entropy of dry saturated steam	S_g	kJ/kg-K

3.8.1 Some Important Points Regarding Steam Tables

- The steam table gives values for 1 kg of water and 1 kg of steam.
- The steam table gives values of properties from the triple point of water to the critical point of steam.
- Either saturation pressure or saturation temperature need to be known. If pressure is known use the table on pressure basis. If temperature is known use the table on temperature basis.
- At low pressure the volume of saturated liquid is very small as compared to the volume of dry steam and usually the specific volume of liquid is neglected. However, at very high pressures the volume of liquid is comparable and should not be neglected.
- The specific enthalpy and specific entropy at 0°C are both taken as zero and measurements are made from 0°C onwards.
- Note that

$$H_g = h_f + h_{fg} \quad \ldots(3.17)$$

and

$$S_g = S_f + S_{fg} \quad \ldots(3.18)$$

- In computing the properties for wet steam remember that only h_{fg} and s_{fg} are affected by dryness fraction but h_f and S_f are not affected by dryness fraction. This means that for steam with dryness fraction x

$$h_g = h_f + x\, h_{fg} \quad \text{and} \quad \ldots(3.19)$$

$$S_g = S_f + x\, S_{fg} \quad \ldots(3.20)$$

- The values of properties for superheated steam can be taken from the table for superheated steam or can be calculated by application of ideal gas equation.

3.8.2 Calculations of Properties of dry Steam :

Properties of saturated water and dry saturated steam are obtained from the steam tables directly.

At a given saturation pressure following properties can be read off directly from the steam tables.

- Saturation temperature
- Specific volume of saturated water
- Specific volume of dry saturated steam
- Enthalpy of saturated water
- Enthalpy of evaporation
- Enthalpy of dry saturated steam
- Entropy of saturated water
- Entropy of evaporation
- Entropy of dry saturated steam.

In steam tables the values are given for 1 kg of water or steam. The values of enthalpy and entropy are measured from 0^0C as a reference point.

Internal Energy of Dry Steam :

This property is not recorded in the steam table. This is to be computed.

Applying the first law of thermodynamics to constant pressure process, we have

$$dh = du + d(Pv) \qquad \ldots(3.21)$$

or $\quad h_2 - h_1 = u_2 - u_1 + (P_2 v_2 - P_1 v_1)$ (unit mass) $\qquad \ldots(3.22)$

or $\quad u_2 - u_1 = (h_2 - h_1) - (P_2 v_2 - P_1 v_1) \qquad \ldots(3.23)$

For given pressure P; h_2, h_1, v_2, v_1 can be read off from the steam table and $u_2 - u_1$ is evaluated.

3.8.3 Calculations of Properties of Wet Steam

Let 'x' be the dryness fraction of the wet steam. Let 'm_g' be the mass of dry steam and 'm_f' be the mass of moisture in given wet steam.

∴ total mass of wet steam = $m_g + m_f$

and dryness fraction $x = \dfrac{m_g}{m_g + m_f}$

(1) Enthalpy :

Let us calculate enthalpy of wet steam. Let 'h' be this enthalpy. We know that,

Total enthalpy of wet steam = enthalpy of moisture + enthalpy of dry steam

∴ $\quad h(m_g + m_f) = h_f \times m_f + h_g \times m_g$

∴ $\quad h = \left(\dfrac{m_f}{m_g + m_f}\right) \times h_f + \left(\dfrac{m_g}{m_g + m_f}\right) \times h_g$ ...(3.24)

but $\quad \dfrac{m_g}{m_g + m_f} = $ 'x' by definition.

∴ $\quad \dfrac{m_f}{m_g + m_f} = \dfrac{m_f + m_g - m_g}{m_g + m_f} = 1 - \dfrac{m_g}{m_g + m_f} = 1 - x$

Substituting in equation (3.24)

$$h = (1 - x) h_f + x h_g \quad ...(3.25)$$

∴ $\quad h = h_f + x(h_g - h_f)$

∴ $\quad h = h_f + x h_{fg}$

as $\quad h_g - h_f = h_{fg}$ ...(3.26)

Equations (3.25) and (3.26) in words can be written as,

$\begin{pmatrix}\text{Enthalpy of}\\ \text{wet steam}\end{pmatrix} = \begin{pmatrix}(1-x) \text{ enthalpy of}\\ \text{liquid}\end{pmatrix} + \begin{pmatrix}x \times \text{ enthalpy of}\\ \text{dry steam}\end{pmatrix}$

or $\begin{pmatrix}\text{Enthalpy of}\\ \text{wet steam}\end{pmatrix} = \begin{pmatrix}\text{Enthalpy of}\\ \text{liquid}\end{pmatrix} + \begin{pmatrix}x \times \text{ enthalpy of}\\ \text{evaporation}\end{pmatrix}$

The Equation (3.26) is more often used.

(2) Specific Volume of Wet Steam :

Let this be v, using the same reasoning as before we have,

$$v = (1 - x) v_f + x v_g \quad ...(3.27)$$

Normally v_f is neglected and,

∴ $\quad v = x v_g$

(3) Entropy of Wet Steam :

Let it be 's' ∴ $\quad s = (1 - x) s_f + x s_g$ ...(3.28)

or $\quad s = s_f + x s_{fg}$ ...(3.29)

(4) Internal Energy of Wet Steam :

We have from equation (3.23)

$$u_2 + u_1 = (h_2 - h_1) - (P_2 v_2 - P_1 v_1)$$

Let x_2 and x_1 be dryness fractions at conditions 2 and 1 respectively. Then,

$\quad h_2 = h_{f2} + x_2 h_{fg2}$ and $\quad v_2 = x_2 v_{g2}$

and $\quad h_1 = h_{f1} + x_1 h_{fg1}$ and $\quad v_1 = x_1 v_{g1}$

Then change in internal energy is,

$$u_2 - u_1 = [(h_{f2} + x_2 h_{fg2}) - (h_{f1} + x_1 h_{fg1})] - (P_2 x_2 v_{g2} - P_1 x_1 v_{g1}) \quad ...(3.30)$$

3.8.4 Calculations of Properties of Superheated Steam

Please refer (Fig. 3.16). Let 'ifgb' be a constant pressure line on a T–H diagram. Let T_{sup} be temperature of superheated steam and T_{sat} be saturation temperature.

Please note that in all the calculations relating to the superheated steam the absolute values of temperatures must be used.

(1) Enthalpy : Let h_{sup} be enthalpy of superheated steam.

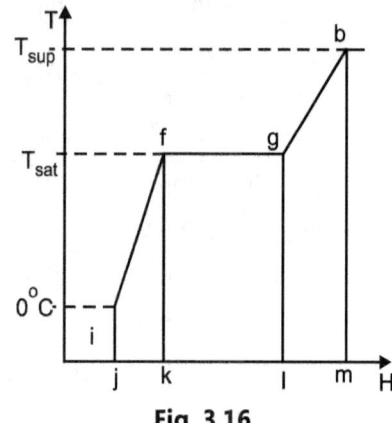

Fig. 3.16

Enthalpy of superheated steam = Enthalpy of dry steam + Enthalpy of superheat

$\therefore \quad h_{sup} = h_g + h_{gb}$ ...(3.31)

Where $\quad h_{gb}$ = enthalpy change from g to b.

but $\quad h_{gb} = m \times C_p \times (T_{sup} - T_{sat})$

or $\quad h_{gb} = C_p \times (T_{sup} - T_{sat})$ as $m = 1$ ...(3.32)

Value of C_p for steam is taken as 2.1 kJ/kgK.

$\therefore \quad h_{sup} = h_g + 2.1\,(T_{sup} - T_{sat})$

h_g can be directly obtained from the steam tables.

(2) Specific Volume :

Let v_{sup} be specific volume of superheated steam at b. We assume that superheated steam obeys gas laws. For constant pressure heating from g to b we have,

$$\frac{v_{sup}}{T_{sup}} = \frac{v_{sat}}{T_{sat}} = \frac{v_g}{T_{sat}} \quad ...(3.33)$$

or $\quad v_{sup} = v_g \times \dfrac{T_{sup}}{T_{sat}}$ ...(3.34)

(3) Entropy : Let v_{sup} be entropy of superheated steam

$\therefore \quad S_{sup} = S_g + S_{gb}$

where S_{gb} is entropy change from g to b,

For constant pressure process g-b

$$S_{gb} = C_p \ln \frac{T_b}{T_g} = C_p \ln \frac{T_{sup}}{T_{sat}} \quad ...(3.35)$$

$$\therefore \quad S_{sup} = S_g + C_p \ln \frac{T_{sup}}{T_{sat}} \qquad \ldots(3.36)$$

where S_g can be directly obtained from the steam tables.

(4) Internal Energy : The change in internal energy is,
$$u_2 - u_1 = (h_2 - h_1) = (P_2 V_2 - P_1 V_1)$$

Let the initial condition of steam be dry and final condition be superheated.

Then,
$$h_2 = h_{sup2} = h_{g2} + C_p (T_{sup2} - T_{sat2})$$

and
$$V_2 = V_{sup2} = V_{sat2} \times \frac{T_{sup2}}{T_{sat2}}$$

And the change in internal energy is,
$$u_2 - u_1 = (h_{sup2} - h_1) - (P_2 V_{sup2} - P_1 V_1) \qquad \ldots(3.37)$$

3.8.5 Finding Values by Interpolation

When steam tables are prepared on pressure or temperature basis, the values of pressure and temperature are selected at a certain convenient interval. For example pressures may be at an interval of 0.1 bar, or 0.5 bar, and 1 bar or temperatures may be at an interval of 1°C. If we wish to find the properties of steam for a value of pressure or temperature which lies in between the values given in the steam table, we have to use a method of interpolation.

Interpolation means to calculate values for in between pressure or temperature using a principle of linear proportion.

This method can be better explained by problems.

SOLVED PROBLEMS

Problem 3.1:

Find enthalpy of dry steam at a pressure of 10.3 bar.

Solution :

In steam tables the values given are at 10.0 bar h_g = 2776.2 kJ/kg and at 10.5 bar h_g = 2778.0 kJ/kg. The difference in enthalpies is 2778.0 − 2776.2 = 1.8 kJ/kg. This corresponds to pressure difference of 10.5 - 10.0 = 0.5 bar. The required pressure difference is 10.3 - 10.0 = 0.3 bar. The enthalpy difference corresponding to 0.3 bar is given by, $h_g = \frac{1.8}{0.5} \times 0.3 = 1.08$ kJ/kg. Adding this to h_g at 10.0 bar we get h_g at 10.3 bar = 2776.2 + 1.08 = 2777.28 kJ/kg which is required value.

This can be expressed by a formula.

$$h_g \text{ (at 10.3 bar)} = 2776.2 + \frac{2778 - 2776.2}{(10.5 - 10.0)} \times (10.3 - 10) = 2777.28 \text{ kJ/kg}.$$

Problem 3.2:
Find specific volume of dry steam at 10.3 bar.
Solution :
By same reasoning we have

$$v_g \text{ at } 10.3 \text{ bar} = 0.19429 + \frac{0.18545 - 0.19429}{10.5 - 10.0} \times (10.3 - 10.0)$$

$$= 0.19429 - 0.005304$$

$$= 0.188986 \text{ m}^3/\text{kg}$$

Please note that V_g decreases as pressure increases and hence, the second term in the expression becomes negative.

Problem 3.3:
Obtain all the properties of steam in the following cases:
- (i) Steam is dry saturated at 11 bar.
- (ii) Steam has a pressure of 8 bar and dryness fraction 0.9.
- (iii) Steam is superheated having pressure 15 bar and temperature 250°C. Assume c_p for superheated steam.

Solution: (i) Dry saturated steam at 11 bar

T_{sat} = 184.1°C from steam table

v_g = 0.17739 m³/kg

v_f = 0.001133 m³/kg

h_f = 781.1 kJ/kg

h_{f_g} = 1998.6 kJ/kg

$h_g = h_f + h_{fg}$ = 2779.7 kJ/kg

s_f = 2.179 kJ/kg·K

$s_{fg} = \dfrac{h_{fg}}{T_{sat}}$ = 4.371 kJ/kg·K

$s_g = s_f + s_{fg}$

= 6.55 kJ/kg·K

(ii) Steam at 8 bar and 0.9 dryness fraction

→ Wet steam

T_{sat} at 8 bar = 170.4°C from steam table

v_f = 0.0011150 m³/kg

$v_x = (1-x) v_f + x \cdot v_g$

= $(1 - 0.9) \times 0.001115 + 0.9 \times 0.24026$

= **0.21635 m³/kg**

$h_x = h_f + xh_{fg}$

$$= 720.9 + 0.9 \times 2046.5$$
$$= \mathbf{2562.75 \text{ kJ/kg}}$$
$$s_f = 2.046 \text{ kJ/kg·K}$$
$$s_x = s_f + x \cdot s_{fg}$$
$$= 2.046 + 0.9 \times 4.614$$
$$= \mathbf{6.1986 \text{ kJ/kg·K}}$$

(iii) Superheated steam at 15 bar and 250°C from steam table, $T_{sat} = 198.3°C$ at 15 bar.

$$v_{sup} = \frac{T_{sup}}{T_{sat}} \cdot v_g$$
$$= \left(\frac{250 + 273}{198.3 + 273}\right) \times 0.13167$$
$$= \mathbf{0.14611 \text{ m}^3/\text{kg}}$$
$$h_{sup} = h_g + c_p (T_{sup} - T_{sat})$$
$$= 2789.9 + 2.1 (250 - 198.3)$$
$$= \mathbf{2898.47 \text{ kJ/kg}}$$
$$s_{sup} = s_g + c_p \cdot \ln\left(\frac{T_{sup}}{T_{sat}}\right)$$
$$= 6.441 + 2.1 \ln\left(\frac{250 + 273}{198.3 + 273}\right)$$
$$= \mathbf{6.6596 \text{ kJ/kg}}$$

Problem 3.4:

Estimate the condition of the steam in the following cases.

(i) p = 20 bar, h = 2797.2 kJ/kg
(ii) p = 14 bar, v = 0.13 m³/kg
(iii) p = 12 bar, s = 6.70 kJ/kg·K

Solution:

(i) For p = 20 bar, h_g = 2797.2 kJ/kg from steam table. Therefore, h_g = h.

∴ **Steam is dry and saturated.**

(**Note:** If h < h_g, it would be wet and if h > h_g, it would be superheated).

(ii) p = 14 bar, v = 0.13 m³/kg,

From steam table, at p = 14 bar, v_g = 0.14073 m³/kg

Comparison of v and v_g:

v < v_g (0.13 < 0.14073)

∴ **Steam is wet.**

∴ $v = v_x = x \cdot v_g$

$$\therefore \quad x = \frac{v_x}{v_g} = \frac{0.13}{0.14073} = \mathbf{0.9237}$$

Note: The steam would have been dry saturated if $v = v_g$ and would be superheated if $v > v_g$.

(iii) p = 12 bar, s = 6.7 kJ/kg·K

Now s_g = 6.519 kJ/kg·K for dry saturated steam (from steam table).

Comparison of s and s_g:

$s > s_g$. Therefore steam is superheated.

(**Note:** It would be dry saturated if $s = s_g$ and wet if $s < s_g$)

$$\therefore \quad s_{sup} = s_g + c_p \ln\left(\frac{T_{sup}}{T_{sat}}\right)$$

$$6.7 = 6.519 + 2.1 \ln\left(\frac{T_{sup}}{188 + 273}\right)$$

$$\therefore \quad T_{sup} = \mathbf{229.496°C}$$

3.9 VAPOUR POWER CYCLES

Thermal power plants use fossil fuels to generate the power. The steam power plant is one of the most successful thermal power plants for the conversion of heat energy into mechanical work. The sequences of various processes that occur in steam power plant are as listed below.

- Heat energy released by the combustion of fuel or by atomic fission is utilized to vaporize water into steam.
- The steam thus produced is expanded in a steam engine or turbine to obtain useful work or power.
- The vapour leaving the turbine is normally condensed and pumped back to its initial state constituting a cycle.
- Thus, the working fluid changes from liquid to vapour and back to its original state.
- This succession of processes is designated as vapour cycle to recognize the state of the working substance during the work output process.

Steam turbines power plants from 1 MW upto 1000 MW units resulting in about 35% to 38% overall thermal efficiency are in current use all over the world. Now a days, combined (gas and steam turbine) cycle plant is gaining popularity as it yields about 55 to 60% overall thermal efficiency. The power developed from steam turbine plant is costlier than hydel-power plant. But one cannot meet the power demand only through hydel power plants, therefore, it is necessary to go for this plant. Also it takes a short time to set up (three to four years) as compared to the hydel which takes nearly ten years and needs a lot of preparatory work in the selection of site. Carnot vapour cycle is the ideal cycle and which consists of the various ideal processes involved to generate the power from thermal energy.

3.10 THE CARNOT VAPOUR CYCLE

The Carnot vapour cycle consists of four fundamental elements namely:
(i) Boiler (Steam generator),
(ii) Turbine,
(iii) Condenser,
(iv) Feed pump handling a two phase mixture-water and its vapour.

Fig. 3.17 shows a steam power plant operating on the Carnot cycle. The processes of the working fluid (steam, i.e. water) are represented on p-v and T-s diagrams as shown in Fig. 3.18.

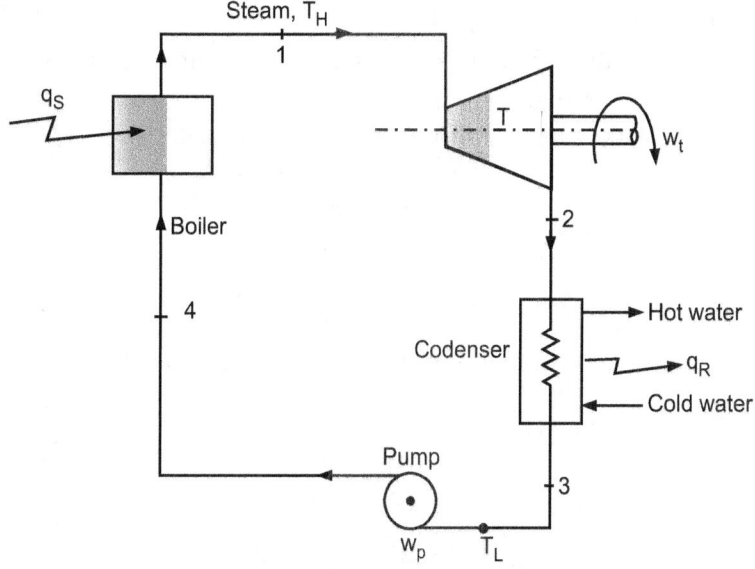

Fig. 3.17: A steam power plant operating on Carnot cycle

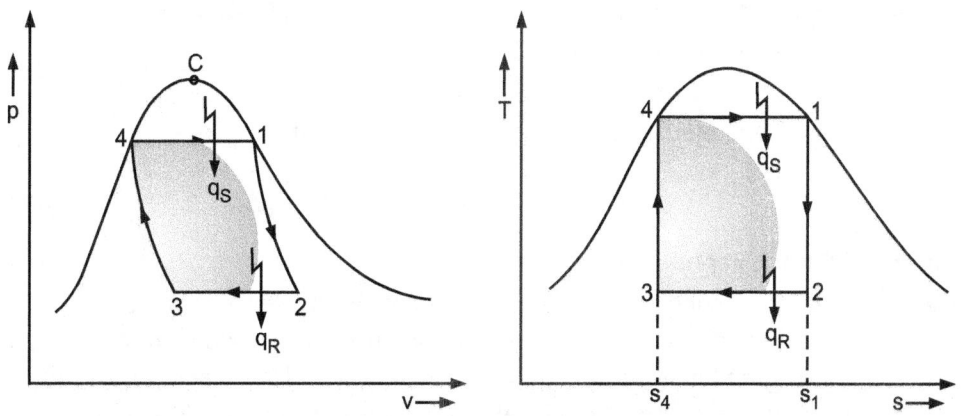

Fig. 3.18: Carnot vapour cycle on p-v and T-s diagrams

Water is heated at constant pressure in the boiler to produce steam. It means heat (q_s) is supplied to the boiler. The condition of steam at the outlet of boiler is at saturated state (represented by point 1 on p-v and T-s diagrams) in Carnot cycle. However, in practice the condition of steam may be superheated one. It is assumed that the condition of water at the outlet of condenser is at point 3. It means a mixture of water and vapour. The mixture is pressurized in the pump such that the condition of water is saturated (point 4). This saturated water is converted to steam in the boiler where it gains (receiver) heat from the burnt gases.

The analysis of Carnot cycle is given below assuming a unit mass of working substance.

Heat supplied in the boiler, $q_s = h_1 - h_{f4}$

Heat rejected in the condenser, $q_R = h_2 - h_3$.

Work is obtained through turbine, where steam expands from its pressure p_1 to pressure p_2.

$$\text{Work, } w_1 = h_1 - h_2$$

$$\text{Work obtained} = \text{Heat supplied} - \text{Heat rejected}$$
$$= (h_1 - h_{f4}) - (h_2 - h_3)$$

$$\text{Thermal efficiency, } \eta_{th} = \frac{\text{Work done}}{\text{Heat supplied}}$$

$$= \frac{(h_1 - h_{f4}) - (h_2 - h_3)}{h_1 - h_{f4}} \qquad \ldots (3.38)$$

Thermal efficiency may also be obtained from turbine and pump work.

For turbine, $\qquad w_t = h_1 - h_2$

For pump, $\qquad w_p = w_{3-4} = h_{f4} - h_3$

$$w_{net} = w_t - w_p = (h_1 - h_2) - (h_{f4} - h_3)$$
$$= (h_1 - h_{f4}) - (h_2 - h_3)$$

$$\therefore \qquad \eta_{th} = \frac{(h_1 - h_{f4}) - (h_2 - h_3)}{h_1 - h_{f4}}$$

Thermal efficiency of a Carnot cycle may be expressed in terms of temperature.

Referring T-s diagram, heat supplied,

$$q_s = T_H (s_1 - s_4)$$

Heat rejected, $q_R = T_L (s_1 - s_4) = T_L (s_2 - s_3)$

$$\therefore \qquad \eta_{th} = \frac{q_s - q_R}{q_s} = \frac{T_H - T_L}{T_H} \qquad \ldots (3.39)$$

Limitations of Carnot Vapour Cycle:

- The condition of working substance at the outlet of condenser is a wet steam. It is a mixture of water and water vapour. The condition of this mixture from state point 3 (p-v and T-s diagram) is to be changed to state 4 (p-v and T-s diagram). This process is carried out through a pump. There is not pump which would handle a mixture of water and water vapour. Therefore, a complete condensation of water vapour in the condenser is desirable.

Further, the pump has to work in such a way that the condition of water at the outlet of pump is saturated (point 4 in p-v and T-s plots). This is also difficult to achieve in practice.

- The saturated steam is expanded in the turbine. The quality of steam decreases while passing through the turbine, therefore, it is also difficult to carry out the expansion of wet steam in the turbine.

3.11 RANKINE CYCLE

Carnot cycle is not a theoretical cycle for steam power plant because it is difficult to build a pump which can pump a mixture of water and vapour and deliver it at a saturated condition. This difficulty is overcome in the Rankine cycle with complete condensation of steam in the condenser. Rankine cycle is the theoretical cycle for steam power plant.

A diagrammatic of Rankine cycle steam turbine power plant is shown in Fig. 3.19. The power plant consists of four basic elements: (i) boiler, (ii) steam turbine, (iii) condenser and (iv) feed pump.

(i) **Boiler:** In the boiler, steam is produced from water at the operating pressure. Fuel is burnt, the heat released is supplied to the water at constant pressure.

(ii) **Steam Turbine:** Here, the steam from the boiler pressure expands and thus performs mechanical work.

(iii) **Condenser:** In the condenser, the exhaust steam from the turbine gives up heat to the cooling water which otherwise cannot be converted into work and is rejected. The condenser enables the exhaust steam to be used as a working fluid of the boiler again. There is a cooling system for condenser consisting of cooling tower and cooling pump. This is not shown in Fig. 3.19.

(iv) **Feed Pump:** The feed pump is used to pump the condensate from the hot-well (in which the condensate is collected) to the boiler at the boiler pressure.

The various processes of the Rankine cycle on p-v, T-s and h-s diagrams are shown in Figs. 3.20, 3.21 and 3.22 respectively. The various processes are:

Process 3-4: The water which is at low pressure p_2 is pumped isentropically into the boiler at high pressure p_1.

Process 4-5: Water is first heated up to the saturation temperature or evaporation temperature T_1 in the boiler and during this process the state point moves along the curve 4-5 called the sensible heating. The heat supplied during the process is $(h_{f5} - h_{f4})$ and is represented by the area L-3-4-5-M on T-s diagram, i.e., the sensible heat of water. Many times point 5 is not shown in power plants because it is the intermediate point in steam generation.

Process 5-1: At constant pressure p_1 and temperature T_1, water is completely vaporized into steam. The heat added in this process is equal to $(h_1 - h_{f5})$ and is represented by M-5-1-N on T-s diagram, i.e. the latent heat of vaporization. The state point 1 shows the dry and saturated condition of steam.

Process 1-2: It is an isentropic expansion of steam in turbine from pressure p_1 to p_2.

Process 2-3: At constant pressure p_2 and temperature T_2, the exhaust steam is condensed in the condenser giving latent heat to cooling water.

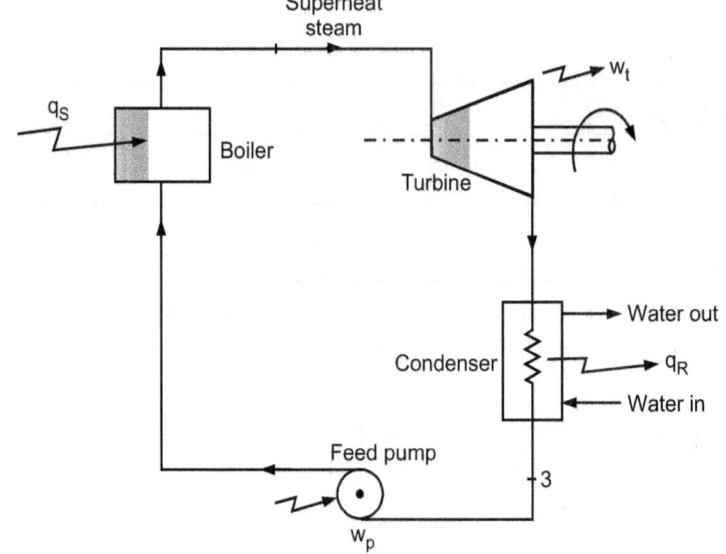

Fig. 3.19: Rankine cycle steam power plant

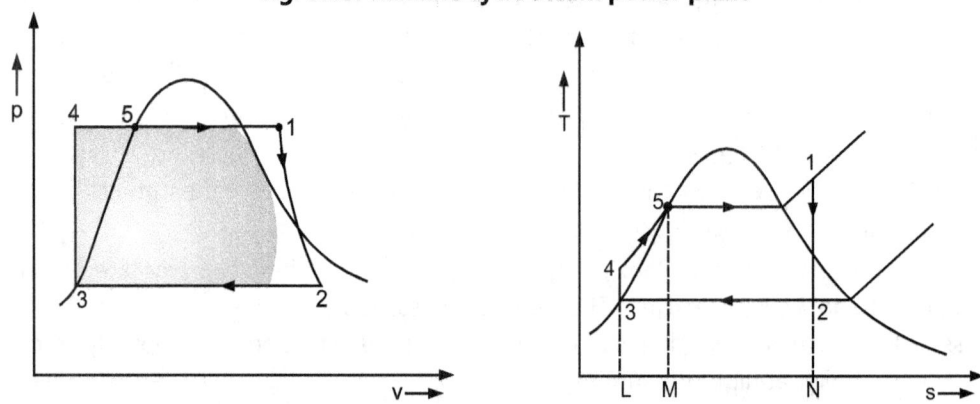

Fig. 3.20: Rankine cycle on p-v diagram   Fig. 3.21: Rankine cycle on T-s diagram

It is possible that steam leaving the boiler may be dry and saturated, wet or superheated. To obtain thermal efficiency of the Rankine cycle, the assumptions made are:

- Steady flow.
- Negligible kinetic and potential energy changes.
- One kg of working fluid flows through the various elements of the cycle.

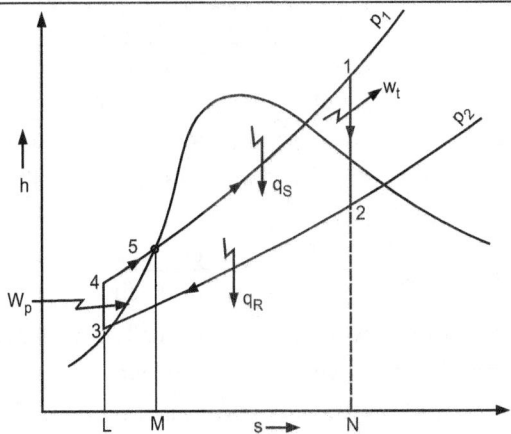

Fig. 3.22: Rankine cycle on h-s diagram

First law of thermodynamics is applied separately to each of the four components of the Rankine cycle. Let us assume that, from first law, $\delta q - \delta u = dh$ or $q - w = \Delta h$.

Heat supplied in the boiler, process 4-1, $q_{4-1} = q_s = q_1 - h_{f4}$

Heat rejected in the condenser, process 2-3, $q_{2-3} = q_R = h_2 - h_{f3}$

Work obtained through turbine, 1-2, $w_{1-2} = w_t = h_1 - h_2$

Work supplied to the pump, 3-4, $w_{3-4} = w_p = h_{f4} - h_{f3}$

Pump work, w_p is also given by, $w_p = h_{f4} - h_{f3} = v_{f3}(p_1 - p_3) = v_{f2}(p_1 - p_2)$

where h_{f2} and h_{f4} are the enthalpy of water at pressures p_2 and p_1 respectively. v_{f2} is the specific volume of water in m³/kg at final pressure p_2.

The net work = Turbine work − Pump work

or $w_{net} = w_t - w_p = (h_1 - h_2) - (h_{f4} - h_{f3})$ kJ/kg

or $w_{net} = (h_1 - h_2) - v_{f2}(p_1 - p_2)$ kJ/kg

While determining the net work from the plant, the work at the pump is to be subtracted from the turbine work output.

$$\eta_{th} = \frac{\text{Net work}}{\text{Head added}} = \frac{w_{net}}{q_A} = \frac{(h_1 - h_2) - (h_{f4} - h_{f3})}{(h_1 - h_{f4})} \quad \ldots (3.40)$$

Thermal efficiency may also be calculated from heat supplied q_A and heat rejected q_R.

$$w_{net} = q_s - q_R = (h_1 - h_{f4}) - (h_2 - h_{f2}) - (h_1 - h_2) - (h_{f4} - h_{f3})$$

∴ $\eta_{th} = \dfrac{w_{net}}{q_A} = \dfrac{(h_1 - h_2) - (h_{f4} - h_{f3})}{(h_1 - h_{f4})}$

or $\eta_{th} = \dfrac{(h_1 - h_2) - (h_{f4} - h_{f3})}{(h_1 - h_{f3}) - (h_{f4} - h_{f3})} = \dfrac{(h_1 - h_2) - w_p}{(h_1 - h_{f2}) - w_p} \quad \ldots (3.41)$

Many times the capacity of steam power plant is expressed in terms of **steam rate**. **Steam rate** is the rate of steam flow (kg/hr) required to produce unit shaft power (1 kW). Therefore,

$$\text{Steam rate} = \frac{1}{w_t - w_p} \times \frac{kg}{kJ} \times \frac{1 \text{ kJ/sec}}{1 \text{ kW}}$$

$$= \frac{1}{w_t - w_p} \cdot \frac{kg}{kW \text{ sec}} = \frac{3600}{w_t - w_p} \cdot \frac{kJ}{kWh}$$

Cycle efficiency is expressed many times as heat rate which is the rate of heat input (Q_s) required to produce work output (1 kW).

$$\text{Heat rate} = \frac{3600 \, Q_s}{w_t - w_p} = \frac{3600 \text{ kJ}}{\eta_{cycle} \cdot kWh}$$

Compared to turbine work, pump work is infinitesimally small and it may be neglected because the specific volume of water is very small. Here, we have

$$w_p = 0 \text{ or } h_{f4} = h_{f3} = h_{f2}$$

$$\therefore \quad \eta_{th} = \frac{h_1 - h_2}{h_1 - h_{f3}} = \frac{h_1 - h_2}{h_1 - h_{f2}} \qquad \ldots (3.42)$$

The thermal efficiency of the Rankine cycle may also be expressed in terms of areas on T-s diagram. Referring to Fig. 3.21,

$$\eta_{th} = \frac{\text{area } 123451}{\text{area } L3451NL} \text{ and neglecting pump work,}$$

$$\eta_{th} = \frac{\text{area } 123451}{\text{area } L351NL}$$

The overall thermal efficiency of a steam power plant varies from 35% to 38%.

In the above analysis, it is assumed that heat additions and rejection take place reversibly. This is, however, not possible in actual power plants. A substantial temperature difference exists between the hot flue gases and working fluid. But the irreversibility associated with this difference is reduced and the thermal efficiency of the cycle is increased by operating a steam generator at a pressure above the critical. The efficiency of the Rankine cycle is shown on T-s plot in Fig. 3.23.

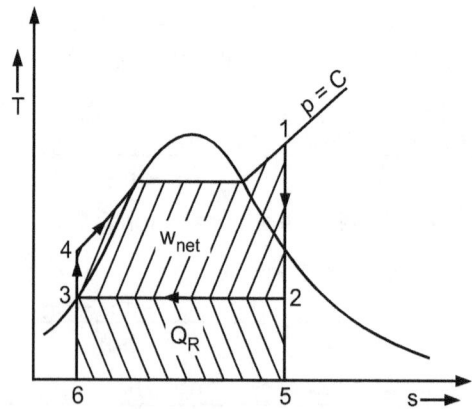

Fig. 3.23 : w_{net} and Q_R are proportional to areas

The heat supplied Q_s is proportional to area 1-5-6-4-1, w_{net} proportional to area 1-2-3-4-1 and the heat rejection Q_s proportional to area 2-5-6-3-2.

3.12 COMPARISON OF RANKINE AND CARNOT CYCLES

Carnot cycle has the maximum possible efficiency operating between the limits of temperature. But it is not suitable in steam power plant. Carnot cycle and Rankine cycle are shown in Fig. 3.24 and Fig. 3.25 respectively with the help of T-s plots.

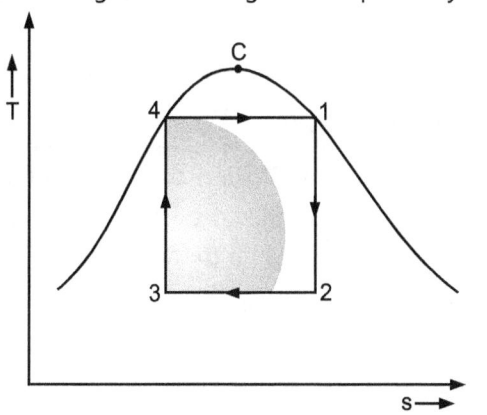

Fig. 3.24: Carnot cycle   **Fig. 3.25: Rankine cycle**

The reversible adiabatic expansion in the turbine, the constant temperature heat rejection in the condenser, and the reversible adiabatic compression in the pump are similar characteristic features of both Rankine and Carnot cycles.

1. The reversible heat addition takes place at constant temperature (process 4-1) in Carnot cycle; while it is at constant pressure (process 4-5-1) in Rankine cycle.
2. The heat supplied per kg of water is more in Rankine cycle than that in Carnot cycle. The heat rejection in condenser of both the cycles is same per unit mass operating between the same temperature limits. Therefore, thermal efficiency of Rankine cycle is less than that of Carnot cycle.
3. In Carnot cycle, it is difficult to control the quality of steam to state 3, so that at the end of isentropic compression, it reaches saturated liquid state. But there is a complete condensation of steam in Rankine cycle.

3.13 IMPROVING THE EFFICIENCY OF THE RANKINE CYCLE

Steam power plants are responsible for the production of most of the electric power in the world. A small increase in the thermal efficiency will lead to a large saving in the fuel requirement. Therefore, every effort is made to improve the efficiency of the cycle on which steam power plants operate.

Thermal efficiency of a power cycle would be increased by two ways:

(i) Increase the average temperature at which heat is transferred to the working fluid in the boiler, or

(ii) Decrease the average temperature at which heat is rejected from the working fluid in the condenser.

Next we discuss three ways of accomplishing this for the simple ideal Rankine cycle.

3.13.1 Lowering the Condenser Pressure (Lowers $T_{low, av}$)

Lowering the operating pressure of the condenser automatically lowers the temperature of the steam and thus the temperature at which heat is rejected. Steam exists as a saturated mixture in the condenser at the saturation temperature corresponding to the pressure inside.

- The effect of lowering the condenser pressure on the Rankine cycle efficiency is illustrated on T-s diagram in Fig. 3.26.
- For comparison purposes, the turbine inlet state is maintained the same.
- The colored area on this diagram represents the increase in net work output as a result of lowering the condenser pressure from p_4 to p'_4.
- The increase in the input requirements is represented by the area under curve 2'-2, but this increase is very small. Thus the overall effect of lowering the condenser pressure is an increase in the thermal efficiency of the cycle.

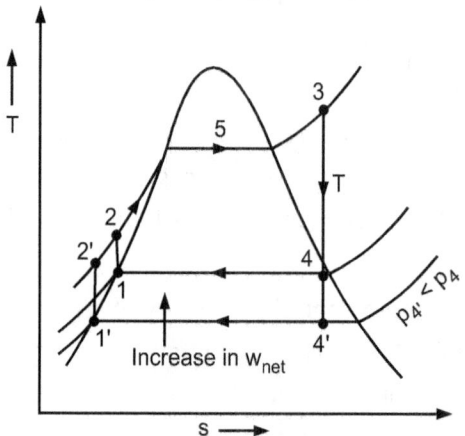

Fig. 3.26: The effect of lower condenser pressure on Rankine cycle

The condensers of steam power plants usually operate well below the atmospheric pressure which increases the efficiency. Vapour power cycles operate in a closed loop therefore, the vacuum pressure in the condenser does not present a major problem. However, there is a lower limit on the condenser pressure that can be used. It cannot be lower than the saturation pressure corresponding to the temperature of the cooling medium. Let us take an example of a condenser is to be cooled by water at 15°C. Allowing a temperature difference of 8°C for effective heat transfer, the steam temperature in the condenser must be above 23°C, thus the condenser pressure must be above 3.5 kPa, which is the saturation pressure at 23°C.

Lowering the condenser pressure it creates the problem of air leakage into the condenser. More importantly, it increases the moisture content of the steam at the last stages of the turbine, as highly undesirable in turbines because it decreases the turbine efficiency and erodes the turbine blades.

3.13.2 Superheating the Steam to High Temperature (Increases $T_{high, av}$)

The average temperature at which heat is added to the steam can be increased without increasing the boiler by superheating the steam to high temperatures.

- The effect of superheating on the performance of vapour power cycles is illustrated on a T-s diagram in Fig. 3.27.
- The colored area on this diagram represents the increase in the heat input.
- Thus both the net work and heat input increase as a result of superheating the steam to a higher temperature.
- The overall effect is an increase in thermal efficiency, however, since the average temperature at which heat is added increases.

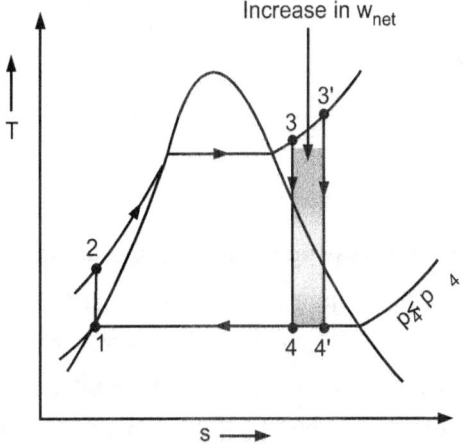

Fig. 3.27: The effect of superheating the steam to higher temperature on the ideal Rankine cycle

Superheating the steam to higher temperature decreases the moisture content of the steam at the turbine exit, as can be seen from the T-s diagram (the quality at state 4' is higher than that at state 4). This is desirable effect. The temperature to which steam can be superheated is limited, however, by metallurgical considerations. Presently the highest steam temperature allowed at the turbine inlet is about 620°C. This value depends on improving the present materials or finding new ones that can withstand higher temperatures. Ceramics are very promising in this regard.

3.13.3 Increasing the Boiler Pressure (Increases $T_{high, av}$)

Another way of increasing the average temperature during the heat addition process is to increase the operating pressure of the boiler. This, in turn, raises the average temperature at which heat is added to the steam and thus raises the thermal efficiency of the cycle.

- The effect of increasing the boiler pressure on the performance of vapour B power cycles is illustrated on a T-s diagram in Fig. 3.28.
- For a fixed turbine inlet temperature, the cycle shifts to the left and the moisture content of steam at the turbine exit increases.
- This undesirable side effect can be corrected, however, by reheating the steam, as discussed in the next section.

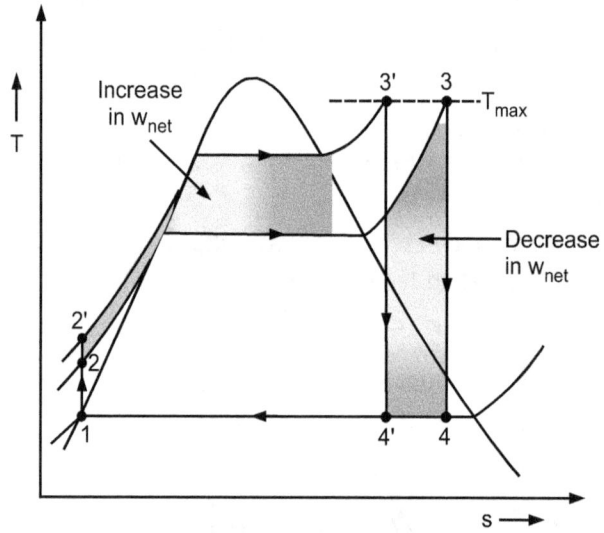

Fig. 3.28: Effect of increasing boiler pressure on ideal Rankine cycle

Operating pressures of boilers have gradually increase over the years from about 2-7 bar in 1922 to over to 300 bar today. Today many modern steam power plants operate at supercritical pressures (P > 22.09 MPa) and have thermal efficiencies of about 40 percent for fossil-fuel plants and 34 percent for nuclear power plants is due to the lower maximum temperatures used in those plants for safety reasons.

SOLVED PROBLEMS

Problem 3.5:

A simple Rankine cycle works between pressure of 25 bar and 0.05 bar. The initial condition of steam is dry saturated. Calculate the cycle efficiency, work ratio and specific steam consumption.

Sat. Temp. °C	Sat. Pr. bar	v_f m³/kg	v_g m³/kg	h_f kJ/kg	h_g kJ/kg	s_f kJ/kg·K	s_g kJ/kg·K
223.9	25	0.001197	0.0799	961.9	2800.9	2.554	6.254
32.9	0.05	0.001005	28.195	137.8	2561.6	0.476	8.396

Solution: The cycle is represented on T-s diagram as shown in Fig. 3.29.

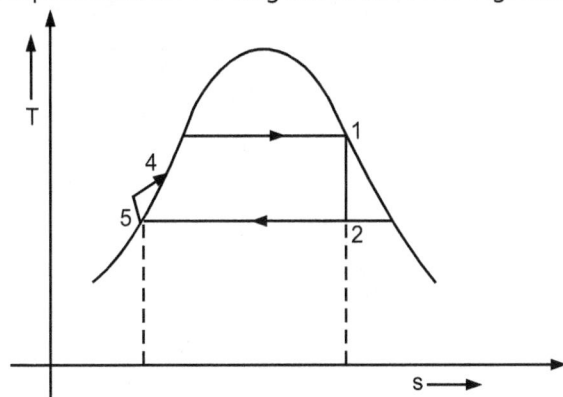

Fig. 3.29

The turbine process being 1-2
From tables,

$$h_1 = 2800.9 \text{ kJ/kg}$$
$$s_1 = 6.254 \text{ kJ/kg·K}$$

The pump work $= v_f [p_4 - p_3]$
$$= 0.001197 [25 + 0.05] \times 10^5 \text{ J}$$
$$= 5.9 \text{ kJ/kg}$$

As $\quad s_1 = s_2 = s_{f2} + x_2 (s_{g2} - s_{f2})$

∴ $\quad x_2 = \dfrac{6.254 - 0.476}{8.396} = 0.6881$

∴ $h_2 = h_{f2} + xh_{fg2} = 137.8 + 0.688 \times 2561.1 = 1812.15 \text{ kJ/kg}$

∴ Turbine work $= 2800.9 - 1812.15 = 988.75 \text{ kJ/kg}$

Cycle efficiency $= \dfrac{(h_1 - h_2) + (h_4 - h_3)}{(h_1 - h_{f4})} = \dfrac{988.75 - 5.9}{2800.9 - (137.8 + 5.9)}$

$= \textbf{0.3698 or 36.98\%}$

Work ratio $= \dfrac{\text{Net work}}{\text{Turbine work}} = \dfrac{982.85}{988.75} = \textbf{0.994}$

Specific steam consumption $= \dfrac{1}{W} \times 3600 = \dfrac{3600}{988.75} = \textbf{3.64 kg/kWh}$

Problem 3.6:

A steam power plant based on simple Rankine cycle works between 50 bar and 0.1 bar. If the steam supplied is dry saturated find (a) Cycle efficiency, and (b) Specific steam consumption.

Solution: The Rankine cycle is shown in Fig. 3.30. The following values are taken from steam tables.

P (sat) bar	T (°C)	v_f m³/kg	v_g m³/kg	h_f kJ/kg	h_g kJ/kg	s_f kJ/kg·K	s_g kJ/kg·K
50	263.9	0.001286	0.039	1154.4	2794.2	2.921	5.974
0.1	45.83	0.00101	14.67	191.8	2584.8	0.649	8.151

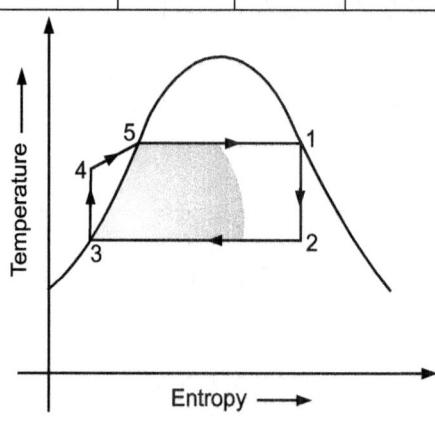

Fig. 3.30

As process 1-2 is isentropic expansion,

$$s_1 = s_2$$

∴ $s_{f1} + s_{fg1} = s_{f2} + x s_{fg2}$

$2.921 + 3.053 = 0.649 + x_2 \times 7.502$

∴ $x_2 = 0.706$

$h_{g1} = h_{f1} + h_{fg1}$
$= 1087 + 1713 = 2794.2$ kJ/kg

∴ $h_{g2} = h_{f2} + x_2 h_{fg2}$
$= 191.8 + 0.906 \times 2392.9 = 1881.19$ kJ/kg

Work done by the pump, $w_p = v_{sw1}(p_4 - p_3)$

$= \dfrac{0.00101 (50 - 0.1) \times 10^5}{1000} = 5.014$ kJ/kg

Net work done per kg of steam

$w_n = h_{g1} - h_{g2} - w_p = 2794.2 - 1881.19 - 5.014 = 907.996$ kJ/kg

$\eta_{rankine} = w_n/(h_{g1} - h_{f4}) = 907.9/[2794.2 - (191.8 + 5.014)]$

$= \mathbf{34.8\%}$

Specific steam consumption $= 1$ kW - hr/[w_{net}] kJ/kg $= 3600/907.9$

$= \mathbf{3.965\ kg/kW\text{-}hr.}$

Problem 3.7:

In a Rankine cycle, the steam at inlet to turbine is saturated at a pressure of 25 bar and the exhaust pressure is 0.1 bar. Determine: (i) The pump work, (ii) Turbine power, (iii) The Rankine efficiency, (iv) The condenser heat flow and (v) The dryness at the end of expansion. Assume flow rate of 10 kg/s.

Solution: From the steam tables:

P (sat) bar	T (sat) °C	v_f m³/kg	v_g m³/kg	h_f kJ/kg	h_g kJ/kg	s_f kJ/kg·K	s_g kJ/kg·K	v_f m³/kg	v_g m³/kg
25	223.9	0.001197	0.0799	961.9	1839	2800.9	2.554	3.699	6.254
0.1	45.83	0.00101	14.67	191.8	2392.9	2584.8	0.649	7.502	8.151

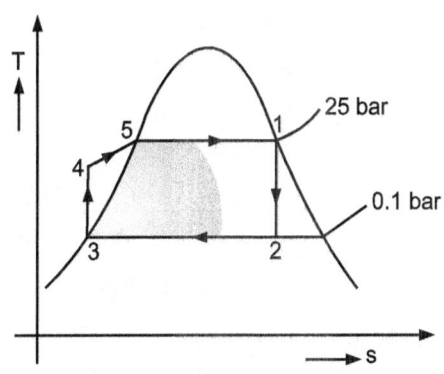

Fig. 3.31

$$h_1 = h_{g1} = 2800.9 \text{ kJ/kg}$$
$$h_3 = h_{f3} \text{ at } 0.1 \text{ bar} = \mathbf{191.8 \text{ kJ/kg}}$$

(i) The pump work $= m (p_4 - p_3) v_f$
$$= 1 \times 10^5 (25 - 0.1) \times 0.00101$$
$$= 2.514 \text{ kJ}$$

As v_f at 0.1 bar $= 0.00101 \text{ m}^3/\text{kg}$

$$h_4 = h_3 + 3 \text{ kJ/kg}$$
$$= 191.8 + 2.514 \text{ kJ/kg}$$

The power required for the pump $= \dfrac{10 \times 2.514 \text{ kJ}}{\text{sec}} = \dfrac{25.14 \text{ kJ}}{\text{sec}}$

$$= \mathbf{25.14 \text{ kW}}$$

(ii) The isentropic enthalpy drop is found using

∴ $\qquad s_1 = s_2 = s_{f2} + x_2 (s_{g2} + s_{f2})$

From steam tables,
$$s_1 = 6.254 \text{ kJ/kg·K}$$
$$s_{f2} = 0.649 \text{ kJ/kg·K}$$
$$s_{g2} = 8.151 \text{ kJ/kg·K}$$

∴ Dryness at the outlet of expansion process

$$x_2 = \frac{s_1 - s_{f2}}{s_{g2} - s_{f2}} = \frac{6.254 - 0.649}{8.151 - 0.649} = 0.747$$

∴ $h_2 = h_{f2} + x_2 h_{fg2} = 1979.2 \text{ kJ/kg}$

∴ Turbine power $= m(h_1 - h_2)$
$$= 10 (2800.9 - 1979.2) \text{ kJ/s}$$
$$= \textbf{8127 kW}$$

Compared to this the pumping power of 30 kW is very small.

(iii) Rankine efficiency:
$$= \frac{(h_1 - h_2) - (h_4 - h_3)}{(h_1 - h_4)}$$
$$= \frac{(2800.9 - 1979.2) - (191.8 - 189.3)}{(2800.9 - 191.8)}$$
$$= 0.3139 \text{ or } \textbf{31.39\%}$$

(iv) The heat flow in the condenser $= m(h_2 - h_3) = 10(1979.2 - 189.3)$
$$= \textbf{17899 kW}$$

(v) Dryness at the end of expansion $= \textbf{0.747 or 74.7\%}$

Problem 3.8:

A steam power plant operating on ideal Carnot cycle uses steam at 5 bar and 90% dryness at the end of the isothermal expansion process. The pressure during isothermal compression is 3 bar. Find the thermal efficiency of the cycle.

Also find the power developed by the engine if the engine uses 1 kg of steam per cycle and makes 200 cycles/min. Assume that the liquid is saturated at the beginning of isothermal expansion (evaporation).

Solution: The cycle is shown on T-s diagram as shown in Fig. 3.32. From steam table, T_1 and T_2 are obtained.

Sat. temp. T_1 at 5 bar = 151.9°C = 424.9 K
Sat. temp. T_2 at 3 bar = 133.5°C = 406.5 K

$$\eta_{th} = \frac{T_1 - T_2}{T_1} = \frac{424.9 - 406.5}{424.9} \times 100 = 4.3\%$$

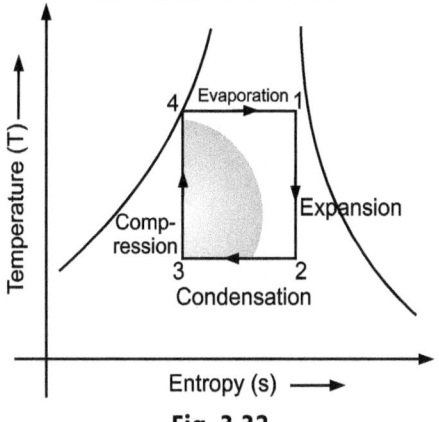

Fig. 3.32

Input during the isothermal expansion per cycle = $m_s \cdot xh_{fg}$

where, m_s = Mass of steam per cycle

x = Dryness fraction of steam at 10 bar

h_{fg} = Latent heat of steam at 10 bar

∴ Input = $1 \times 0.9 \times 2163.2$ = 1446.8 kJ/cycle

where, h_{fg} = 2163.2 kJ

∴ Output/cycle = 906×0.043 = 83.715

∴ Output per minute = 83.715×200

= 16743.168 kJ/m

∴ Power = $\dfrac{16743.168}{60}$

= **279.05 kW**

Problem 3.9:

A steam turbine operates on ideal Carnot cycles using dry saturated steam at 15 bar. The exhaust takes place at 0.05 bar into a condenser. Assume that the expansion and compression are isentropic and liquid enters the boiler as saturated liquid. Find the (a) Power developed by the turbine if the steam consumption is 20 kg/min. and (b) The efficiency of the operating cycle.

Solution: h_1 = Enthalpy of dry saturated steam at 15 bar (from steam tables).

Sat. Temp °C	v_f m³/kg	v_g m³/kg	h_f kJ/kg	h_g kJ/kg	S_f kJ/kg·K	S_g kJ/kg·K	v_f m³/kg
198.3	15 bar	0.001154	0.13167	144.6	2789.9	2.314	6.441
32.90	0.05 bar	0.001005	28.194	137.8	2561.6	0.476	8.396

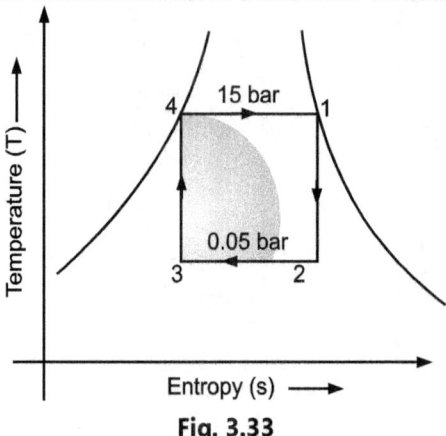

Fig. 3.33

$$h_1 = h_g = 2789.9 \text{ kJ/kg}$$

The expansion 1-2 is isentropic.

$$s_1 = s_2$$
$$s_1 = s_{g1} = s_{f2} + x_2 s_{fg}$$

Substituting the values from steam tables,

$$6.441 = 0.476 + x_2 (7.92)$$

∴ $$x_2 = 0.753$$

$$h_2 = h_{f2} + x_2 h_{fg2}$$

∴ (at 0.05 bar) $= 137.8 + 0.753 \times 2561.6 =$ **2066.68 kJ/kg**

For isentropic compression process 3-4,

∴ $s_3 = s_4 = s_{f4}$ as point 4 is on saturated liquid line

$$s_3 = s_{f3} + x_3 s_{fg3}$$

Substituting the values from steam tables,

$$0.476 + x_3 (7.920) = 2.314$$

∴ $$x_3 = 0.232$$

$$h_3 = h_{f3} + x_3 h_{fg3} = 137.8 + 0.232 \times 2423.8 = \textbf{700.12 kJ/kg}$$

Work of expansion is given by,

$$w_e = h_1 - h_2 = 2789.9 - 2066.68 = \textbf{723.22 kJ}$$

Work of compression is given by,

$$w_c = h_4 - h_3 = h_{f4} - h_3$$
$$= 844.6 - 700.12 = \textbf{144.48 kJ/kg}$$

w_n (Net work done) $= w_e - w_c$

$$= 723.22 - 144.48 = \textbf{578.74 kJ/kg}$$

∴ Work done per minute = 578.74 × 20 = **11574.8 kJ/min**

∴ Power developed by the engine = $\dfrac{11574.8}{60}$ = **192.91 kW**

Heat supplied = $h_1 - h_4 = h_1 - h_{f4}$

= 2789.9 − 844.6 = **1945.3 kJ/kg**

∴ Cycle efficiency = $\dfrac{578.74}{1945.3}$ = 0.2975 = **29.75%**

The Carnot efficiency is also given by

= $\dfrac{T_1 - T_2}{T_1}$

where, T_1 saturation temperature of steam at 15 bar = (273 + 198.3) K and T_2 (saturation temperature of steam at 0.05 bar = 273 + 33) K.

∴ Carnot efficiency = $\dfrac{(198.3 + 273) - (33 + 273)}{(198.3)} = \dfrac{165.3}{471.3}$

= 0.3507 or **35.07%**

Problem 3.10:

A boiler feed pump works on the (full admission) non-expansive cycle. Steam is supplied at 12 bar and dry saturated condition. The exhaust takes place at 1 bar. Draw the cycle of operation on p-v and T-s diagrams and find:
(a) The steam consumption per kW-hour
(b) Theoretical efficiency of the cycle.
(c) Heat removed in the condenser per kg of steam.
(d) If the feed pump supplies 50 kg of water per minute to the boiler, find the power required to run the pump.

Solution: Non-expansive cycle means that there is no expansion of the steam in the cylinder, and high pressure steam is admitted throughout the stroke.

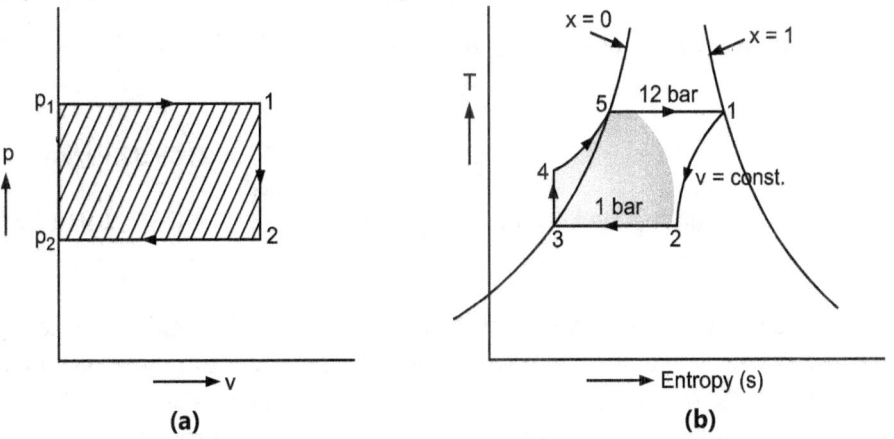

Fig. 3.34

(a) Work done per kg of steam:

$$W = \frac{(p_1 - p_2) v_1}{J}$$

where, $v_1 = v_{s1}$ (as dry steam is supplied)

$$= \frac{[(12 - 1) \times 10^5] \times 0.16321}{1000} = \mathbf{179.53 \text{ kJ/kg}}$$

Pump work per kg of steam:

$$w_p = \frac{v_s (p_1 - p_2)}{J}$$

where, v_s is the specific volume of saturated water at 1 bar.

∴ $$w_p = \frac{0.001043 (12 - 1) \times 10^5}{1000} = \mathbf{1.1473 \text{ kJ/kg}}$$

Net work available is,

$$w_n = 179.53 - 1.1473 = 178.38 \text{ kJ/kg}$$

$$\text{Steam consumption per kWh} = \frac{3600}{178.38} = \mathbf{20.18 \text{ kg/kWh}}$$

(b) Heat supplied per kg of steam is

$$h_s = h_1 - h_{f4}$$
$$= h_1 - (h_{f3} + w_p)$$
$$h_1 = 2782.7$$

∴ $h_2 = 2782.7 - (417.5 + 1.1473) = 2364.05 \text{ kJ/kg}$

$$\text{The cycle efficiency} = \frac{178.38}{2364.05} \times 100 = \mathbf{7.54\%}$$

(c) Heat removed in the condenser per kg of steam

$$= h_2 - h_{f3} = (h_1 - w_n) - h_{f3}$$
$$= 2782.7 - 178.38 - 417.5 = \mathbf{2186.82 \text{ kJ/kg}}$$

(d) Power required to run the feed pump $= \left(\frac{100}{60}\right) \times w_p = \left(\frac{100}{60}\right) \times 1.1473 = \mathbf{1.912 \text{ kW.}}$

Problem 3.11:

Dry saturated steam at 12 bar is supplied to a steam turbine. The exhaust takes at 1 bar. Determine the following: (a) Rankine efficiency, (b) Steam consumption per kWh if the efficiency ratio is 0.65, (c) Carnot efficiency for the given pressure limit using steam as a working fluid. (d) If the exhaust pressure is reduced to 0.1 bar by introducing a jet condenser, find the percentage increase in Rankine efficiency and percentage decrease in specific steam consumption. Neglect the pump work.

Solution: Enthalpy of dry saturated steam at 12 bar.
From steam table, $h_g = 2782.7$ kJ/kg.

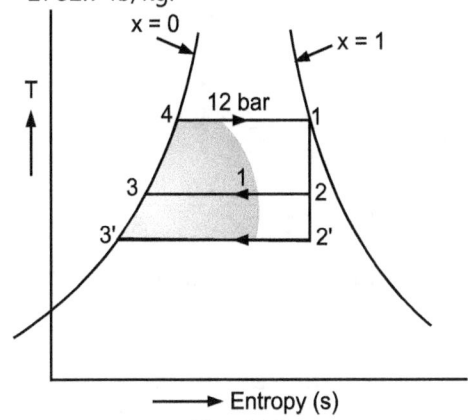

Fig. 3.35

The isentropic expansion from 12 bar to 1 bar is represented by 1-2.

∴ $\quad S_{g1} = S_{f2} + x_2 S_{fg2}$
∴ $\quad 6.519 = 1.303 + x_2 \times 6.057$
∴ $\quad x_2 = 0.8611$

Similarly, for exhaust pressure 0.1 bar, the process is 1-2.

∴ $\quad S_{g1} = S'_{f2} + x'_2 \times S'_{fg2}$

∴ $\quad 6.519 = 0.649 + x'_2 \times 7.502$

∴ $\quad x'_2 = 0.7824$

The enthalpies at 2 and 2' are calculated as,
$h_2 = h_{f2} + x_2 h_{fg2} = 417.5 + 0.8611 \times 2257.9 = 2361.77$ kJ/kg

$h'_2 = h'_{f2} + x'_2 h'_{fg2} = 191.8 + 0.7824 \times 2392.9 = 2064.0$ kJ/kg

(a) Rankine efficiency when exhaust pressure is 1 bar is,
$$\eta_r = \frac{h_1 - h_2}{h_1 - h_{f2}} = \frac{2782.7 - 2361.77}{2782.7 - 417.5} = \frac{420.93}{2365.2} = 0.1779 = 17.79\%$$

Rankine efficiency when exhaust pressure is 0.1 bar is,
$$\frac{h_1 - h'_2}{h_1 - h'_{f2}} = \frac{2782.7 - 2064}{2782.7 - 191.8} = \frac{718.7}{2590.9} = 0.2773 = 27.73\%$$

(b) Efficiency ratio = $\dfrac{\text{Indicated thermal efficiency}}{\text{Rankine efficiency}}$

(i) When exhaust pressure is 1 bar

Indicated thermal efficiency, η_i = 0.1779 × 0.65 = 0.115635

Indicated thermal efficiency, $\eta_i = \dfrac{3600}{m_s (h_1 - h_{f2})}$

where, m_s is specific steam consumption in kg/kWh.

$$0.115635 = \dfrac{3600}{m_s (2782.7 - 417.5)}$$

$\therefore \quad m_s = \dfrac{3600}{0.115635 \times 2365.2} = 13.08 \text{ kg/kWh}$

(ii) When the exhaust pressure is 0.1 bar, then η_i (indicated thermal efficiency)

$$= 0.2773 \times 0.65 = 0.18024$$

$\therefore \quad m_s = \dfrac{3600}{\eta_i (h_1 - h'_{f2})} = \dfrac{3600}{0.18024 (2782.7 - 191.8)}$

$$= 7.709 \text{ kg/kWh}$$

$\therefore$ Percentage decrease in specific steam consumption

$$= \dfrac{13.08 - 7.709}{13.08} \times 100 = 41.06\%$$

(c) Carnot efficiency when exhaust pressure is 1 bar

$$= \dfrac{T_1 - T_2}{T_1} = \dfrac{188 - 100}{188 + 273} = \dfrac{88}{461.0}$$

$$= 0.190 = 19.08\%$$

Carnot efficiency when exhaust pressure is 0.1 bar

$$= \dfrac{T_1 - T_2}{T_1} = \dfrac{188 - 46}{188 + 273} = \dfrac{142}{461}$$

$$= 0.3080 = 30.80\%$$

Percentage increase in Carnot efficiency

$$= \dfrac{30.80 - 19.8}{19.8}$$

$$= 0.3571$$

$$= 35.71\%$$

Exhaust pressure	Carnot efficiency	Rankine efficiency
1 bar	19.08	17.79
0.1 bar	30.80	27.73

Problem 3.12 :

In a Rankine engine, the specific steam consumption is 6 kg/kWh. The enthalpy of steam supplied is 2000 kJ/kg and condensate is at a temperature of 60°C. Find thermal efficiency of the engine.

Solution: The Rankine engine working on Rankine cycle is shown in Fig. 3.36.

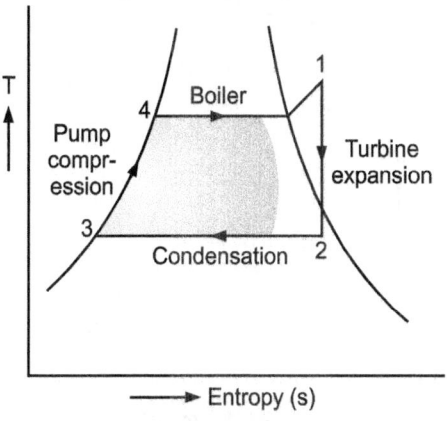

Fig. 3.36

$$h_1 = 2500 \text{ kJ/kg}$$
$$h_{f3} = 4.2 \times (60 - 0) = 252 \text{ kJ/kg}$$

The thermal efficiency is given by,

$$\eta = \frac{kW}{m'_s (h_1 - h_{f3})}$$

where, h_1 and h_{f3} are in kJ and m'_s is steam consumption per second.

$$\therefore \quad \eta = \frac{kW \times 3600}{3600 \, m'_s (h_1 - h_{f3})} = \frac{kW \times 3600}{m_s (h_1 - h_{f3})}$$

where, m_s is steam consumption per hour.

$$\eta = \frac{3600}{\frac{m_s}{kW}(h_1 - h_{f3})} = \frac{3600}{\dot{m}(h_1 - h_{f3})}$$

where, $\dot{m}_s$ is the steam consumption per kW per hour which is known as specific steam consumption.

$$\therefore \quad \eta = \frac{3600}{6(2000 - 252)} = 0.34 = \mathbf{34\%}$$

Problem 3.13:
Dry saturated steam is supplied to a turbine at 16 bar. The isentropic expansion continues to 1.1 bar. Determine (i) The Rankine efficiency, (ii) How is the Rankine efficiency affected if the exhaust is sent to condenser where pressure is maintained at 0.3 bar?
Solution: Refer to Fig. 3.37.

(i) The Rankine efficiency is, $\eta_r = \dfrac{h_1 - h_2}{h_1 - h_{f2}}$, $h_1 = h_g = 2791$

$h_1 = 2791.7$ kJ/kg

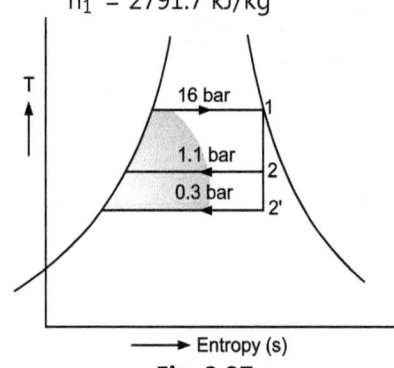

Fig. 3.37

As expansion 1-2 is isentropic,
∴ $\qquad s_1 = s_2$
$\qquad s_{g1} = s_{f2} + x_2 \, s_{fg2}$ (values are taken from steam table)
$\qquad 6.418 = 1.33 + x_2 \times 5.9947$
∴ $\qquad x_2 = 0.8482$
∴ $\qquad h_2 = h_{f2} + x_2 \, h_{fg2} = 428.84 + 1 + 2250.8 = 2680.64$ kJ/kg

$\eta_r = \dfrac{2791.7 - 2346.5}{2791.7 - 428.84} = 0.1884 =$ **18.8%**

(ii) When the expansion is continued to 0.3 bar, then,

$$s_1 = s_2' = s_{f2}' + x_2' \, h_{fg2}'$$

∴ $\qquad 6.44 = 0.944 + x_2' \times 6.825$

∴ $\qquad x_2' = 0.805$

∴ $\qquad h_2' = h_{f2}' + x_2' \cdot h_{fg2}' = 289.3 + 0.805 \times 2336.1 = 2169.86$ kJ/kg

∴ $\qquad \eta_r' = \dfrac{h_1 - h_2'}{h_1 - h_{f2}'} = \dfrac{2791.7 - 2169.86}{2791.7 - 289.3} = \dfrac{621.84}{2502.4} = 0.248 =$ **24.84%**

Alternately, h_2 and h_2' can also be directly obtained from h-s chart after drawing vertical line from point '1' and making the points 2 and 2' which is more easy than this method.

Problem 3.14:

The enthalpy of steam at inlet to a turbine of a power plant is 3000 kJ/kg and enthalpy of steam leaving the turbine is 2600 kJ/kg.

(a) If the temperature of saturated condensate is 50°C, find (i) Rankine efficiency and (ii) Specific steam consumption.

(b) If the highest temperature of steam supplied in the above power plant is 400°C, what would be the maximum possible efficiency of the plant?

(c) If the mass flow rate of steam in the above power plant is 1 kg/sec. find

(i) Power developed by the turbine, (ii) Heat transfer in the condenser, (iii) Work required for he feed pump if the boiler pressure is 10 bar, (iv) Heat supplied in the boiler.

Solution: Refer to Fig. 3.38.

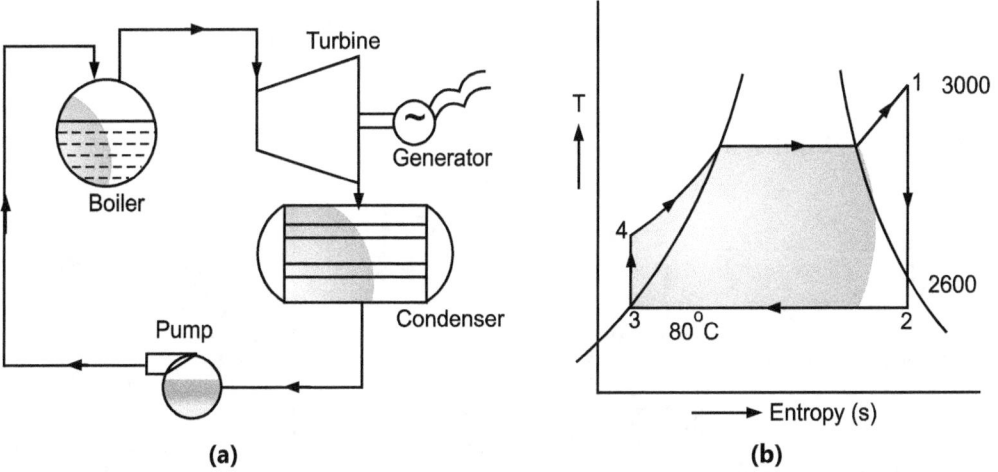

Fig. 3.38

Rankine efficiency is given by,

$$\eta_r = \frac{h_1 - h_2}{h_1 - h_{f2}} = \frac{3000 - 2600}{3000 - 50} = \frac{400}{2950} = 0.1355 = 13.55\%$$

$$\eta_r = \frac{3000}{\dot{m}_s (h_1 - h_{f3})} = \frac{3000}{\dot{m}_s (3000 - 50)} \quad \text{where, } \dot{m}_s \text{ is in kg/kW-hr.}$$

$$\dot{m}_s = \frac{3000}{0.1355 \times 2950} = 7.505 \text{ kg/kW-hr}$$

(b) The highest possible efficiency is as per Carnot efficiency

$$\therefore \quad \eta_c = \frac{T_1 - T_2}{T_1} = \frac{400 - 50}{400 + 273} = \frac{350}{673} = 0.52 = \mathbf{52\%}$$

(c) (i) Power developed by the turbine = $1 \times (3000 - 2600) = 400$ kW

(ii) Heat transfer in the condenser per kg of steam

$$= h_2 - h_{f2} = 2600 - 50 = \mathbf{2550 \text{ kJ/kg}}$$

(iii) Work required to run pump = $(v_w \cdot dp) \, m_w$

where, v_w is specific volume of saturated water at 50°C

$$= \frac{0.001012 \times (10 - 0.12335) \times 10^5 \times (1)}{10^3} \, kW = \mathbf{1 \, kW}$$

(iv) Heat supplied in the boiler per kg of steam

$$= h_2 - h_{f3} = 3000 - 50 = \mathbf{2950 \, kJ/kg}$$

Problem 3.15:

A steam turbine plant operates on the Rankine cycle. Steam is delivered from the boiler to the turbine at a pressure of 3.5 MN/m² and with a temperature of 350°C. Steam from the turbine exhausts into a condenser at a pressure of 10 kN/m² condensate from the condenser is returned to the boiler by means of a feed pump.

Determine:

   (i) The dryness fraction of the steam entering the condenser.
   (ii) Rankine efficiency.
   Draw T-s diagram.

Solution: Given Data: Rankine cycle

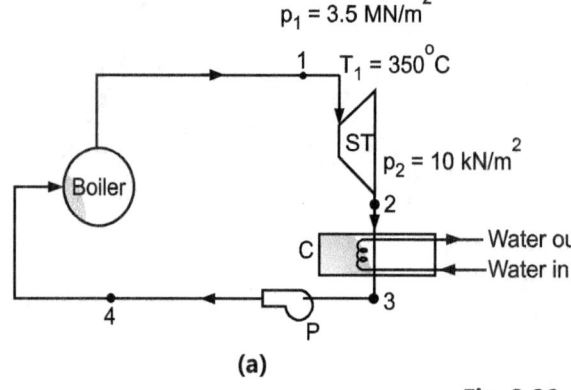

Fig. 3.39

Determine:

   (i) Dryness fraction of steam at point 2.
   (ii) Rankine efficiency.

At 35 bar and 350°C from steam table (superheated),

$$h_1 = 3106.45 \, kJ/kg$$
$$s_1 = 6.663 \, kJ/kg \cdot K$$

To find h_2, from isentropic expansion process 1-2,

$$s_1 = s_2$$
$$= s_{f2} + x_2 \cdot s_{fg2}$$

∴ $6.663 = 0.649 + x_2 \times 7.502$ ... (at 0.1 bar)

$$\therefore \quad x_2 = \frac{6.663 - 0.649}{7.502} = 0.8016$$

Now,
$$h_2 = h_{f2} + x_2 \cdot h_{fg2}$$
$$= 191.8 + 0.8016 \times 2392.9 \quad \ldots \text{(at 0.1 bar)}$$
$$h_2 = 2110.075 \text{ kJ/kg}$$

From steam table, at 0.1 bar,
$$h_3 = h_{f2} = 191.8 \text{ kJ/kg}$$

Also, Pump (w_p) work) $= v_4 (p_4 - p_3)$
$$= 0.001010 \times (35 - 0.1) \times 10^2 \text{ kJ/kg}$$
$$= 3.5249 \text{ kJ/kg}$$

$\therefore \quad h_4 - h_3 = 3.5249$

$\therefore \quad h_4 = h_3 + 3.5249$
$$= 191.8 + 3.5249$$
$$h_4 = \mathbf{195.3249 \text{ kJ/kg}}$$

Now, Rankine cycle efficiency (η_R):

$$= \frac{\text{Turbine work} - \text{Pump work}}{\text{Heat supplied}}$$

$$= \frac{(h_1 - h_2) - w_p}{h_1 - h_4}$$

$$= \frac{(3106.45 - 2110.075) - 3.5249}{(3106.45 - 195.3249)}$$

$$= \frac{992.85}{2911.1251} = 0.341 \text{ or } \mathbf{34.1\%}$$

Problem 3.16:

The feed water to a boiler enters an economiser at 32°C and leaves at 120°C, being fed into the boiler at this temperature. The steam leaves the boiler 0.95 dry at 2 MPa and passes through a superheater where its temperature is raised to 250°C without change of pressure. The steam output is 8.2 kg/kg of coal burned and the calorific value of the coal is 28000 kJ/kg. Determine the energy received per kilogram of water and steam in: (i) The economiser, (ii) The boiler, (iii) The superheater expressing the answers as percentages of the energy supplied by the coal.

Solution:

Heat released per kg of coal = Q = 28000 kJ/kg

Energy received per kg of water in economiser = Q_1
$$= c_{pw} (T_{w2} - T_{w1}) = 4.18 \times (120 - 32) = 367.84 \text{ kJ/kg}$$

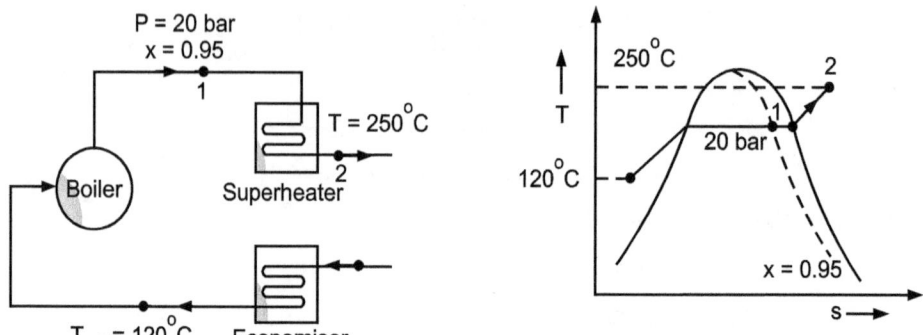

Fig. 3.40

Energy received per kg of water in boiler = Q_2

$$= h_1 - h_{f\,(at\,120°C)}$$
$$= (h_{f1} + xh_{fg1}) - h_{f\,(at\,120°C)}$$
$$= (908.6 + 0.95 \times 1888.6) - 504.1$$
$$= 2198.67 \text{ kJ/kg} \qquad \ldots (7.85\% \text{ of } Q)$$

Energy received per kg of steam in superheater = Q_3

$$= (h_2 - h_1) = (2902.4 - 2702.77)$$
$$= 199.63 \text{ kJ/kg} \qquad \ldots (0.713\% \text{ of } Q)$$

Problem 3.17:

A steam power plant is operated at a boiler pressure of 7 MPa and the condenser pressure of 20 kPa. Calculate:

(i) Pump work
(ii) Turbine work
(iii) Heat added
(iv) Rankine cycle efficiency
(v) Net power produced in MW if the steam is produced at the rate of 37.8 kg/sec and at 550°C.

Solution: Rankine cycle:

Steam pressure at inlet to turbine = p_1 = 7 MPa = 70 bar

Steam temperature at inlet to turbine = T_2 = 550°C

Steam pressure at exit of turbine = p_2 = 20 kPa = 0.2 bar

Mass flow rate of steam = m_s = 37.8 kg/sec

Calculate:

(i) Pump work = w_p, (ii) Turbine work = w_T, (iii) Heat added = Q_A, (iv) Rankine cycle efficiency = η_{cycle}, (v) Net power produced in MW.

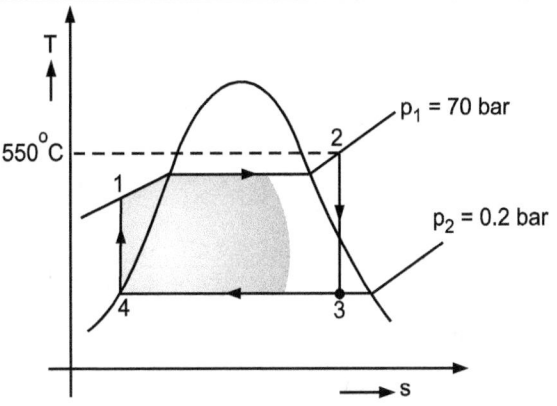

Fig. 3.41

The following properties are taken from superheat steam table.

At $p_1 = 70$ bar and $T_1 = 550°C$.

Enthalpy of steam at point 2 = h_2 = 3530.9 kJ/kg.

Entropy of steam at point 2 = s_2 = 6.9486 kJ/kg·K

From saturated steam table,

At $p_3 = 0.2$ bar,

Entropy of steam at point 3 = $s_3 = s_{f3} + x_3 \cdot s_{fg3}$
$$= 0.8320 + x_3 \cdot (7.0766)$$

For, isentropic expansion (2-3) process,

$$s_2 = s_3$$

∴ $\quad 6.9486 = 0.8320 + x_3 \cdot (7.0766)$

∴ $\quad x_3 = 0.864$

Now, Enthalpy of steam at exit of turbine = $h_3 = h_{f3} + x_3 \cdot h_{fg3}$
$$= 251.4 + 0.864 \times 2358.3$$
$$= 2288.96 \text{ kJ/kg}$$

Enthalpy at point 4 = $h_4 = h_{f3}$ = 251.4 kJ/kg

For finding 'h_1',

Pump work = $w_p = v_f \cdot (p_1 - p_2)$

∴ $\quad h_1 - h_4 = v_f (p_1 - p_2)$

∴ $\quad h_1 = v_f (p_1 - p_2) + h_4$
$$= (0.001017)(70 - 0.2) \times 10^2 + 251.4$$

$\quad h_1 = 258.881$ kJ/kg

(i) $\quad$ Pump work = $w_p = v_f (p_1 - p_2)$
$$= 0.001017 \times (70 - 0.2) \times 10^2 = \mathbf{7.48256 \text{ kJ/kg}}$$

(ii) $\quad$ Turbine work = $w_T = h_2 - h_3$
$$= 3530.9 - 2288.97 = \mathbf{1241.93 \text{ kJ/kg}}$$

(iii)   Heat supplied $= Q_s = h_2 - h_1$

$$= 3530.9 - 258.88 = \mathbf{3272.02 \text{ kJ/kg}}$$

(iv)   Rankine cycle efficiency $= \eta_{cycle}$

$$= \frac{w_T - w_p}{Q_A}$$

$$= \frac{1241.93 - 7.48256}{3272.02} = \mathbf{0.3773 \text{ or } 37.73\%}$$

(v)   Net power developed:

Net work done $= w_T - w_p$

$$= 1241.93 - 7.48256 = \mathbf{1234.45 \text{ kJ/kg}}$$

Given that,

Steam flow rate $= m_s = 37.8$ kg/sec

∴   Net power developed $=$ Net work done $\times m_s$

$$= 1234.45 \times 37.8$$

$$= 46662.113 \text{ kJ/sec or kW} = \mathbf{46.66 \text{ kW}}$$

Problem 3.18:

A steam power plant operates between boiler pressure of 30 bar and condenser pressure of 0.04 bar with dry saturated steam supplied at inlet to the turbine. Calculate:
(i)   The cycle efficiency
(ii)   Specific steam consumption
(iii)   Work ratio
(iv)   Plot the cycle on T-s diagram.

Solution: Given:

Boiler pressure, $p_1 = 30$ bar

Condenser pressure $= p_2 = 0.04$ bar

At inlet to turbine, dry saturated steam.

Calculate:
(i)   The cycle efficiency $= \eta_{cycle}$
(ii)   Specific steam consumption $=$ S.S.C.
(iii)   Work ratio
(iv)   Plot the cycle on T-s diagram.

At pressure, $p_1 = 30$ bar

Enthalpy at inlet of turbine $= h_2 = h_g = 2804.2$ kJ/kg

Entropy at inlet of turbine $= s_2 = s_g = 6.1869$ kJ/kg

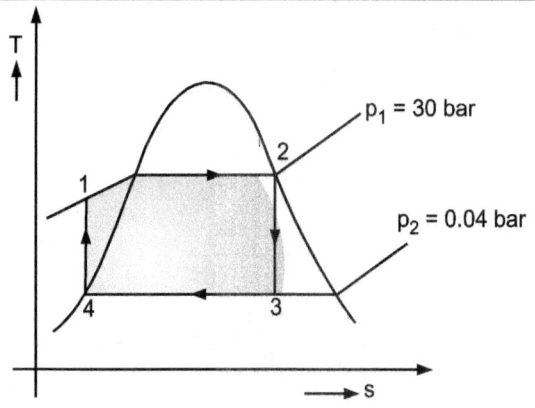

Fig. 3.42

For process 2-3:

$$s_2 = s_3$$
$$\text{at 30 bar} = \text{at 0.04 bar}$$

∴ $\quad s_2 = s_{f3} + x_3 \cdot s_{fg3}$

∴ $\quad 6.1869 = 0.4226 + x_3 \times 8.0520$

$$x_3 = 0.7159$$

Now,

Enthalpy at point 3 $= h_3 = h_{f3} + x_3 \cdot h_{fg3}$

$= 121.46 + 0.7159 \times 2432.9 = 1863.1$ kJ/kg

Enthalpy at point 4 $= h_4 = h_{f3} = 121.46$ kJ/kg

For finding h_1:

Pump work $= w_p = h_1 - h_4$

∴ $\quad v_f (p_1 - p_4) = h_1 - h_4 \qquad \qquad \ldots (1)$

At 0.04 bar, $\quad v_f = 0.001004$ m³/kg

Then equation (1) becomes,

$(0.001004) \times (30 - 0.04) \times 10^2 = h_1 - 121.46$

∴ $\quad h_1 = 124.47$ kJ/kg

(i) Rankine cycle efficiency $= \eta_{cycle} = \dfrac{(h_2 - h_3) - (h_1 - h_4)}{(h_2 - h_1)}$

$= \dfrac{(2804.2 - 1863.135) - (124.47 - 121.46)}{(2804.2 - 124.47)}$

$= \dfrac{(941.065 - 3.01)}{2679.73} = \mathbf{0.35 \text{ or } 35\%}$

(ii) Specific steam consumption (SSC):

$$S.S.C = \frac{3600}{W_{net}} \text{ kg/kW-hr.}$$

$$= \frac{3600}{(w_T - w_p)}$$

$$= \frac{3600}{(h_2 - h_3) - (h_1 - h_4)}$$

$$= \frac{3600}{(941.065 - 3.01)} = \mathbf{3.84}$$

(iii) Work Ratio (WR):

$$WR = \frac{W_{net}}{W_T}$$

$$= \frac{(h_2 - h_3) - (h_1 - h_4)}{(h_2 - h_3)}$$

$$= \frac{941.065 - 3.01}{941.065} = \mathbf{0.997}$$

(iv) Cycle on T-s diagram is shown in Fig. 3.47.

Problem 3.19:

A steam turbine receives superheated steam at 100 bar and 600°C. It is exhausted at 2 bar and then used for process of humidity control. If the steam flow rate is 7200 kg/hr, find the ideal cycle efficiency of the plant. Also find the input in kW and specific steam consumption.

Solution: Given Data: p_2 = 100 bar, T_2 = 600°C, p_3 = 2 bar, m_s = 7200 kg/hr

From steam table,

At 100 bar, T_2 = 600°C

$$h_2 = 3622.7 \text{ kJ/kg}$$
$$s_2 = 6.9013 \text{ kJ/kg·K}$$

At 2 bar,
$$s_f = 1.5301$$
$$s_{fg} = 5.5967 \text{ kJ/kg·K}$$

Adiabatic expansion 2-3,

$$s_2 = s_3$$
$$6.9013 = s_f + x_3 \, s_{fg}$$
$$6.9013 = 1.5301 + x_3 \times 5.5967$$
$$x_3 = 0.9591$$

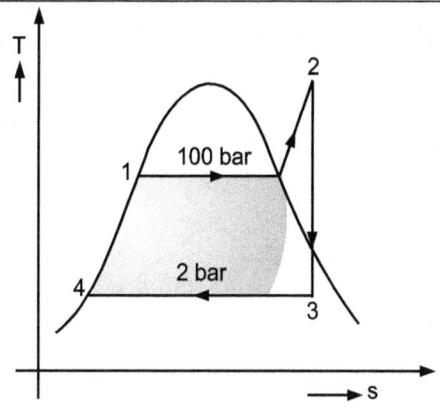

Fig. 3.43

The enthalpy of steam at point '3'

$$h_3 = h_f + x_3 h_{fg} \text{ at 2 bar}$$
$$= 504.7 + 0.9591 \times 2201.6 = 2617.59 \text{ kJ/kg}$$

Heat supplied $= h_2 - h_1$
$$= 3622.7 - 1408.04 = 2214.66 \text{ kJ/kg}$$

Turbine work $= h_2 - h_3$
$$= 3622.7 - 2617.59$$
$$= 1005.11 \text{ kJ/kg}$$

$$\text{Ideal cycle efficiency} = \frac{\text{Turbine work}}{\text{Heat supplied}}$$
$$= \frac{1005.11}{2214.66} = \mathbf{45.38\%}$$

$$\text{Output in kW} = 1005.11 \times \frac{7200}{3600}$$
$$= \mathbf{0.2010.2 \text{ kW}}$$
$$= \mathbf{2010.22 \text{ kW}}$$

$$\text{Specific steam consumption} = \frac{7200}{2010.22}$$
$$= \mathbf{3.582 \text{ kg/kW-h}}$$

Problem 3.20:

Steam of mass 10 kg and pressure 1000 kPa, 0.85 dry, is heated at constant pressure till the volume is doubled. Determine:

(i) Final quality of steam.

(ii) Heat added.

(iii) Change in internal energy.

Solution: Given Data: m = 10 kg, p_1 = 1000 kPa, x = 0.85, $v_2 = 2v_1$

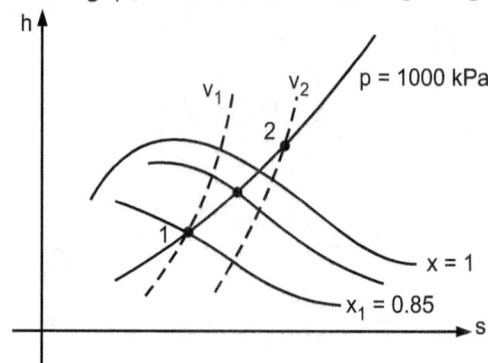

Fig. 3.44

At 10 bar pressure,
$$v_g = 0.19429 \text{ m}^3/\text{kg}$$
$$T_s = 179.88°C$$
$$v_1 = x \times 0.19429$$
$$= 0.85 \times 0.19429$$
$$v_1 = \mathbf{0.1651465}$$

The specific volume at point 2 (after heating),
$$v_2 = 2 \times v_1 = 2 \times 0.1651465$$
$$= 0.3303 \text{ m}^3/\text{kg}$$

But, $v_2 > v_g$ at 10 bar pressure.
Therefore, steam is in superheat state.

∴ Final quality of steam is **superheated**.

From superheat steam table,
At v_2 = 0.3303 m³/kg, p_2 = 1000 kPa
$$T_2 = 450.11°C$$

Now,
$$h_1 = h_{f1} + xh_{fg}$$
$$= 762.61 + 0.85 \times 2013.6 = 2474.17 \text{ kJ/kg}$$
(∵ at 10 bar)

and
$$h_2 = 3371.35 \text{ kJ/kg}$$
... (∵ at T_2 = 450.11°C)

Heat added = $h_2 - h_1$ = 3371.35 − 2475.17
$$= 897.18 \text{ kJ/kg}$$
$$= 897.18 \times 10 \text{ kJ} = \mathbf{8971.8 \text{ kJ}}$$

Change in internal energy,
$$u_2 - u_1 = (h_2 - h_1) + (p_1v_1 - p_2v_2)$$
$$= 8971.8 + 10 \times 1000 \times (0.1651465 - 0.3303)$$
$$= \mathbf{7320.335 \text{ kJ}}$$

(i) Final quality of steam = Superheated steam with temperature 450.11°C.
(ii) Heat added = 8971.8 kJ.
(iii) Change in IE = 7320.335 kJ.

Problem 3.21:

A Carnot steam cycle operates between a source temperature of 311.06°C for a boiler pressure of 10 MPa and a sink temperature of 32.88°C (condenser pressure 5 kPa). Determine the ratio of net work to turbine work and the thermal efficiency of the cycle when all processes are reversible. Also determine specific steam consumption.

Solution: Given Data: Carnot cycle

$T_1 = 311.06°C = 311.06 + 273 = 584.06$ K
$T_2 = 32.88°C = 32.88 + 273 = 305.88$ K
$p_1 = 10$ MPa $= 100$ bar
$p_2 = 5$ kPa $= 0.05$ bar

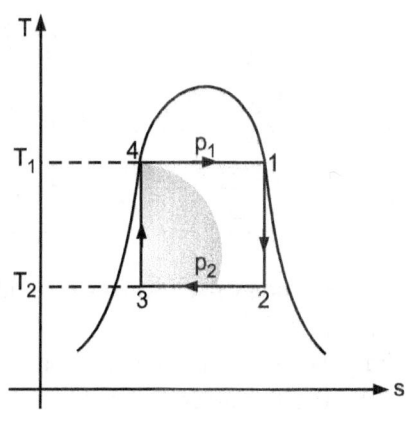

Fig. 3.45

At 100 bar pressure, from steam table,

$$T_s = 310.96°C$$
$$h_1 = h_g = 2727.70 \text{ kJ/kg}$$
$$h_4 = h_f = 1407.04 \text{ kJ/kg}$$
$$s_1 = s_g = 5.6198 \text{ kJ/kg·K}$$
$$s_4 = s_f = 3.3605 \text{ kJ/kg·K}$$

At 0.05 bar pressure, $T_s = 32.898°C$, $h_f = 137.77$ kJ/kg
$$h_{fg} = 2423.8 \text{ kJ/kg}$$
$$s_f = 0.4763 \text{ kJ/kg·K}$$
$$s_{fg} = 7.9197 \text{ kJ/kg·K}$$

To find dryness fraction at point 2, equate entropies at point 1 and point 2.

$$s_1 = s_{f2} + x_2 s_{fg2}$$
$$5.6198 = 0.4763 + x_2 \times 7.9197$$
$$x_2 = 0.64945$$
$$h_2 = h_{f2} + x_2 h_{fg2}$$
$$= 137.77 + 0.64945 \times 2423.8 = 1711.9 \text{ kJ/kg}$$

To find dryness fraction at point '3', equate entropies at point 4 and point 3.

$$s_4 = s_{f3} + x_3 s_{fg3}$$

∴ $\quad 3.3605 = 0.4763 + x_3 \times 7.9197$

∴ $\quad x_3 = 0.3642$

∴ $\quad h_3 = h_{f3} + x_3 h_{fg3}$
$\quad\quad = 137.77 + 0.3642 \times 2423.8 = 1020.7$ kJ/kg

Turbine work = $w_T = h_1 - h_2 = 2727.70 - 1711.92 = 1015.78$ kJ/kg
Pump work = $w_p = h_4 - h_3 = 1408.04 - 1020.67 = 387.37$ kJ/kg
Heat supplied = $Q_s = h_1 - h_4 = 2727.70 - 1408.04 = 1319.66$ kJ/kg
Net work = $w_{net} = w_T - w_p = 1015.78 - 387.37 = 628.41$ kJ/kg

Work ratio $= \dfrac{w_T - w_p}{w_T} = \dfrac{w_{net}}{w_T} = \dfrac{628.41}{1015.78} = \mathbf{0.6186}$

Thermal efficiency $= \eta_{th} = \dfrac{w_{net}}{Q_s} = \dfrac{628.41}{1319.66} = \mathbf{0.4762\ or\ 47.62\%}$

Specific steam consumption $= \dfrac{3600}{w_{net}} = \dfrac{3600}{628.41} = \mathbf{5.729\ kg/kW\text{-}hr}$

Problem 3.22:

A steam power plant operating on Rankine cycle receives steam from a boiler at 3.5 MPa and 350°C. It is exhausted to condenser at 10 kPa. Calculate:
 (i) Energy supplied per kg of steam generated in a boiler.
 (ii) Quality of steam entering the condenser.
 (iii) Rankine cycle efficiency considering feed pump work.
 (iv) Specific steam consumption.

Solution: Given:
$\quad p_1 = 3.5$ MPa = 35 bar
$\quad T_1 = 350°C$
$\quad p_2 = 10$ kPa = 0.1 bar

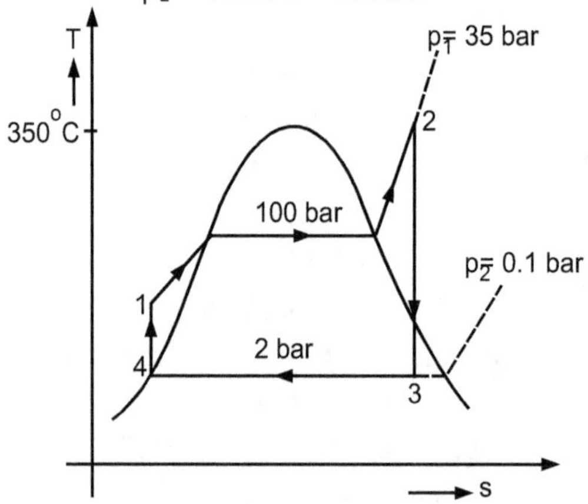

Fig. 3.46

From steam table, at 0.1 bar,

$$h_4 = h_f = 191.8 \text{ kJ/kg}$$

$$w_p = \frac{p_1 - p_2}{10} = 3.49 \text{ kJ/kg} = h_1 - h_4$$

$$\therefore \quad h_1 = 195.29 \text{ kJ/kg}$$

and h_2 corresponding to 35 bar and 350°C = 3106.45 kJ/kg

For isentropic process, $\quad s_2 = s_3$

$$s_2 = s_{f3} + x_3 \, s_{fg3}$$

s_2 at 35 bar and 350°C = 6.663 kJ/kg by interpolation.

$$\therefore \quad 6.663 = 0.649 + x_3 \times 7.502$$

$$\therefore \quad x_3 = 0.8016$$

and $\quad h_3 = h_{f3} + x_3 \, h_{fg3}$

$$= 191.8 + 0.8016 \times 2392.9 = 2110.075$$

$$= 2110.075 \text{ kJ/kg}$$

$\therefore$ Heat supplied = $h_2 - h_1$ = 2911.16 kJ/kg

Work of turbine = $w_T = h_2 - h_3$

$$= 3106.45 - 2110.075 = \mathbf{996.375 \text{ kJ/kg}}$$

Rankine efficiency = $\eta_{rankine} = \dfrac{w_T - w_p}{\text{Heat supplied}}$

$$= \frac{996.375 - 3.49}{2911.6} = \mathbf{0.3410 \text{ or } 34.10\%}$$

Specific steam consumption = $55 = \dfrac{3600}{w_{net}} = \dfrac{3600}{992.88} = \mathbf{3.63 \text{ kg/kW-hr}}$

Problem 3.23:

A steam plant using Rankine cycle generated steam at 10 bar and 380°C. Condensation occurs at 0.06 bar. Find out Rankine efficiency. What will be Carnot efficiency? Neglect feed pump work.

Solution: Rankine cycle,

$$p_1 = 10 \text{ bar}, T_{sup3} = 380°C,$$

$$p_b = 0.06 \text{ bar}$$

Neglecting pump work,

At p_1 = 10 bar, T_{sup3} = 380°C from steam table,

$$h_3 = 3240 \text{ kJ/kg}$$
$$s_3 = 7.4 \text{ kJ/kg·K}$$
$$T_{s3} = 179.88°C$$

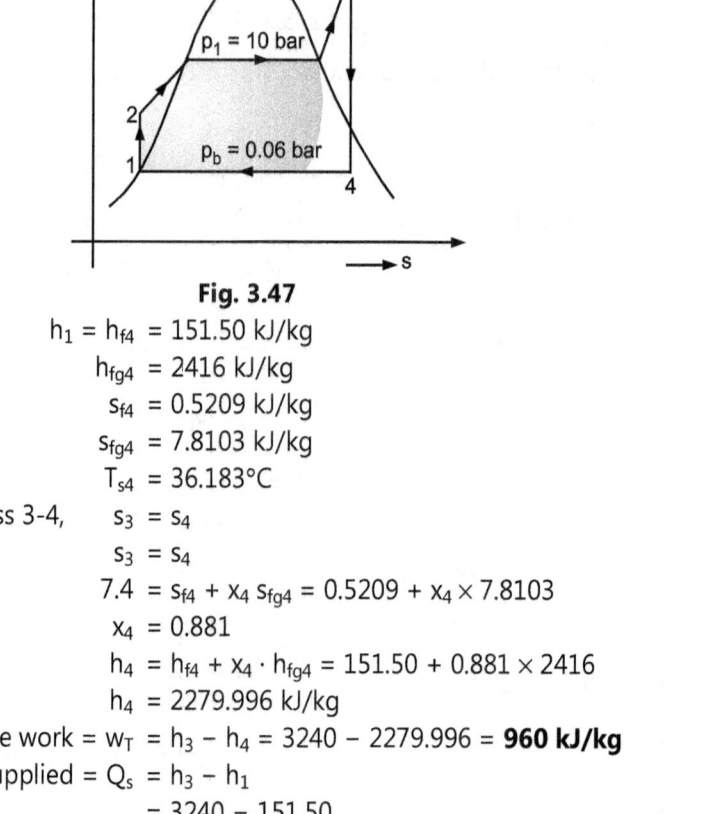

Fig. 3.47

At $p_b = 0.06$ bar, $\quad h_1 = h_{f4} = 151.50$ kJ/kg
$\qquad\qquad\qquad\qquad h_{fg4} = 2416$ kJ/kg
$\qquad\qquad\qquad\qquad s_{f4} = 0.5209$ kJ/kg
$\qquad\qquad\qquad\qquad s_{fg4} = 7.8103$ kJ/kg
$\qquad\qquad\qquad\qquad T_{s4} = 36.183°C$

For isentropic process 3-4, $\quad s_3 = s_4$
$\qquad\qquad\qquad\qquad s_3 = s_4$
∴ $\qquad\qquad\qquad 7.4 = s_{f4} + x_4\, s_{fg4} = 0.5209 + x_4 \times 7.8103$
∴ $\qquad\qquad\qquad x_4 = 0.881$
∴ $\qquad\qquad\qquad h_4 = h_{f4} + x_4 \cdot h_{fg4} = 151.50 + 0.881 \times 2416$
$\qquad\qquad\qquad\qquad h_4 = 2279.996$ kJ/kg

Turbine work $= w_T = h_3 - h_4 = 3240 - 2279.996 =$ **960 kJ/kg**
Heat supplied $= Q_s = h_3 - h_1$
$\qquad\qquad\qquad\qquad = 3240 - 151.50$
$\qquad\qquad\qquad\qquad =$ **3088.5 kJ/kg**

$$\text{Rankine efficiency} = \frac{w_T}{Q_s} = \frac{960}{3088.5} = 0.3108 = \mathbf{31.08\%}$$

$$\text{Carnot efficiency} = \frac{T_1 - T_2}{T_1}$$

$$= \frac{T_{s3} - T_{s4}}{T_{s3}} = \frac{179.88 - 36.183}{179.88} = 0.7988 = \mathbf{79.88\%}$$

Problem 3.24:

In a Rankine cycle, the steam at inlet to turbine is saturated at a pressure of 35 bar and the exhaust pressure is 0.2 bar.

Determine:
- (i) Pump work
- (ii) Turbine work
- (iii) Rankine efficiency
- (iv) Condenser heat flow
- (v) Dryness at the end of expansion.

Assume flow rate of 9.5 kg/s.

Solution: Pressure and conditions of steam, at inlet to the turbine,
$$p_1 = 35 \text{ bar}$$
$$x = 1$$

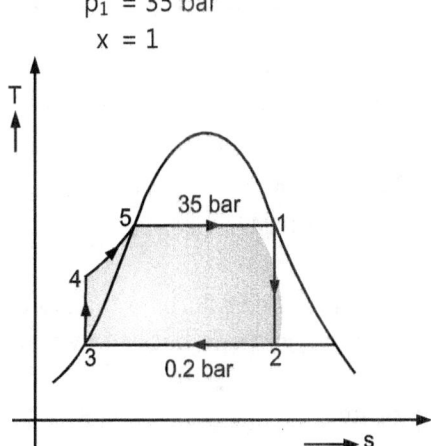

Fig. 3.48

Exhaust pressure, $p_2 = 0.2$ bar

Flow rate, $\dot{m} = 9.5$ kg/sec

From steam table,

At 35 bar, $h_1 = h_{g1} = 2802$ kJ/kg

$s_{g1} = 6.1228$ kJ/kg·K

At 0.2 bar, $h_f = 251.5$ kJ/kg

$h_{fg} = 2358.4$ kJ/kg

$v_f = 0.001017$ m³/kg; $s_f = 0.8312$ kJ/kg·K

$s_{fg} = 7.0773$ kJ/kg·K

(i) The pump work: Pump work = $(p_4 - p_3) v_f = (35 - 0.2) \times 10^5 \times 0.001017$

= 3.54 kJ/kg

∴ Power required to drive the pump = 9.5×3.54 kJ/sec

= 33.63 kW

(ii) The turbine work: $s_1 = s_2 = s_{f2} + x_2 \cdot s_{fg2}$

$6.1228 = 0.8321 + x_2 \times 7.0773$

$x_2 = 0.747$

∴ $h_4 = h_{f2} + x_2 \cdot h_{fg2}$

$= 251.5 + 0.747 \times 2358.4 = 2013$ kJ/kg

∴ Turbine work = $\dot{m}(h_1 - h_2) = 9.5 \times (2802 - 2013)$

= **7495.5 kW**

(iii) Rankine efficiency: $\eta_{Rankine} = \dfrac{h_1 - h_2}{h_1 - h_{f2}} = \dfrac{2802 - 2013}{2802 - 251.5}$

$$= \frac{789}{2550.5} = 0.3093 \text{ or } 30.93\%$$

(iv) Condenser heat flow:

The condenser heat flow $= \dot{m}(h_2 - h_{f3}) = 9.5 \times [(2013) - 251.5]$

$$= 16734.25 \text{ kW}$$

(v) The dryness at the end of expansion, x_2:

$$x_2 = 0.747 \text{ or } 74.7\%$$

Problem 3.25:

Steam at 20 bar and 360° expands in a steam turbine to 0.08 bar. It is then condensed in a condenser to saturated water. The pump feeds back the water to the boiler. Assume ideal Rankine cycle and determine:

(i) The net work done per kg of steam.
(ii) The Rankine efficiency.

Solution:

Given Data:

$p_1 = 20$ bar
$T_1 = 360°C$
$p_b = 0.08$ bar

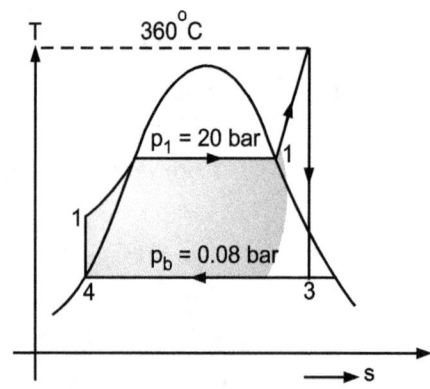

Fig. 3.49

From steam tables corresponding to condenser pressure of 8 bar,

$$h_4 = h_f = 173.86 \text{ kJ/kg}$$

We have,
$$W_p = \left[\frac{p_1 - p_b}{10}\right] \text{ kJ/kg} = h_1 - h_4$$

$$= \frac{20 - 0.08}{10} = 1.992 \text{ kJ/kg} = h_1 - h_4$$

∴
$$h_1 = W_p + h_4 = 1.992 + 173.86$$
$$h_1 = 175.852 \text{ kJ/kg}$$

∴ h_2 corresponding to 20 bar and 360°C = 3160.62 kJ/kg

At 350°C = 3138.6 kJ/kg and at 400°C = 3248.7 kJ/kg

Difference is $\dfrac{110.1}{50°C}$ = 2.202 kJ/kg

∴   2.202 × 10 = 22.02 kJ/kg

∴   At 360°C = 3138.6 + 22.02 = 3160.62 kJ/kg

Now, for isentropic process 2-3:

Entropy before expansion s_2 = Entropy after expansion s_3

To find s_2 = 7.1296 at 400°C

6.9596 at 350°C $\dfrac{0.17}{50}$ = 0.0034 kJ/kg·K

0.0034 × 10 = 0.034 kJ/kg·K

6.9596 + 0.034 = 6.9936 kJ/kg·K

∴   6.9936 = $s_{f3} + x_3 \cdot s_{fg3}$ at condenser pressure

                 = 0.5925 + x_3 × 7.6371

∴ x_3 = 0.8382

$h_3 = h_{f3} + x_3 \cdot h_{fg3}$ at condenser pressure

     = 173.86 + 0.8382 × 2403.2 = 2188.15 kJ/kg

∴   Work done = $w_s = w_T - w_p = (h_2 - h_3) - w_p$

           = (3160.62 − 2188.15) − 1.992 = 970.478 kJ/kg

and $\eta_{Rankine} = \dfrac{w_s}{q_i} = \dfrac{970.478}{h_2 - h_1}$

           = $\dfrac{970.478}{3160.62 - 175.852}$ = **32.51%**

EXERCISE

1. Explain phase transformation of water at constant pressure with the help of T-s diagram.
2. What is the effect of pressure on boiling point?
3. Draw p-v, T-v, h-s and T-s diagrams for water.
4. What is meant by sensible heat, latent heat and enthalpy of water?
5. What is dryness fraction? How do you calculate specific volume, enthalpy and entropy of wet steam?
6. How do you find enthalpy and specific volume of superheated steam?
7. What is internal energy? How do you calculate it for a wet steam and superheated steam?
8. Represent the following processes on p-v and T-s diagrams.
   (a) Constant volume
   (b) Constant pressure
   (c) Hyperbolic
   (d) Isentropic
9. What are the four basic components of a steam power plant?

10. What is the reversible cycle that represents the simple steam power plant? Draw the flow rate, p-v, T-s and h-s diagrams of this cycle.
11. What do you understand by steam rate and heat rate? What are their units?
12. Why is Carnot cycle not practicable for a steam power plant?
13. What do you understand by the mean temperature of heat addition?
14. For a given T_2, show how the Rankine cycle efficiency depends on the mean temperature of heat addition.
15. What is metallurgical limit?
16. Explain how the quality at turbine exhaust gets restricted.
17. How are the maximum temperature and maximum pressure in the Rankine cycle fixed?
18. When is reheating of steam recommended in a steam power plant? How does the reheat pressure get optimized?
19. What is the effect of reheat on (a) the specific output, (b) the cycle efficiency, (c) steam rate, and (d) heat rate, of a steam power plant?
20. Give the flow and T-s diagrams of the ideal regenerative cycle. Why is the efficiency of this cycle equal to Carnot efficiency? Why is this cycle not practicable?
21. What is the effect of regeneration on the (a) specific output, (b) mean temperature of heat addition, (c) cycle efficiency, (d) steam rate and (e) heat rate of a steam power plant?
22. How does the regeneration of steam carnotite the Rankine cycle?
23. What are open and closed heaters? Mention their merits and demerits.
24. Why is one open and closed heaters used in a steam plant? What is it called?
25. How are the number of heaters and the degree of regeneration get optimized?
26. Draw the T-s diagram of an ideal working fluid in a vapour power cycle.
27. Discuss the desirable characteristics of working fluid in a vapour power cycle.
28. Mention a few working fluids suitable in the high temperature range of a vapour power cycle.
29. What is a binary vapour cycle?
30. What are topping and bottoming cycles?
31. Show that the overall efficiency of two cycles coupled in series equals the sum of the individual cycle efficiencies minus their product.
32. What is a back pressure turbine? What are its applications?
33. What is a cogeneration plant? What are the thermodynamic advantages of such a plant?
34. What is the biggest loss in a steam plant? How can this loss be reduced?
35. What is a pass-out turbine? When is it used?
36. Express the overall efficiency of a steam plant as the product of boiler, turbine, generator and cycle efficiencies.

Unit - IV

STEAM CONDENSERS

4.1 INTRODUCTION

In any heat engine the amount of work done per kg of working fluid depends on the range of temperature of the fluid in the engine, being greater the greater the range.

We know that the thermal efficiency of a closed cycle power developing plant using steam as the working fluid and working on **Carnot cycle** is given by an expression $\left(\dfrac{T_1 - T_2}{T_1}\right)$ where T_1 is the maximum temperature in the cycle and T_2 is the lowest temperature reached in the cycle. This efficiency expression shows that an efficiency increases as T_1 increases and T_2 decreases. We understand that the maximum temperature T_1 of the steam supplied to the steam prime-mover is limited by the material of the turbine blades used. Similarly, the temperature T_2 at which the heat is rejected, is limited by the atmospheric conditions. Pressure of steam corresponding to atmospheric temperature will be very much less than atmospheric pressure. (For example : at atm-temperature of 27°C, the saturation pressure is 0.03564 bar.)

Stated in another way, the work done is greater the greater amount of expansion of the fluid. In any heat engine, it is a more or less simple matter to expand the working fluid to a small absolute pressure, but the difficulty is to get rid of the fluid after it has expanded to a pressure less than atmospheric pressure. In internal combustion engine, the working fluid cannot be used over again, and it has therefore to be discharged into the atmosphere, and the pressure of the atmosphere, therefore, fixes the lower limit of expansion. When steam is the working fluid, however, it may be returned to the boiler and used over again and this can be done most conveniently and most economically by first condensing it and then pumping the resulting water into the boiler.

It is not the condensation of the steam in a condenser which causes the low pressure of the steam as it enters the condenser should, for greatest thermodynamic efficiency, be the same as that in the condenser, and condensing it need not lower its pressure of atmosphere. But by condensing the steam, it may then be more economically removed to make way for more steam from the engine. The heat taken from the steam in condensing it is generally entirely lost.

4.2 NECESSITY OF CONDENSERS

Condenser is, basically, a vacuum vessel in which steam is condensed by abstracting the heat and the pressure is maintained below atmospheric pressure.

The primary object of condensing exhaust steam is to make it possible to remove it economically at a pressure less than that of the atmosphere after it has done its work in the prime-mover, and therefore to enable the steam to expand to a greater extent and do more work.

A secondary object is the obtaining of hot feed-water for the boiler. The amount of heat available for conversion into work, with different back pressures and different initial pressures, is given in the table below. The amounts of heat given are the enthalpy drops due to isentropic expansions. The specific volumes of the steam at the back pressures are also given. The steam is assumed to be initially dry and saturated, but it will of course be wet after expansion.

Abs. initial press bar	Abs. back press bar	*Vacuum mm of Hg	Available heat/kg steam kJ	Sp. vol. at back pre cu-m
20	1.0	00	505	1.3888
20	0.15	647.50	750	7.7678
20	0.07	707.50	827	15.3161
10	1.0	00	381	1.4786
10	0.15	647.50	645	8.0585
10	0.07	707.50	720	16.1168
1	0.15	647.50	295	9.1209
1	0.07	707.50	380	18.2110
* Vacuum referred to 760 mm of Hg				

It will be seen from the table that the advantage due to lowering the back pressure, made possible by condensing the exhaust steam, is relatively greater the lower the initial pressure. Also the gain per bar reduction in back pressure is greater the lower the back pressure.

Although the thermodynamic efficiency is greater, the lower the back pressure, the ultimate efficiency may be reduced when the back pressure is reduced beyond a limit depending on the cost of producing and utilizing that back pressure. In reciprocating engines there is generally no saving by increasing the vacuum beyond 690 mm of Hg and 664 mm of Hg is often taken as the limit, but in steam turbines, the vacuum may with advantage be 715 mm of Hg and in special cases it may exceed 740 mm of Hg.

4.3 VACUUM MEASUREMENT

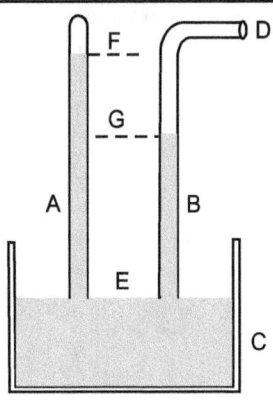

Fig. 4.1

The measure of a vacuum in a vessel is the difference between the atmospheric pressure and the absolute pressure in the vessel. To make this measurement definite it must be converted to correspond with a standard atmospheric pressure. The standard atmospheric pressure generally taken in connection with vacuum measurement is the barometric pressure of 760 mm of Hg which corresponds to 1.01325 bar.

The conversion of a vacuum gauge reading to standard will be best understood by referring to Fig. 4.1. A is a mercury barometer and B a mercury vacuum gauge, both dipping into an open basin of mercury C. The vacuum gauge is connected at D to the condenser or other vessel, the vacuum in which is to be measured. The column of mercury EF in A balances the pressure of the atmosphere acting on the surface of the mercury in C. The column of mercury EG in B plus the absolute pressure P in the vessel connected to B at D acting on the top of the column EG also balances the pressure of the atmosphere, therefore, the height GF measures the absolute pressure p above the mercury in B. But the pressure p is independent of the pressure of the atmosphere. Hence, if the reading of the vacuum gauge, corrected to standard, is Z

$$760 - Z = EF - EG \text{ or } Z = 760 - EF + EG$$

For example, if the gauge shows a vacuum of 710 mm of Hg when the barometer shows 750 mm of Hg, the vacuum corrected to standard is 760 – 750 + 710 = 720 mm of Hg. The vacuum gauge reading, corrected to standard, is sometimes expressed as a percentage of the standard barometric height, thus, in the above example 720 mm is 94.74 percent of 760 mm. A vacuum so expressed must not, however, be confused with vacuum efficiency as defined in this chapter. The vacuum gauges used in practice are similar to pressure gauges and are of the Bourdon type, but the dials are graduated either to read centimeters or millimetre of mercury.

4.4 ELEMENTS OF A CONDENSING PLANT

For the purpose of maintaining a vacuum by the condensation and removal of the exhaust steam, the principal requirements are :

    (a) A condenser in which the steam is condensed.

    (b) A supply of injection or cooling water.

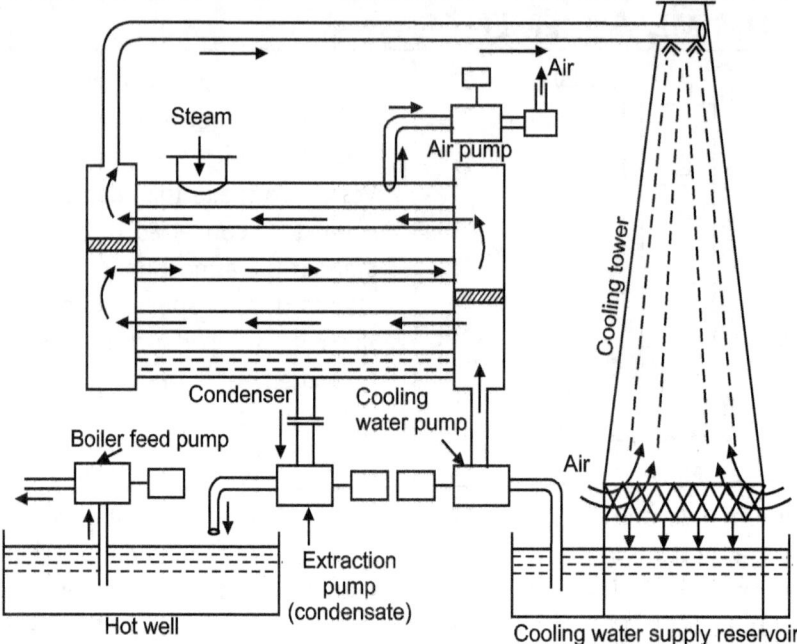

Fig. 4.2

(c) A pump to circulate the cooling water when a surface condenser is used.
(d) A pump, called the **air pump**, for removing the condensed steam and the air and uncondensed water vapour from the condenser. [Separate pumps may be used for (a) the condensed steam and (b) the air and uncondensed water vapour].
(e) A reservoir or a receptacle for the condensed steam discharged by the air pump, called the **hot-well**, from which the boiler feed is taken.
(f) Arrangement for recooling the cooling water of a surface condenser or the excess injection water not required for boiler feed, in cases where the water is to be used over and over again for cooling or injection purposes.

The condensing plant incorporating these elements is as shown in Fig. 4.2

4.5 TYPES OF CONDENSERS

The first class may be subdivided into –

Parallel flow condensers in which the jet or spray of water and the steam enter the condenser at the top and fall together to the bottom.

Counter current or flow condensers in which the steam flows upwards through the condenser, meeting the water which streams downwards from the top. The air is removed at the top and the water, separately, at the bottom.

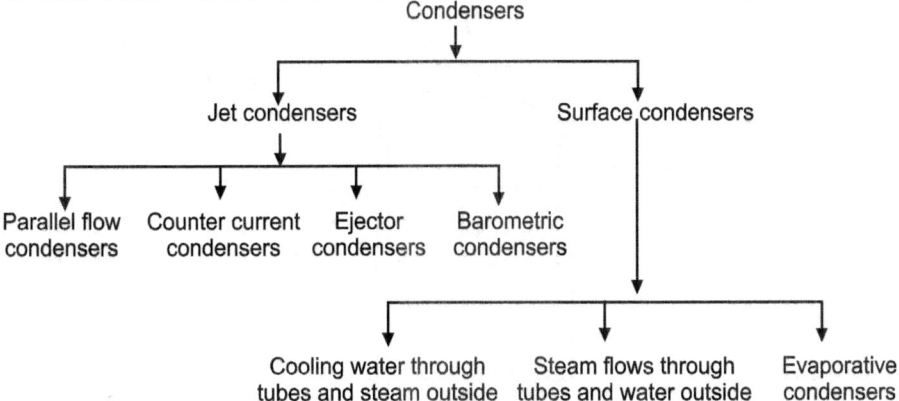

Ejector condensers in which the steam and water mix in a series of combining cones and the kinetic energy of the steam is utilized to assist in moving water through condenser into the hot-well against the pressure of the atmosphere.

Barometric condensers in which a jet condenser at a high level is provided with a long vertical discharge pipe delivering the hot water into a sump at the bottom without the aid of a pump, but an air pump is required to remove the air at the top.

The second class may be subdivided into –

Surface condensers in which the steam flows through tubes while the steam flows around them.

Surface condensers in which the steam flows through the tubes while the cooling water flows around them.

Evaporative condensers in which the steam flows through the tubes which are comparatively cool by water trickling over them, the cooling water being evaporated and taking its latent heat of vaporisation from the tubes.

Jet condensers are only used when the supply of condensing water is resonably pure because it goes with the condensed steam to the hot-well from which the boiler feed water is taken. In modern condensing plants, the most common types of condensers are, the counter current jet condenser and the surface condenser in which the cooling water flows through the tubes and the steam flows around them.

4.5.1 Parallel-flow Jet Condensers

In this jet condenser, the water and steam are flowing or passing through the condenser in the same direction and thus water and steam come in contacted with each other. Steam is condensed and both cooling water and condensate is collected at the bottom of the condenser and is admitted to the condensate extraction pump and air is removed with the help of air pump.

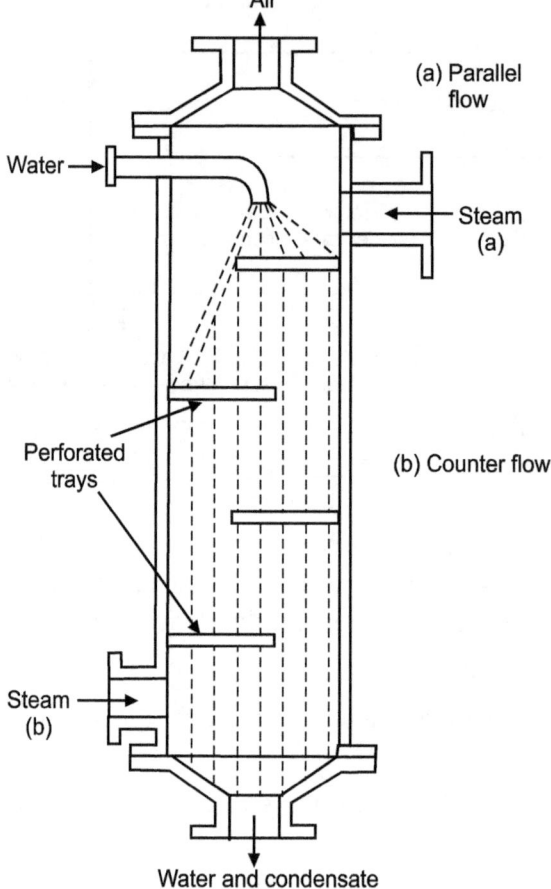

Fig. 4.3

A schematic diagram of parallel flow jet condenser is shown in figure where dotted lines are shown for steam admission in case of a parallel flow jet condenser. The condensate falls to the bottom of the condenser and flows to the condensate extraction pump which removes it to the hot well and air is taken at the top by an air pump as shown.

4.5.2 Counter-flow Type Condenser

In this counter-flow type condenser, water and steam flow in the direction opposite to each other. The schematic diagram of such a condenser is shown in Fig. 4.3 (b). A vertical section of another counter-flow jet condenser is shown in Fig. 4.4.

The main parts of this type of condenser are as –

- Water entry compartment.
- Perforated conical shaped plate for water to flow in number of jets.
- Tray.

- Short pipe through which water jets flows to the bottom of condenser.

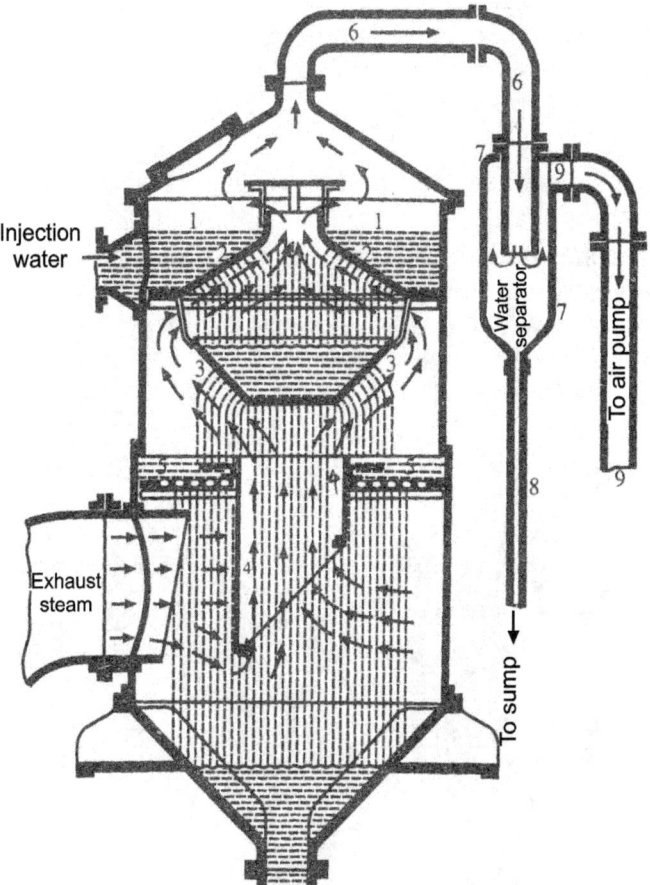

Fig. 4.4

- Collection tray from where water jets also come to the bottom of condenser.
- The air and uncondensed water vapour are led further through pipe 6.
- The separator where water vapour drops suspendender are separator.
- Pipe through which separated water particles are taken to the sump.
- Pipe 9 leads the moist air to the air pump.

If the condenser is a **low-level one**, when it is placed near the level of the engine or turbine (generally it will be slightly below the level of turbine or engine-nearly 5-6 ft or 1.5 to 2 metres), the water is taken from a tank or reservoir below it by a pump, generally of the centrifugal type. This low-level condensers are further divided into two categories as **low-vacuum** and **high-vacuum jet condensers.**

In these condensers, the air pump has only to deal with the moist air.

4.5.3 Ejector Condensers

The main principle of this condenser is that the momentum of flowing water removes the mixture of condensate and cooling water against the atmospheric pressure. The water enters at the top and flows through a number of nozzles (co-axial) fixed in a tube in which there are steam ports leading into the spaces between the nozzles. The exhaust steam enters at the top and surrounds the cones through which cooling water flows at high velocity. Steam is drawn into it due to the vacuum produced by this flow of water, thereby condensing the steam. The mass of condensate, cooling water and air is discharged out of the condenser, due to this velocity, against the atmospheric pressure.

Ledward's well known **ejector condenser** is shown in Fig. 4.5.

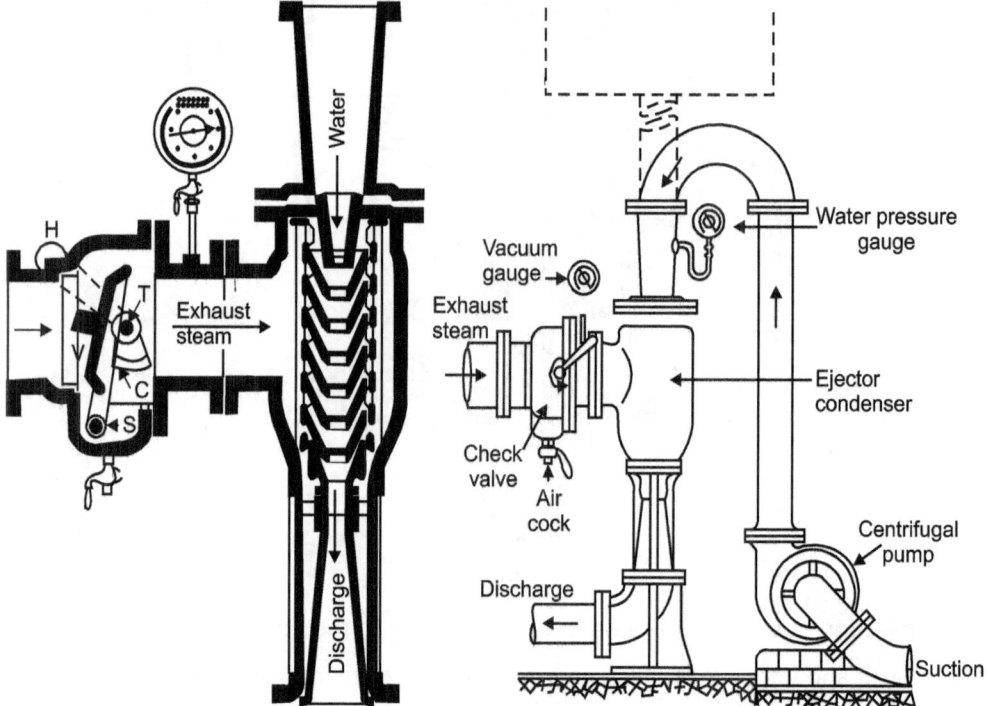

Fig. 4.5

It is usual to fit a check valve V in the exhaust pipe near to the condenser. This is a non-return valve hinged on a spindle S. The use of this valve is to prevent the backward rush of water from the discharge tank to the engine which would follow a sudden failure of the water supply to the condenser.

Such a backward rush of water would close the check valve. An addition to the check valve is a can C attached to a spindle T operated by a handle H by which means the check valve may be locked in its closed position.

The ejector condenser is small in comparison with other types of condensers and there being no air pump, the first cost is low. It is also simple and reliable, but it is generally used for comparatively small engines. The vacuum obtained is generally about 60 cm of Hg.

4.5.4 Barometric or High-level Jet Condenser

In this condenser, the condensing chamber is elevated above 34–35 feet or 10.36 – 10.5 metres above the level of the water in the collecting tank or sump, and the condenser is self discharging so far as the water is concerned. But a pump is necessary to force the injection water up to the condenser.

This is shown in Fig. 4.6. The condenser itself is generally counter-flow type.

4.5.5 Surface Condensers

Surface condenser has a great advantage over the jet condenser as the condensate does not mix with the cooling water; the whole of the condensate can, therefore, be reused in the boiler. This is very necessary in ships which can carry only a limited amount of fresh water for the boilers, and use sea water for cooling water.

With land installations, the cooling water can be allowed to cool again after use and thus be reused continuously through the condenser; this reduces the water consumption of the plant. The necessary high vacuum pressure in the condenser is maintained by the extraction pump and air pump too.

Sometimes an ejector is used for this purpose in place of a pump.

We have before classified surface condenser depending upon the relative positions of steam and cooling water with respect to tubes.

(a) Standard Surface Condensers :

In standard surface condensers, the steam to be condensed is made to flow over the outside of tubes, while the cooling or circulating water is made to flow inside the tubes. This flow pattern is used because the clean steam does not contaminate the outside of the tubes.

This type of the surface condenser may be further classified as **single-pass** or **multi-pass** condensers.

In single-pass condensers, the water flows in one direction only through all the tubes or it traverses the length of the tubes only once. In multi-pass condensers, the water flows or travels the lengths of tubes many times (twice in case of a two-pass condenser or four times in case of a four pass condensers).

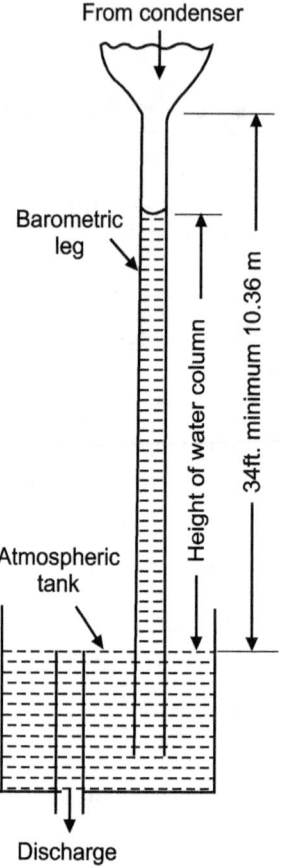

Fig. 4.6

Fig. 4.7 (a) shows one form of standard type of surface condenser having two passes. The steam enters at the top of surface condenser and passing downwards over the tubes, through which cooling water is flowing, is condensed and the condensate is removed at the bottom by means of an extraction pump.

The cooling water enters at one end of the tubes situated in the bottom half of the condenser and after passing to the other end returns back through the tubes situated in the top half of the condenser.

This condenser is also called as **Down flow type** condenser.

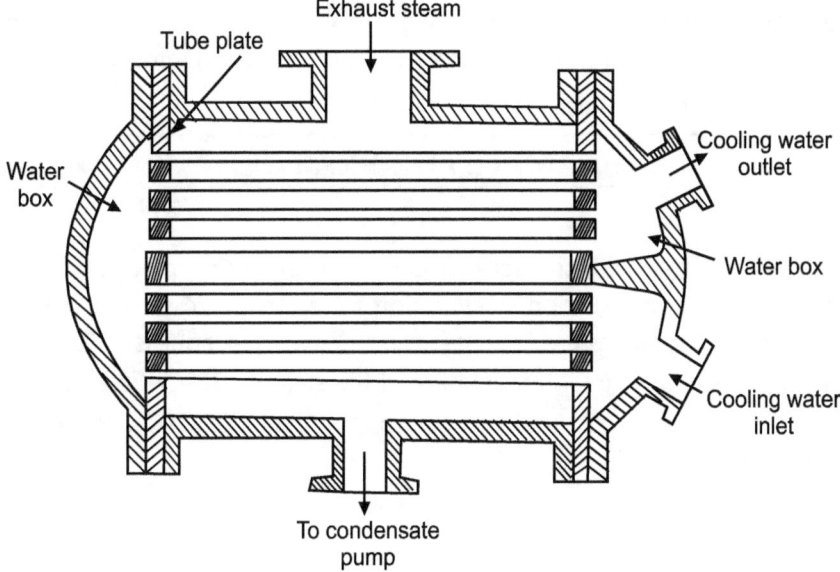

Fig. 4.7 (a)

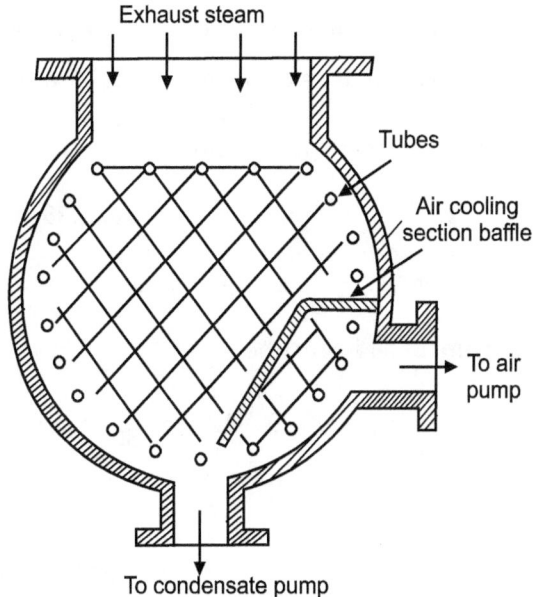

Fig. 4.7 (b)

The salient features of the modern trend in the design of the condenser is to shield the air exit from the downstream of condensate by means of a baffle and thus air is extracted with only a comparatively small amount of water vapour. A section of tubes is screened by the baffle to form an air cooling section as shown in Fig. 4.7 (b). The air cooling section reduces the required capacity of the air pump and the weight of the steam removal by the air pump. See an illustrated example for this.

EXAMPLE FOR PRACTICE

Example :

A surface condenser fitted with separate air and water extraction pumps, has a portion of the tubes near the air pump suction screened off from the steam so that the air is cooled below the condensate temperature. The steam condensed per hour is 2500 kg and the air leakage is 2 kg per hour. The inlet temperature of the steam is 38°C, the temperature at the entrance to the air cooler is 37°C and at the air pump section is 31°C. Assuming a constant vacuum throughout the condenser, find :

(a) the weight of steam condensed in the air cooler per minute,

(b) the volume of air to be dealt with by the air pump per minute.

Solution :

Assume that the steam entering the condenser is dry and saturated.

∴ Partial pressure of steam at 38°C = 0.06624 bar

Specific volume of steam = 21.627 cu.m./kg

∴ Volume of steam per minute = $\dfrac{2500}{60} \times 21.627$

= **901.125 cu.m.**

This is also the volume of air $\left(\dfrac{2}{60} = \dfrac{1}{30} \text{ kg}\right)$ per minute.

If p_a is the partial pressure of air in bar, then,

$$p_a \times 10^5 \times 901.125 = \dfrac{1}{30} \times 287 \times (273 + 38)$$

∴ $p_a = \dfrac{287 \times 311}{901.125 \times 10^5}$

= **0.0009905 bar**

Hence condenser pressure = $p_a + p_s$

= 0.0009905 + 0.06624

= **0.0672305 bar**

At entry to cooler :

Temperature is 37°C.

∴   Partial pressure of steam = 0.06274 bar

∴   Partial pressure of air = 0.0672305 − 0.06274

$$= 0.0044905 \text{ bar}$$

∴   Volume of air per minute $= \dfrac{m_a R_a T_a}{p_a}$

$$= \dfrac{1}{30} \times \dfrac{287 \times 410}{0.0044905 \times 10^5}$$

$$= \mathbf{8.7347 \text{ cu.m./min}}$$

This is also the volume of steam with this air.

∴   Weight of steam associated with this air $= \dfrac{8.7347}{22.763}$

$$= \mathbf{0.3837 \text{ kg/min}}$$

At air pump suction :

Temperature is 31°C.

∴   Partial pressure of steam = 0.04491 bar

∴   Partial pressure of air = 0.0672305 − 0.04491

$$= \mathbf{0.0223205 \text{ bar}}$$

∴   Volume of air per minute $= \dfrac{m_a R_a T_a}{p_a}$

$$= \dfrac{1}{30} \times \dfrac{287 \times 304}{2232.05}$$

$$= \mathbf{1.3030 \text{ cu.m.}} \quad \text{... Ans.}$$

∴   Steam associated with this air $= \dfrac{1.3030}{31.199}$

$$= \mathbf{0.04176 \text{ kg}}$$

∴   Weight of steam condensed in the air cooler per minute

$$= 0.3837 - 0.04176$$

$$= \mathbf{0.34194 \text{ kg}} \quad \text{... Ans.}$$

(b) Central flow type surface condenser :

In this type of condenser, the suction pipe of the air extraction pump is placed in the centre of the tube nest as shown in Fig. 4.7 (c).

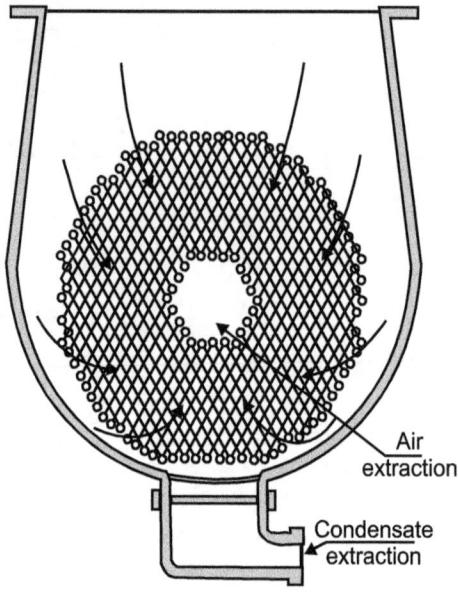

Fig. 4.7 (c)

This causes the condensate to flow radially towards the centre of the tube nest. It then leaves at the bottom where the condensate extraction pump is situated. This method is an improvement on the downward flow type as the steam is directed radially inwards by a volute casing around the tube nest. It has thus access to the whole periphery of the tubes.

(c) Inverted type of surface condenser :

Inverted type of surface condenser has the air suction at the top. The steam enters near the bottom and flows outwards; it then returns to the bottom of the condenser by flowing near the outer surface. The condensate extraction pump is at the bottom.

(d) Regenerative type of surface condenser :

This term is applied to condensers adopting a regenerative method of heating of condensate. After leaving the tube banks the condensate is passed through the entering exhaust steam from the engine or turbine, thus the temperature of the condensate is raised and is used as feed water for the boilers.

4.5.6 Evaporative Condenser

The principle of the evaporative condenser may be explained as shown in Fig. 4.8.

The steam to be condensed enters at the top of series of tubes around which a spray of cold water is falling. At the same time a current of air circulates over the water film formed on the surface of tubes. A natural or forced air current causes rapid evaporation of the water film with the result that the steam flowing through the tubes gets condensed. The vapour of the cooling water passes off with the heated air. The remainder of the cooling water at increased temperature is collected and used again after its temperature is restored to the original value by the addition of the requisite quantity of cold make-up water.

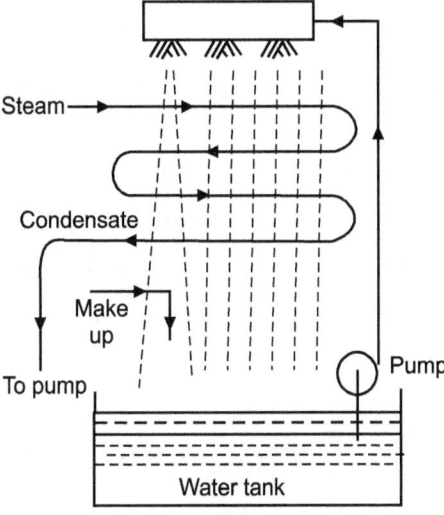

Fig. 4.8

This type of the condenser is restricted to small powers on account of nuisance which would result from the production of cloud in a populated area. It can take overload for a short period without seriously affecting the vacuum.

4.5.7 Comparison of Jet and Surface Condensers

(I) Surface Condensers :

(a) Advantages :
- Vacuum obtained is comparatively high with consequent higher plant efficiency.
- As cooling water does not mix with steam, any water can be used with treating the water.
- Condensate being very pure, it can be used as boiler feed.
- It is more suitable for high power capacity plants.

(b) Disadvantages :
- It requires more space.
- Maintenance is costly.

(II) Jet Condensers :

(a) Advantages :
- Mixing of steam and cooling water is more perfect.
- Requires comparatively less quantity of cooling water.

- The condensing plant is simple and less costly.
- Maintenance is easy and less.
- Condensate extraction pump is eliminated in case of high-level or barometric condensers.

(b) Disadvantages :
- If condensate is to be used, the cooling water should be clean and pure so that it can be used directly in the boiler.
- If water is not pure, condensate is wasted.
- The power required for extraction pumps is comparatively high.
- The high level or barometric condenser has a long pipe and is costly.
- Vacuum in jet condenser seldom exceeds 650 mm of Hg due to liberation of dissolved gases in the cooling water.

4.6 DALTON'S LAW OF PARTIAL PRESSURES AND MIXTURE OF AIR AND WATER VAPOUR

Dalton (1766–1844) demonstrated experimentally the following laws which were known as Dalton's Law of partial pressure. These laws were afterwards verified by Gay-Lussac. The laws are –
- The pressure, and, consequently, the quantity, of vapour which saturates a given space are the same for the same temperature, whether there is or is not any other gaseous substance in the space.
- The pressure of the mixture of a gas and a vapour is equal to the sum of the pressures which each would exert if it occupied the same space, and same temperature, alone.

Here the second law is a consequence of the first and is known as the law of partial pressures. The application of the above laws to condenser and air pump problems is illustrated by the following problems.

SOLVED PROBLEMS

Problem 4.1 :

The vacuum in a condenser is found to be 71.12 cm of Hg (barometer 76 cm of Hg) and the temperature is 30°C. To find the weight of air present per kg of uncondensed steam.

Solution : From the steam tables, 1 kg of steam at 30°C will exert a pressure of 0.04242 bar and have a volume of 32.939 cu.m. The air present per kg of steam will, by Dalton's first law, have a volume of 32.939 cu.m.

THERMAL SCIENCE (S.E. MECH. & AUTO. SEM. III SU)   STEAM CONDENSERS

The combined pressure of air and steam is $76 - 71.12 = 4.88$ cm of Hg or $\dfrac{4.88 \times 1.01325}{76}$
$= 0.0651$ bar. By Dalton's second law, the pressure of the air is $0.06510 - 0.04242 = 0.02268$ bar.

For air, $10^5 \, pv = mRT$

∴ Mass of air associated with 1 kg of steam is given by –

$$m = \dfrac{10^5 \times 0.02268 \times 32.939}{287 \times 303}$$

$$= 0.8591 \text{ kg} \quad \text{... Ans.}$$

Problem 4.2 :

A surface condenser deals with 5000 kg of steam per hour and the air leakage amounts to 2 kg per hour. The temperature of the air pump suction is 35°C and the vacuum is 68.58 cm of Hg (barometer 76 cm of Hg). To determine the discharging capacity of the air pump in cu.m. per minute to remove the air and condensed steam. Assume volumetric efficiency of the air pump to be 80%.

Solution : At 35°C, the pressure of steam is 0.05622 bar.

The combined pressure of air and steam is

$$(76 - 68.58 = 7.42 \text{ cm of Hg} = 0.09893 \text{ bar.})$$

∴   Partial pressure of air $= 0.09893 - 0.05622$

$$= 0.04271 \text{ bar}$$

Weight of air per minute $= \dfrac{2}{60}$ kg

∴ Volume of air per minute $= v$

We have, $10^6 \, p_a v_a = m_a R_a T_a$

$$10^5 \times 0.04271 \times v = \dfrac{2}{60} \times 287 \times 308$$

∴ $v = \dfrac{2}{60} \times \dfrac{287 \times 308}{0.04271 \times 10^5}$

$$= 0.69 \text{ cu.m./min}$$

Again weight of steam condensed per minute $= \dfrac{5000}{60}$ kg

∴ Volume of condensate per minute

$$= \frac{5000}{60} \times \frac{1}{1000} = \frac{5}{60} = \frac{1}{12}$$

$$= 0.0833 \text{ m}^3/\text{min}$$

∴ Theoretical capacity of the air pump

$$= \text{volume of condensate + volume of air}$$

$$= 0.69 + 0.0833$$

$$= 0.7733 \text{ cu.m./min}$$

As the volumetric efficiency of the air pump is 80%, the effective capacity of the air pump

$$= \frac{\text{Theoretical capacity}}{\text{Volumetric efficiency}}$$

$$= \frac{0.7733}{0.8}$$

$$= 0.9667 \text{ cu.m./min.} \quad \text{... Ans.}$$

4.7 CONDENSER VACUUM AND VACUUM EFFICIENCY

The minimum absolute pressure at the steam inlet to a condenser is that corresponding to the temperature of the condensed steam, and the corresponding vacuum is the maximum obtainable in the perfect condensing plant, with no air present, at that temperature. The ratio of the actual vacuum obtained at the steam inlet to the condenser to this maximum vacuum is called the **vacuum efficiency.**

For example, if the temperature of the condensed steam is 36°C, the corresponding absolute pressure of the steam is 0.0594 bar, and the corresponding vacuum for barometer reading as 760 mm of Hg is (1.01325 − 0.0594 = 0.95385 bar = 715.45 mm of Hg). If the actual vacuum at the steam inlet to the condenser is 700 mm of Hg, then the vacuum efficiency will be given as

$$\text{Vacuum efficiency} = \frac{\text{Actual vacuum}}{\text{Maximum vacuum}}$$

$$= \frac{700}{715.45}$$

$$= 0.9784 \text{ or } 97.84\%$$

Condenser Efficiency :

There is no standard method of ascertaining the efficiency of condenser. According to the method adopted by Messrs. C.A. Parsons and Co., the thermal efficiency of a condenser is the ratio of the difference between the outlet and inlet temperatures of the cooling water to the difference between the temperature corresponding to the vacuum in the steam space and the inlet temperature of the cooling water.

For example, let the inlet temperature of the cooling water be 27°C and outlet temperature 37°C, and let the vacuum be 71 cm of Hg with barometer reading 76 cm of Hg.

The absolute pressure corresponding to the vacuum is (76 – 71) i.e. 5 cm of Hg = $\frac{5}{76}$ × 1.01325 = 0.06666 bar pressure, and the corresponding saturation temperature is approximately 38°C.

Hence the condenser efficiency is given as

$$\text{Condenser efficiency} = \frac{37-27}{38-27} = \frac{10}{11} = 0.9091 = \textbf{90.91\%}$$

4.8 SOURCES OF AIR IN CONDENSERS

The air found in condensers comes in –

- with the steam from the boiler in which it enters dissolved in the feed water,
- by leakage from the atmosphere at the various joints of parts which are internally under a pressure less than that of the atmosphere,
- the porous castings used for condensers, and
- in the case of jet condensers, with the injection water in which it is dissolved.

4.9 AIR PUMPS

If non-condensable gases like air are present in the condenser, heat transfer action is very badly or adversely affected. The quantity of air present or the pressure of air is a very serious factor and should be reduced as far as possible. It is practically impossible to get rid off all the air. Therefore, this air is to be removed continuously by air pump by sucking the air from the condenser, then compressing it above the atmospheric pressure and delivering it in the atmosphere.

The presence of air reduces the vacuum in the condenser and obviously the work done is reduced and therefore air removal plays a very important process in maintaining the vacuum in the condenser.

Thus the **primary function** of an air pump is to remove the air which would otherwise accumulate in the condenser and choke it. **Another common but not essential function** of the air pump is to remove the water as well as air from the condenser.

It is becoming increasingly common to have separate pumps for extracting the air and water from a condenser. An air pump which extracts both air and water is called a **Wet Air Pump**. An air pump which extracts only air from a condenser is called a **Dry Pump.**

4.9.1 Types of Air Pumps

Air pumps may be divided into –

(a) **reciprocating** piston or bucket pumps which may be either **wet** or **dry** pumps.

(b) rotary pumps which are generally dry pumps.

(c) water jet pumps which are nearly always wet pumps. and

(d) steam jet pumps which are dry pumps.

(a) Reciprocating Air Pump :

A design of reciprocating air pump, which has been largely used, and which is highly efficient, is the **Edward's air Pump**. This is shown in Fig. 4.9 (a).

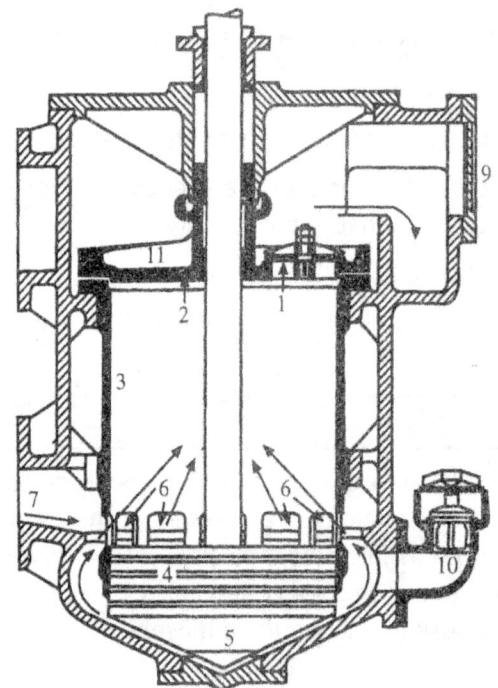

Fig. 4.9 (a)

This pump has no foot or bucket valves and since there is no passage through it the bucket becomes a piston. There are head or delivery valves of which one is shown at 1. These valves are placed in the cover 2, which is on the top of the pump barrel 3. The piston 4 has a conical bottom 5, and the bottom of the pump casing follows the contour of this part of the piston. Circumferential grooves formed on the piston hold water and form a labryinth packing. Ports 6 are made in the barrel near its lower end. Connection with the condenser is made at 7.

During the downward stroke of the piston, a vacuum is produced in the barrel above the piston, the head valves being closed, and as soon as the piston begins to uncover the ports 6, the air and water vapour from the condenser rush into the space above the piston. The conical part of the piston enters the water which has flowed into the bottom of the pump from the condenser and drives it over the lower part of the barrel and through the ports 6. The pump is now charged, and during the up stroke of the piston the charge is expelled through the head valves and then over the weir 8 on its way to the hot-well. The weir 8 ensures a head of water over the head valves so that if there is any leakage through these valves into the barrel it is a leakage of water and not air. The head valves are accessible, even when the pump is working, through the door 9.

The water-sealed relief valve 10 opens to the atmosphere when for any reason the pressure below the piston exceeds the pressure of the atmosphere.

The cover 2 is stiffened by having radial ribs 11 cast on it between the head valves.

(b) Leblanc Rotary Dry Air Pump :

The air pump shown in Fig. 4.9 (b) is invented by Prof. Maurice Leblanc and is a rotary air pump. This is a dry air pump, although it is charged with water for the purpose of its operation.

A cross-section of the pump is shown at (a) and a longitudinal section of the upper half at (b). A wheel or impeller 1, keyed to a shaft, carries a ring of vanes 2 which is overhung. The pump chamber 3, which is inside the ring of vanes is charged with water which escapes through the nozzle 4 on to the vanes. As the wheel revolves, the water from the nozzle is caught up between the vanes and thrown out by the centrifugal force in thin sheets which fly into the collecting cone 5 with a velocity of about 40 m/sec.

These sheets of water become pistons in the collecting cone, and the air from the condenser coming in at 6 is drawn downwards and entrained between the successive sheets of water. After passing through the collecting cone, the air and water enter the diffuser 7, only a portion of which is shown, where the velocity is gradually reduced and the kinetic energy converted into pressure energy, so that by the time the air and water reach the outer end of the diffuser, which is a divergent pipe, the pressure is sufficient to overcome the pressure of the atmosphere, and, if necessary, a head of water in addition.

The discharge takes place into a tank where the air is liberated and the water returns to the pump chamber 3 and is used over and over again.

The shaft carrying the impeller is, generally, most conveniently driven by an electric motor.

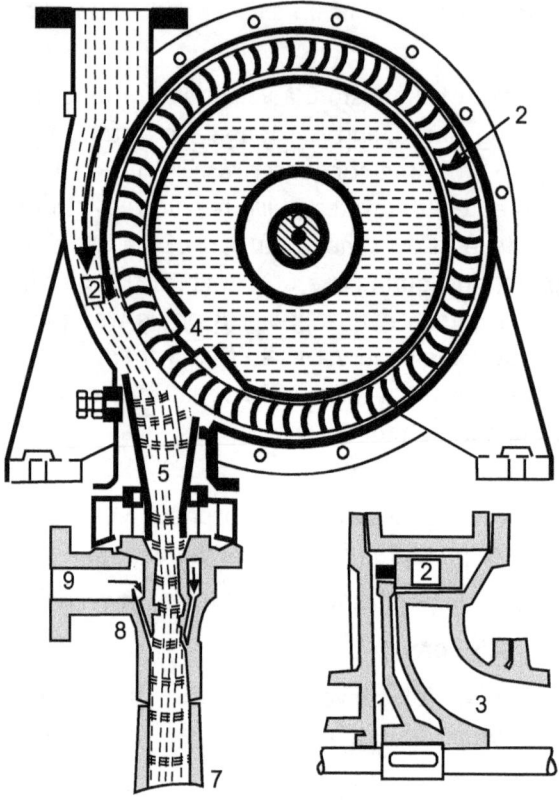

Fig. 4.9 (b)

(d) Steam Jet Ejectors :

Very good results are now obtained by using jets of steam to withdraw the air from the condensers. Although this method is an old one it is only in recent years that it has been perfected. One of the successful applications of this method is found in **Leblanc's Steam air ejector**, as shown in Fig. 4.9 (c).

The moist air from the condenser is drawn in at 1 and then compressed and discharged at not less than atmospheric pressure. The compression takes place in two stages. In the first stage there is one steam nozzle 2 and in the second stage there is a group of nozzles 3. All the steam nozzles are of the de Laval type.

Steam, generally at a pressure of not less than 7 bar enters at 4 and feeds directly the second stage nozzles 3. The steam reaches the first stage nozzle 1 through the pipe 5 in which there is a controlling valve 6.

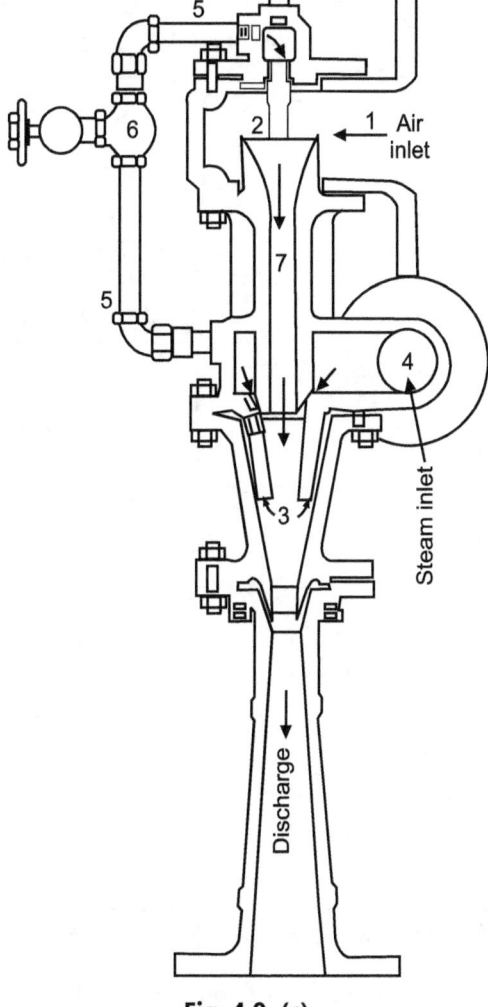

Fig. 4.9. (c)

The steam expanding in the nozzles issues from them with a velocity of from 900 to 1200 metres per second and at a small pressure depending on the vacuum in the condenser. The first stage steam jet inducts the air at 1, mixed and the mixture of steam and air rushes forward into the diffuser 7 where the kinetic energy of the mixture is converted into pressure energy and before reaching the second stage, both air and steam are compressed to about seven times the pressure in the space 1. The further compression required takes place in the second stage, aided by the action of the steam jets from the nozzles 3.

Discharge takes place into the boiler feed tank where the steam is condensed and its heat utilized. The steam air ejector is characterised by extreme simplicity and it occupies a very small space compared with other forms of air pumps.

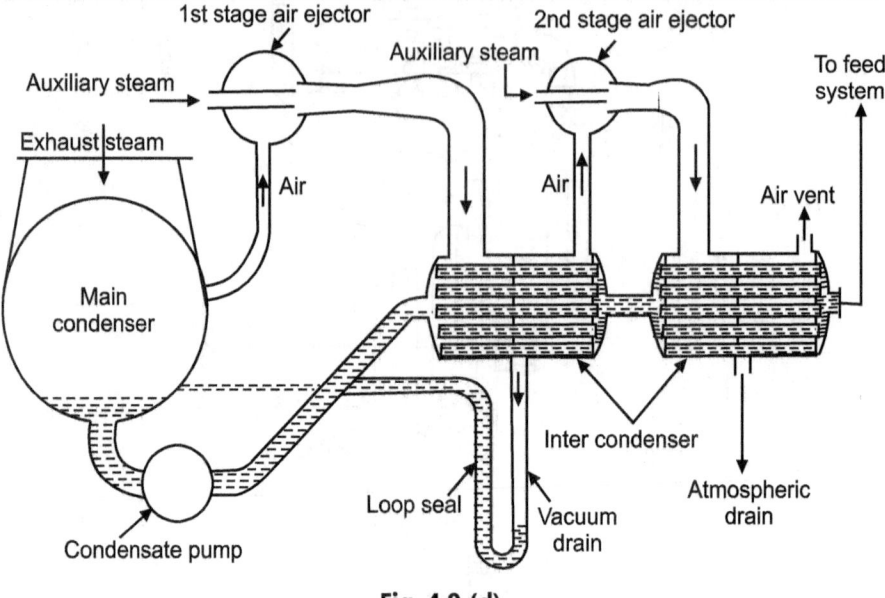

Fig. 4.9 (d)

Fig. 4.9 (d) shows the flow diagram for a two stage air ejector with inter and after condensers. A small surface condenser is placed between the first stage and the second stage to condense steam used to work the first stage of air ejector. This surface condenser is known as inter-condenser. The second stage air ejector takes suction from the inter-condenser shell and discharges to the after-condenser shell.

The working of this air ejector is self explanatory.

4.10 CAPACITY OF AIR EXTRACTION PUMPS

Air extraction capacity of the air pumps can be found out thus –

Let p = Atmospheric pressure

X = Actual vacuum at condenser inlet

From this actual absolute pressure at the condenser inlet can be found. Let it be p_c.

Let t = temperature of steam entering the condenser

From this absolute pressure of steam corresponding to t can be found from steam tables.

Let p_s is pressure of steam if no air is present.

∴ Applying Dalton's Law of partial pressures, we get –

$$\begin{bmatrix} \text{Condenser} \\ \text{absolute pressure} \end{bmatrix} = [\text{Partial pressure of steam + Partial pressure of air}]$$

$$p_c = p_s + p_a$$

∴ p_a = partial pressure of air is found.

Knowing the condition of steam at inlet of the condenser, specific volume of steam can be obtained from steam tables.

Specific volume = $x V_g$ at 't' temperature

= This is also the volume of air associated with 1 kg steam

∴ Knowing the partial pressure of air, temperature and volume of air, we can find the weight of air associated with 1 kg steam entering the condenser.

m_a = mass of air/kg steam

$$= \frac{p_a V_a}{R_a T_a}$$

If Y is the quantity of steam consumption of turbine (kg/hour), then weight of air that has to be handled by the air pump is given by

$$m_a = \frac{p_a V_a}{R_a T_a} \times Y \text{ kg/hour}$$

= Capacity of the air pump

4.11 COOLING TOWERS

The majority of large power plants are built adjacent to rivers where cooling water in large quantities is available. But for many plants the source of cooling water is the local water supply. In such cases, the same water is circulated over and over again. It must be cooled by means of cooling ponds or cooling towers. In cooling ponds method, hot water is discharged into the pond of sufficient area so that water is cooled by the air passing over the surface of the pond. This requires ponds of larger sizes. In order to reduce the area, the water is sprayed into the air over the pond thus increasing the rate of cooling. In this 'spray-ponds', atmosphere round the plant becomes humid which is objectionable. This has led to the development of the cooling tower. In the cooling tower, the water is delivered to the top of the tower and then allowed to drop to a tank below, the water being broken into spray during the fall.

The natural draught and forced draught towers are shown in Fig. 4.10. In natural draught towers, the circulation of air is brought about by the difference in pressure between the air inside and outside the tower. This is exactly identical in principle with the boiler chimney draught. In the forced draught towers, the air circulation depends on the fans placed at the bottom of the tower. In the induced draught tower, the fan and motor is placed at the top of the tower and draws air through the tower.

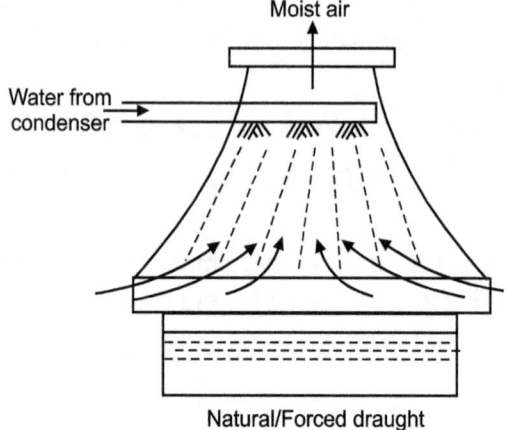

Fig. 4.10

There are three general types of cooling towers that are commonly used.

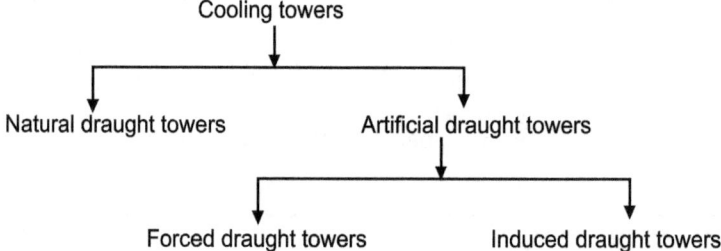

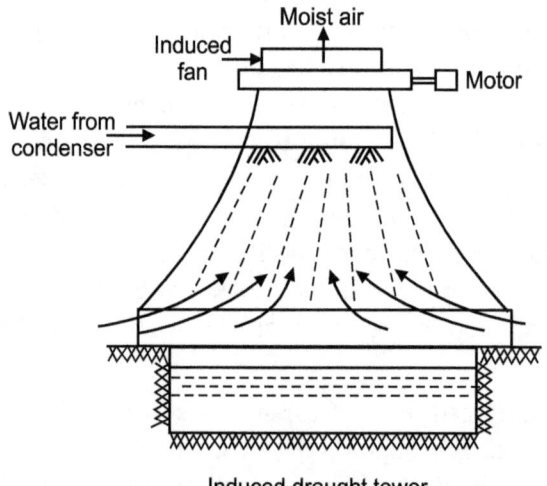

Induced draught tower

Fig. 4.11

This arrangement for induced draught tower is shown in Fig. 4.11. Cooling towers are also, sometimes, classified as Wet towers and Dry towers. Wet towers are those towers where water and air come in contact with each other. While in dry towers, water and air do not come in contact with each other. In this case, water is made to pass through tube coils while air is circulated outside the tube coil.

4.12 COOLING WATER REQUIREMENTS

We have seen that in a condenser the circulating water receives or abstracts heat from the steam to be condensed and the temperature of the circulating water is raised. In a jet condenser as the cooling water and the steam to be condensed come in direct contact, the temperature of the condensate is the same as that of the outlet temperature of the circulating water.

Let m_w be the quantity of circulating water required per kg of steam, t_{w_1} be the temperature of circulating water at inlet and t_{w_2} be the temperature of circulating water at outlet from the condenser.

∴ Heat received by circulating water from 1 kg of steam is given by the relation $W c_{pw} (t_{w_2} - t_{w_1})$ kJ.

If h_i is the total heat or enthalpy of one kg steam entering the condenser and h_{fo} be the heat or enthalpy of condensate leaving the condenser, then we can equate these quantities of heat.

∴ Heat gained by water = Heat lost or given by steam

$$m_w c_{pw} (t_{w_2} - t_{w_1}) = h_i - h_{fo}$$

Generally, the steam entering the condenser is wet and then $h_i = h_{f_i} + x \, h_{fg_i}$ where x is the dryness fraction of steam entering the condenser. From this equation, either quantity of cooling water can be calculated if the condition of steam is given or the condition of steam entering the condenser can be calculated if quantity of circulating water is given. The above equation can be used for both the jet and surface condensers.

The quantity of cooling water per kg of steam entering a surface condenser is more than that used in a jet condenser. The quantity of water used varies from 20 to 60 kg of water per kg of steam and the temperature rise of the circulating cooling water may also vary from 12 to 18°C.

Problem 4.3 :

A steam engine developing 150 kW uses 9.8 kg of steam per kWh. If exhaust steam at a pressure of 0.15 bar (abs), the condensate leaves at 36°C, the cooling water to the condenser enters at 17°C and leaves at 34°C, determine the weight of cooling water used per hour if the dryness fraction of steam is 0.85.

Solution : Let m_w be the amount of circulating water required per kg of steam condensed. Steam pressure is 0.15 bar abs.

$\therefore$ h_i = enthalpy of 1 kg steam entering the condenser

$= h_f + x \, h_{fg}$ [at 0.15 bar]

$= 226 + 0.85 \times 2373.2$

$= 226 + 2017.22$

$= \mathbf{2243.22 \text{ kJ}}$

Enthalpy of condensate at 36°C

$h_o = \mathbf{150.7 \text{ kJ/kg}}$

$\therefore$ Heat gained by water = Heat given by steam

$m_w \times 4.187 \, (34 - 17) = 2243.22 - 150.7$

$m_w \times 71.179 = 2092.52$

or $m_w = \dfrac{2092.52}{71.179}$

$= 29.398 \text{ kg}$

$= \mathbf{29.4}$ ... **Ans.**

$\therefore$ Total circulating water used per hour

$= 29.398 \times$ weight of steam/hr

$= 29.398 \times (150 \times 9.8)$

$= \mathbf{43215 \text{ kg/hr}}$ ... **Ans.**

Problem 4.4 :

In a surface condenser the pressure of steam is 0.12 bar. The rate of cooling water flow is 40 kg/kg of steam condensed. Condensate leaves at 44°C and the rise in temperature of circulating water is 13°C. Determine the dryness fraction of steam entering the condenser.

Solution :

Let x be the dryness fraction of steam.

$\therefore$ Enthalpy of steam entering the condenser is

$h_i = h_f + x \, h_{fg}$ [at 0.12 bar]

$= 206.9 + x \times 2384.3$

Similarly, enthalpy of condensate at 44°C is

$$h_o = 184.2 \text{ kJ/kg}$$

∴ Heat given by 1 kg steam = 206.9 + x × 2384.3 − 184.2

$$= 22.7 + 2384.3 \, x$$

Also, heat received or gained by circulating water per kg steam

$$= m_w \, c_{pw} \, (t_{w_2} - t_{w_1})$$

$$= 40 \times 4.187 \times 13$$

$$= 2177.24 \text{ kJ}$$

∴ Heat lost by steam = Heat gained by water

$$22.7 + 2384.3 \, x = 2177.24$$

$$x = \frac{2177.24 - 22.7}{2384}$$

$$= \frac{2154.54}{2384}$$

$$= 0.90375 \quad \text{... Ans.}$$

Problem 4.5 :

The vacuum in the condenser is 716 mm of Hg when the barometer reads 748 mm of Hg. In another case, the vacuum in the condenser is 705 mm of Hg and barometer reads 754 mm of Hg. Correct these vacuum readings to standard vacuum of 760 mm of Hg.

Solution :

(Remember here that absolute pressure in the condenser remains same.)

Case I :   Vacuum = 716 mm of Hg

and barometer reads 748 mm of Hg.

∴ Absolute pressure = 748 − 716

$$= \textbf{32 mm of Hg}$$

Absolute pressure = Barometer reading − Vacuum

∴ Vacuum in the condenser = Barometer reading − Absolute pressure

$$= 760 - 32$$

$$= \textbf{728 mm of Hg} \quad \text{... Ans.}$$

Case II :   Vacuum = 705 mm of Hg

∴ Absolute pressure = 754 − 705

$$= 49 \text{ mm of Hg}$$
$$= 760 - \text{New Vac}$$
∴ New vacuum $= 760 - 49$
$$= \mathbf{711 \text{ mm of Hg}} \qquad \text{... Ans.}$$

Problem 4.6 :

The vacuum at the steam inlet to a condenser was found to be 716 mm of Hg and the temperature of steam in the condenser is 35°C, when barometer reads 760 mm of Hg. Find the vacuum efficiency.

Solution :

If no air would have present in the condenser, the maximum vacuum pressure or minimum absolute pressure would be corresponding to temperature of 35°C.

∴ Minimum absolute pressure of steam
$$= 0.05622 \text{ bar}$$
$$= \frac{0.05622 \times 760}{1.01325}$$
$$= \mathbf{42.168 \text{ mm of Hg}}$$

∴ Maximum vacuum would be
$$= 760 - 42.168$$
$$= \mathbf{717.832 \text{ mm of Hg}}$$

But actual vacuum in the condenser
$$= 716 \text{ mm of Hg}$$

∴ Vacuum efficiency $= \dfrac{\text{Actual vacuum}}{\text{Max. vacuum}}$
$$= \frac{716}{717.832}$$
$$= \mathbf{0.9974}$$
$$= \mathbf{99.74\%} \qquad \text{... Ans.}$$

Problem 4.7 :

The following particulars relate to a test of the surface condenser of a steam turbine.

Absolute pressure of the exhaust steam entering the condenser was 0.06 bar. Temperature of condensate = 32°C; temperature of circulating water at inlet and outlet = 15°C and 30°C respectively. Weight of cooling water per kg of steam = 32 kg. Assuming no losses, determine the dryness fraction of the steam as it enters the condenser.

Solution :

Heat gained by circulating water through condenser per kg of steam

$$= m_w \times c_{pw} \times \text{Rise in temperature}$$
$$= 32 \times 4.187 \times (30 - 15)$$
$$= \textbf{2009.76 kJ/kg steam}$$

Heat given by steam in the condenser

$$= h_f + x h_{fg} - h_c$$

where, x = Dryness fraction of steam entering the condenser

h_c = enthalpy of 1 kg condensate at 32°C

∴ Heat given by steam

$$= 151.5 + x \times 2416 - 134.02$$
$$= 17.48 + x \times 2416$$

With no losses,

Heat given by steam = Heat gained by water

$$17.48 + 2416 \, x = 2009.76$$
$$x = \textbf{0.8246} \quad \text{... Ans.}$$

Problem 4.8 :

Taking the data of the preceding problem except the final temperature of the cooling water is to be taken to apply to a jet condenser, calculate the weight of injection (cooling) water required per kg of steam.

Solution :

In jet condenser, water mixes with steam and the temperature of water and condensate will be same. Here that temperature is 30°C i.e. the temperature of the condensate is also 30°C.

Let W be the weight of injection water per kg of steam.

∴ Heat gained by water $= W \times 4.187 \times 15$

$$= \textbf{62.805 W kJ}$$

Heat given by 1 kg of steam $= h_f + x \, h_{fg} - h_e$

$$= 151.5 + 0.8246 \times 2416 - 125.66$$
$$= 2018.07$$

$$\therefore \quad W = \frac{2018.07}{62.805}$$

$$= 32.13 \text{ kg/kg steam} \quad \ldots \text{Ans.}$$

Problem 4.9 :

The temperature in a surface condenser is 37.651°C and a vacuum is 700 mm of Hg. Barometer reads 755.2 mm of Hg. Correct the vacuum to a standard barometer of 760 mm of Hg and hence determine (1) The partial pressure of steam and air. (2) Weight of air associated with 1 kg of steam.

Solution : (1) Partial pressure of steam and air :

$$\text{Absolute pressure} = 755.2 - 700 = 55.2 \text{ mm of Hg}$$

For standard barometer of 760 mm of Hg,

$$\text{Absolute pressure} = \text{Barometer reading} - \text{Vacuum (New)}$$

$$55.2 = 760 - \text{New vacuum}$$

$\therefore$ New vacuum for standard barometer

$$= 760 - 55.2$$

$$= \textbf{704.8 mm of Hg} \quad \ldots \text{Ans.}$$

Absolute steam pressure at 37.651°C is 0.065 bar (with no air present).

$$\text{Total pressure in condenser} = \frac{55.2 \times 1.03125}{760}$$

$$= \textbf{0.0736 bar}$$

$$= p_a + p_s$$

$\therefore$ Partial pressure of steam = **0.065 bar** ... Ans.

$$\text{Partial pressure of air} = 0.0736 - 0.065$$

$$= \textbf{0.0086 bar} \quad \ldots \text{Ans.}$$

(2) Weight of air/kg of steam : Assuming dryness fraction of steam entering the condenser as 1, the volume of 1 kg steam entering the condenser is **22.016 m³**. This is also the volume of air associated with 1 kg of steam.

$$\therefore \quad \text{Weight of air} = \frac{p_a V_a}{R_a T_a}$$

$$= \frac{10^5 \times 0.0086 \times 22.016}{287 \times 310.651}$$

$$= \textbf{0.2124 kg/kg steam} \quad \ldots \text{Ans.}$$

Problem 4.10 :

Steam enters a condenser at a temperature of 36.183°C and the barometer stands at 749 mm of Hg. A vacuum of 703 mm of Hg was produced. Determine the vacuum efficiency.

Solution :

Minimum absolute pressure in the condenser with no air is corresponding to steam temperature of 36.183°C and is 0.06 bar.

$$\therefore \quad 0.06 \text{ bar} = 45 \text{ mm of Hg}$$

$$\therefore \quad \text{Maximum vacuum} = 749 - 45$$
$$= 704 \text{ mm of Hg}$$

$$\text{Actual vacuum} = 703 \text{ mm of Hg}$$

$$\therefore \quad \text{Vacuum efficiency} = \frac{\text{Actual vacuum}}{\text{Maximum vacuum}}$$

$$= \frac{703}{704}$$

$$= \mathbf{0.9986} \quad \text{... Ans.}$$

$$\text{or} = \mathbf{99.86\%}$$

Problem 4.11 :

The following data were obtained from a test of a surface condenser :
Inlet temperature of circulating water = 21°C
Outlet temperature of circulating water = 35°C
Vacuum in the condenser = 704.7 mm of Hg
Barometer reading = 760 mm of Hg
Compute the efficiency of the condenser.

Solution :

$$\text{Absolute pressure of steam} = 760 - 704.7$$
$$= 55.3 \text{ mm of Hg}$$
$$= \mathbf{0.07373 \text{ bar}}$$

Saturation temperature at this pressure is 40°C.

$$\therefore \quad \text{Condenser efficiency} = \frac{\text{Actual rise in temperature of water}}{\text{Maximum rise in temperature of water}}$$

$$= \frac{35 - 21}{40 - 21}$$

$$= \frac{14}{19} = 0.7368 = \mathbf{73.68\%} \quad \text{... Ans.}$$

Problem 4.12 :

Exhaust steam having a dryness fraction of 0.85 enters a surface condenser at a pressure of 0.1 bar and is condensed to water at 38°C. The circulating water enters at 15°C and leaves at 30°C. Calculate the weight of circulating water required per kg of steam.

Solution :

Heat gained by circulating water/kg of steam

$$= m_w \times c_{pw} \times (t_o - t_i)$$
$$= m_w \times 4.187 \times (30 - 15)$$
$$= 62.885 \, m_w$$

Considering the pressure of steam entering the condenser as absolute pressure of 0.1 bar,

Heat given by 1 kg steam $= h_f + x h_{fg} - h_c$
$$= 191.83 + 0.85 \times 2392.9 - 159.09$$
$$= 2066.705 \text{ kJ}$$

∴ Assuming that there are no losses, we have

$$m_w \times 62.885 = 2066.705$$

$$m_w = \frac{2066.705}{62.885}$$

$$= 32.865 \text{ kg} \quad \text{... Ans.}$$

Mass of circulating water required per kg of steam is **32.865 kg.**

Problem 4.13 :

In a particular steam power plant air is believed to leak into the condenser. To check whether this is so, the plant is run until the conditions are steady and then the steam supply from the engine is shut off; simultaneously the air and condensate extraction pumps are closed down, so that the condenser is isolated. At shut down, the temperature and vacuum are observed to be 38°C and 703 mm of Hg respectively. After five minutes, these values were 26°C and 483 mm of Hg. The effective volume of the condenser is 0.57 cu.m.

Determine from these data, the weight of air leakage into the condenser during observed period. Assume R = 287 N-m/kg-°C for air.

Solution : Initially

Partial pressure of steam corresponding to **38°C** is **0.06624** bar.

Condenser absolute pressure = 757 – 703 = 54 mm of Hg

= **0.07199 bar**

∴ Partial pressure of air = 0.07199 − 0.06624

= **0.00575 bar**

∴ Weight of air present = $\dfrac{10^5 \times 0.00575 \times 0.57}{287 \times 311}$

= **0.003672 kg**

After 5 minutes :

Steam pressure corresponding to 26°C = **0.03360 bar**

Condenser pressure = 757 − 483 = **274 mm of Hg**

= $\dfrac{274 \times 1.01325}{760}$ bar

= **0.3653 bar**

∴ Partial pressure of air = 0.3653 − 0.0336

= **0.3317 bar**

∴ Mass of air present = $\dfrac{0.3317 \times 10^5 \times 0.57}{287 \times 299}$

= **0.2203 kg**

∴ Mass of air leaked = 0.2203 − 0.003672

= **0.216628 kg** ... Ans.

Problem 4.14 :

The temperature of the steam entering the surface condenser is 46°C and the temperature of the air pump suction is 42°C. The barometer reading is 752 mm of Hg. Find : (a) the condenser vacuum and (b) the vapour pressure and air pressure near to the air pump suction. If the effective capacity of the air pump on the suction stroke is 11 m³/min, find : (i) the weight of air entering the condenser per minute, and (ii) the weight of steam carried over per minute in the air discharged from the air pump.

Assume that the air pump deals with moist air only and not with the condensate.

Solution : (a) Condenser vacuum :

Absolute partial pressure of steam at condenser inlet temperature of 46°C is **0.10086** bar i.e. **75.65** mm of Hg.

∴ Condenser vacuum = 752 − 75.65

= **676.35 mm of Hg** ... Ans.

(b) Air pump suction :

Partial vapour pressure at 42°C = 0.08198 bar

∴ Partial air pressure = 0.10086 − 0.08198

= 0.01888 bar ... **Ans.**

(i) Weight of air/min.

$$\text{Wt. of air entering the condenser per minute} = \frac{p_a V_a}{R_a T_a}$$

$$= \frac{10^5 \times 0.01888 \times 11}{287 \times 315}$$

= **0.2297 kg/min** ... **Ans.**

(ii) Weight of vapour carried over :

Volume of steam = Volume of air

= **11 cu.m./min.**

Assuming steam to be dry and saturated at the suction of air pump, specific volume of steam at 42°C = **17.59 m³/kg.**

∴ Weight of vapour carried over per minute in the air discharged from the air pump

$$= \frac{11}{17.59} = \textbf{0.6253 kg/min} \qquad \ldots \textbf{Ans.}$$

Problem 4.15 :

In a condenser a vacuum of 68.5 cm of Hg was obtained with the barometer reading 75 cm of Hg. The temperature of condenser was 35°C and 19.6 kg of steam was condensed per minute; 532 kg of cooling water was circulated per minute and its temperature rise was 20°C; the temperature of hot well was 29°C. Calculate :

(i) Weight of air per cu.m. of condenser.

(ii) Condition of steam entering the condenser.

(iii) Vacuum efficiency.   [P.U. 1965]

Solution : (i) Weight of air/cu.m. of condenser :

With no air present in the condenser, the minimum absolute pressure of steam entering the condenser would be pressure corresponding to temperature of 35°C.

∴ Absolute pressure of steam = **0.05622 bar**

Actual vacuum produced = 68.5 cm of Hg

∴ Absolute pressure in condenser = 75 − 68.5 = 6.5 cm of Hg

$$= \frac{6.5 \times 1.01325}{76} \text{ bar}$$

$$= \mathbf{0.08666 \text{ bar}}$$

∴ Partial pressure of air in condenser

$$= 0.08666 - 0.05622$$

$$= \mathbf{0.03044 \text{ bar}}$$

∴ Weight of air/cu.m. of condenser

$$= \frac{p_a V_a}{R_a T_a} = \frac{0.03044 \times 10^5 \times 1}{287 \times 308}$$

$$= \mathbf{0.03444 \text{ kg}} \qquad \text{... Ans.}$$

(ii) Condition of steam entering the condenser :

Let x be the dryness fraction of steam entering the condenser.

Heat gained by circulating water/min

$$= m_w \, c_{pw} \, (t_2 - t_1)$$

$$= 532.0 \times 4.187 \times 20$$

$$= \mathbf{44549.7 \text{ kJ}}$$

Heat given by steam in condensing

$$= (h_f + x h_{fg} - h_c) \times \text{weight of steam condensed/min}$$

$$= 19.6 \, [146.56 + x \times 2418.8 - 121.48]$$

$$= 19.6 \, [25.08 + 2418.8x]$$

Neglecting any loss of heat, we have

Heat gained by water = Heat lost by steam

$$44549.7 = 19.6 \, [25.08 + 2418.8x]$$

$$2418.8x = \frac{44549.7}{19.6} - 25.08$$

$$= 2247.86$$

$$x = \mathbf{0.9293} \qquad \text{... Ans.}$$

(iii) Vacuum efficiency :

Maximum vacuum that can be obtained is

$$= 75 - \frac{76 \times 0.05622}{1.01325}$$

$$= 75 - 4.2168$$

$$= \mathbf{70.7832 \text{ cm of Hg}}$$

Actual vacuum produced = 68.5 cm of Hg

∴ Vacuum efficiency = $\dfrac{\text{Actual vacuum}}{\text{Maximum vacuum}}$

$$= \frac{68.5}{70.7832}$$

$$= \mathbf{0.9677 \text{ or } 96.77\%} \qquad \text{... Ans.}$$

Problem 4.16 :

The temperature of steam entering a condenser is 50°C with the barometer at 76 cm of Hg. The vacuum throughout the condenser is 66 cm of Hg. The condenser requires 30 kg of circulating water per kg of steam condensed when the rise of temperature is 18°C. Condensate temperature is 47°C. The air pump suction is screened off and the suction temperature is 45°C. Volume of air at 76 cm of Hg and 0°C is 0.774 m³/kg.

Determine : (i) Condition of steam entering the condenser.

    (ii) Weight of air per kg of steam.

    (iii) Air pump capacity assuming separate air pump.

Solution : (i) Condition of steam :

Let x be the dryness fraction of steam entering the condenser.

Heat given by 1 kg steam at 50°C $= (h_f + x h_{fg} - h_c)$

$$= 209.26 + x \times 2382.9 - 196.71 \text{ at } 47°C$$

$$= 12.55 + 2382.9 \, x \text{ kJ/kg}$$

Heat gained by circulating water /kg steam

$$= m_w \, c_{pw} \text{ (Rise in temperature)}$$

$$= 30 \times 4.187 \times 18 = \mathbf{2260.98 \text{ kJ/kg steam}}$$

Neglecting any loss of heat due to radiation etc. we have,

    Heat gained by water = Heat lost by steam

∴ $2260.98 = 12.55 + 2382.9 \, x$

    $x = 0.9436$

$$= \mathbf{94.36\%} \qquad \text{... Ans.}$$

(ii) Weight of air per kg of steam :

Specific volume of dry steam at

Condenser pressure = 12.05 cu.m. at 50°C

Dryness fraction of steam = 0.9436

∴ Volume of 1 kg steam = 0.9436 × 12.05

= **11.37 cu.m.**

By Dalton's law, this is also the volume of air accompanying the steam = 11.37 cu.m.

As the pump suction is screened off, the temperature of air and the vapours accompanying the air is 45°C.

∴ Steam pressure corresponding to 45°C = 0.09582 bar

Actual condenser absolute pressure

$$= 76 - 66 = 10 \text{ cm of Hg}$$

$$= \frac{1.01325 \times 10}{76} = \mathbf{0.1333 \text{ bar}}$$

∴ Partial pressure of air = 0.1333 − 0.09582

= **0.03748 bar**

∴ Weight of air/kg steam $= \dfrac{p_a V_a}{R_a T_a} = \dfrac{0.03748 \times 10^5 \times 11.37}{287 \times 318}$

= **0.4669 kg** ... Ans.

(iii) Air pump capacity :

Air pump capacity assuming separate air pump = **11.37 m³/kg of steam** ... Ans.

Problem 4.17 :

A surface condenser maintains a vacuum of 72 cm of mercury, barometer 76.6 cm of Hg, and deals with 318 kg of steam per minute, which on entering the condenser is 0.87 dry. The air leakage into the system is at the rate of 0.4 kg per 1000 kg of steam. The condensate temperature is 30°C. The circulating water undergoes a rise of 20°C. Determine the weights per minute to be dealt with, respectively, by the dry air pump and the circulation pump.

Solution :

Assuming no undercooling, the temperature of condensate and the temperature of steam entering the condenser are same i.e. 30°C.

∴ Pressure of steam corresponding to the condensate temperature of 30°C is 0.04241 bar.

	Actual vacuum pressure	= 72 cm of Hg
∴	Absolute pressure	= 76.6 – 72
		= 4.6 cm of Hg
		= **0.06133**
∴	Partial pressure of air	= 0.06133 – 0.04241 bar
		= **0.01892 bar**
	Weight of air leakage	$= \dfrac{318}{1000} \times 0.4$
		= **0.1272 kg/min**

∴ Volume of air leakage/min $= \dfrac{m_a R_a T_a}{p_a} = \dfrac{0.1272 \times 287 \times 303}{0.01892 \times 10^5}$

= **5.8464 m³/min**

∴ Capacity of air pump = **5.8464 m³/min** ... Ans.

For finding the weight of circulating water required, we have

Heat gained by circulating water = Heat lost by steam

$m_w \times c_{pw} (t_2 - t_1) = m(h_f + x h_{fg} - h_c)$

$m_w \times 4.187 \times 20 = 318 [125.66 + 0.87 \times 2430.7 - 125.66]$

$83.74\, m_w = 672477.46$

∴ m_w = weight of circulating water/min

$= \dfrac{672477.46}{83.74}$

= **8030.54 kg/min**

= **8.03054 m³/min**

∴ Capacity of the water circulating pump = **8.03054 cu.m./min** ... Ans.

Problem 4.18:

A jet condenser has to condense 910 kg of steam per hour. The quantity of injected water used is 31800 kg/hour and its initial temperature is 24°C. The volume of air, at atmospheric pressure, dissolved in injection water is 4% of the volume of injection water. The air which comes in with the steam and leaks into the condenser amounts to 0.5 kg/1000 kg of steam. The vacuum in the air pump suction is 63.25 cm of Hg with barometer reading 76 cm of Hg, and the temperature of the condensate is 45°C. Determine the suction capacity in cu.m. per minute to remove air and water from the condenser. Assume volumetric efficiency of the air pump is 80%.

Solution :

Condenser pressure (absolute) = 76 − 63.25

= 12.75 cm of Hg

= **0.16999 bar**

The absolute pressure of steam (partial) corresponding to the condensate temperature of 45°C is **0.09582 bar**.

∴ Partial pressure of air, p_a = 0.16999 − 0.09582

= **0.07417 bar**

Volume of condensate/min = $\dfrac{910}{60} \times \dfrac{1}{1000}$ = **0.01517 cu.m./min**

Volume of injected water/min = $\dfrac{31800}{60 \times 1000} = \dfrac{318}{600}$ = **0.53 m³/min**

Volume of air dissolved in injection water = 0.04 × 0.53 = **0.0212 cu.m./min.**

This air is at 24°C and 1.01325 bar.

∴ Volume of air present in injection water at condenser pressure and temperature is given by

$$\dfrac{p_1 V_1}{T_1} = \dfrac{p_2 V_2}{T_2} = \dfrac{1.01325 \times 10^5 \times 0.0212}{297}$$

∴ $V_1 = \dfrac{45 + 273}{297} \times \dfrac{1.01325 \times 10^5 \times 0.0212}{0.07417 \times 10^5}$

= **0.31 cu.m.**

From the pressure and temperature of air in the steam and leakage, the volume of the air per minute is found from the relation

$$pV = mRT$$

$$V = \dfrac{mRT}{p}$$

$$= \left(\dfrac{0.5}{1000} \times \dfrac{910}{60}\right) \times \dfrac{287 \times 318}{0.07417 \times 10^5}$$

= 0.007583 × 12.305

= **0.09331 cu.m.**

∴ Total volume to be discharged from the condenser

$$= 0.01517 + 0.53 + 0.31 + 0.09331$$

$$= \textbf{0.94848 cu.m.}$$

This is the actual volume dealt with by the air pump. But the volumetric efficiency of the air pump is given as 0.8.

∴ Capacity of the air pump $= \dfrac{0.94848}{0.8}$

$$= \textbf{1.1856 cu.m./min} \qquad \text{... Ans.}$$

Example 4.19 :

A vacuum of 700 mm of Hg was maintained in a condenser when barometer reads 754 mm of Hg. The mean temperature in the condenser is 22°C. Determine the vacuum efficiency and mass of air associated with 1 kg of steam.

Solution :

Minimum absolute pressure that can be produced at 22°C is 0.02642 bar

$$\left(= \dfrac{760 \times 0.02642}{1.01325} = 19.82 \text{ mm Hg}\right)$$

∴ Maximum vacuum that can be produced at 22°C

$$= 754 - 19.82$$

$$= \textbf{734.18 mm of Hg}$$

Actual vacuum produced $= 700$ mm Hg

∴ Vacuum efficiency $= \dfrac{\text{Actual vacuum}}{\text{Theoretical vacuum}}$

$$= \dfrac{700}{734.18}$$

$$= \textbf{0.9534} \qquad \text{... Ans.}$$

$$= \textbf{95.34\%} \qquad \text{... Ans.}$$

Assuming steam to be dry and saturated,

Volume of 1 kg steam $=$ Volume of air associated with steam

$$= \textbf{51.492 cu.m.}$$

Actual absolute pressure $= 754 - 700 = 54$ mm of Hg

$$= \dfrac{54 \times 1.01325}{760} \text{ bar}$$

$$= 0.071994 = p_a + p_s$$

∴ $\quad p_a = 0.071994 - 0.02642$

$$= \mathbf{0.045574 \text{ bar}}$$

∴ Amount of air associated with 1 kg of steam

$$m_a = \frac{p_a V_a}{R_a T_a} = \frac{10^5 \times 0.045574 \times 51.492}{287 \times 295}$$

$$= \mathbf{2.7717 \text{ kg}} \qquad \text{... Ans.}$$

Problem 4.20 :

The following observations were recorded during a test on a steam condenser.

Barometer reading – 765 mm Hg

Condenser vacuum – 710 mm Hg

Mean condenser temperature – 35°C

Temperature of Hot well – 28°C

Condensate collected – 2000 kg/hr

Cooling water circulated – 60,000 kg/hr

Temperature of cooling water at inlet – 14°C

Temperature of cooling water at outlet – 30°C

Determine :
1. Vacuum corrected to standard barometric pressure of 760 mm Hg.
2. Quality of steam entering the condenser.
3. Condenser efficiency.
4. Mass of air present per kg of steam.

Solution :

1. Corrected vacuum :

$\quad$ Condenser absolute pressure $= 765 - 710$

$$= 55 \text{ mm Hg}$$

$$= 760 - \text{corrected vacuum}$$

∴ $\quad$ Corrected vacuum $= 760 - 55$

$$= \mathbf{705 \text{ mm Hg}} \qquad \text{... Ans.}$$

2. Quality of steam :

Heat lost by steam = Heat gained by cooling water

$2000 [h_f + x h_{fg} - c_{pw} t_w] = 60000 \times c_{pw} [t_{c_2} - t_{c_1}]$

$(146.6 + x \times 2418.8 - 117.3) = 30 \times 4.187 [30 - 14]$

$2418.8x + 29.3 = 125.61 \times 16 = 2009.76$

$$x = \frac{2009.76 - 29.3}{2418.8}$$

$$= \frac{1980.46}{2418.8}$$

$$= 0.819 \qquad \text{... Ans.}$$

3. Condenser efficiency :

$$\text{Condenser efficiency} = \frac{\text{Temperature rise of cooling water}}{\text{(Condenser temperature)} - \text{(Inlet of cooling water)}}$$

$$= \frac{16}{35 - 14} = \frac{16}{21}$$

$$= 0.762 \qquad \text{... Ans.}$$

4. Mass of air present/kg steam :

Absolute pressure of steam when no air is present = **0.05622 bar.**

Actual absolute pressure = 55 mm Hg

= **0.07333 bar**

= $p_s + p_a$

$\therefore \quad p_a = 0.07333 - 0.05622$

= 0.01711 bar = partial pressure of air

$V_a = V_s = x V_g = 0.819 \times 25.245$

$\therefore \quad m_a = \dfrac{p_a V_a}{R_a T_a} = \dfrac{10^5 \times 0.01711 \times 0.819 \times 25.245}{287 \times 308}$

= **0.4 kg** ... Ans.

Problem 4.21 :

A barometric jet condenser handles 5000 kg of 0.9 dry steam per hour, and maintains a vacuum of 630 mm Hg when barometer reads 750 mm of Hg. The cooling water enters the condenser at 16°C and the mixture of condensate and cooling water leaves at 44°C. Find the minimum height of the tail pipe above the hot-well and the cooling water circulated in kg/hour.

Solution : Absolute pressure in the condenser = 750 – 630 = 120 mm Hg

$$= 0.16 \text{ bar}$$

∴ Heat gained by cooling water = Heat given by steam

$$m_w \times c_{pw} (t_{out} - t_{in})_w = m_s [(h_f + x \, h_{fg})_{0.16 \text{ bar}} - (h_f)_{44°C}]$$

$$m_w \times 4.187 (44 - 16) = 5000 [231.6 + 0.9 \times 2370 - 184.2]$$

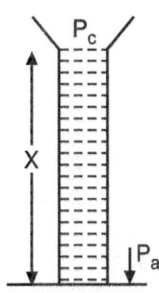

Fig. 4.12

$$m_w = \text{cooling water/hour}$$

$$= \frac{5000 [231.6 + 2133 - 184.2]}{4.187 \times 28}$$

$$= \frac{5000 \times 2180.4}{4.187 \times 28}$$

$$= \textbf{92992 kg/hour} \quad \text{... Ans.}$$

Let $\quad x = $ height of tail pipe necessary

$\rho_w = $ Density of mixture (condensate & cooling water)

$$= 1000 \text{ kg/m}^3$$

∴ $\quad p_a = p_c + \rho_w x$

∴ $\quad p_a - p_c = 1.01325 - 0.16 = \textbf{0.85325 bar}$

$$= g_0 \, \rho_w \times \left[\frac{kg}{m^3} \times m = \frac{kg}{m^2} \right]$$

∴ $\quad x = \dfrac{0.85325 \text{ (bar)} \times 10^{-5}}{1000 \times 9.81}$

$$= \textbf{8.7 m} \quad \text{... Ans.}$$

Problem 4.22 :

A steam turbine has a steam-flow rate of 10,000 kg/hr. Steam enters the surface condenser at 40°C and 0.85 dryness. Air leakage is 30 kg/hr.

The condensate is at 30°C. Find –

   (i) the **quantity** of cooling water circulated, if the rise in temperature is 10°C, in **kg/min**.

   (ii) the capacity of the wet air pump in m³/min.

State the assumptions made if any.

Solution :

1. Quantity of water :

Enthalpy of 1 kg steam entering the condenser

$$= 167.5 + 0.85 \times 2406.9$$
$$= 167.5 + 2045.87$$
$$= \mathbf{2213.37 \text{ kJ/kg}}$$

∴ Heat lost by steam per min = Heat gained by water in min.

$$\frac{10000}{60} \times [2213.37 - 4.187 \times 30125.61] = W_w \times (4.187 \times 10)$$

$$\frac{1000}{6} [2088.76] = W_w \times 4.187 \times 10$$

W_w = Weight of water circulated/min

$$= \frac{1000}{6} \times \frac{2088.76}{41.87}$$

$$= \mathbf{8314.5 \text{ kg/min}} \qquad \ldots \text{Ans.}$$

2. Capacity of air pump (wet) :

At inlet to the air pump (wet), the temperature of condensate is 30°C.

p_s = partial pressure of steam at 30°C

$$= \mathbf{0.04242 \text{ bar}}$$

At inlet to condenser –

$t = 40°C \quad \therefore p_s = 0.07375 \text{ bar}$

$V_g = 19.546 \text{ m}^3/\text{kg}$

∴ Volume of steam at inlet/hour = 19.546 × 10000 = **195460 cu.m./hr.**

= Volume of air/hr

∴ $p_a = \dfrac{m_a R_a T_a}{V_a} = \dfrac{30 \times 287 \times 313}{195460}$

= 13.79 N/m²

= **0.0001379 bar**

∴ Total condenser pressure = 0.07375 + 0.0001379

= **0.07389 bar**

∴ Partial pressure of air at air pump inlet

= 0.07389 − 0.04242

= **0.03147 bar**

∴ Volume of air dealt with by air pump

$= \dfrac{m_a R_a T_a}{p_a} = \dfrac{30 \times 287 \times 303}{0.03147 \times 10^5}$

= **828.99 m³/hour**

Volume of condensate dealt with by air pump = $\dfrac{10000}{1000}$ = **10 cu.m./hr.**

∴ The total capacity of the wet air pump = 828.99 + 10 = **838.99 m³/hr.**

≈ **839 cu.m./hr.** ... Ans.

Example 4.23 :

Dry steam is condensed at a rate of 6800 kg/hour and the air leakage amounts to 12 kg/hr. The air pump suction is screened off. The exhaust steam temperature is 32°C. The condensate temperature is 30°C and the temperature at the air pump suction is 25°C.

Determine :

(i) The mass of steam condensed in the air cooler suction per hour,

(ii) The volume of air handled by the pump, and

(iii) The percentage reduction in the air pump capacity due to cooling of air.

Solution : p_s = partial pressure of steam at 32°C at inlet to condensate.

= **0.04753 bar**

V_g = 29.572 cu.m./kg (dry and sat. steam)

∴ Volume of steam at inlet/hour

$= 6800 \times 29.572$

$= \mathbf{201089.6 \text{ cu.m./hr.}}$

$= $ Volume of air/hour

∴ Partial pressure of air at inlet

$$p_a = \frac{m_a \cdot R_a T_a}{V_a} = \frac{12 \times 287 \times 305}{201089.6}$$

$= 5.2236 \text{ N/m}^2 = \mathbf{0.000052236 \text{ bar}}$

∴ Total pressure (absolute) in condenser

$= p_s + p_a = 0.04753 + 0.000052236$

$= \mathbf{0.04758 \text{ bar}}$

At air pump suction, t = 25°C

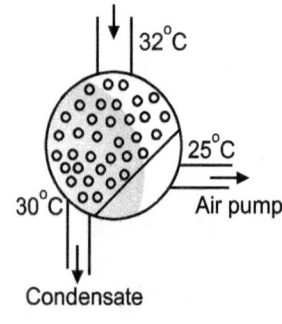

Fig. 4.13

$p_s = $ partial pressure of steam

$= 0.03166 \text{ bar}$

$V_g = 43.402 \text{ m}^3/\text{kg at 25°C}$

$p_a = $ partial pressure of air at air pump suction

$= 0.04758 - 0.03166$

$= \mathbf{0.01592 \text{ bar}}$

$V_a = $ Volume of air/hr at air pump inlet

$$= \frac{12 \times 287 \times 298}{10^5 \times 0.01592}$$

$= \mathbf{644.7 \text{ cu.m./hour}}$

$= $ steam volume/hour

∴ Weight of steam at air pump inlet

$$= \frac{644.7}{43.402} = \mathbf{14.853 \text{ kg/hr}}$$

$p_s = $ steam partial pressure at 30°C

$= 0.04242 \text{ bar}$

$V_g = 32.929 \text{ m}^3/\text{kg}$

$p_a = $ partial pressure of air

∴

= 0.04758 − 0.04242 = **0.00516 bar**

$$V_a = \frac{12 \times 287 \times 303}{0.00516 \times 10^5} = \mathbf{2022.35 \text{ cu.m./hr}}$$

and mass of steam $= \dfrac{2022.35}{32.929} = \mathbf{61.42 \text{ kg/hour}}$

1. Mass of steam condensed in cooler section

   = 61.42 − 14.853

   = **46.567 kg/hr** ... Ans.

2. The volume of air handled by the pump

   = **644.7 cu.m./hr** ... Ans.

3. Percentage reduction in the air pump capacity due to cooling of air

   $= \dfrac{2022.35 - 644.7}{2022.35} \times 100$

   = **68.12%** ... Ans.

Problem 4.24 :

Following readings were noted during a trial on a surface condenser. Condenser vacuum = 70 cm Hg. Barometer reading = 76.5 cm Hg. Mean temperature of condenser = 35°C. Hot well temperature = 28°C, mass of condensate collected = 1800 kg/hr. Air leakage = 1 kg per 1000 kg of steam, cooling water used = 44.5 kg/kg of steam condensed.

Temperature rise of cooling water = 12°C

Inlet temperature of cooling water = 15°C

Calculate : (i) Vacuum efficiency.

(ii) Condenser efficiency.

(iii) Quality of steam entering the condenser.

(iv) Capacity of wet extraction pump in m³/min.

Solution : (i) Vacuum efficiency :

Minimum absolute pressure of steam at 35°C (in absence of air)

= 0.05622 bar

= **4.217 cm Hg**

∴ Maximum vacuum = 76.5 − 4.217

= **72.283 cm Hg**

Actual vacuum = 70 cm Hg

∴ Vacuum efficiency = $\dfrac{\text{Actual vacuum}}{\text{Maximum vacuum}}$

$= \dfrac{70}{72.283} = 0.9684 = $ **96.84%** ... Ans.

(ii) Condenser efficiency :

Condenser efficiency = $\dfrac{\text{Act. rise in temp. of cooling water}}{\text{Max. possible temp. rise}}$

$\dfrac{t_2 - t_1}{t_c - t_1} = \dfrac{12}{35 - 15} = \dfrac{12}{20}$

= **0.6 or 60%** ... Ans.

(iii) Quality of steam entering the condenser :

We have,

Heat gained by water = Heat given by steam

$44.5 \times 4.187 \times 12 = h_f + x\, h_{fg} - 4.187 \times 28$

$2235.86 = 146.6 + x \times 2418.8 - 117.236$

$= 129.364 + 2418.8\, x$

$x = \dfrac{2235.86 - 129.364}{2418.8} = \dfrac{2106.496}{2418.8}$

= **0.871** or dryness fraction

= **0.871** ... Ans.

(iv) Capacity of wet extraction pump :

Actual absolute pressure = 76.5 − 70 = 6.5 cm Hg

= **0.087 bar**

p_s = steam pressure = 0.05622 bar

∴ p_a = air pressure = 0.087 − 0.05622

= **0.03078 bar**

Mass of air = $\dfrac{1800}{1000} \times 1$ = 1.8 kg

∴ Volume of air/hr = $\dfrac{mRT}{p} = \dfrac{1.8 \times 287 \times 308}{0.03078 \times 10^5}$

= **51.694 cu.m./hr**

∴ Total volume to be dealt with by wet extraction pump

= 1.8 (water) + 51.694 (air) = **53.494 m³/hr**... Ans.

= Capacity of wet extraction pump.

Problem 4.25 :

The following observations were recorded during a trial on condenser –

Temperature of condensate	= 40°C
Hot-well temperature	= 32°C
Condenser vacuum	= 690 mm Hg
Barometer reading	= 760 mm Hg
Flow rate of condensate	= 15 kg/min
Flow rate of cooling water	= 35000 kg/hr
Rise in temperature of cooling water	= 14°C
Inlet temperature of cooling water	= 26°C

Calculate :
(i) Vacuum efficiency of the condenser.
(ii) Effectiveness of condenser.
(iii) Condition of steam entering the condenser.

Solution : (i) Vacuum efficiency of the condenser :

The lowest absolute pressure of steam in the condenser or maximum vacuum in the condenser

$$= \text{Saturated pressure at } 40°C$$
$$= 0.07375 \text{ bar}$$
$$= 55.32 \text{ mm of Hg}$$

∴ Maximum vacuum = 760 – 55.32
= **704.68 mm/Hg**

Actual vacuum obtained = 690 mm/Hg

∴ Vacuum efficiency = $\dfrac{690}{704.68}$

= 0.9791 = **97.91%** ... **Ans.**

(ii) Effectiveness of the condenser :

$$\epsilon = \dfrac{\text{Actual drop in temperature of condensate}}{\text{Maximum rise in temperature of cooling water}}$$

$$= \dfrac{40-32}{40-26} = \dfrac{8}{14} = 0.5714 \text{ or } \mathbf{57.14\%} \quad \text{... \textbf{Ans.}}$$

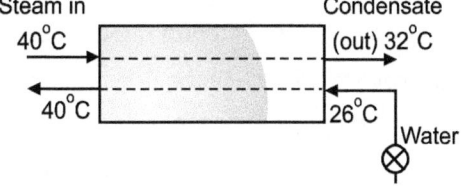

Fig. 4.14

(iii) Condition of steam entering the condenser :

Let x be the dryness fraction of steam entering the condenser.

$$\text{Heat lost by steam} = \text{Heat gained by water}$$

$$15\,[167.5 + x \times 2406.9 - 4.187 \times 32] = \frac{35000}{60} \times 4.187\,[14]$$

$$167.5 + 2406.9x - 133.984 = \frac{34193.833}{15}$$

$$33.516 + 2406.9x = 2279.6$$

$$x = \frac{2279.6 - 33.516}{2406.9}$$

$$= \frac{2246.084}{2406.9}$$

$$= 0.9332 = \mathbf{93.32\%} \qquad \text{... Ans.}$$

Problem 4.26 :

The following observations were recorded on a trial on a condenser –

Barometer reading	– 760 mm Hg
Recorded vacuum	– 690 mm Hg
Mean temperature of condensation	– 33°C
Hot well temperature	– 26°C
Mass of condensate	– 2200 kg/hr
Mass of cooling water circulated	– 70500 kg/hr

Rise in temperature of cooling water – 15°C

Find : (i) Dryness fraction of steam entering condenser.

(ii) Mass of air present per cu.m. of condenser.

(iii) Vacuum efficiency.

Solution : (i) Dryness fraction :

Let x be the dryness fraction of steam entering the condenser.

∴   Heat lost by steam = Heat gained by water

$$2200\,[h_f + x\,h_{fg} - 4.187 \times 26] = 70500 \times 4.187 \times 15$$

$$2200\,[138.2 + x \times 2423.6 - 4.187 \times 26] = 70500 \times 4.187 \times 15$$

$$138.2 + 2423.6x - 108.862 = \frac{705}{22} \times 4.187 \times 15$$

$$29.338 + 2423.6x = 2012.61$$

$$\therefore \quad x = \frac{2012.61 - 29.338}{2423.6} = \frac{1983.272}{2423.6} = 0.8183 \ldots \textbf{Ans.}$$

(ii) Mass of air present :

Absolute pressure of steam if no air is present

$$= \text{Sat. pressure at mean condenser temperature}$$
$$= 0.05029 \text{ bar} = \textbf{37.72 mm Hg}$$

Actual absolute pressure $= 760 - 690 = 70 \text{ mm Hg}$

$$= \textbf{0.09333 bar}$$

Air pressure $= 0.09333 - 0.05029$

$$= \textbf{0.04304 bar}$$

$\therefore$ Mass of air per cu.m. of condenser

$$= \frac{p_a V_a}{R_a T_a} = \frac{0.04304 \times 10^5 \times 1}{287 \times 306}$$

$$= \textbf{0.049 kg of air} \qquad \ldots \textbf{Ans.}$$

(iii) Actual vacuum produced = 690 mm Hg

Maximum vacuum that can be produced

$$= 760 - 37.72$$
$$= 722.28 \text{ mm Hg}$$

$\therefore$ Vacuum efficiency $= \dfrac{\text{Actual vacuum}}{\text{Theoretical}}$

$$= \frac{690}{722.28} = 0.9553$$

or $= \textbf{95.53\%} \qquad \ldots \textbf{Ans.}$

Problem 4.27 :

A test was conducted on a steam condenser and gave the following results :

Mass flow rate of condensate	= 14 kg/min
Mass flow rate of cooling water	= 35000 kg/hr
Mean temperature of condensate	= 40°C

Hot well temperature		=	32°C
Condenser vacuum		=	690 mm Hg
Barometer reading		=	760 mm Hg
Rise in temperature of cooling water		=	14°C
Inlet temperature of cooling water		=	26°C

Find : (i) Vacuum efficiency.

(ii) Condenser efficiency.

(iii) Dryness fraction of steam entering the condenser.

Solution : (i) Vacuum efficiency :

Mean temperature of condensate = 40°C

∴ Maximum absolute pressure of steam (at 40°C) = 0.07377 bar = 55.332 mm Hg

∴ Maximum vacuum that can be obtained = 760 − 55.332 = **704.668 mm Hg**

Actual vacuum = 690 mm Hg

∴ Vacuum efficiency = $\dfrac{\text{Actual vacuum}}{\text{Maximum vacuum without air}}$

$= \dfrac{690}{704.668} = 0.9792 =$ **97.92 %** ... **Ans.**

(ii) Condenser efficiency :

Rise in cooling water temperature = 14°C

Actual absolute pressure = 760 − 690 = 70 mm Hg

= **0.09333 bar**

Corresponding saturation temperature = 44.2°C

∴ Condenser efficiency = $\dfrac{\text{Actual rise in temperature of cooling water}}{\text{Maximum temperature rise that can be obtained}}$

$= \dfrac{14}{44.2 - 26}$

$= 0.7692$

$=$ **76.92%** ... **Ans.**

(iii) Dryness fraction of steam entering condenser :

Heat gained by cooling water = Heat lost by steam

$$\frac{35000}{60} \times 4.187 \times 14 = 14\,[167.5 + x \times 2407.91 - 4.187 \times 32]$$

$$ h_f h_{fg}$$

$$34193.833 = 14\,[33.516 + 2407.91\,x]$$

$$\frac{34193.833}{14} - 33.516 = 2407.91\,x$$

$$(2442.426 - 33.516) = 2407.91\,x$$

$$\frac{2408.91}{2407.91} = x \approx 1$$

Dryness fraction of steam entering the condenser = **1** ... **Ans.**

Problem 4.28 :

A condenser of a steam power plant indicates a vacuum of 65 cm of Hg when barometer reads 75 cm Hg. The condensing steam has a temperature of 45°C and a dryness fraction 0.9. Calculate :

(i) the amount of air to be handled by the pump per min. if the rate of steam condensation is 2000 kg/hr.

(ii) vacuum efficiency of the condenser.

Solution : (i) Amount of air handled :

Without any air present, the minimum absolute pressure of steam in condenser would be absolute pressure corresponding to steam temperature of 45°. i.e. **0.09582 bar.**

Actual absolute pressure in the condenser

$$= 75 - 65 = 10 \text{ cm Hg}$$

$$= \frac{10}{76} \times 1.01325$$

$$= \mathbf{0.1333 \text{ bar}}$$

∴ Absolute pressure of air in condenser

$$= 0.1333 - 0.09582$$

$$= \mathbf{0.03748 \text{ bar}}$$

∴ Mass of air to be handled per min

$$= \frac{p_a V_a}{R_a T_a} = \frac{(0.03748 \times 10^5) \times x V_g\,(0.9 \times 15.276)}{287 \times 318} \times \frac{2000}{60}$$

$$= 0.04107 \times 13.75 \times 33.33$$

$$= \mathbf{18.82 \text{ kg/min}} \quad \text{... Ans.}$$

(ii) Vacuum efficiency :

$$\text{Actual vacuum} = 65 \text{ cm Hg}$$

Maximum vacuum that can be obtained

$$= 1.01325 - 0.09582$$
$$= 0.91743 \text{ bar} = 68.813 \text{ cm Hg}$$

$$\therefore \quad \text{Vacuum efficiency} = \frac{65}{68.813}$$
$$= 0.9446$$
$$\text{or} = \textbf{94.46\%} \quad \text{... Ans.}$$

Problem 4.29 :

A surface condenser receives 18 kg steam per minute. The steam enters the condenser at 34°C having a dryness fraction of 0.9. Cooling water inlet temperature is 10°C and the exit temperature is 30°C. Estimate the quantity of cooling water required in kg/min., assuming no undercooling of condensate. What is the mass of air present per cu.m. (m³) of condenser value ? Absolute pressure in the condenser is 55 mm of Hg. **[P.U. Dec. 1998]**

Solution :

$$\text{Heat lost by steam/min} = m (h - h_f) \text{ at 34°C}$$
$$= 18 [h_f + x \, h_{fg} - h_f]$$
$$= 18 \times 0.9 \times 142.4$$
$$= \textbf{2306.88 kJ/min}$$

$$\text{Heat gained by water/min} = m_w \times c_{pw} \times [T_f - T_i]$$
$$= m_w \times 4.187 \, [30 - 10]$$
$$= m_w \times 4.187 \times 20$$

$$\therefore \quad \text{Heat lost by steam} = \text{Heat gained by circulating water}$$
$$2306.88 = m_w \times 4.187 \times 20$$

$$\therefore \quad m_w = \frac{2306.88}{20 \times 4.187}$$
$$= \textbf{27.55 kg/min} \quad \text{... Ans.}$$

If steam condenser is not having any air, then the pressure in condenser would have been 0.05318 bar but because of the presence of air, the absolute pressure is 55 mm Hg

$$= \frac{55}{760} \times 1.01315$$

= **0.7333 bar**

∴ Partial pressure of air present = 0.7333 − 0.05318

$$p_a = 0.02015 \text{ bar}$$

∴ Mass of air per cu.m. volume of condenser

$$= \frac{p_a V_a}{R_a T_a} = \frac{10^5 \times 0.02015 \times 1}{287 \times (273 + 34 = 307)}$$

$$= \textbf{0.02287 kg} \quad \text{... Ans.}$$

Example 4.30 :

The following readings relate to a test on a surface condenser –

Condenser vacuum	= 71.5 cm Hg
Barometer reading	= 76 cm Hg
Mean condenser temperature	= 33°C
Hot well temperature	= 27.5°C
Condensate collected	= 1785 kg/hr
Cooling water circulated	= 51250 kg/hr
Inlet temperature of cooling water	= 9°C
Outlet temperature cooling water	= 29°C

Determine : (i) Vacuum efficiency, (ii) Condenser efficiency, (iii) Quality of steam entering the condenser, (iv) Air present/m³ of condenser volume, (v) Capacity of wet extraction pump required if the air leakage is 1 kg/1000 kg of condensate.

Solution : (i) Vacuum efficiency :

Minimum absolute present of steam if air is absent

= Sat. pressure at 33°C = 0.05029 bar

= 3.772 cm Hg

∴ Maximum vacuum = 76 − 3.772 = 72.228 cm Hg

Actual vacuum = 71.5 cm Hg

∴ Vacuum efficiency = $\dfrac{\text{Actual vacuum}}{\text{Maximum vacuum}}$

$$= \frac{71.5}{72.228}$$

$$= 0.9899 \approx \textbf{99\%} \quad \text{... Ans.}$$

(ii) Condenser efficiency :

$$\text{Condenser efficiency} = \frac{\text{Actual temp. rise of cooling water}}{\text{Maximum temp. rise of cooling}}$$

$$= \frac{29 - 9}{33 - 9}$$

$$= \frac{20}{24} = 0.8333$$

$$= \textbf{83.33\%} \qquad \text{... Ans.}$$

(iii) Quality of steam entering the condenser :

Let x be the dryness fraction of steam.

∴ Heat lost by steam = Heat gained by water

$$1785\ [138.2 + 2423.6x - 4.187 \times 27.5] = 51250 \times 4.185\ (29 - 9)$$

$$138.2 - 115.14 + 2423.6x = 2404.3$$

$$x = \frac{2404.3 - 23.06}{2423.6} = 0.9825$$

$$= \textbf{98.25\%} \qquad \text{... Ans.}$$

(iv) Air present :

Actual absolute /pressure = 76 − 71.5 = 4.5 cm Hg (abs.) = **0.06 bar**

∴ Partial pressure of air = 0.06 − 0.05029

= **0.00971 bar**

∴ Weight of air/m³ $= \dfrac{p_a V_a}{R_a T_a} = \dfrac{0.00971 \times 10^5 \times 1}{287 \times 306}$

= **0.0111 kg** ... Ans.

(v) Capacity of wet extraction pump :

Mass of condensate = 1785 kg/hr = 1.785 cu.m./hr

Mass of air/hr = 1.785 kg

∴ Volume of air/hr $= \dfrac{1.785 \times 287 \times 306}{10^5 \times 0.00971} = 161.44\ m^3/hr$

∴ Capacity of wet extraction pump = 1.785 + 161.44

= **163.225 kg/hr** ... Ans.

EXAMPLES OF PRACTICE

1. The following observations were made during a test on surface condenser.
   Barometer reading = 760 mm of Hg
   Condenser vacuum = 705 mm of Hg
   Mean temperature of condenser = 35°C
   Rise in cooling water temperature = 16°C
   Condensate collected = 2000 kg/hr
   Inlet temperature of cooling water = 15°C
   Hot well temperature = 28°C
   Determine :
   (i) Vacuum efficiency.
   (ii) Condenser efficiency.
   (iii) Quality of steam entering condenser.
   (iv) Mass of air present per cu.m. of condenser volume.
   Ans. (i) 98.2%, (ii) 64%, (iii) x = 0.8139, (iv) 0.02 kg/m^3.

2. The absolute pressure in the surface condenser is 11.56 kPa when barometer reads 100 kPa. The condenser temperature is 40°C.
   Determine :
   (i) Partial pressure of air.
   (ii) Vacuum efficiency.
   (iii) Mass of air present per kg of steam.
   Ans. (i) 0.04185 bar, (b) 95.6%, (c) 0.91 kg.

3. The following observations were made during the test on surface condenser :
   Barometer reading = 760 mm of Hg
   Condenser vacuum = 705 mm of Hg
   Mean condenser temperature = 35°C
   Condensate collected = 2000 kg/hr
   Cooling water circulated = 60,000 kg/hr
   Rise in temperature of cooling water = 16°C
   Hot well temperature = 28°C
   Inlet water temperature = 15°C
   Determine :
   (a) Vacuum efficiency
   (b) Condenser efficiency
   (c) Mass of air present per 1 m^3 of condenser volume.
   Ans. (a) 98.2%, (b) 80%, (c) 0.01932 kg/m^3.

4. The following data refers to a surface condenser :

Vacuum in condenser	= 710 mm of Hg
Temperature of condenser	= 32°C
Barometer reading	= 760 mm of Hg
Hot well temperature	= 30°C
Cooling water	= 48000 kg/hr
Cooling water inlet and outlet temperature	= 20 and 34.5°C
Condensate	= 1500 kg/hr

Determine :
(a) Mass of air in 1 m³ of condenser volume.
(b) Dryness fraction of steam at inlet.
(c) Vacuum efficiency.
Ans. (a) 0.029 kg/m³, (b) 0.7617, (c) 0.9735 or 97.35%.

5. The following data were obtained during a test on a steam condenser :

Condenser vacuum recorded	= 705 mm of Hg
Barometer reading	= 750 mm of Hg
Mean condenser temperature	= 35°C
Hot well temperature	= 30°C
Mass of cooling water circulated	= 54000 kg/hr
Inlet temperature of cooling water	= 9°C
Outlet temperature of cooling water	= 28.5°C
Mas of condensate	= 1850 kg/hr

Find :
(i) Vacuum efficiency corrected to standard barometric pressure.
(ii) Condenser efficiency.
(iii) Quality of steam entering the condenser.
(iv) Mass of air present per m³ of condenser volume.
Ans. (i) 99.6%, (ii) 75%, (iii) 0.9769, (iv) 0.004315 kg/m³.

6. The following observations refer to a test on a condensing plant :

Recorded vacuum	= 700 mm of Hg
Barometer reading	= 760 mm of Hg
Mean condenser temperature	= 30°C
Condensate collected	= 22000 kg/hr

The air entering the condenser is given by the relation
$$\frac{\text{Steam condensation} + 2}{2000} \text{ kg/hr.}$$
Compute the discharge capacity of a wet air pump which removes the air and condensate in m³/min. Take volumetric efficiency of the pump equal to 80%.
Ans. 6.723 m³/min.

7. The following observations were made on a steam condensing plant :

   Barometer reading = 760 mm of Hg
   Recorded vacuum = 700 mm of Hg
   Mean temperature of condenser = 34°C
   Hot well temperature = 27°C
   Mass of condensate = 2120 kg/hr
   Mass of cooling water = 66000 kg/hr
   Rise in temperature of cooling water = 16°C

   Find :
   (1) the state of steam entering the condenser
   (2) mass of air present per m^3 of condenser volume
   (3) vacuum efficiency.

   Ans. (1) 0.849, (2) 0.03304, (3) 97.2%.

8. The following results were noted during a trial on surface condenser :

   Mean temperature of condenser = 30°C
   Condensate temperature = 23°C
   Barometer pressure = 72 cm of Hg
   Condenser vacuum = 66.375 cm of Hg
   Condensate collected = 550 kg/hr
   Cooling water circulated = 18000 kg/hr
   Rise in temperature of cooling water = 14°C

   Calculate :
   (a) Dryness fraction of steam entering the condenser.
   (b) Capacity of air pump in m^3/min
   (c) Mass of air discharged in kg/min.

   Ans. (a) 0.865, (b) 237 m^3/min, (c) 8.88 kg/min.

9. The steam is supplied at 3 MPa and 300°C to a steam turbine. The expansion of steam is carried out isentropically to a condenser vacuum of 738.528 mm of Hg. Barometer reads 755 mm of Hg. The condenser temperature is 19°C and rise in temperature of cooling water through the condenser is 10°C.

Determine :

(1) Quality of steam entering the condenser.

(2) Quantity of cooling water circulated per kg of steam.

Assume no air is present in the condenser.

Ans. 43.8 kg/kg steam.

10. The following observations were recorded during a test on the surface condenser :

Vacuum in the condenser	= 710 mm of Hg
Barometer	= 760 mm of Hg
Condenser temperature	= 32°C
Hot well temperature	= 30°C
Mass of cooling water circulated through condenser per kg of steam condensed	= 32 kg
Inlet temperature of cooling water	= 15°C
Exit temperature of cooling water	= 29°C

Determine :

(i) Dryness fraction of steam in the condenser.

(ii) Mass of air present per m³ of condenser volume.

(iii) Mass of air present/kg steam present in the condenser.

(iv) Condenser efficiency.

(v) Vacuum efficiency.

Ans. (i) 0.77, (ii) 0.02183, (iii) 0.51, (iv) 0.823, (v) 98%.

Unit - V

STEAM NOZZLES

5.1 INTRODUCTION

A nozzle is a device which serves two purposes :

1. To convert thermal energy into kinetic energy.
2. To direct mass flow from it at a specified angle.

There are many applications which require high velocity jet of fluid.

Nozzles are used in steam and gas turbines, jet engines, etc. The other applications of the nozzle are the injectors for pumping feed water into the boiler and the ejectors for removing air from the condensers.

Steam Turbine Layout :

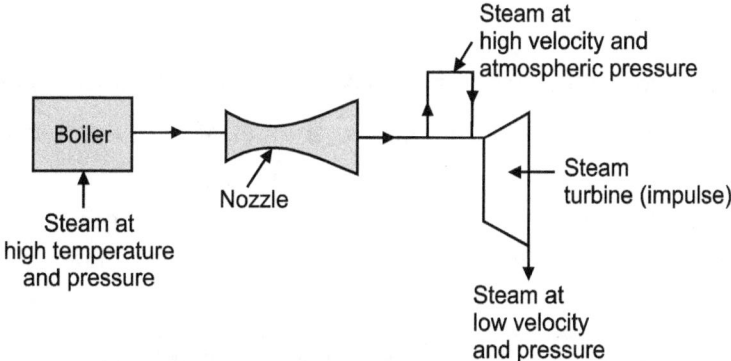

Fig. 5.1 : Steam Turbine Layout

5.2 NOZZLE SHAPES

There are two types of nozzle shapes.

(i) Convergent Nozzle :

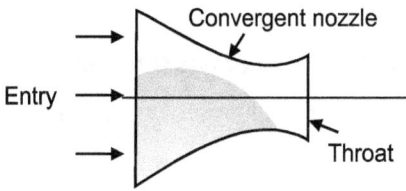

Fig. 5.2 : Convergent Nozzle

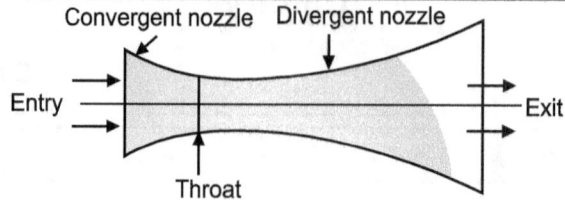

Fig. 5.3 : Convergent - divergent nozzle

The cross-section of the nozzle can be circular, rectangular, square or elliptical.

5.3 NOZZLE FLOW CONDITIONS

The nozzle is an open system in which flow of fluid is a steady flow process.

Hence, the flow of fluid through the nozzle should satisfy following conditions :
- Mass flow rate into and out of system are equal and do not vary with time.
- State and energy of the fluid at entrance and exit should not vary with time.
- The rates of heat and work transfer into and out of the system should not change with time.

We will derive relations for exit velocity and discharge for ideal gas flowing through the nozzle and apply these relations to steam by using suitable value of index 'n'.

5.4 FLOW OF AN IDEAL GAS THROUGH NOZZLE

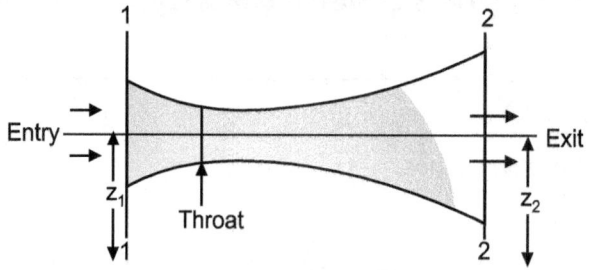

Fig. 5.4 : Flow of gas through nozzle

Let, A_1, A_2 – cross sectional area of nozzle at entrance and exit respectively

$\dot{m}$ – mass flow rate in kg/sec.

P_1, P_2 – pressure absolute in N/m²

v_1, v_2 – specific volume in m³/kg

u_1, u_2 — specific internal energy in J/kg
c_1, c_2 — velocity in meters/sec.
z_1, z_2 — elevation above arbitrary datum in meter
q — net rate of heat transfer in J/kg
w — net rate of work transfer in J/kg

Applying steady state flow energy equation to nozzle

$$\frac{c_1^2}{2} + z_1 \cdot g + h_1 + q = \frac{c_2^2}{2} + z_2 \cdot g + h_2 + w \qquad \ldots (5.1)$$

Assumptions :

(i) Normally nozzle is horizontal $\qquad \therefore z_1 = z_2$
(ii) Flow is isentropic $\qquad \therefore q = 0$
(iii) No work is done $\qquad \therefore w = 0$

$\therefore$ Equation (5.1) reduces to,

$$\frac{c_1^2}{2} + h_1 = \frac{c_2^2}{2} + h_2$$

or
$$\frac{c_2^2 - c_1^2}{2} = h_1 - h_2 \qquad \ldots (5.2)$$

Velocity of fluid when it enters the nozzle is known as velocity of approach (c_1). Normally, velocity of approach is very small as compared with exit velocity and hence can be neglected.

$$\therefore \quad c_2 = \sqrt{h_1 - h_2}$$

In the above equation, unit of every term is in J/kg. However, as the enthalpy for ideal gas is given in kJ/kg, the equation can be written with each term in kJ/kg.

$$\therefore \quad \frac{c_2^2}{1000} = 2(h_1 - h_2) \qquad \ldots (5.3)$$

$$\therefore \quad c_2^2 = 2000(h_1 - h_2)$$

$$\therefore \quad c_2 = 44.7\sqrt{h_1 - h_2} \qquad \ldots (5.4)$$

By using equation (5.4), exit velocity of the fluid can be found out when the enthalpy drop across the nozzle is known.

5.5 MASS FLOW RATE THROUGH THE NOZZLE

The change in kinetic energy of fluid flowing through the nozzle is given by the equation (5.2)

$$\frac{c_2^2 - c_1^2}{2} = h_1 - h_2$$

$$\therefore \frac{c_2^2 - c_1^2}{2} = u_1 + P_1 v_1 - u_2 - P_2 v_2$$

$$\therefore \frac{c_2^2 - c_1^2}{2} = (P_1 v_1 - P_2 v_2) + (u_1 - u_2)$$

$$= (P_1 v_1 - P_2 v_2) + c_v (T_1 - T_2)$$

$$(\because du = c_v dt)$$

For ideal gas $P_1 v_1 = RT_1$ per kg and $c_p - c_v = R$.

$$\therefore \frac{c_2^2 - c_1^2}{2} = (P_1 v_1 - P_2 v_2) + \frac{c_v \cdot R}{R}(T_1 - T_2)$$

$$\therefore \frac{c_2^2 - c_1^2}{2} = (P_1 v_1 - P_2 v_2) + \frac{c_v}{c_p - c_v}(RT_1 - RT_2)$$

$$\therefore \frac{c_2^2 - c_1^2}{2} = (P_1 v_1 - P_2 v_2) + \frac{1}{r-1}(P_1 v_1 - P_2 v_2)$$

(In expression $\frac{c_v}{c_p - c_v}$, dividing numerator and denominator by c_v).

$$\therefore \frac{c_2^2 - c_1^2}{2} = (P_1 v_1 - P_2 v_2)\left[1 - \frac{1}{\gamma - 1}\right]$$

$$\therefore \frac{c_2^2 - c_1^2}{2} = (P_1 v_1 - P_2 v_2)\left(\frac{\gamma}{\gamma - 1}\right)$$

If the velocity of approach c_1 is neglected,

$$\frac{c_2^2}{2} = (P_1 v_1 - P_2 v_2)\frac{\gamma}{\gamma - 1}$$

$$\therefore c_2 = \sqrt{\frac{2 \cdot \gamma}{\gamma - 1}(P_1 v_1 - P_2 v_2)}$$

$$\therefore \quad c_2 = \sqrt{2 \cdot \frac{\gamma}{\gamma-1} \cdot P_1 v_1 \left(1 - \frac{P_2 v_2}{P_1 v_1}\right)}$$

As
$$P_1 v_1^\gamma = P_2 v_2^\gamma$$

$$\therefore \quad \frac{v_2}{v_1} = \left(\frac{P_2}{P_1}\right)^{-1/\gamma}$$

Substituting for $\frac{v_2}{v_1}$,

We get,
$$c_2 = \sqrt{2 \cdot \frac{\gamma}{\gamma-1} P_1 v_1 \left\{1 - \left(\frac{P_2}{P_1}\right)^{\frac{\gamma-1}{\gamma}}\right\}} \quad \ldots (5.5)$$

$$\text{Mass flow rate in kg/sec.} = \frac{\text{Area} \times \text{Velocity}}{\text{Specific volume}}$$

Hence, the mass flow rate in kg/sec. when the fluid flows through cross sectional area A_2 and where specific volume of fluid is v_2 is given by

$$\dot{m} = \frac{A_2}{v_2} \sqrt{2 \frac{\gamma}{\gamma-1} P_1 v_1 \left\{1 - \left(\frac{P_2}{P_1}\right)^{\frac{\gamma-1}{\gamma}}\right\}} \quad \ldots (5.6)$$

We will convert this expression in terms of P_1, v_1, A_2 and ratio $\frac{P_1}{P_2}$ which are known *quantities*.

Now,
$$P_1 v_1^\gamma = P_2 v_2^\gamma$$

$$\therefore \quad \left(\frac{v_2}{v_1}\right)^\gamma = \frac{P_1}{P_2}$$

$$\therefore \quad \frac{v_2}{v_1} = \left(\frac{P_1}{P_2}\right)^{1/\gamma}$$

$$\therefore \quad v_2 = v_1 \left(\frac{P_1}{P_2}\right)^{1/\gamma} = v_1 \left(\frac{P_2}{P_1}\right)^{-1/\gamma}$$

Substituting this value of v_2 in equation (5.6), we get

$$\dot{m} = \frac{A_2}{v_1} \left(\frac{P_2}{P_1}\right)^{1/\gamma} \sqrt{2 \cdot \frac{\gamma}{\gamma-1} \cdot P_1 v_1 \left\{1 - \left(\frac{P_2}{P_1}\right)^{\frac{\gamma-1}{\gamma}}\right\}}$$

$$= A_2 \sqrt{2 \cdot \frac{\gamma}{\gamma-1} \cdot P_1 v_1 \left(\frac{P_2}{P_1}\right)^{\frac{2}{\gamma}} \cdot \frac{1}{v_1^2} \left\{1 - \left(\frac{P_2}{P_1}\right)^{\frac{\gamma-1}{\gamma}}\right\}}$$

$$= A_2 \sqrt{2 \cdot \frac{P_1}{v_1} \cdot \frac{\gamma}{\gamma-1} \left\{ \left(\frac{P_2}{P_1}\right)^{\frac{2}{\gamma}} - \left(\frac{P_2}{P_1}\right)^{\frac{\gamma+1}{\gamma}} \right\}} \qquad \ldots (5.7)$$

This is a very important relation which gives mass flow rate in kg/sec. in terms of known quantities P_1, P_2, v_1 and A_2.

5.6 CONDITIONS FOR MAXIMUM DISCHARAGE THROUGH NOZZLE

Nozzles are always designed for maximum discharge conditions. The maximum discharge condition determines the pressure at throat and area at throat. The pressure and volume at entry are constant and considering maximum discharge conditions, pressure and volume at throat are determined.

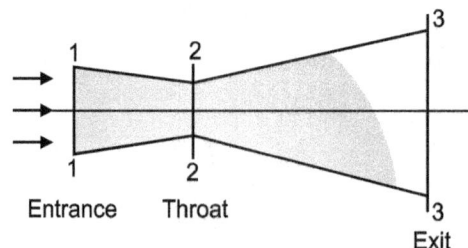

Fig. 5.5 : Nozzle

In the expression

$$\dot{m} = A_2 \sqrt{\frac{P_1}{v_1} \cdot \frac{\gamma}{\gamma-1} \cdot \left\{ \left(\frac{P_2}{P_1}\right)^{\frac{2}{\gamma}} - \left(\frac{P_2}{P_1}\right)^{\frac{\gamma+1}{\gamma}} \right\}}$$

P_1, v_1 and γ are all constants so the mass flow rate per unit area is dependent on ratio $\frac{P_2}{P_1}$ where P_2 is the pressure at throat and P_1 is pressure at entrance.

Hence there is only one value of $\frac{P_2}{P_1}$ which will give maximum discharge.

Hence differentiating the term $\left\{ \left(\frac{P_2}{P_1}\right)^{\frac{2}{\gamma}} - \left(\frac{P_2}{P_1}\right)^{\frac{\gamma+1}{\gamma}} \right\}$ with respect to $\frac{P_2}{P_1}$ and equating it to zero will give the value of $\frac{P_2}{P_1}$ at which discharge will be maximum.

$$\therefore \quad \frac{d}{d\left(\frac{P_2}{P_1}\right)}\left\{\left(\frac{P_2}{P_1}\right)^{\frac{2}{\gamma}} - \left(\frac{P_2}{P_1}\right)^{\frac{\gamma+1}{\gamma}}\right\} = 0$$

$$\therefore \quad \frac{2}{\gamma}\left(\frac{P_2}{P_1}\right)^{\frac{2}{\gamma}-1} - \frac{\gamma+1}{\gamma}\left(\frac{P_2}{P_1}\right)^{\frac{\gamma+1}{\gamma}-1} = 0$$

$\therefore$ Simplifying, $\quad \dfrac{P_c}{P_1} = \dfrac{P_2}{P_1} = \left(\dfrac{2}{\gamma+1}\right)^{\frac{\gamma}{\gamma-1}}$ ... (5.8)

$$\therefore \quad P_2 = P_1\left(\frac{2}{\gamma+1}\right)^{\frac{\gamma}{\gamma-1}} = P_c \quad \ldots (5.9)$$

This is known as critical pressure which gives maximum discharge and $\dfrac{P_c}{P_1} = \left(\dfrac{2}{\gamma+1}\right)^{\frac{\gamma}{\gamma-1}}$ is called critical pressure ratio.

5.7 CRITICAL TEMPERATURE RATIO

This is the ratio of temperature at throat and at entrance for maximum discharge condition. Let T_c be the temperature at throat and T_1 be the temperature at entrance.

For maximum discharge, $\quad \dfrac{P_c}{P_1} = \left(\dfrac{2}{\gamma+1}\right)^{\frac{\gamma}{\gamma-1}}$

Now, general relation between pressure and temperature for an ideal gas is

$$\frac{T_c}{T_1} = \left(\frac{P_c}{P_1}\right)^{\frac{\gamma-1}{\gamma}}$$

Substituting $\dfrac{P_c}{P_1} = \left(\dfrac{2}{\gamma+1}\right)^{\frac{\gamma}{\gamma-1}}$ in the above equation, we get

$$\frac{T_c}{T_1} = \left[\left(\frac{2}{\gamma+1}\right)^{\frac{\gamma}{\gamma-1}}\right]^{\frac{\gamma-1}{\gamma}} = \frac{2}{\gamma+1} \quad \ldots (5.10)$$

The ratio $\dfrac{T_c}{T_1}$ is called *critical temperature ratio*.

5.8 FLOW OF STEAM THROUGH NOZZLE

The expression for critical pressure and maximum discharge derived earlier apply to perfect gas and not vapours. This is due to the fact that in case of vapours the exponent of expansion is no longer constant but depends upon initial and final states of vapour.

Close approximation is achieved for expansion of steam through nozzle if the expansion is assumed to follow the law $Pv^n = C$.

1. For steam initially superheated, $n = 1.3$
2. For steam initially dry saturated, $n = 1.135$
3. For steam initially wet with dryness fraction 'X', $n^* = 1.035 + X(0.10)$

   * This is known as Zener's equation.

Using these values of n, we can write expression of critical pressure ratios as under

1. For superheated steam,

$$\dfrac{P_c}{P_1} = \left(\dfrac{2}{1.3+1}\right)^{\frac{1.3}{0.3}} = 0.546 \qquad \ldots (5.11)$$

2. For dry saturated steam,

$$\dfrac{P_c}{P_1} = \left(\dfrac{2}{1.135+1}\right)^{\frac{1.135}{1.135-1}} = 0.578 \qquad \ldots (5.12)$$

3. For wet steam, $n = 1.035 + (0.6)(0.1)$

$\begin{pmatrix}\text{say with dryness}\\ \text{fraction} = 0.6\end{pmatrix} = 1.095$

$$\dfrac{P_c}{P_1} = \left(\dfrac{2}{1.095+1}\right)^{\frac{1.095}{1.095-1}} = (0.9546)^{11.52} = 0.585$$

5.9 EFFECT OF FRICTION ON NOZZLE EFFICIENCY

When the steam expands through the nozzle, there is friction present which will increase entropy and process cannot be expressed by a vertical line on enthalpy-entropy diagram.

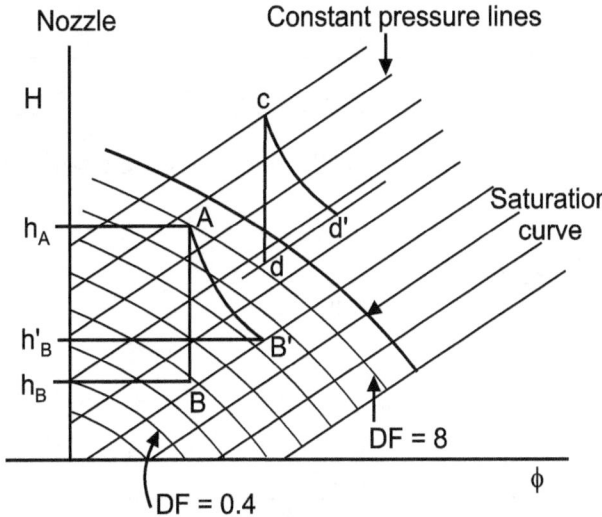

The friction is between steam and inner surface of the nozzle.

Consider expansion of steam. The expansion without friction is expressed by AB and expansion with friction is expressed by AB'. During expansion AB', entropy increases.

Fig. 5.6 : Flow with friction

5.10 EFFECTS OF FRICTIONAL LOSSES

(I) During expansion with friction from A to B',

   Enthalpy drop = $h_A - h_B'$

During expansion without friction from A to B,

   Enthalpy drop = $h_A - h_B$.

Hence reduction in enthalpy drop due to friction = $h_{B'} - h_B$.

(II) When the expansion takes place with friction, the heat due to friction is utilized in heating the steam. As such steam which is wet, its dryness fraction improves. Steam which is dry saturated gets superheated and for superheated steam its temperature increases.

(III) When steam expands with friction its dryness fraction improves which in turn increases its volume as compared with volume during expansion without friction.

All these observations can be better understood with the help of H-S or Mollier chart.

5.11 NOZZLE EFFICIENCY

The nozzle efficiency can be explained as, it is the efficiency with which pressure energy can be converted into kinetic energy.

$$\text{Nozzle efficiency (Referring to Fig. 5.6)} = \frac{\text{Actual enthalpy drop}}{\text{Theoretical enthalpy drop}}$$

$$H_A = \frac{h_A - h_{B'}}{h_A - h_B} \qquad \ldots (5.13)$$

5.12 VELOCITY COEFFICIENT

It is defined as the *ratio of actual exit velocity to isentropic velocity for the same pressure drop.*

$$\therefore \quad \text{Velocity coefficient} = \frac{\text{Actual velocity}}{\text{Isentropic velocity}} = \frac{44.7\sqrt{h_A - h_{B'}}}{44.7\sqrt{h_A - h_B}} = \sqrt{\frac{h_A - h_{B'}}{h_A - h_B}}$$

But $\dfrac{h_A - h_{B'}}{h_A - h_B}$ is nozzle efficiency.

$$\therefore \quad \text{Velocity coefficient} = \sqrt{\text{Nozzle efficiency}} \qquad \ldots (5.14)$$

5.13 COEFFICIENT OF DISCHARGE

It is defined as actual discharge in kg per second divided by discharge in kg/sec. when the expansion is isentropic.

$$\text{Coefficient of discharge} = \frac{m_{\text{actual}}}{m_{\text{isentropic}}} \qquad \ldots (5.15)$$

5.14 VARIATION OF VELOCITY, AREA AND SPECIFIC VOLUME

We can plot the graph of nozzle length versus specific volume, velocity, nozzle area in the following manner.

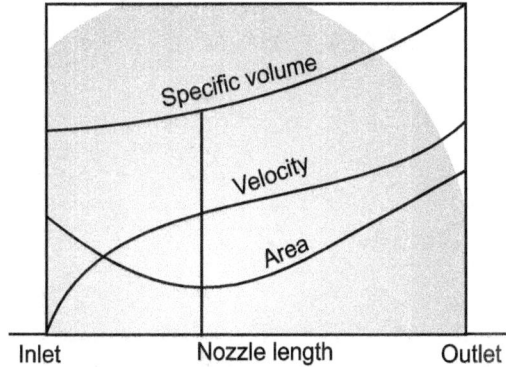

Fig. 5.7 : **Nozzle length Vs Specific volume, area and velocity**

Assumptions :

(i) The inlet conditions are fixed.

(ii) The process of expansion of fluid is known.

From this we can find enthalpy with the help of Mollier chart or using process equations. Then specific volume of the fluid can be calculated at any section.

As you know discharge and specific volume, cross-sectional area of the nozzle at any section can be calculated.

The velocity can be calculated by using equation (5.4).

Area and specific volume can be calculated as described above.

Hence, we can plot graphs of nozzle length versus specific volume, velocity, area.

Important Observations :

1. Velocity increases continuously from inlet to outlet. This is obvious as pressure energy is converted into kinetic energy.
2. The rate of increase of specific volume is gradual.

5.15 CHOCKING OF NOZZLES AND GENERAL COMMENTS

The application of nozzle is to convert pressure energy into kinetic energy and we require flow of steam to attain supersonic velocity as it enters the turbine. The initial velocity of steam as it comes out from the boiler is subsonic.

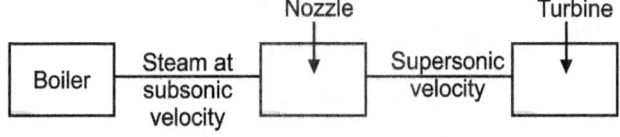

Fig. 5.8 : **Steam plant layout**

We will study how to get this change by using nozzle. Let us consider any flow passage of varying sectional area in the direction of flow.

It is a duct with varying cross-sectional area which gives increase in velocity.

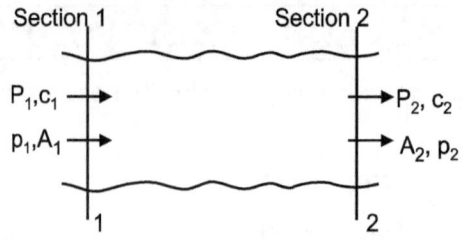

Fig. 5.9 : Flow through duct

Consider section 1 - 1 and section 2 - 2 and applying continuity equation and using usual notation for P_1, c_1, ρ_1 and A_1, we get

$$\rho_1 A_1 c_1 = \rho_2 A_2 c_2$$

Similarly, applying energy equation (2.1) to this flow,

$$\frac{c_1^2}{2} + z_1 \cdot g + h_1 + q = \frac{c_2^2}{2} + z_2 \cdot g + h_2 + w$$

As $z_1 = z_2$, and since no work is done, $w = 0$.

We get,
$$\frac{c_1^2}{2} + h_1 + q = \frac{c_2^2}{2} + h_2$$

$\therefore \qquad q = \dfrac{c_2^2}{2} - \dfrac{c_1^2}{2} + h_2 - h_1$

$\therefore \qquad dq = dK + dh$

where $\dfrac{c_2^2}{2} - \dfrac{c_1^2}{2} = dK$ and $h_2 - h_1 = dh$

$\therefore \qquad dq = dK + du + d(Pv)$

$\therefore \qquad dq = dK + du + Pdv + vdP$

but $\qquad dq = du + Pdv$

$\therefore \qquad du + Pdv = dK + du + Pdv + vdP$

$\therefore \qquad 0 = dK + vdP$

$\left(\text{Change in kinetic energy} = \dfrac{c_2^2}{2} \text{ neglecting } \dfrac{c_1^2}{2}\right)$

The differential form, $\quad dK = \dfrac{2c}{2} \cdot dc = c\, dc$

$\therefore \qquad 0 = c\, dc + v\, dP$

$\therefore \qquad c\, dc = -v\, dP \qquad \qquad \ldots (5.15\ A)$

Now, consider continuity equation which is

$$\rho_1 A_1 c_1 = \rho_2 A_2 c_2 = \rho A c = \text{constant}$$

where $\qquad \rho = $ density, kg/m^3

A = area, m²
c = velocity in m/sec.

By partial differentiation, we get,

$$0 = \frac{1}{v} \cdot A\, dc + \frac{c}{v} dA - A\frac{c}{v^2} \cdot dv$$

Dividing both sides of this equation by $\frac{Ac}{v}$, we get

$$0 = \frac{A\, dc}{v \cdot Ac} v + \frac{c}{v} dA \cdot \frac{v}{Ac} - \frac{Ac}{v^2} \cdot dv \cdot \frac{v}{Ac}$$

$$0 = \frac{dc}{c} + \frac{dA}{A} - \frac{dv}{v} \quad \ldots (5.15\ B)$$

Now, substituting the value of dc from equation (5.15 A), we get,

$$0 = -\frac{v\, dP}{c} \cdot \frac{1}{c} + \frac{dA}{A} - \frac{dv}{v}$$

$$\therefore \quad 0 = -\frac{v\, dP}{c^2} + \frac{dA}{A} - \frac{dv}{v}$$

$$\therefore \quad \frac{dA}{A} = \frac{dv}{v} + \frac{v dP}{c^2} = \frac{v dP}{c^2}\left[\frac{dv}{v} \cdot \frac{c^2}{v dP} + 1\right]$$

But $\quad \dfrac{dv}{v^2 - dP} = -\dfrac{1}{(\text{sonic velocity})^2}$

$$= -\frac{1}{a^2} \quad (\text{From sonic velocity derivation})$$

where a is the sonic velocity.

$$\therefore \quad \frac{dA}{A} = \frac{v dP}{c^2}\left[-\frac{c^2}{a^2} + 1\right]$$

$$= \frac{v dP}{c^2}[1 - M^2]$$

Substituting for vdP from equation (5.15 A), we get

$$\frac{dA}{A} = -\frac{c\, dc}{c^2}[1 - M^2]$$

$$\therefore \quad \frac{dA}{A} = \frac{dc}{c}[M^2 - 1] \quad \ldots (5.15\ C)$$

This is an important relation between velocity, area and *acoustic velocity* at any particular case.

Now, $\quad M = \dfrac{\text{Velocity}}{\text{Velocity of sound}} = \text{Mach Number} = \dfrac{c}{a}$.

Case I :

If $\quad M < 1$ i.e. velocity is less than one mach number

$\quad M^2 < 1$ and $M^2 - 1$ is negative.

i.e. $\quad \dfrac{dA}{A} = \dfrac{dc}{c}$ (–ve quantity)

∴ $\quad \dfrac{dc}{c} = -\dfrac{dA}{A}$

Now, if we want velocity to increase, $\dfrac{dc}{c}$ will be +ve and $\dfrac{dA}{A}$ will be negative. Therefore sectional area is decreasing in the direction of flow. Such a flow passage is called nozzle and the velocity is then sonic velocity, the nozzle is called subsonic nozzle.

In the subsonic nozzle the flow is accelerated while the area is reducing and the limit is that the velocity equal velocity of sound when $M = 1$.

Case II :

If $\quad M > 1$, i.e. the velocity is greater than sonic velocity

$\quad M^2 > 1$ and $M^2 - 1$ is positive.

i.e. $\quad \dfrac{dA}{A} = \dfrac{dc}{c}$ (+ve quantity)

∴ $\quad \dfrac{dc}{c} = +\dfrac{dA}{A}$

Now, if we want velocity to increase, $\dfrac{dc}{c}$ will be +ve and $\dfrac{dA}{A}$ will be positive. Therefore sectional area is increasing in the direction of flow and such a passage is called diverging nozzle. Here supersonic flow is further accelerated and the nozzle is called supersonic nozzle.

Therefore subsonic nozzle will be accelerated to sonic velocity and it will be further accelerated to supersonic velocity. Thus, if a fluid with subsonic velocity enters convergent-divergent nozzle we will get supersonic velocity at the outlet.

Hence, following conclusions can be drawn,

- For subsonic velocities (M < 1) dA and dc must be opposite in sign i.e. an increase of cross-sectional area causes a reduction of velocity and vice versa.
- For supersonic velocities (M > 1) dA and dc are of same sign. An increase of cross-sectional area then causes an increase of velocity and vice versa.
- When M = 1, dA must be zero and since the second derivative is positive, A must be minimum. Thus, if the velocity of flow equals the sonic velocity anywhere, it must be at minimum area which is throat.

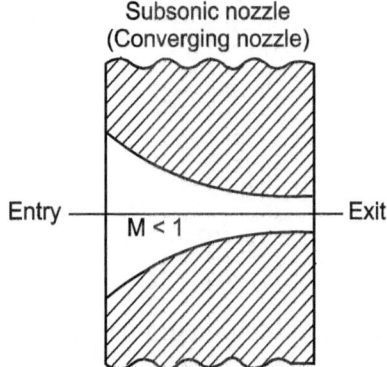

Fig. 5.10 : Subsonic nozzle

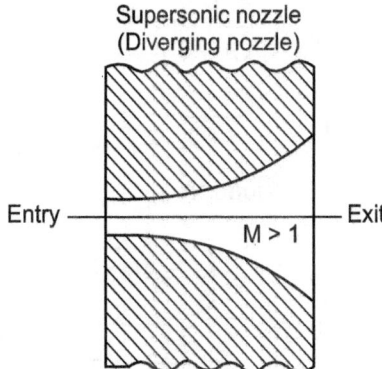

Fig. 5.11 : Supersonic nozzle

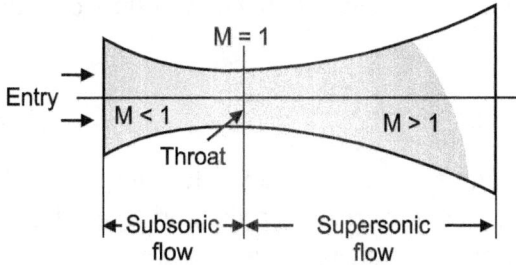

Fig. 5.12 : Convergent-divergent nozzle

Nozzles are used for increasing the velocity of steam. At the exit of the boiler, velocity is negligible. Then steam passes through subsonic nozzle and its velocity increases to sonic velocity (M = 1) and it reaches throat. We still want higher velocity, hence divergent nozzle has to be used.

5.16 FLOW CHARACTERSTIC OF A NOZZLE AND CHOCKING OF NOZZLE

$$m = \text{Mass flow rate} = \frac{\text{area} \times \text{velocity}}{\text{specific volume}} = \frac{Ac}{v}$$

Now, velocity, $c = M \times a$

$$= M\sqrt{\gamma R T}$$

and $\dfrac{1}{v} = \dfrac{P}{RT}$

We get $m = \dfrac{APM}{\sqrt{T}}\sqrt{\dfrac{\gamma}{R}}$

For sonic velocity M = 1, pressure and temperature at the throat will have critical values. The critical values are

$$P_c = \left(\frac{2}{\gamma+1}\right)^{\frac{\gamma}{\gamma-1}} \cdot P_1$$

and

$$T_c = \left(\frac{2}{\gamma+1}\right) T_1$$

Substituting these values in the above equation,

$$m = \frac{A \cdot \left(\frac{2}{\gamma+1}\right)^{\frac{\gamma}{\gamma-1}} \cdot P_1}{\sqrt{\frac{2}{\gamma+1} \cdot T_1}} \cdot \sqrt{\frac{\gamma}{R}}$$

If R and γ are fixed for a gas, mass flow is a function of upstream pressure and temperature only.

The mass flow rate increases as ratio $\dfrac{P_c}{P_1}$ increases. At throat $\dfrac{P_c}{P_1}$ = 0.528 for perfect gas, 0.546 for superheated steam, and 0.578 for dry saturated steam. When this ratio increases beyond this value, the mass flow starts decreasing and when this ratio is 1, i.e. when throat pressure is equal to inlet pressure the discharge is zero.

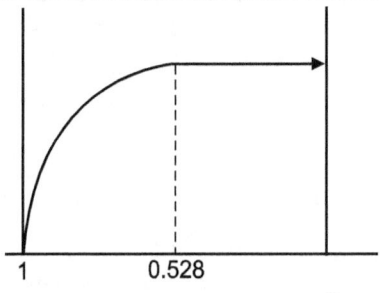

Fig. 5.13 : Pressure ratio, $\dfrac{P_c}{P_1}$

The nozzles are always designed for maximum discharge and the discharge at point B is maximum and at this point the nozzle is said to be chocked. The discharge of nozzle cannot be more than this value.

5.17 EFFECT OF CHANGE IN BACK PRESSURE ON NOZZLE PERFORMANCE

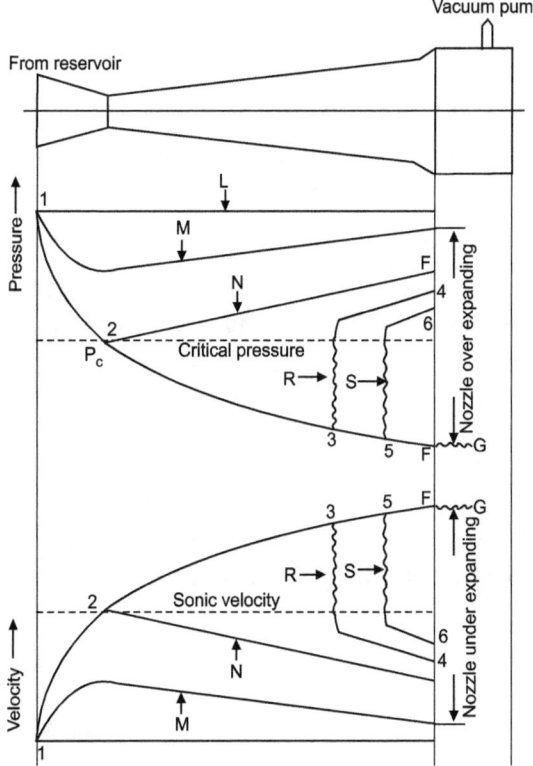

Fig. 5.14 : Effect of back pressure on nozzle performance

The nozzles are always designed for maximum discharge. When nozzle is used in an impulse turbine, inlet pressure is high. (Range 100 – 200 bar). The throat pressure for maximum discharge is critical pressure.

(P_c/P_1 = 0.546 or 0.578 etc.) The discharge pressure is condenser pressure of the turbine which is 0.1 to 0.5 bar. So the steam expands from 200 Bar to 0.1 Bar in a convergent-divergent nozzle.

It is interesting to know what happens to the flow of steam if exit/back pressure is not the designed pressure.

To study this, nozzle is connected to a very large reservoir at one end and to a vacuum pump at the other end. By means of vacuum pump, back pressure can be changed.

(1) Condition L :

When the back pressure is equal to inlet pressure there will not be flow of steam.

(2) Condition M :

The discharge pressure is reduced to such a value that throat pressure is above critical pressure, the flow is entirely subsonic. The convergent-divergent nozzle performs like a venturi.

(3) Condition N :

Discharge pressure is such that, at throat velocity of steam is sonic and remains subsonic in divergent portion. Hence, in the convergent portion there is isentropic expansion to critical pressure and in divergent portion there is isentropic diffusion.

(4) Design Condition :

When the discharge pressure is equal to nozzle designed outlet pressure, there is steady acceleration in the entire passage. The velocity is subsonic in convergent portion and supersonic in divergent portion and pressure diagram is 1 – 2 – F and velocity diagram is 1 – 2 – F. This is an ideal condition.

(5) Condition R and S :

When due to any condition back pressure is above designed pressure, the expansion will be as shown in curve R and S and expansion takes place inside the nozzle. This is called over expanding nozzle. The expansion is with turbulence. The expansion curves are 1234 or 1256.

When due to any reason back pressure is below designed pressure, the expansion takes place as 1 FG and it is under expanding nozzle. The expansion takes place outside the nozzle in the passage connecting end of nozzle and intake of turbine and expansion is with turbulence.

The ideal expansion is as shown by curve 1 – 2 – F.

5.18 SUPER SATURATED FLOW THROUGH STEAM NOZZLES

Consider expansion of steam in a nozzle from condition a to condition c. At a the steam is superheated at pressure P_1 and temperature T_a. As the steam expands from a to b the steam is cooled and at point b it is saturated. When steam expands from b to c, the temperature of steam drops down from T_b to T_c and steam becomes wet with a certain dryness fraction.

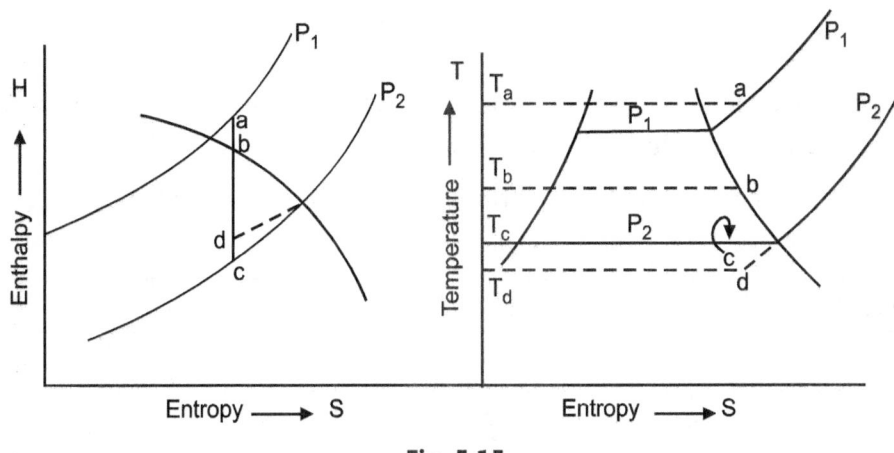

Fig. 5.15

The expansion of steam from A to B to C is expansion under thermal equilibrium.

However, in actual practice, the condensation of steam from b to c does not take place as steam has extremely less time available for condensation. If we consider that steam expands from point a to c, the time available is as small as $\frac{1}{10000}$ th of a second and this time is not sufficient for steam to condense. Hence, instead of following the path abc, it follows the path abd. d is the point of intersection of ac and pressure line P_2 extended. At point 'd' steam is not wet but in a gaseous form. Hence, it is not in equilibrium condition because at that temperature it should be partly wet.

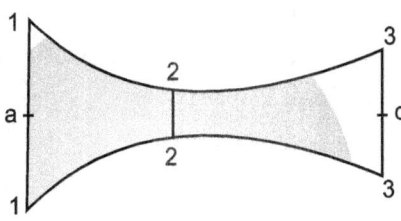

Fig. 5.16

Hence the expansion abd is non-equilibrium or metastable or supersaturated flow. The temperature of steam will be T_d instead of T_c. As T_d is less than T_c, the steam is undercooled or supercooled.

Degree of Undercooling :

It is defined as *difference between the saturation temperature corresponding to pressure P_2 and the actual temperature of the supersaturated vapour at point 'd'.* $T_c - T_d$ is called *degree of undercooling.*

Degree of Supersaturation :

It is defined as the *ratio of actual pressure P_2 and the saturation pressure corresponding to actual temperature of the supersaturated vapour at point 'd'.*

These definitions will be clear when we solve a problem on supersaturated flow.

5.19 WILSON LINE

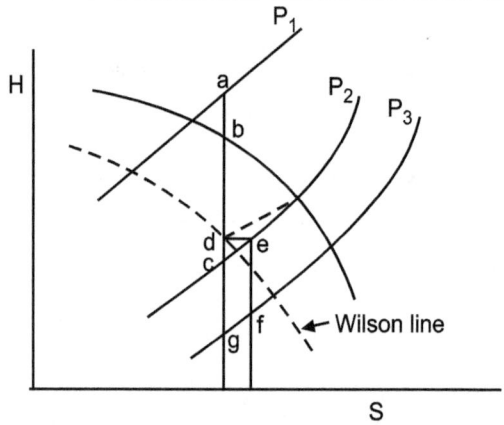

Fig. 5.17

There is however limit to the degree of undercooling and the limit of supersaturated flow is represented by WILSON LINE. That is supersaturated flow cannot continue beyond point d. At point 'd' the steam immediately comes back to pressure P_2 following the path de. Further expansion of the steam takes place like ef. Hence supersaturated flow will be abdef. Flow under thermal equilibrium will be abcg

    I.   Hence loss in heat drop = $H_f - H_g$

   II. Increase in entropy   = $S_f - S_g$

During supersaturated adiabatic expansion of steam (bd), the steam vapour expands according to the law $Pv^{1.3}$ = constant i.e. as superheated steam.

SOLVED PROBLEMS

Problem 5.1

Steam enters a convergent-divergent nozzle at pressure of 22 bar and temperature of 300°C. The exit pressure is 4 bar. Steam flow rate is 11 kg/sec. Find (a) velocity of steam at throat and exit. (b) Area of nozzle at throat and exit in mm².

Solution :

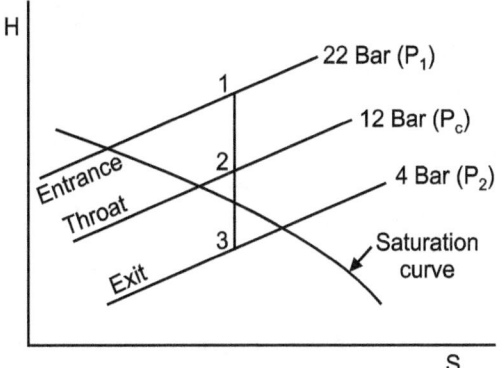

Fig. 5.18

From steam tables at pressure of 22 Bar, saturation temperature is 217.24° C. As the temperature of steam is 300°C, it is superheated.

Nozzles are always designed for maximum discharge and throat pressure P_C for superheated steam of maximum discharge will be $P_C = 0.546 \cdot P_1$

$$\therefore \quad P_C = (0.546)(22)$$
$$= 12.012 \text{ Bar.}$$

From Mollier chart, $h_1 = 3019$ kJ/kg

$h_2 = 2890$ kJ/kg, Temp. 225°C

$h_3 = 2675$ kJ/kg, dryness fraction 0.97

1. Velocity at throat $= 44.7\sqrt{h_1 - h_2} = 44.7\sqrt{3019 - 2890}$

   $= 507.69$ m/sec.   ... Ans.

2. Velocity at exit $= 44.7\sqrt{h_1 - h_3} = 44.7\sqrt{3019 - 2675}$

   $= 829.06$ m/sec   ... Ans.

3. Rate of discharge in kg/sec. $= \dfrac{\text{Area} \times \text{Velocity}}{\text{Specific volume}}$

At throat steam is superheated at 12 Bar pressure and 225°C temperature.

Specific volume in m³/kg $= v_{sup} = v_{sat} \cdot \dfrac{T_{sup}}{T_{sat}}$

$$= (0.1632)\left(\dfrac{225 + 273}{187.96 + 273}\right)$$

$$= (0.1632)(1.080)$$

$$= 0.1763 \text{ m}^3/\text{kg}$$

$$\text{Discharge} = \frac{\text{Area} \times \text{Velocity}}{\text{Specific volume}}$$

$$\therefore \quad \text{Area} = \frac{\text{Discharge} \times \text{Specific volume}}{\text{Velocity}}$$

$$= \frac{(11)(0.1763)}{507.69} \, m^2$$

$$= 3819.85 \, mm^2 \qquad \text{... Ans.}$$

At exit steam is wet at a pressure of 4 Bar and dryness fraction 0.97.

Specific volume in $m^3/kg = (X \, v_g) = (0.97 \times 0.4622)$

$$= 0.4483 \, m^3/kg$$

$$\text{Area at exit} = \frac{(11)(0.4483)}{829.06} = 5948.06 \, mm^2 \qquad \text{... Ans.}$$

Problem 5.2

Steam which is at a pressure of 3 Bar and dry saturated expands in a convergent nozzle to a pressure of 2 Bar. The area of throat is 3 cm². Neglecting approach velocity, calculate the exit velocity and mass flow rate if

(a) Equilibrium flow is assumed

(b) Supersaturated flow is assumed.

Also calculate degree of supersaturation.

Solution : (a) Equilibrium Flow :

Note : Remember that nozzle is convergent and as throat pressure is 0.66 times initial pressure, maximum discharge conditions do not apply.

From steam tables, $\quad h_1 = 2724.7 \, kJ/kg$

$$S_1 = S_g = 6.9909 \, kJ/kg/K$$

As flow is isentropic to 2 Bar,

$$S_1 = S_2 = 6.9909 = S_f + X(S_{fg}) = 1.5301 + X_2(5.597)$$

$$\therefore \quad X_2 = 0.9756$$

$$h_2 = h_f + X_2(h_{fg})$$

$$= 504.7 + (0.9756)(2201.6)$$

$$= 2652.58 \, kJ/kg$$

$$V_2 = X_2 \, v_g = (0.9756)(0.8854) = 0.8637 \, m^3/kg$$

$$c_2 = 44.7\sqrt{(h_1 - h_2)} = 44.7\sqrt{(2724.7 - 2652.58)}$$
$$= 379.6 \text{ m/sec.}$$

Mass flow rate in kg/sec. $= \dfrac{\text{area} \times \text{velocity}}{\text{specific volume}} = \dfrac{3 \times 10^{-4} \times 379.6}{0.8637}$

$$= 0.1318 \text{ kg/sec.} \qquad \text{... Ans.}$$

(b) Supersaturated flow :

For supersaturated flow the fluid behave like gas and expansion takes place as per law

$$(P_1 v_1^{1.3}) = (P_2 v_2^{1.3})$$

$$\therefore \quad [(3 \times 100)(0.6055)^{1.3}] = [(2 \times 100)(v_2)^{1.3}]$$

$$\therefore \quad v_2 = 0.6055 \left(\dfrac{3}{2}\right)^{\frac{1}{1.3}} = (0.6055)(1.5)^{0.7692}$$

$$= 0.8271 \text{ m}^3/\text{kg}$$

As per equation (5.5),

$$c_2 = \sqrt{2 \cdot \dfrac{n}{n-1} P_1 v_1 \left\{1 - \left(\dfrac{P_2}{P_1}\right)^{\frac{n-1}{n}}\right\}}$$

$$= \sqrt{2 \times \dfrac{1.3}{1.3-1} \times 3 \times 10^5 \times 0.6055 \left\{1 - \left(\dfrac{2}{3}\right)^{\frac{0.3}{1.3}}\right\}}$$

$$= \sqrt{15.7 \times 10^5 (1 - 0.910)} = 373.8 \text{ m/sec.}$$

Mass flow rate, $m = \dfrac{A_2 c_2}{v_2} = \dfrac{(3)(10)^{-4}(373.8)}{0.8271} = 0.135 \text{ kg/sec.}$

From the steam tables saturation temperature at 3 Bar is 133.54°C and as steam expands as per law $Pv^{1.3} = c$,

$$T_2 = T_1 \left(\dfrac{P_2}{P_1}\right)^{\frac{1.3-1}{1.3}} = (133.54 + 273)\left(\dfrac{2}{3}\right)^{\frac{0.3}{1.3}}$$

$$= 369.95 \text{ K} = 96.95°\text{ C}$$

From the steam tables at 96.95°C, saturation pressure is 0.9094 Bar (Use temperature tables).

$$\therefore \quad \text{Degree of supersaturation} = \dfrac{2}{0.9094} = 2.199 \qquad \text{... Ans.}$$

Problem 5.3

Steam nozzle supplied with pressure of 7 Bar and 275°C discharges steam at 1 Bar. If the diverging portion of the nozzle is 60 mm long and the throat diameter is 5 mm, determine the cone angle of the divergent portion. Assume 10% of the total available enthalpy drop to be lost in friction in the divergent portion. Also determine the velocity and temperature of steam at the throat.

Solution :

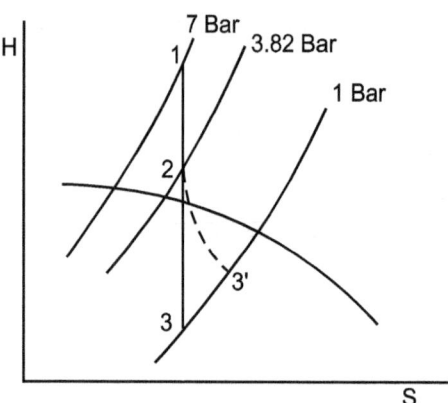

Fig. 5.19

The steam is initially superheated.

Throat pressure for maximum discharge = $P_c = 0.546 \, P_1$

$= (0.546)(7)$

$= 3.82$ Bar

From Mollier chart,

$h_1 = 3000$ kJ/kg

$h_2 = 2850$ kJ/kg

$T_2 = 195°C$

∴ $h_1 - h_2 = 3000 - 2850 = 150$ kJ/kg

At point 2, $\quad v_{sup.} = v_{sat.} \cdot \dfrac{T_{sup.}}{T_{sat}} = 0.485 \times \dfrac{195 + 273}{141.78 + 273}$

$= 0.485 \times \dfrac{468}{414.78} = 0.5472 \text{ m}^3/\text{kg}$

Velocity at throat $= c_2 = 44.7 \sqrt{h_1 - h_2}$

$= 44.7 \sqrt{150}$ m/sec

$= 547.46$ m/sec. ... **Ans.**

From Mollier chart, $h_3 = 2615$ kJ/kg

$X_3 = 0.972$

Velocity at exit $= c_3 = 44.7 \sqrt{(h_1 - h_3)(0.9)}$

$= 44.7 \sqrt{(3000 - 2615)(0.9)}$

$= 831.86$ m/sec. ... **Ans.**

[**Note :** When results are obtained by using Mollier chart, error will be about ± 5 percent]

Now, mass flow rate = $\dfrac{\text{Area} \times \text{Velocity}}{\text{Specific volume}}$

$$= \dfrac{\dfrac{\pi}{4} \cdot d^2 \times (547.46)}{0.5472} = \dfrac{(0.7854)\left(\dfrac{5}{1000}\right)^2 (547.46)}{0.5472}$$

$$= 0.01964 \text{ kg/sec.}$$

From this information we can calculate diameter at exit.

Mass flow rate = $0.01964 = \dfrac{\dfrac{\pi}{4} \cdot D^2 \times 831.86}{1.6937 \times 0.972}$

∴ $\quad 0.01964 = \dfrac{(0.7854)(D^2)(831.86)}{1.6937 \times 0.972}$

∴ $\quad D_3^2 = 4.948836 \times 10^{-5} \text{ m}^2$

$\quad\quad\quad = 4.948836 \times 10^{-5} \times 10^6 \text{ mm}^2$

$\quad\quad\quad = 49.488 \text{ mm}^2$

∴ $\quad D_3 = 7.034 \text{ mm}$

$\tan\theta = \dfrac{\dfrac{(7.034 - 5)}{2}}{60} = 0.01695$

∴ $\quad \theta = 0.97°$

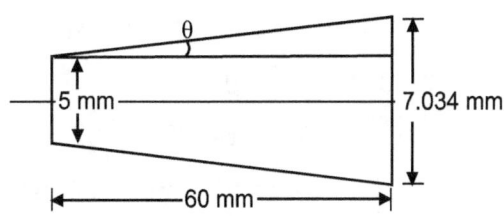

Fig. 5.20

∴ Cone angle = $2\theta = 0.97 \times 2 = 1.94°$ ... **Ans.**

Problem 5.4

Steam at a pressure of 10 Bar and 200°C expands in a convergent-divergent nozzle to a pressure of 0.1 Bar. The flow rate is 5 kg/min. The expansion is supersaturated upto throat and in the thermal equilibrium afterwards. Calculate (a) Diameter of nozzle at exit, (b) Degree of supersaturation, (c) Degree of undercooling at throat.

Solution :

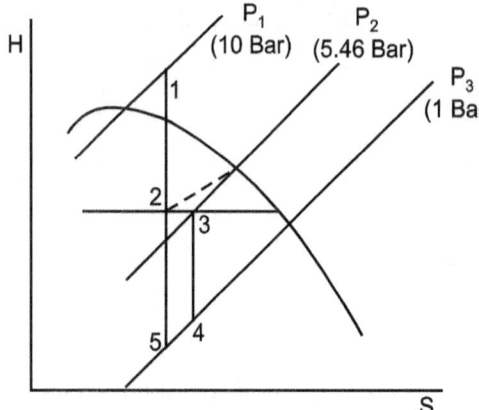

Fig. 5.21

The supersaturated expansion upto throat is 1 – 2.

The expansion in thermal equilibrium is 34.

From superheated steam tables at 10 Bar and 200° C,

$h_1 = 2826.8$; $v_1 = 0.2059$

Expansion 1 – 2 is as per law,

$$P_1 v_1^{1.3} = P_2 v_2^{1.3}$$

$$h_1 - h_2 = \frac{n}{n-1} \cdot P_1 v_1 \left[1 - \left(\frac{P_2}{P_1}\right)^{\frac{n-1}{n}}\right], \text{ take } n = 1.3$$

$$= \frac{1.3}{1.3-1} \times 10 \times 100 \times 0.2059 \left[1 - \left(\frac{5.46}{10}\right)^{\frac{1.3-1}{1.3}}\right]$$

$$= 4.33 \times 1000 \times 0.2059 \left[1 - (0.546)^{0.23}\right]$$

$$= 4.33 \times 1000 \times 0.2059 \,(0.13) \text{ kJ/kg}$$

$$= 115.9 \text{ kJ/kg}$$

∴ $h_2 = 2826.8 - 115.9 = 2710.9$ kJ/kg

From Mollier chart, $h_4 = 2120$ kJ/kg, $X_4 = 0.807$

$v_4 = v_g \times 0.807 = ^*14.675 \times 0.807 = 11.84$ m³/kg

(* This value is taken from steam tables)

Velocity at exit $= c_4 = 44.7 \sqrt{h_1 - h_4}$

$= 44.7 \sqrt{2826.8 - 2120}$

$= 1188.12$ m/sec.

Now, for calculating diameter at exit, we will have to calculate area at exit.

Mass flow rate in kg/sec.$= \dfrac{\text{Area} \times \text{Velocity}}{\text{Specific volume}}$

$$\therefore \quad \frac{5}{60} = \frac{\text{Area} \times 1188.12}{11.84}$$

$$\therefore \quad \text{Area} = \frac{5 \times 11.84}{1188.12 \times 60} \text{ m}^2 = 830.443 \text{ mm}^2$$

$$\therefore \quad d^2 = \frac{830.443}{0.7854} = 1057.35 \text{ mm}^2$$

$$\therefore \quad d = 32.51 \text{ mm} \qquad \text{... Ans.}$$

As 1 – 2 is supersaturated expansion, it follows the law $Pv^{1.3} = c$

$$\therefore \quad \frac{T_2}{T_1} = \left(\frac{P_2}{P_1}\right)^{\frac{1.3-1}{1.3}}$$

$$\therefore \quad T_2 = (200 + 273)\left(\frac{5.46}{10}\right)^{\frac{0.3}{1.3}} = (473)(0.87)$$

$$= 411.5° \text{ K} = 138.54° \text{ C}$$

The saturation temperature corresponding to pressure of 5.46 Bar is 154.76°C (This value is taken from steam tables for pressure of 5.4 Bar).

$$\therefore \quad \text{Degree of undercooling} = 154.76 - 138.54$$

$$= 16.22° \text{ C} \qquad \text{...Ans.}$$

Degree of Supersaturation :

The pressure corresponding to temperature of 138.54° C is 3.45 Bar by interpolation (rough estimate).

$$\therefore \quad \text{Degree of supersaturation} = \frac{\text{Pressure } P_2}{\text{Pressure corresponding to saturation temperature}}$$

$$= \frac{5.46}{3.45} = 1.582 \qquad \text{... Ans.}$$

(Note : As values are taken from Mollier diagrams and exact values from steam tables are difficult to evaluate, approximation is ± 5%.)

Problem 5.5

Steam is supplied through a group of six nozzles at 35 Bar and 300°C. The exit pressure is 3 Bar. The mass flow rate is 5.2 kg/sec. The flow is supersaturated. Determine :

1. Exit area and diameter for circular cross-section
2. Enthalpy loss due to supersaturation
3. Mass flow rate increase due to supersaturation.

Solution : P_1 = 35 Bar, t_1 = 300° C,

P_2 = 3 Bar

From steam tables,

h_1 = 2978.9 kJ/kg

v_1 = 0.06849 m³/kg

s_1 = 6.4492 kJ/kgK

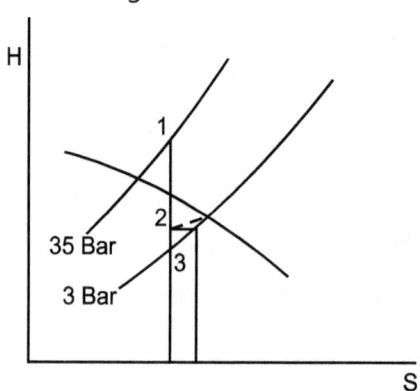

Fig. 5.22

The expansion 1 – 2 is supersaturated flow according to the law $P_1 v_1^{1.3} = P_2 v_2^{1.3}$

∴ $$\frac{v_2}{v_1} = \left(\frac{P_1}{P_2}\right)^{1/n}$$

∴ $$\frac{v_2}{v_1} = \left(\frac{35}{3}\right)^{1/1.3} = (11.66)^{0.7692} = 6.6146$$

∴ $v_2 = v_1 \times 6.6146 = (0.06849 \times 6.6146)$

= 0.453 m³/kg

$$h_1 - h_2 = \frac{n}{n-1} [P_1 v_1 - P_2 v_2]$$

$$= \frac{1.3}{1.3 - 1} [35 \times 100 \times 0.06849 - 3 \times 100 \times 0.453]$$

$$= 4.33 [239.715 - 135.9]$$
$$= 449.518 \text{ kJ/kg}$$
$$c_2 = 44.7\sqrt{449.518} = 947.64 \text{ m/sec.}$$

$$\text{Mass flow rate} = \frac{A_2 c_2}{v_2} = \frac{A_2 \times 947.64}{0.453} = \frac{5.2}{6}$$

$$\therefore \quad A_2 = \frac{(5.2)(0.453)}{(6)(947.64)} \text{ m}^2 = 414.29 \text{ mm}^2$$

$$\therefore \quad \frac{\pi}{4} D_2^2 = 414.29$$

$$\therefore \quad D_2 = 22.97 \text{ mm} \qquad \text{... Ans.}$$

When the flow is in equilibrium by using Mollier chart,

$$h_3 = 2505 \text{ kJ/kg}$$

and h_2
$$= h_1 - 449.518 = 2529.38 \text{ kJ/kg}$$

Loss of enthalpy due to supersaturation

$$= h_2 - h_3 = 2529.38 - 2505$$
$$= 24.38 \text{ kJ/kg} \qquad \text{... Ans.}$$

Increase in mass flow rate due to supersaturation :

Mass flow rate under equilibrium condition has to be calculated.

$$\text{Mass flow rate (Equilibrium condition)} = \frac{\text{area} \times \text{velocity}}{\text{sp. volume}} \qquad \text{Here } A_3 = A_2$$

$$= \frac{414.29 \times 10^{-6} \times 44.7\sqrt{2978.9 - 2505}}{0.9 \times 0.60556}$$

(Dryness fraction from Mollier chart, specific volume of dry saturated steam is from steam tables.)

$$= \frac{414.29 \times 10^{-6} \times 44.7 \times 21.76}{0.545} \text{ kg/sec.}$$

Mass flow rate (Equilibrium condition) $= 0.7393$ kg/sec.

Mass flow rate (Supersaturated condition) $= \frac{5.2}{6} = 0.8666$ kg/sec.

$$\therefore \quad \% \text{ increase} = \frac{0.8666 - 0.7393}{0.7393} \times 100 = 17.21 \% \quad \text{... Ans.}$$

Problem 5.6

Dry saturated steam is expanded in a nozzle from a pressure of 10 Bar to a pressure of 4 Bar. If the expansion is supersaturated, find :

1. The degree of undercooling
2. The degree of supersaturation.

Solution :

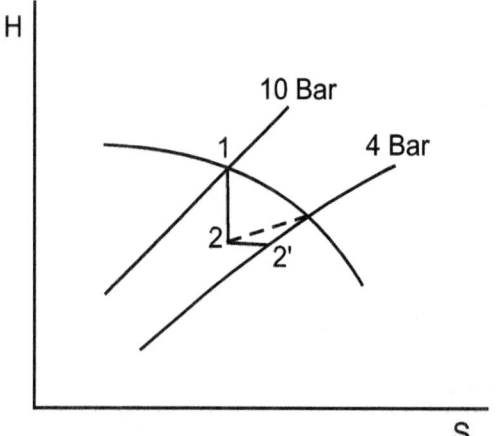

Fig. 5.23

The expansion 1 – 2 is supersaturated, hence it is according to the equation

$$\therefore \quad Pv^{1.3} = \text{constant}$$

$$\therefore \quad P_1 v_1^{1.3} = P_2 v_2^{1.3}$$

$$\therefore \quad \frac{T_1}{T_2} = \left(\frac{P_1}{P_2}\right)^{\frac{1.3-1}{1.3}}$$

$$= \left(\frac{10}{4}\right)^{0.23}$$

$$= 1.234$$

$$\therefore \quad T_2 = \frac{T_1}{1.234} = \frac{179.88 + 273}{1.234} = 367°K = 94°C$$

$$\therefore \quad \text{Degree of undercooling} = \text{Saturation temperature corresponding to pressure 4 Bar} - \text{Actual temperature}$$

$$= 143.62 - 94 = 49.62° \text{ C} \quad \text{...Ans.}$$

Now, saturation pressure corresponding to temperature of 94°C is 0.8146 Bar.

$$\therefore \quad \text{Degree of supersaturation} = \frac{\text{Actual pressure}}{\text{Saturation pressure corresponding to actual temperature}}$$

$$= \frac{4}{0.8146} = 4.91 \quad \text{... Ans.}$$

Problem 5.7

Steam enters the nozzle of an impulse turbine at 10 Bar and 250°C and leaves at 1 Bar. The turbine develops 225 kW with specific steam consumption of 16. If the throat diameter is 8 mm find the number of nozzles and the exit diameter, assuming that 10 % of the total enthalpy drop is lost in overcoming friction in the divergent portion only. Neglect velocity of approach.

Solution :

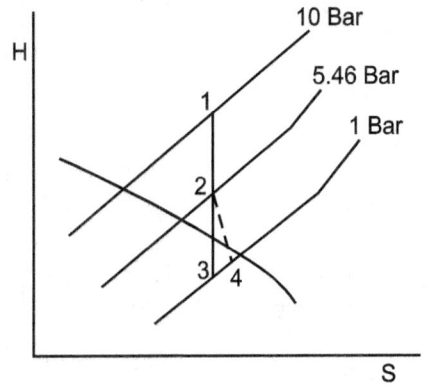

Fig. 5.24

The steam is initially superheated. Hence assuming maximum discharge condition,

$$P_2 = 0.546 \; P_1 = 5.46 \text{ Bar}$$

From steam tables, for 10 Bar and 250°C temperature,

$$h_1 = 2943 \text{ kJ/kg}$$
$$s_1 = 6.9259 \text{ kJ/kgK}$$

$$s_1 = s_2 = s_g + c_p \ln \frac{T_{sup}}{T_{sat}}$$

$$6.9259 = 6.7870 + 2.1 \ln \frac{T_{sup}}{155.46 + 273}$$

$$6.9259 - 6.7870 = 2.1 \ln \frac{T_{sup}}{155.46 + 273}$$

∴ $$\frac{0.1389}{2.1} = \ln \frac{T_{sup}}{155.46 + 273} = \ln \frac{T_{sup}}{428.46}$$

∴ $$0.06614 = \ln \frac{T_{sup}}{428.46}$$

∴ $$1.06837 = \frac{T_{sup}}{428.46}$$

∴ $$T_{sup} = 457.75° \text{ K} = T_2 = 184.75° \text{ C}$$

Enthalpy at point 2 = h_2 = 2751.7 + 2.1 (184.75 − 155.46)

= 2813.2 kJ/kg

Now, velocity at 2 = $c_2 = 44.7\sqrt{h_1 - h_2} = 44.7\sqrt{2943 - 2813.2}$

= 509.13 m/sec.

Specific volume at point 2 = $v_2 = v_{sat} \cdot \dfrac{T_{sup}}{T_{sat.}} = 0.3425 \times \dfrac{457.75}{428.46}$

= 0.3659 m³/kg

Flow through the nozzle = $\dfrac{\text{Area} \times \text{Velocity}}{\text{Specific volume}} = \dfrac{\frac{\pi}{4} \times (0.008)^2 \times 509.13}{0.3659}$ kg/sec.

= 0.0699 kg/sec.

The actual discharge = $\dfrac{225 \times 16}{3600}$ kg/s = 1 kg/sec.

Number of nozzles = $\dfrac{\text{Actual discharge in kg/sec.}}{\text{Discharge per nozzle/sec.}} = \dfrac{1}{0.0699} = 14.306$

= 15 nozzles are required

From steam tables,

$s_3 = s_f + X\, s_{f_g}$

s_3 = 1.3027 + X (6.0571)

But $s_1 = s_2 = s_3$ = 6.9259

∴ 6.9259 = 1.3027 + X (6.0571)

∴ X = $\dfrac{6.9259 - 1.3027}{6.0571}$ = 0.928

∴ Enthalpy at point 3 = $h_f + X \cdot h_{f_g}$

= 417.51 + (0.928) (2257.9)

= 2512.84 kJ/kg

Enthalpy drop in friction = (0.1) ($h_1 - h_3$) = (0.1) (2943 − 2512.84)

$$= 43.016 \text{ kJ/kg}$$

∴ $\quad h_4 = h_3 + 43.016 = 2555.8 \text{ kJ/kg}$

∴ $\quad$ Velocity at exit $= 44.7\sqrt{h_1 - h_4} = 44.7\sqrt{2943 - 2555.8}$

$$= 879.24 \text{ m/sec.}$$

Now, Discharge per nozzle $= \dfrac{\text{Area} \times \text{Velocity}}{\text{Specific volume}}$

We will have to find condition of steam at point 4.

$$h_4 = 2555.8 = h_f + X \, h_{fg} = 417.51 + X \, (2257.9)$$

∴ $\quad X = \dfrac{2555.8 - 417.51}{2257.9} = 0.948$

∴ $\quad 0.0699 = \dfrac{\text{Area} \times 879.24}{0.948}$

∴ $\quad \text{Area} = \dfrac{(0.0699)(0.948)}{879.24} = 753.66 \text{ mm}^2 = \dfrac{\pi}{4} \cdot D_{exit}^2$

∴ $\quad$ Diameter at exit $= 30.97 \text{ mm}$ ... **Ans.**

Problem 5.8

A steam nozzle admits steam at 7 Bar and 275°C. The throat diameter is 5 mm. Expansion of steam upto throat is frictionless. The velocity at throat and exit are 533 m/sec. and 838 m/sec. respectively. The steam leaves the nozzle at 1 Bar. Determine :

1. Throat pressure   2. Exit diameter.

Solution : From Mollier diagram,

$$h_1 = 3010 \text{ kJ/kg}$$

Velocity at throat $= c_2 = 44.7\sqrt{h_1 - h_2} = 533$

∴ $\quad 533 = 44.7 \sqrt{3010 - h_2}$

∴ $\quad \sqrt{3010 - h_2} = 11.92$

∴ $\quad 3010 - h_2 = 142$

∴ $\quad h_2 = 3010 - 142 = 2868 \text{ kJ/kg}$

∴ From Mollier chart, throat pressure = 4.1 Bar ... **Ans.**

Condition of steam at throat is superheated at 200°C.

∴ $$v_2 = v_{sat} \cdot \frac{T_{sup}}{T_{sat}}$$

$$= 0.45162 \times \frac{200 + 273}{144.52 + 273}$$

$$= 0.5112 \ m^3/kg$$

Now, $c_3 = 44.7\sqrt{h_1 - h_3}$

∴ $838 = 44.7\sqrt{3010 - h_3}$

∴ $\dfrac{838}{44.7} = \sqrt{3010 - h_3} = 18.74$

∴ $3010 - h_3 = 351.18$

∴ $h_3 = 3010 - 351.18 =$ **2658.82 kJ/kg**

Now for 7 Bar and 275°C temperature, entropy of steam from steam tables = 7.2031 kJ/kgK

∴ $s_1 = 7.2031 = s_3 = s_f + X \, s_{fg}$

∴ $7.2031 = 1.3027 + X \cdot 6.0571$

∴ $X = 0.974$

∴ $v_3 = X \cdot v_g = (0.974)(1.6937) = 1.649 \ m^3/kg$

For steady flow, $\dfrac{A_2 \, c_2}{v_2} = \dfrac{A_3 \, c_3}{v_3}$

∴ $A_3 = \dfrac{A_2 \, c_2}{v_2} \cdot \dfrac{v_3}{c_3}$

$$= \frac{\left(\dfrac{\pi}{4}\right)(0.005)^2 \, 533 \times 1.649}{0.5112 \times 838} \times 10^6$$

$A_3 = 40.28 \ mm^2 = \dfrac{\pi}{4} d_3^2$

∴ $d_3 = 7.16 \ mm$ ... **Ans.**

EXAMPLES FOR PRACTICE

1. Steam at a pressure of 3 bar and 10°C superheat is passed through a convergent nozzle. The velocity of steam before entering the nozzle is 100 m/sec. The back pressure is
   1.5 Bar. Assuming nozzle efficiency of 92 % and specific heat of superheated steam as 2.3 kJ/kg. K, determine the area of nozzle at throat for a discharge of 0.45 kg/sec.

   [Ans. 10.509 cm^2]

2. Steam enters a group of convergent-divergent nozzles at a pressure of 2.2 MN/m^2 and with a temperature of 260°C. Equilibrium expansion through the nozzles to an exit pressure of 0.4 MN/m^2 takes place. Upto the throat of the nozzles the flow can be considered frictionless. From the throat to exit, however, there is an efficiency of expansion of 85 %. The rate of steam flow through the nozzle is 11 kg/sec. Using enthalpy-entropy chart for steam, determine :

   (a) The throat and exit velocities.

   (b) The throat and exit areas.

   [Ans. 547.7 m/sec, 799.97 m/sec., 3210 mm^2, 6050 mm^2]

3. Steam expands through a convergent-divergent nozzle from 5 bar and dry saturated to a back pressure of 0.2 bar. Mass flow is 2 kg/sec. Calculate the exit and throat areas when the friction loss in the divergent part is 10% of the total heat drop. Neglect approach velocity.

   [Ans. Throat area = 33.74 cm^2, Exit area = 142.8 cm^2]

4. Dry saturated steam is expanded in a nozzle from a pressure of 10 Bar to a pressure of
   5 Bar. If the expansion is supersaturated, find the degree of (i) undercooling, (ii) supersaturation.

   [Ans. 39.8°C, 3.2]

5. Compare the mass of discharge from a CD nozzle expanding from 8 bar and 250°C to 2 bar absolute when (i) the expansion takes place under thermal equilibrium, (ii) metastable expansion.

[Ans. 2.37 %]

6. The nozzles in the stage of an impulse turbine receive steam at 12 bar, superheat 62°C. The pressure in the wheel chamber is 4 bar. State whether the nozzle is convergent, divergent or convergent-divergent. Assuming negligible approach velocity and 10 % frictional loss, suggest suitable number of nozzles to be used for a flow rate of
450 kg/min approximately with the exit area of 2.4 cm². Also find rate of discharge through the nozzles.

   [Ans. Convergent-divergent, number of nozzles = 24, 0.3125 kg/sec/nozzle]

Unit - VI

STEAM TURBINES

6.1 INTRODUCTION

Steam turbine is a device to transform heat energy into mechanical work. The steam turbine is superior to steam engines used earlier because of its better efficiency. Steam turbines can develop upto 1,00,000 kW for a single rotor. Steam turbines are extensively used in power generation, on ships, in sugar industry. In steam turbines the enthalpy is first converted wholly or partially into kinetic energy which is later transformed into mechanical work.

6.2 COMPARIOSON OF STEAM TURBINES AND STEAM ENGINES

Advantages of Steam Turbines over Steam Engines :

- In steam turbines there are no reciprocating parts, hence frictional losses are less. The vibrations are also less.
- Steam turbines work on rankine cycle, whereas steam engine works on modified rankine cycle as it is uneconomical to expand the steam upto atmospheric pressure in the cylinder as it will need a very long cylinder. The efficiency of rankine cycle is more than modified rankine cycle.
- Number of parts are less in steam turbine as compared with steam engine. Hence the construction of steam turbine is simpler as compared with steam engine.
- Power to weight ratio is higher for steam turbines.
- The turning movement developed by turbine is uniform, whereas turning movement developed by steam engine is not uniform. Hence steam engine needs a flywheel whereas steam turbine does not need a flywheel.
- Steam turbine can take overloads with slight reduction in thermal efficiency.

Disadvantages of Steam Turbines :

The turbines can operate efficiently at higher speeds, whereas actual applications need lower speed and as such speed reduction is essential for utilising power developed by the steam turbine. There are considerable losses in the reduction gear boxes.

6.3 CONSTRUCTION OF STEAM TURBINE

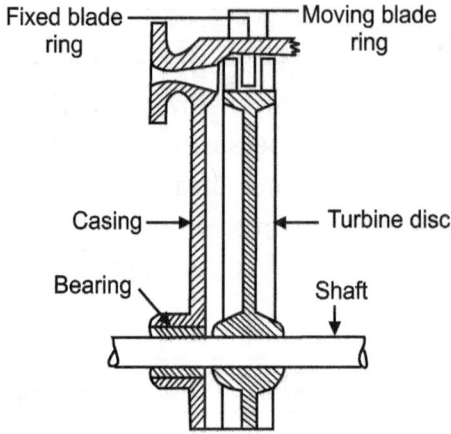

Fig. 6.1 : Construction of steam turbine

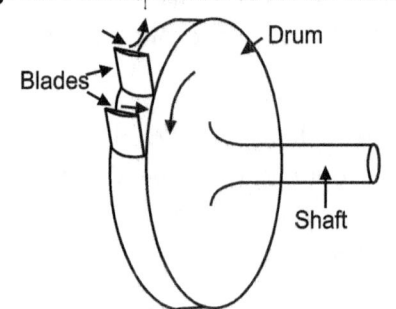

Fig. 6.2 : Construction of steam turbine

The steam turbine consists of casing, drum, shaft, blades, bearings and packings. The drum is keyed to the shaft which is supported on bearings. The moving blades are fixed on the drum whereas fixed blades are attached to the casing. The packings are used to stop leakage of steam from the space between the shaft and hole in the casing.

6.4 TYPES OF TURBINES

The size of the turbine is limited by the centrifugal force acting on the turbine disc. If we expand the steam at one stretch then the velocity of the steam turbine blades will be very high and due to limitation of centrifugal force, the size of the turbine will be small. Due to high speed of rotation of the turbine, a direct drive between turbine shaft and external equipment is not possible. For this reason, a reduction gear box is used. The problem in steam turbine development is to reduce the speed of rotation and at the same time to make full use of energy in the steam, thus allowing production of turbines of large size and high power output. The turbines are classified into two basic types.

1. Impulse turbine.
2. Reaction turbine.

6.5 IMPULSE TURBINE

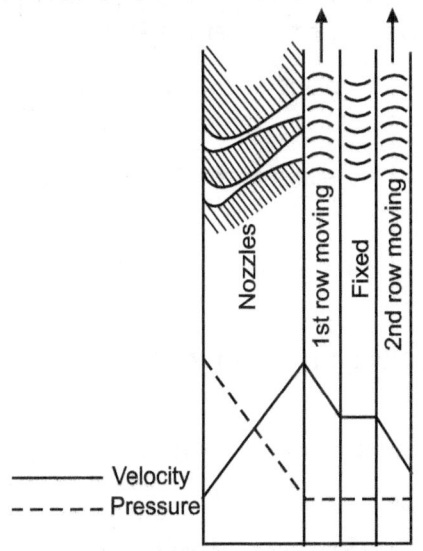

This type of turbine requires a set of nozzles and pressure drop of steam takes place in a nozzle and then throughout expansion. The pressure of the steam does not change over the moving blades. The velocity increases due to pressure drop in the nozzle. Some of the kinetic energy is imparted to moving blades to produce motion of the shaft and as such velocity decreases when flowing over the moving blades.

Fig. 6.3 : Impulse turbine pressure velocity variation

6.6 VELOCITY DIAGRAM FOR IMPULSE TURBINE

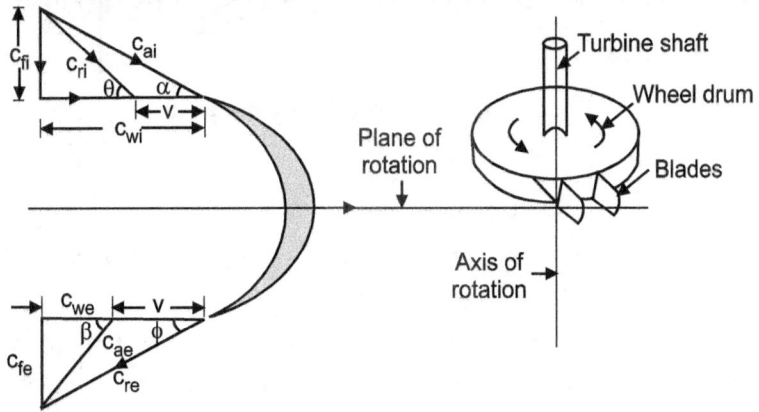

Fig. 6.4 : Velocity diagram

Let
- c_{ai} – Absolute velocity of steam at inlet.
- v – Mean blade speed.
- c_{ri} – Velocity of steam relative to the blade at inlet.
- α – Angle absolute velocity makes with plane of rotation.
- θ – Inlet angle of the blade.
- c_{ae} – Absolute velocity of steam at outlet.
- c_{re} – Velocity of steam relative to the blade at outlet.
- c_{wi} – The component of c_{ai} in the plane of rotation of blades (velocity of whirl at inlet).
- c_{we} – The component of c_{ae} in the plane of rotation of blades (velocity of whirl at outlet).
- c_{fi} – The component of c_{ai} which is along axis of rotation (velocity of flow at inlet).
- c_{fe} – The component of c_{ae} along the axis of rotation (velocity of flow at outlet).
- β – Angle absolute velocity makes with plane of rotation.
- ϕ – Outlet angle of the blade.

The combination of inlet and outlet velocity diagrams is as shown in Fig. 6.5.

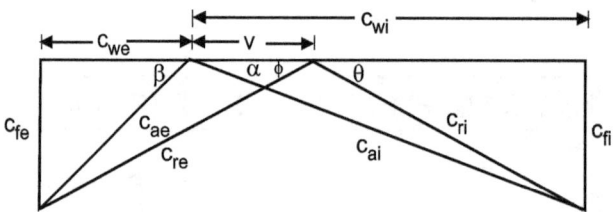

Fig. 6.5 : Combined velocity diagram

Expression for work done :

The absolute velocity has two components.

- The component in the direction of motion is called velocity of whirl or tangential velocity. This is responsible for producing motion.
- The component in the direction right angles to the direction of blade motion is called velocity of flow and is responsible for maintaining flow of steam along the axis of the steam to turbine in an axial flow turbine.

Now, Force = Rate of change of momentum
= mass × change in velocity of whirl
= mass × (− c_{we} − c_{wi})

(c_{we} is negative because it is opposite to the direction of motion of blades. The velocities in the direction of motion of blades are considered to be positive.)

∴ Tangential force = − m (c_{we} + c_{wi})

where m is mass of steam flowing through the blades in kg/sec and reaction to this force gives driving thrust on the wheel.

∴ Driving force on the wheel = m (c_{we} + c_{wi}) ... (6.1)

The rate of doing work is product of driving force multiplied by blade velocity.

= force × distance moved per second
= m (c_{we} + c_{wi}) · v

The axial thrust is given by product of mass of steam flowing parallel to the axis of rotation multiplied by change in velocity of flow.

∴ Axial thrust = m (c_{fe} − c_{fi}) ... (6.2)

If c_{fe} > c_{fi} the end thrust is in the opposite direction to the velocity of flow and vice versa.

6.7 EFFICIENCY OF IMPULSE TURBINE

The efficiency of impulse turbine is the ratio of work done to the energy supplied. It is also called diagram efficiency or blading efficiency or utilisation factor.

∴ Diagram efficiency = $\dfrac{\text{Work done by blades}}{\text{Energy supplied to the blades}}$

$$= \dfrac{(c_{wi} + c_{we})(v)}{c_{ai}^2/2}$$

$$= \dfrac{2 \cdot v \cdot (c_{wi} + c_{we})}{c_{ai}^2/2} \quad \text{... (6.3)}$$

It is now necessary to know on what factors diagram efficiency depends and to find out maximum value of diagram efficiency.

From velocity diagram,

c_{wi} = c_{ai} cos α = c_{ri} cos θ + v

c_{we} = c_{ae} cos β = c_{re} cos φ − v

$$\therefore \quad c_{wi} + c_{we} = c_{ri} \cos\theta + c_{re} \cos\phi$$

$$= c_{ri} \cos\theta \left[1 + \frac{c_{re} \cos\phi}{c_{ri} \cos\theta}\right]$$

$$= c_{ri} \cos\theta \, [1 + kc] \quad \ldots (6.4)$$

where $\quad k = \dfrac{c_{re}}{c_{ri}} \quad$ and $\quad c = \dfrac{\cos\phi}{\cos\theta}$

Now, $\quad c_{ri} \cos\theta = c_{ai} \cos\alpha - v$

Substituting this value of $c_{ri} \cos\theta$ in equation (3.4), we get

$$c_{wi} + c_{we} = (c_{ai} \cos\alpha - v)(1 + kc)$$

Hence work done per kg of steam per second will be

$$W = (c_{ai} \cos\alpha - v)(1 + kc) \, v \quad \ldots (6.5)$$

Hence diagram efficiency $= \dfrac{\text{Work done}}{\text{Energy supplied}}$

$$= \frac{(c_{ai} \cos\alpha - v)(1 + kc) \, v}{c_{ai}^2 / 2}$$

$$= \frac{2(c_{ai} \cos\alpha - v)(1 + kc)(v)}{c_{ai}^2}$$

$$= (1 + kc) \cdot \frac{v}{c_{ai}} \cdot 2 \left[\cos\alpha - \frac{v}{c_{ai}}\right]$$

Now, let $\quad \rho = \dfrac{v}{c_{ai}}$

This factor is called blade speed ratio and is an important factor in the design of turbine blades.

$\therefore \quad$ Diagram efficiency $= [2(1 + kc) \rho (\cos\alpha - \rho)]$

$$= 2(1 + kc)(\rho \cos\alpha - \rho^2) \quad \ldots (6.6)$$

Hence from equation (6.6), it will be seen that diagram efficiency is a function of Nozzle angle α, blade speed ratio ρ, blade velocity coefficient k and blade angles θ and ϕ.

Now as per equation (6.5),

$$\text{Work done} = (c_{ai} \cos\alpha - v)(1 + kc) \, v$$

Other parameters remaining the same, the work done is maximum if $\cos\alpha = 1$ i.e. if $\alpha = 0$. But if α is reduced, c_f decreases which means reduced axial flow of steam. Hence for maintaining same quantity of flow we have to increase annulus area. The increased annular area increases friction in the passage which is not desirable. It is to be understood that velocity of flow is responsible for continuous flow of steam over the blades. Hence optimum value of nozzle angle lies within limits of 14° to 20°.

6.8 MAXIMUM DIAGRAM EFFICIENCY

If α, k, c are assumed to be constant, the diagram efficiency depends upon the value of ρ. In order to determine the optimum value of ρ for maximum diagram efficiency, differentiate equation (6.6) with respect to ρ and equate to zero. Let diagram efficiency be denoted by η_d.

Hence, $\quad \dfrac{d}{d\rho}$ (diagram efficiency) $= 2(1 + kc)(\cos \alpha - 2\rho) = 0$

or $\quad \rho = \dfrac{\cos \alpha}{2}$ since $1 + kc$ is not equal to zero.

Now substituting $\quad \rho = \dfrac{\cos \alpha}{2}$ in equation (6.6) we get,

$$\eta_{d\,(max)} = 2(1 + kc)\left[\dfrac{\cos \alpha}{2} \cdot \cos \alpha - \dfrac{\cos^2 \alpha}{4}\right]$$

$$= (1 + kc)\dfrac{\cos^2 \alpha}{2}$$

If we assume that blades are symmetrical, $\theta = \phi$.

$\therefore \quad \dfrac{\cos \phi}{\cos \theta} = 1$

and if we assume that friction is absent, $c_{ri} = c_{re}$

$\therefore \quad \dfrac{c_{ri}}{c_{re}} = k = 1$

$\therefore \quad \eta_{d\,(max)} = \cos^2 \alpha \quad \ldots (6.7)$

6.9 MAXIMUM WORK CORRESPONDING MAXIMUM EFFICIENCY CONDITION

Now as per equation (6.5),

Work done $= (c_{ai} \cos \alpha - v)(1 + kc)v$

Substituting $\quad \rho = \dfrac{\cos \alpha}{2} = \dfrac{v}{c_{ai}}$ in this equation,

$\therefore \quad W_{max} = \left(\dfrac{2v}{\cos \alpha} \cdot \cos \alpha - v\right)(1 + kc)v$

$$= (v)(1 + kc)v = (1 + kc)v^2$$

If blades are symmetrical $\theta = \phi$, $\therefore \dfrac{\cos \phi}{\cos \theta} = 1 = c$

If we assume that friction is absent, $c_{ri} = c_{re}$

$$\therefore \quad \dfrac{c_{ri}}{c_{re}} = k = 1$$

$$W_{max} = (1 + 1)v^2 = 2v^2 \qquad \ldots (6.8)$$

6.10 DIAGRAM EFFICIENCY AND MAXIMUM WORK VERSUS BLADE SPEED RATIO

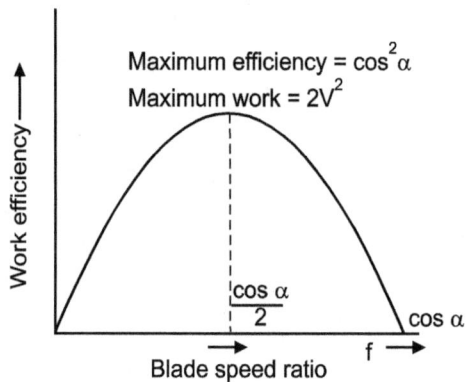

Fig. 6.6 : Maximum diagram efficiency and maximum work versus blade speed ratio

Observations :

1. When $\rho = \dfrac{\cos \alpha}{2}$, we get maximum efficiency and maximum work as derived earlier.

2. When $\rho = 0$, $\dfrac{v}{c_{ai}} = 0$.

   Now according to equation (3.5),
   $$W = (c_{ai} \cos \alpha - v)(1 + kc)v$$
   Substitute $v = 0$
   $$W = 0$$

3. When $\rho = \cos \alpha$ $\therefore \dfrac{v}{c_{ai}} = \cos \alpha$ or $v = c_{ai} \cos \alpha$.

   Now according to equation (6.5),

$$W = (c_{ai} \cos \alpha - v)(1 + k_c) v$$

Substitute $v = c_{ai} \cos \alpha$

∴
$$W = (v - v)(1 + k_c) v$$
$$= 0$$

Similarly, diagram efficiency will be zero when $\rho = 0$ and $\rho = \cos \alpha$.

According to equation (6.6),

$$\text{Diagram efficiency} = 2(1 + k_c)(\rho \cos \alpha - \rho^2)$$

Substitute $\rho = 0$

$$\text{Diagram efficiency} = 0$$

Substitute $\rho = \cos \alpha$

$$\text{Diagram efficiency} = 2(1 + k_c)(\cos^2 \alpha - \cos^2 \alpha)$$
$$= 0$$

6.11 EFFECT OF FRICTION

As the steam passes over the turbine blades, there will be friction between steam and the blades. This friction will result in a reduction of relative velocity. Thus c_{re} will be less than c_{ri}. The frictional loss is commonly expressed as a percentage loss of relative velocity.

SOLVED PROBLEMS

Problem 6.1

The nozzles of the simple impulse turbine are inclined at an angle of 20° to the direction of the path of moving blades and steam leaves nozzles at 420 m/sec. The blade speed is 180 m/sec. Find suitable inlet and outlet angles for the blades in order that there shall be no axial thrust on the blades allowing for the velocity of steam passing over the blades being reduced by 15%.

Determine also power developed for a steam flow of one kg/sec. Find kinetic energy of steam leaving the wheel.

Solution :

Axial thrust is given by difference between c_{fi} and c_{fe} multiplied by steam flow rate.
As axial thrust is zero, $c_{fi} = c_{fe}$.

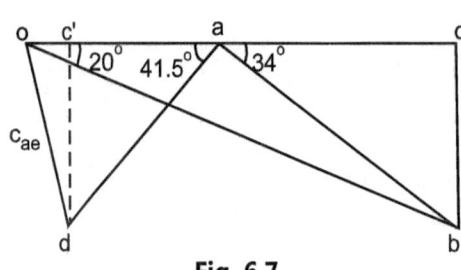

Fig. 6.7

Draw the velocity diagram using suitable scale.

$oa = v = 180$ m/sec
$ob = c_{ai} = 420$ m/sec
$ab = c_{ri} = 255$ m/sec

As frictional losses are 15%,

$$\frac{c_{re}}{c_{ri}} = 0.85$$

$c_{re} = ad = 0.85 \times c_{ri} = 0.85 \times ab = 216.75$ m/sec

1. Work done/kg $= (c_{wi} + c_{we}) \cdot v = (oc - oc')(v) = 370 \times 180$
   $= 66.6$ kJ/kg

As mass flow rate is 1 kg/sec.

Power developed $=$ Work done in $\dfrac{kJ}{kg} \times$ steam flow rate in $\dfrac{kg}{sec}$

$= 66.6 \times 1 = 66.6$ kJ/sec $= 66.6$ kW ... **Ans.**

2. Blade angle at inlet $= \angle cab = 34°$ (measured from diagram) ... **Ans.**
3. Blade angle at outlet $= \angle oad = 41.5°$ (measured from diagram) ... **Ans.**
4. K.E. of steam leaving the turbine $= \dfrac{c_{ae}^2}{2} = \dfrac{(145)^2}{2} = 10512.5$ Nm $= 10.512$ kJ.

Example 6.2

The following data refers to one stage of an impulse turbine.
Isentropic heat drop 190 kJ/kg. Friction in nozzle is 10% isentropic heat drop. Nozzle angle 20°. Ratio of blade speed to whirl component of steam speed is 0.4. Velocity coefficient for blades 0.90. The velocity of steam at entry to nozzle is 35 m/sec. Find the blade angles so that steam may enter them without shock and leave them in axial direction. Draw an energy balance per kg of steam.

Solution :

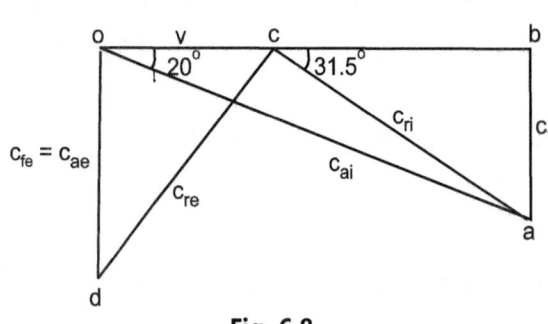

Fig. 6.8

$ob = c_{wi} = 560$ m/sec
$oa = c_{ai} = 585$ m/sec
$oc = v = 224$ m/sec
$ca = c_{ri} = 380$ m/sec
$od = c_{ae} = c_{fe} = 260$ m/sec
$cd = c_{re} = 342$ m/sec

Draw velocity diagram using the data.

Useful heat drop which is converted into kinetic energy
$$= 190 \times 0.9 = 171 \text{ kJ}$$

If c_{ai} is the steam velocity issuing from the nozzle,

then
$$\frac{c_{ai}^2 - 35^2}{2 \times 10^3} = 171$$

$\therefore \qquad c_{ai} = 585.85 \text{ m/sec}$

Blade velocity, $\quad v = (0.4)(c_{wi}) = (0.4)(560)$
$$= 224 \text{ m/sec}$$

$c_{ve} = (0.9)(c_{ri}) = (0.9)(380) = 342 \text{ m/sec}$

$c_{ae} = c_{fe} = 260 \text{ m/sec}$

As discharge is axial, $\angle \beta = 90°$ $\therefore c_{ae} = c_{fe}$.

c_{ae}, c_{fe}, c_{ri} are measured from the diagram.

(I) Work done/kg $= (c_{wi} + c_{we})(v) = (c_{wi} + 0)(v)$
$$= (560)(224) = 125400 \text{ Nm/kg} = 125.4 \text{ kJ/kg}$$

(II) Frictional loss $= \dfrac{c_{ri}^2 - c_{re}^2}{2} = \dfrac{380^2 - 342^2}{2} = 13718 \text{ J/kg} = 13.718 \text{ kJ/kg}$

(III) Kinetic energy loss at exit $= \dfrac{c_{ae}^2}{2} = \dfrac{260^2}{2} = 33800 \text{ J/kg} = 33.8 \text{ kJ/kg}$

(IV) K.E. supplied at inlet $= \dfrac{(\text{Velocity of approach})^2}{2} = \dfrac{35^2}{2} = 612.5 \text{ J/kg}$
$$= 0.6125 \text{ kJ/kg}$$

Heat balance on kg basis

Energy supplied		Energy spent	
Heat supplied –	190 kJ	Useful work	– 125.4 kJ
K.E. supplied –	0.6125 kJ	Nozzle friction	– 19 kJ
		Blade friction	– 13.7 kJ
		K.E. loss at exit	– 33.8 kJ
190.6125 kJ		**191.9 kJ**	

The error of 191.9 – 190.6125 = 0.2875 kJ/kg is in the scaling of velocity diagram.

Problem 6.3

In a velocity compounded impulse turbine, the steam leaves the nozzle at 500 m/sec and after passing through the fixed and moving blade ring it is discharged from the second moving blade ring in an axial direction. The axial velocity of flow in the first moving ring is twice that in the second moving blade ring. The discharge angle of the second moving blade ring is 30° to the plane of rotation. The relative velocity of steam falls by 10% in the passage through each blade ring, fixed and moving. The blade angles are such that the flow is shockless and that there is no end thrust on either moving ring. Find (1) Blade speed, (2) Nozzle angle, (3) Blade angles, (4) Work done per kg of steam.

Solution :

Draw outlet triangle for second row moving blade to any scale.

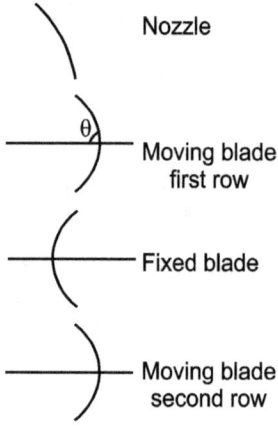

Fig. 6.9

Measure $c_{re\,II}$ on the diagram which is 29 units.

$$c_{ri\,II} = \frac{c_{re\,II}}{0.9} = 32 \text{ units}$$

Measure $c_{ai\,II}$ on the diagram which is 56 units.

As the losses in the fixed blade are 10%, inlet to fixed blade is $\frac{56}{0.9}$ = 62 units.

This is also outlet velocity of first ring of moving blades.

As axial velocity of first ring of moving blades is two times the axial velocity of second ring of moving blades,

$$c_{fe\,I} = c_{fe\,II} \times 2 = 2 \times 14 = 28 \text{ units}$$

Measure $c_{re\,I}$ from the diagram which is 84 units.

As frictional losses in moving blades are 10%,

$$c_{ri\,I} = \frac{c_{ri\,I}}{0.9} = \frac{84}{0.9} = 93 \text{ units}$$

Measure $c_{ai\,I}$ from the diagram which is 116 units.

$$116 \text{ unit} = 500 \text{ m/sec}$$

Now measure other velocities in the diagram using this scale

$$1 \text{ units} = \frac{500}{116} = 4.3 \text{ m/sec}$$

1. Blade speed = v = 25 units × 4.3 = 107.5 m/sec. ... Ans.
2. Nozzle angle α from the diagram = 15° ... Ans.
3. Inlet blade angle = θ = 17.5°. ... Ans.
4. Outlet blade angle = φ = 20°. ... Ans.
5. Work done per kg of steam = $(c_{wi\,I} + c_{we\,I}) + (c_{wi\,II} + c_{we\,II}) \, v$

$$= \frac{[(170 \times 4.3) + (55 \times 4.3)](107.5)}{1000}$$

$$= 104 \text{ kJ/kg}$$ ... Ans.

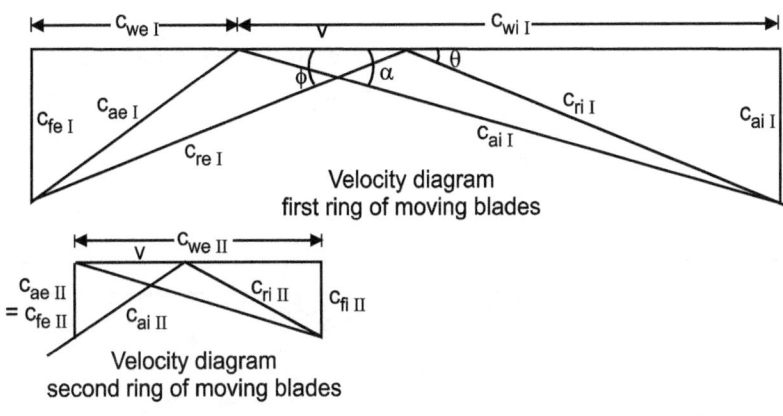

Fig. 6.10 : Velocity diagram

Problem 6.4

The following particulars refer to a velocity compounded impulse turbine with two rows of moving blades with a fixed row of guide blades between them.

Velocity of steam leaving nozzles is 1000 m/sec. Nozzle angle is 20°. Blade speed is 200 m/sec. Blade angles of first moving blades are symmetrical and blade outlet angle of the fixed blade is 23°. Blade outlet angle of the second moving blade is 30°. Friction factor for all rows is 0.9.

Determine : (a) Power output in kW. (b) Axial thrust on rotor.

Steam consumption of the turbine is 4000 kg/hour.

Solution :

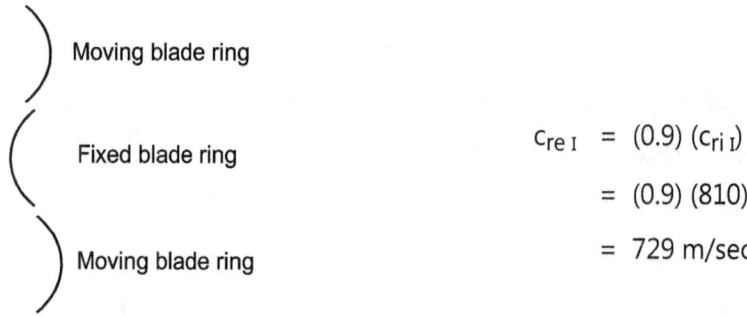

Fig. 6.11

$$c_{re\,I} = (0.9)(c_{ri\,I})$$
$$= (0.9)(810)$$
$$= 729 \text{ m/sec}$$

$$ab = v = 200 \text{ m/sec}$$
$$bc = c_{ri\,I} = 810 \text{ m/sec}$$
$$ac = c_{ai\,I} = 1000 \text{ m/sec}$$
$$\angle cbd = \angle abf = 26° \text{ as blades are symmetrical}$$
$$af = c_{ae\,I} = 550 \text{ m/sec}$$
$$c_{we\,I} + c_{wi\,I} = 1390 \text{ m/sec}$$

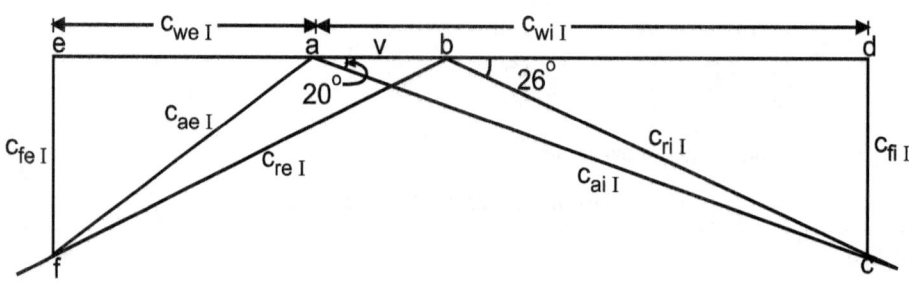

Fig. 6.12

Blade outlet angle of fixed blade is inlet angle with which steam enters second ring of moving blades. This angle is 23°. The steam enters second ring of moving blades with velocity $0.9 \times c_{ae\,I} = (0.9)(550) = 495$ m/sec.

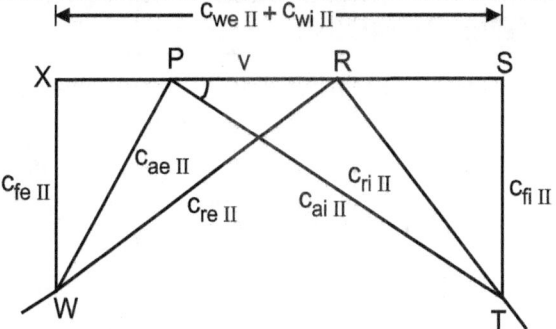

Fig. 6.13

$$c_{re\,II} = (0.9)(c_{ri\,II}) = (0.9)(310) = 279 \text{ m/sec}$$

$$c_{we\,II} + c_{wi\,II} = 500 \text{ m/sec}$$

I. Power output $= \dfrac{\text{mass flow rate in kg}}{\text{sec}} \cdot \left(c_{w\,stage\,I} + c_{w\,stage\,II}\right) v$

$$= \dfrac{4000}{3600} \cdot \dfrac{(1390 + 500)(200)}{1000} \text{ kW}$$

$$= \dfrac{40}{36}\left(\dfrac{1890 \times 200}{1000}\right) = \dfrac{40}{36}(189 \times 2)$$

$$= 420 \text{ kW} \quad \text{... Ans.}$$

II. Axial thrust on rotor $= $ m in kg/sec $[(c_{fi\,I} + c_{fi\,II}) - (c_{fe\,I} + c_{fe\,II})]$

$$= \dfrac{4000}{3600}[(360 + 200) - (320 + 140)]$$

$$= \dfrac{4000}{3600}[(560 - 460)] = \dfrac{4000 \times 100}{3600} \text{ Newtons}$$

$$= 111.1 \text{ Newtons} \quad \text{... Ans.}$$

6.12 COMPOUNDING OF TURBINES

As mentioned in earlier articles, the disadvantage of steam turbine is its high speed. Hence methods to reduce to turbine speed have been used. These methods are compounding of turbines. There are three methods of compounding of turbines.

(a) Velocity compounding. (b) Pressure compounding.

(c) Pressure - velocity compounding.

6.13 VELOCITY COMPOUNDING

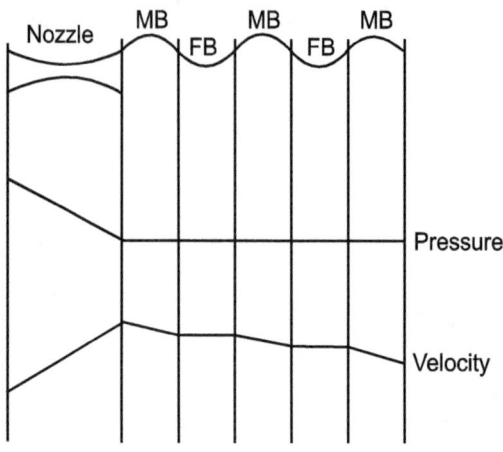

Fig. 6.14 : Velocity compounding

Steam is expanded in a single row of nozzles. The high velocity steam leaving the nozzles passes on to the first row of moving blades where its velocity is only partially reduced.

The steam leaving first row of moving blades passes into a row of fixed blades which are mounted in the turbine casing. Velocity remains constant in fixed blades. The velocity change is only in moving blades. The velocity compounded impulse turbine runs at constant pressure. This type of turbine is known as 'CURTIS' turbine.

6.14 PRESSURE COMPOUNDING

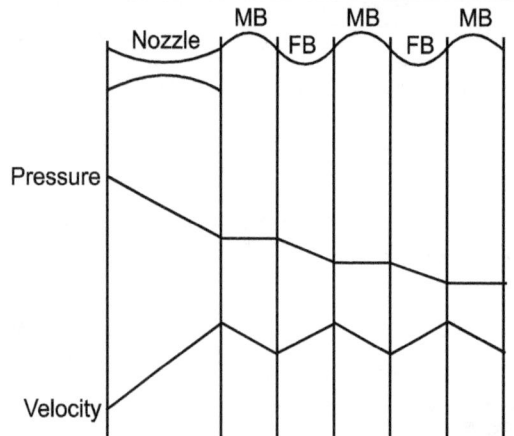

Pressure decreases in nozzles in stages. The pressure remains constant when steam passes over moving blades.

Velocity increases in nozzles and decreases in moving blades only.

As only part of pressure drop occurs in each stage, the steam velocities will not be high and turbine will run slower. This type of turbine is known as 'RATEAU' turbine.

Fig. 6.15 : Pressure compounding

In pressure compounded turbine, pressure decreases progressively and hence specific volume of steam also increases progressively. Hence to keep same rate of steam flow, blade height has to be increased progressively to accommodate this higher volume of steam.

6.15 PRESSUSRE VELOCITY COMPOUNDING

In this type, both the two previous methods are used.

Pressure : Pressure drops in nozzles only and remains constant over fixed and moving blades.

Velocity : Velocity increases in nozzles and remains constant over fixed blades and decreases over moving blades.

The total pressure drop of the steam is divided into stages and velocity obtained in each stage is also compounded. This has the advantage of allowing a bigger pressure drop in each stage and consequently less stages are required, hence a shorter turbine will be obtained for a given total pressure drop.

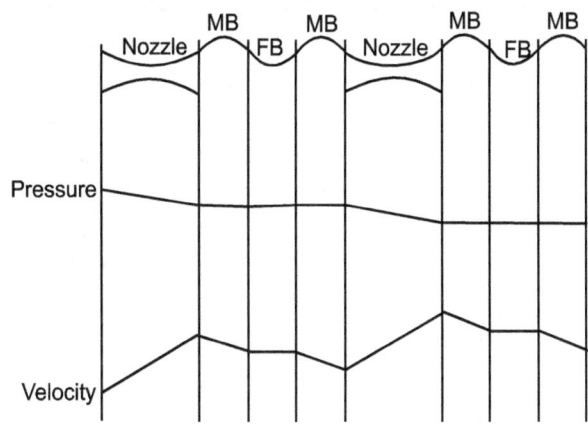

Fig. 6.16 : Pressure velocity compounding

6.16 ADVANTAGES AND DISADVANTAGES OF VELOCITY COMPOUNDING

Advantages	Disadvantages
1. As all pressure drop is taking place in nozzles, turbine operates at atmospheric pressure. Hence turbine housing need not be strong.	1. As all energy is converted into kinetic energy in one stroke itself, the frictional losses in the nozzle are large which decreases the efficiency of the turbine.
2. The arrangement needs little space.	2. The efficiency of the turbine goes on decreasing with increase in number of stages.
3. There are fewer number of stages and hence initial cost is less.	3. Power developed in last stages is only fraction of power developed in first low, still all stages require same space and material.

6.17 IMPULSE REACTION TURBINE

A pure impulse turbine based on principle of famous Hero wheel was built in 1883 by Gustaf delaval. The tip speed was 180 meters per second and speed of rotation was 42000 r.p.m. This turbine was not efficient and hence was not practical. Hence in practice an impulse-reaction turbine which derives its energy partly due to impulse and partly due to reaction of exit steam is used. Each stage of reaction turbine consists of a fixed row of blades over the whole of the circumferential annulus and an equal number of blades on a wheel. The fixed blade channels are of nozzle shape and there is a small drop of pressure which is accompanied by increase in velocity. The steam then passes over the moving blades. Due to increasing area of blades (since X > Y), there is pressure drop.

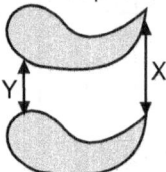

Fig. 6.17 : Reaction turbine blades

6.18 WORKING OF REACTION TURBINE

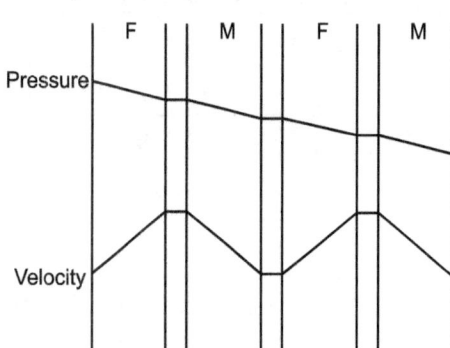

Fig. 6.18 : Reaction turbine

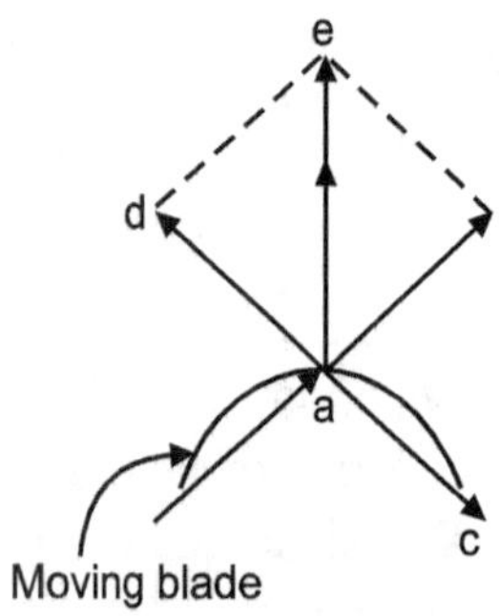

As the steam passes over the fixed blades pressure drops and there is increase in velocity. As the steam impinges on moving blades, just as in impulse turbine, it gives impulse to the blades.

As stated earlier due to increase in area through which steam flows there is drop in pressure. When pressure decreases the velocity increases. But as this energy has to drive the load this energy is utilised in decreasing the velocity as the steam passes over the moving blades.

ab is the force acting on the blade due to impulse. ac is the force of the exit steam. ad is the reaction to this force, hence the resulting force is ae which rotates the blades.

Fig. 6.19 : Force diagram

6.19 DEGREE OF REACTION

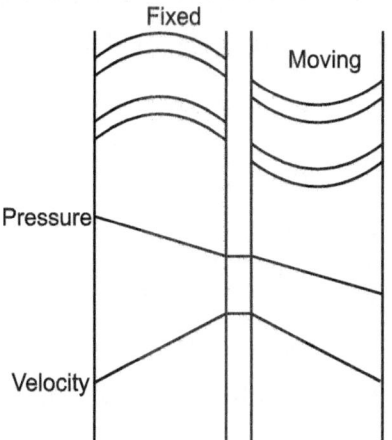

Fig. 6.20 (A) : Reaction turbine pressure- velocity variation

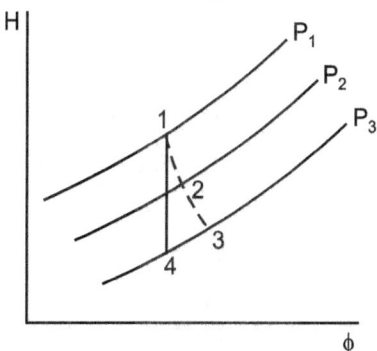

Fig. 6.20 (B) : Reaction turbine H- ϕ diagram

The degree of reaction is defined as the ratio of isentropic heat drop in the moving blades to the isentropic heat drop in the entire stage of the reaction turbine.

(**Note** : A set of fixed and moving blades is called a stage.)

$$\therefore \quad \text{Degree of reaction} = \frac{h_2 - h_3}{h_1 - h_3}$$

Fig. 6.21 : Velocity diagram reaction turbine

The enthalpy drop $h_2 - h_3$ represents the increase in relative kinetic energy in the moving blade.

The enthalpy drop $h_1 - h_3$ represents work output of the stage.

$$\therefore \quad \text{Degree of reaction} = \frac{\dfrac{C_{re}^2 - C_{ri}^2}{2}}{(C_{wi} + C_{we}) \cdot v} = \frac{C_{re}^2 - C_{ri}^2}{2 \cdot C_w \cdot v}$$

Referring to the velocity diagram,

$$C_{re} = C_{fe} \operatorname{cosec} \phi, \quad C_{ri} = C_{fi} \operatorname{cosec} \theta$$

and

$$C_w = C_f (\cot \phi + \cot \theta)$$

$C_{fi} = C_{fe} = C_f$ is the velocity of flow which remains constant throughout a stage.

$$\therefore \quad R = \frac{(C_f \operatorname{cosec} \phi)^2 - (C_f \operatorname{cosec} \theta)^2}{2 \cdot v \cdot C_f (\cot \phi + \cot \theta)}$$

$$R = \frac{C_f^2 (\operatorname{cosec}^2 \phi - \operatorname{cosec}^2 \theta)}{C_f \cdot 2 \cdot v (\cot \phi + \cot \theta)}$$

$$= \frac{C_f (\cot \phi - \cot \theta)}{2v}$$

For 50% degree of reaction,

$$\frac{1}{2} = \frac{C_f \cdot (\cot \phi - \cot \theta)}{2v}$$

$$\therefore \quad v = C_f (\cot \phi - \cot \theta) \quad \ldots (6.9)$$

From the velocity diagram,

$$v = C_f (\cot \phi - \cot \beta)$$

and

$$v = C_f (\cot \alpha - \cot \theta)$$

but from equation (6.9),

$$v = C_f (\cot \phi - \cot \theta)$$

$\therefore$ Equating,

$$(\cot \phi - \cot \beta) = (\cot \phi - \cot \theta)$$

$$\therefore \quad \beta = \theta$$

Similarly,

$$C_f (\cot \alpha - \cot \theta) = C_f (\cot \phi - \cot \theta)$$

$$\therefore \quad \alpha = \phi$$

Hence when degree of reaction is 50%, $\alpha = \phi$ and $\beta = \theta$ and inlet and outlet velocity diagrams are symmetrical and blades are symmetrical. This type of turbine is called Parson reaction turbine.

6.20 EFFICIENCY OF REACTION TURBINE

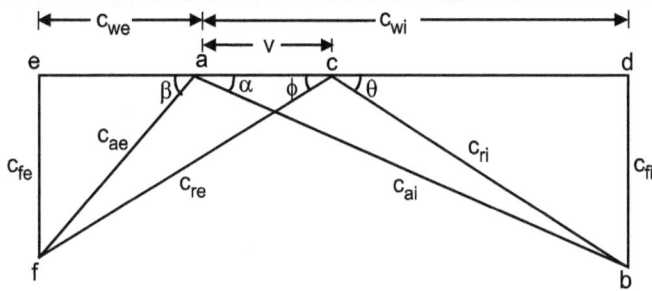

Fig. 6.22 : Efficiency of reaction turbine

$$\text{Kinetic energy supplied to fixed blade} = \frac{c_{ai}^2}{2}$$

$$\text{Kinetic energy supplied to moving blade} = \frac{c_{re}^2 - c_{ri}^2}{2}$$

$$\text{Total energy supplied} = \frac{c_{ai}^2}{2} + \frac{c_{re}^2 - c_{ri}^2}{2}$$

For Parson turbine with 50% degree of reaction, Δ abd and Δ cfe are similar

$\therefore \qquad c_{ai} = c_{re}$

$$\text{Total energy supplied} = \frac{c_{ai}^2}{2} + \frac{c_{ai}^2}{2} - \frac{c_{ri}^2}{2}$$

$$= c_{ai}^2 - \frac{c_{ri}^2}{2}$$

From velocity diagram,

$$c_{ri}^2 = c_{ai}^2 + v^2 - 2 \cdot v \cdot c_{ai} \cos \alpha$$

$\therefore \qquad \text{Total energy supplied} = c_{ai}^2 - \left[\frac{c_{ai}^2 + v^2 - 2 \cdot v \cdot c_{ai} \cos \alpha}{2} \right]$

$$= \frac{c_{ai}^2 - v^2 + 2 \cdot v \cdot c_{ai} \cos \alpha}{2} \qquad \ldots (6.10)$$

Now, $\qquad \text{Work done} = c_w \cdot v$

$$= v \cdot [c_{ai} \cos \alpha + c_{re} \cos \phi - v]$$

but $c_{ai} = c_{re}$ and $\alpha = \phi$ and $\theta = \beta$

$$\therefore \quad W = v\,[2\,c_{ai} \cos \alpha - v]$$

$$\therefore \quad \text{Diagram efficiency} = \frac{\text{Work done}}{\text{Energy supplied}} = \frac{v\,[2\,c_{ai} \cos \alpha - v]}{\left(\dfrac{c_{ai}^2 - v^2 + 2v\,c_{ai} \cos \alpha}{2}\right)}$$

$$= \frac{2 \cdot v \cdot [2 \cdot c_{ai} \cos \alpha - v]}{c_{ai}^2 - v^2 + 2v\,c_{ai} \cos \alpha}$$

Dividing numerator and denominator by c_{ai}^2, we get

$$DE = \frac{2\left(\dfrac{2 \cdot v \cdot c_{ai} \cos \alpha}{c_{ai}^2} - \dfrac{v^2}{c_{ai}^2}\right)}{1 - \dfrac{v^2}{c_{ai}^2} + \dfrac{2v \cos \alpha}{c_{ai}}} = \frac{2\left(\dfrac{2 \cdot v}{c_{ai}} \cos \alpha - \dfrac{v^2}{c_{ai}^2}\right)}{1 - \dfrac{v^2}{c_{ai}^2} + \dfrac{2 \cdot v}{c_{ai}} \cos \alpha}$$

Now, let
$$\rho = \frac{v}{c_{ai}} = \text{blade speed radio}$$

$$\therefore \quad DE = \left[\frac{2\,(2\rho \cos \alpha - \rho^2)}{1 - \rho^2 + 2 \cdot \rho \cos \alpha}\right] \quad \ldots (6.11)$$

The efficiency is maximum when $1 - \rho^2 + 2\rho \cos \alpha$ is minimum.

or when $\dfrac{d}{d\rho}\,[1 - \rho^2 + 2\rho \cos \alpha] = 0$

$$\therefore \quad -2\rho + 2 \cos \alpha = 0$$

$$\therefore \quad \rho = \cos \alpha$$

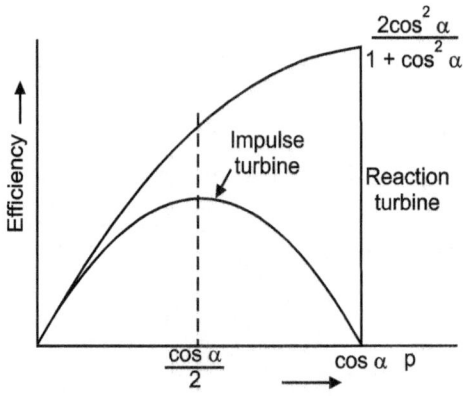

Fig. 6.23 : Efficiency versus ρ

As the curve of efficiency versus ρ for reaction turbine is flat and hence a small variation in ρ from optimum value will not cause much change in the value of efficiency.

For getting the maximum value of efficiency, put $\rho = \cos \alpha$ in equation (6.11).

We get
$$\eta_{max} = \frac{2 \cdot \rho(\rho)}{1 - \rho^2 + 2\rho^2} = \frac{2\rho^2}{1 + \rho^2} = \frac{2 \cdot \cos^2 \alpha}{1 + \cos^2 \alpha} \quad \ldots (6.12)$$

6.21 REHEAT FACTOR

Steam expands through the turbine accompanied by friction. There are other losses such as leakage, which gives rise to throttling. Due to this the flow of steam does not remain isentropic but becomes irreversible accompanied by increase in entropy. Hence referring to HS diagram the expansion will not be AD but $A_1 A_2 A_3 A_4 A_5 A_6$.

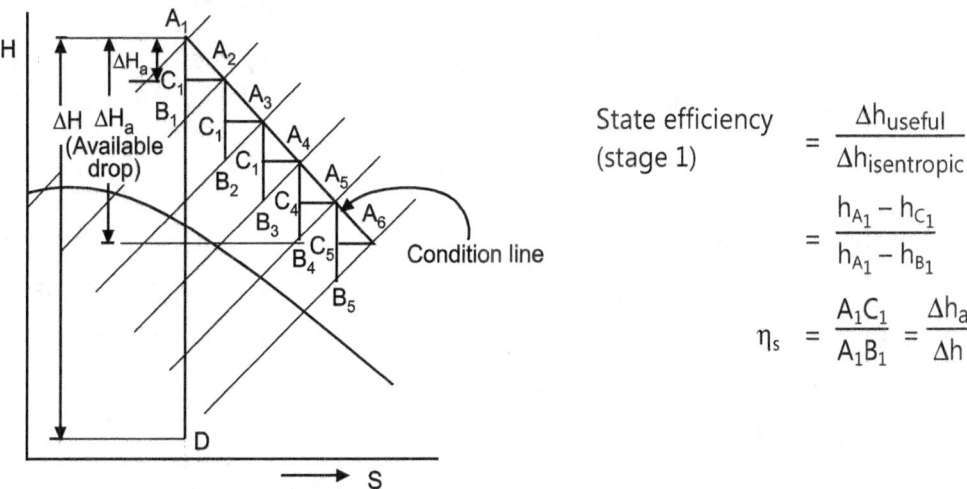

State efficiency (stage 1) $= \dfrac{\Delta h_{useful}}{\Delta h_{isentropic}}$

$= \dfrac{h_{A_1} - h_{C_1}}{h_{A_1} - h_{B_1}}$

$\eta_s = \dfrac{A_1 C_1}{A_1 B_1} = \dfrac{\Delta h_a}{\Delta h}$

Fig. 6.24 : Reheat factor

Overall efficiency $= \dfrac{\text{Actual enthalpy drop in turbine}}{\text{Isentropic enthalpy drop}}$

$\eta_o = \dfrac{\Delta H_a}{\Delta H}$

The overall efficiency indicates with what degree thermal energy is converted into useful work in the turbine.

Reheat factor $= \dfrac{A_1 B_1 + A_2 B_2 + A_3 B_3 + A_4 B_4 + A_5 B_5}{AD}$

$= \dfrac{\text{Cumulative enthalpy drop}}{\text{Total isentropic enthalpy drop}}$

The reheat factor is usually between 1.02 to 1.06.

6.23 LOSSES IN TURBINE

The losses are difference between isentropic heat drop and available heat drop.

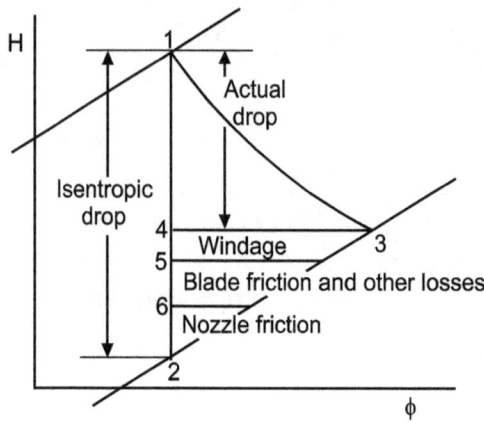

Fig. 6.25 : Losses in turbine

The losses are due to following reasons :

(1) Losses in Nozzle : When the steam passes through nozzle due to friction between steam and inside wall of nozzle there is enthalpy loss.

(2) Losses in Blade Ppassage : When steam passes over the blades there is a loss of enthalpy due to friction.

(3) Residual Velocity Loss : Steam leaves the turbine with velocity c_{ae}. Hence energy loss is $\dfrac{c_{ae}^2}{2}$.

(4) Windage and Disc Friction :

When steam turbine disc rotates, steam is thrown towards the casing due to centrifugal force which causes friction between steam and blade surface. When the turbine rotor moves at high speed in the casing there is windage loss.

(5) Losses in Regulating Valves :

Steam has to pass through the valves where throttling action takes place which gives rise to some loss of enthalpy.

(6) Losses due to Leakage :

The leakage of steam takes place through annular area between shaft and hole in casing of the turbine.

(7) Losses Due to Mechanical Friction :

There is friction between rotor shaft and bearings due to which there is loss of power.

(8) Loss Due to Radiation :

The heat is lost due to radiation from turbine casing. Every effort is made to minimise these losses.

6.24 GOVERNING OF STEAM TURBINES

Purpose of Governing the Turbine :

The turbine is designed to operate at most economic capacity. (The capacity at which steam consumption is minimum).

However in operation, the turbine is required to run at different loads. At different loads the speed of the turbine should be maintained at the desired speed.

There are five different methods of governing a turbine.

1. Throttle governing.
2. Nozzle control governing.
3. By-pass governing.
4. Combination of throttle and nozzle governing.
5. Combination of throttle and by-pass governing.

(1) Throttle Governing :

Please refer to Fig. 3.26.

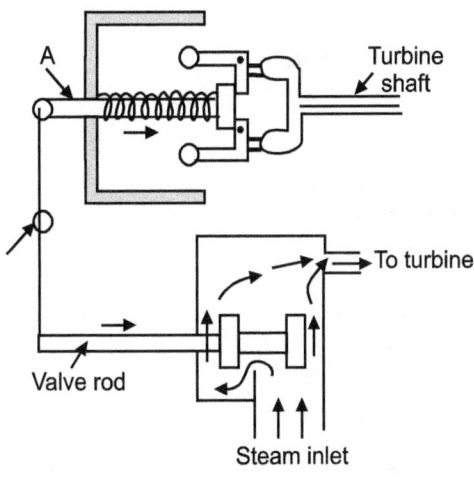

Fig. 6.26 : Throttle Governing

When the load on the turbine decreases, the speed of the turbine increases. This increases speed of centrifugal governor. The governor balls try to move out which moves the shaft to the left against force of spring. The throttle valve rod and valve moves to the right and decreases opening thereby throttling the steam. This will decrease steam supply pressure and then speed will drop down at desired value.

The mechanism of throttle governing is simple but due to irreversible throttling process, the throttle governing is not efficient.

This type of governing is used in small turbines only.

(2) Nozzle Control Governing :

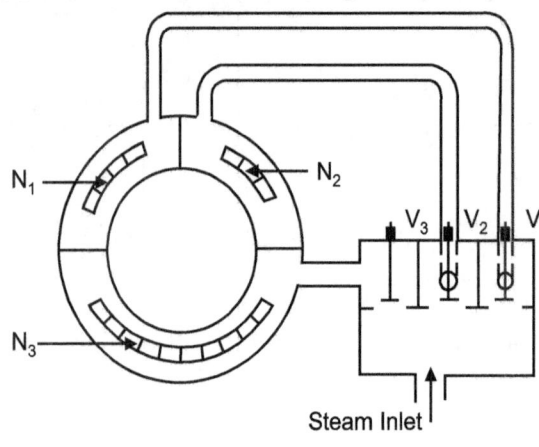

N_1, N_2, N_3 are three different sets of nozzles controlled by valves V_1, V_2 and V_3. Each set has different number of nozzles.

When load on the turbine increases a set with more number of nozzles supplies the steam to the turbine and remaining sets are shut off. By this way desired speed is obtained.

With the nozzle governing the enthalpy drop available as the load is decreased, is greater than throttle governing.

Fig. 6.27 : Nozzle governing

(3) By-pass Governing :

Steam turbines are designed for economic load with full admission of steam at high pressure stages. When the turbine is required to operate at maximum load, additional steam supply is required. Additional steam cannot be admitted in the first stage as additional nozzles are not available.

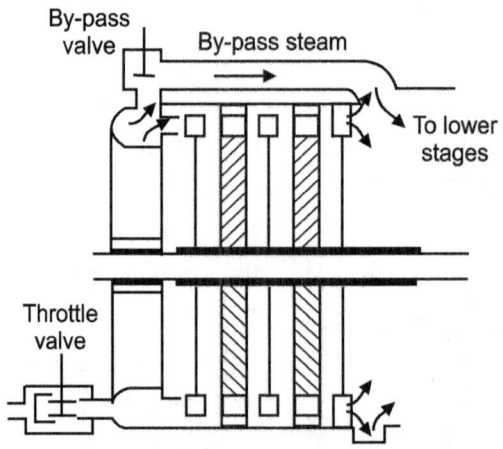

Fig. 6.28 : By-pass governing

Hence a bye-pass valve is provided which by-passes intermediate stages and is directly led to lower stages through a by-pass valve. The by-pass valve is under the control of turbine governor. The by-pass governing is done in turbines which have throttle valve governing.

Nozzle control governing is not possible in reaction turbine as reaction turbines require pressure drop in moving blades, throttle governing plus by by-pass governing is used.

Note :

1. Only in the case of Parson reaction turbine $\angle \alpha = \angle \phi$.
2. In all reaction turbines $c_{fi} = c_{fe}$.
3. When the steam leaves the turbine in axial direction $\angle \beta = 90°$.

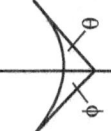

SOLVED PROBLEMS

Problem 6.5

In a Parson turbine running at 1500 RPM the available enthalpy drop for expansion is 62.8 kJ/kg. If the mean diameter of the rotor is 90 cm, find the number of rows of moving blades required. Assume stage efficiency of 75%. Blade outlet angle is 20° and speed ratio is 0.7.

Solution :

As it is a Parson turbine, inlet and outlet velocity triangles are symmetrical.

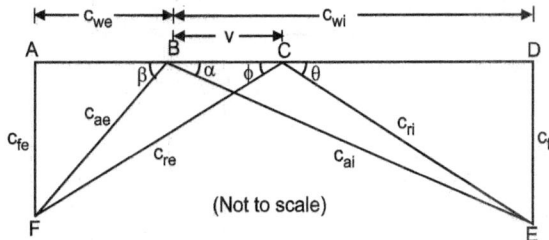

$\angle \alpha = \phi$
$\angle \theta = \angle \beta$
$c_{ai} = c_{re}$

Fig. 6.29

$$\text{Blade velocity, } v = \frac{\pi DN}{60} = \frac{(3.14)(0.9)(1500)}{60} = 70.65 \text{ m/sec}$$

$$\rho = \frac{v}{c_{ai}} = 0.7$$

$$\therefore \quad c_{ai} = \frac{v}{0.7} = \frac{70.65}{0.7} = 100.92 \text{ m/sec}$$

From velocity diagram,

$$AB = c_{re} \cos 20 - v = (100.92)(0.9397) - 70.65$$
$$= 24.184$$

$$c_w = c_{we} + c_{wi} = v + AB + CD$$
$$= (70.65) + (24.184) + (24.184) = 119.018 \text{ m/sec}$$

Work done per stage $= c_w \cdot v = (119.018)(70.65)$ Joules/kg
$$= 8.40 \text{ kJ/kg}$$

Useful enthalpy drop/stage = Work done per stage × Stage efficiency
$$= 8.4 \times 0.75 = 6.3 \text{ kJ/kg}$$

∴ Available enthalpy drop per kg for all stages $= 62.8$ kJ

∴ No. of stages $= \dfrac{62.8}{6.3} = 9.96$ say 10 ... **Ans.**

Problem 6.6 :

At a stage of reaction turbine, the mean rotor diameter is 1.3 m. The speed ratio is 0.7. Rotor speed is 3000 RPM. Blade outlet angle is 20°.

Find : (i) Inlet angle.
(ii) Diagram efficiency.
(iii) Maximum diagram efficiency.

Solution :

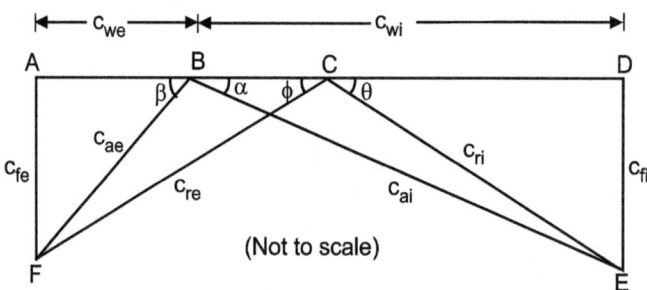

Fig. 6.30

Assuming turbine to be Parson turbine, $\alpha = \phi = 20°$

$$v = \frac{\pi DN}{60} = \frac{\pi \times 1.3 \times 3000}{60} = 204.1 \text{ m/sec}$$

$$\text{Speed ratio} = 0.7 = \frac{v}{c_{ai}}$$

∴ $$c_{ai} = \frac{v}{0.7} = \frac{204.1}{0.7} = 291.57 \text{ m/sec.}$$

$$\cos 20° = \cos \alpha = \frac{BD}{c_{ai}} = \frac{BD}{291.57} = 0.9397$$

$\therefore \quad BD = (291.57)(0.9397) = 273.98 \text{ m/sec}$

$c_{ri}^2 = c_{ai}^2 + v^2 - 2 c_{ai} v \cos 20$

$\therefore \quad c_{ri} = \sqrt{(291.57)^2 + (204.1)^2 - (2)(291.57)(204.1)(0.9397)}$

$\therefore \quad c_{ri} = \sqrt{85013 + 41656.8 - 111842}$

$\therefore \quad c_{ri} = \sqrt{14827.8} = 121.76 \text{ m/sec}$

$CD = BD - BC = 273.98 - 204.1 = 69.88 \text{ m/sec}$

$c_{wi} = v + CD = 204.1 + 69.88 = 273.98 \text{ m/sec}$

$\therefore \quad$ Work done/kg $= c_w \cdot v$ Joules/kg $= \dfrac{(343.7)(204.1)}{1000} \dfrac{kJ}{kg}$

$= 70.149 \text{ kJ/kg}$

Energy supplied $= \dfrac{c_{ai}^2 + (c_{re}^2 - c_{ri}^2)}{2}$

$= \dfrac{2 c_{ai}^2 - c_{ri}^2}{2}$ as $c_{re} = c_{ai}$

$= \dfrac{(2)(291.57)^2 - 121.76^2}{2}$ J/kg

$= 170026 - 14825.49 = \dfrac{155200.5}{2}$ J/kg

$= 77600.2$ J/kg $= 77.6$ kJ/kg

Diagram efficiency $= \dfrac{\text{Work done}}{\text{Energy supplied}} = \dfrac{70.14}{77.6} = 90.38\%$ ... **Ans.**

$\sin \alpha = \dfrac{c_{fi}}{c_{ai}}$

$\therefore \quad c_{fi} = c_{ai} \sin \alpha = 291.57 \times 0.342 = 99.71 \text{ m/sec}$

$\tan \theta = \dfrac{c_{fi}}{CD} = \dfrac{99.71}{69.88} = 1.426$

$\therefore \quad \theta = 54.95° \approx 55°$ ... **Ans.**

The condition for maximum efficiency is

$$\rho = \frac{V}{C_{ai}} = \cos\alpha$$

and η_{max}
$$= \frac{2\cos^2\alpha}{1+\cos^2\alpha} = \frac{(2)(0.9397)^2}{1+(0.9397)^2}$$
$$= \frac{(2)(0.883)}{1.883} = 93.79\% \qquad \text{... Ans.}$$

Problem 6.7

The following data refers to a stage of a Parson's reaction turbine consisting of one ring of fixed blades and one ring of moving blades.

1. Speed of blade ring – 3000 RPM
2. Mean diameter of blade ring – 80 cm
3. Inlet absolute velocity – 290 m/sec
4. Blade outlet angle – 20°
5. Rate of steam flow – 7 kg/sec.

Find : (i) Blade inlet angle, (ii) Tangential force, (iii) Power developed.

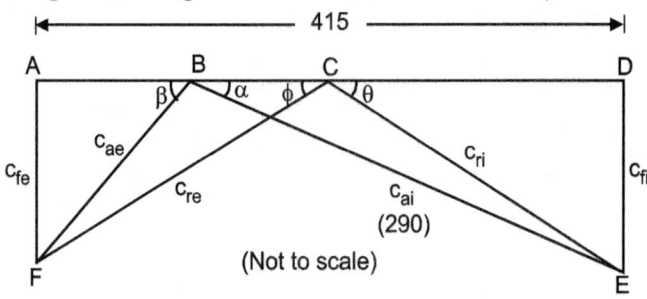

Fig. 6.31

Solution :

1. Blade speed $= \frac{\pi DN}{60} = \frac{(3.14)(0.8)(3000)}{60} = 125.6$ m/sec

As it is a Parson's turbine, $\angle\alpha = \angle\phi = 20°$.

Draw velocity diagram to some scale and complete $\triangle$ BCE and measure $\angle\theta$.

$\angle\theta$ = Blade inlet angle = 34° ... Ans.

2. Tangential force = $m(c_{wi} + c_{we})$
   $= 7(415)$
   $= 2905$ Newtons ... Ans.

3. Power developed = $\dfrac{m \cdot (C_{wi} + C_{we})(v)}{1000}$ kW

   = $\dfrac{(7)(415)(125.6)}{1000}$

   = 364.86 kW ... **Ans.**

Problem 6.8 :

A reaction turbine has identical blading. It delivers dry saturated steam at 2.5 bar. The velocity of steam is 90 m/sec. The mean blade height is 3 cm and exit angle of the moving blade is 20°.

At the mean radius the axial flow velocity equals $\dfrac{3\text{th}}{4}$ blade speed. For a steam flow rate of 9000 kg/hour, calculate :

1. The power output of stage, 2. Rotor speed in rev/min, 3. Diagram efficiency,
4. Enthalpy drop in a stage/kg,
5. % increase in relative velocity in the moving blades due to expansion in the blades.

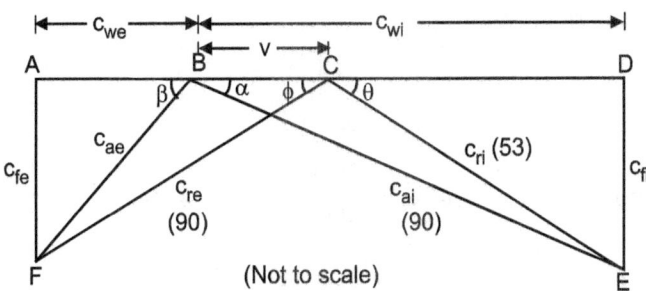

Fig. 6.32

Solution : Data :

C_{ai} = 90 m/sec $\alpha = \phi = 20°$

$C_f = \dfrac{3}{4} v$, $C_{fi} = C_{fe}$

$C_f = C_{ai} \sin 20 = (90)(0.342) = 30.78$ m/sec

$C_f = \dfrac{3}{4} \cdot v = 30.78$

∴ $v = 30.78 \times \dfrac{4}{3} = 41.04$ m/sec

Mass flow rate in kg/sec = $\dfrac{\text{Area through which steam flows} \times \text{Velocity of flow}}{\text{Specific volume}}$

$\therefore \quad \dfrac{9000}{3600} = \dfrac{(\pi D \cdot h)(30.78)}{0.7184}$

where
$\quad D$ = diameter of wheel in meters
$\quad h$ = height of blades in meters

$\therefore \quad \pi Dh = \dfrac{(1.796)}{30.78} = 0.0583 \text{ m}^2$

$\therefore \quad (3.14)(D)\dfrac{(3)}{100} = 0.0583$

$\therefore \quad D = 0.6188 \text{ m}$

$\quad = 61.88 \text{ cm}$ ... **Ans.**

Blade speed, $v = 41.04 = \dfrac{\pi DN}{60} = \dfrac{(3.14)(0.6188)(N)}{60}$

$\therefore \quad N = \dfrac{(41.04)(60)}{(3.14)(0.6188)} = 1267.2 \approx 1270 \text{ RPM}$ ... **Ans.**

Measure from the diagram –

$\quad c_{wi} + c_{we} = 128 \text{ m/sec}$

$\quad c_{ri} = 53 \text{ m/sec}$

Work done = $m(c_{wi} + c_{we})v = \dfrac{9000}{3600} \times 128 \times 41.04$

$\quad = 13132.8 \text{ W} = 13.132 \text{ kW}$ ... **Ans.**

Energy input = $m\left(\dfrac{c_{ai}^2}{2} + \dfrac{c_{re}^2 - c_{ri}^2}{2}\right)$

$\quad = \dfrac{2.5}{2}(c_{ai}^2 + c_{ai}^2 - c_{ri}^2)$

$\quad = \dfrac{2.5}{2}(2 \times 90^2 - 53^2)$

$\quad = 1.25(16200 - 2809) = 16738 \text{ watts}$

$\quad = 16.738 \text{ kW}$

Diagram efficiency = $\dfrac{\text{Work done}}{\text{Energy supplied}} = \dfrac{13.13}{16.738} = 78.48\%$ ... **Ans.**

% increase in relative velocity $= \dfrac{C_{re} - C_{ri}}{C_{ri}} = \dfrac{90 - 53}{53}$

$= 69.8\%$

Enthalpy drop in moving blades per kg $= \dfrac{C_{re}^2 - C_{ri}^2}{2} = \dfrac{90^2 - 53^2}{2}$

$= 2645$ J/kg

$= 2.645$ kJ/kg

Enthalpy drop per stage = Enthalpy drop in moving blades + Enthalpy drop in fixed blades

$= 2.645 + 2.645$ (As blades are identical)

$= 5.29$ kJ/kg ... **Ans.**

Problem 6.9 :

A reaction turbine develops 4 kW. The steam consumption is 240 kg/min. Leakage of steam 10%, steam condition at inlet 2.5 bar, 0.95 dry, exit angle 20° for both fixed and moving blades. Rotor speed 300 RPM. Axial velocity 0.7 of blade velocity.

Find the turbine drum diameter and height of the blades.

Solution :

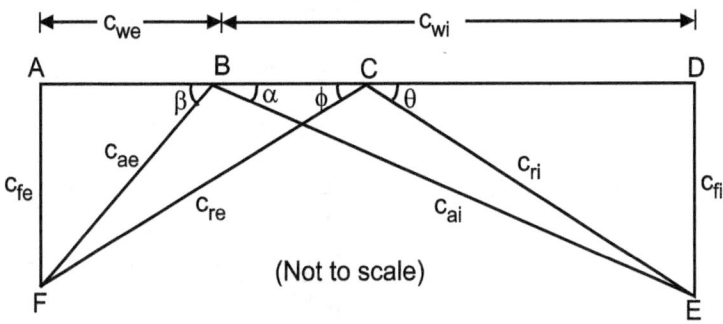

Fig. 6.33

Exit angle of fixed blade is the angle with which steam enters moving blade.

∴ $\alpha = 20°$

Exit angle of moving blade is the angle with which steam leaves the moving blade

∴ $\phi = 20°$

Steam flow rate through the blades = $\dfrac{240 \times 0.9}{60}$ = 3.6 kg/sec

(As leakage is 10%)

$$\text{Power output in kW} = \dfrac{m \cdot (C_{wi} + C_{we})\, v}{1000}$$

$$4 = \dfrac{(3.6)\,(AB + BC + BC + CD - v)\, v}{1000}$$

$$4 = \dfrac{3.6\,(AC + BD - v)\, v}{1000}$$

(AC = BD as Δ^sBED and CFA are similar)

$$4 = \dfrac{3.6\,(2\, C_f \cot 20 - v)\, v}{1000} \qquad \ldots (1)$$

Now,
$$v = \dfrac{\pi DN}{60} = \dfrac{(3.14)\,(D)\,(300)}{60} = 15.7\, D$$

$$C_f = (0.7)(v) = (0.7)(15.7\, D) = 10.99\, D$$

Substituting these values in equation (1),

$$4 = \dfrac{(3.6)\,(2 \times 10.99\, D \cot 20 - 15.7\, D)\, 15.7\, D}{1000}$$

Solving,   D = 1.258 m   ... Ans.

Hence C_f = 13.83 m/sec

   v = 19.75 m/sec

$$\text{Mass flow rate} = \dfrac{\pi D h}{\text{Sp. volume}} \times C_f \qquad (h \text{ is height of the blade})$$

$$\therefore \quad 3.6 = \dfrac{(3.14)\,(1.258)\,(h)\,(13.83)}{(0.95)\,(0.7184)}$$

Solving   h = 0.0449 m = 44.9 mm   ... Ans.

Problem 6.10 :

Steam is supplied to a three stage turbine at 35 bar and 400°C and exhausts at 0.05 bar and 0.9 dry. If the work developed per stage is equal, find : (i) Condition at entry to each stage. (ii) Stage efficiencies, (iii) Reheat factor, (iv) Overall efficiency.

Assume condition line to be straight.

Solution :

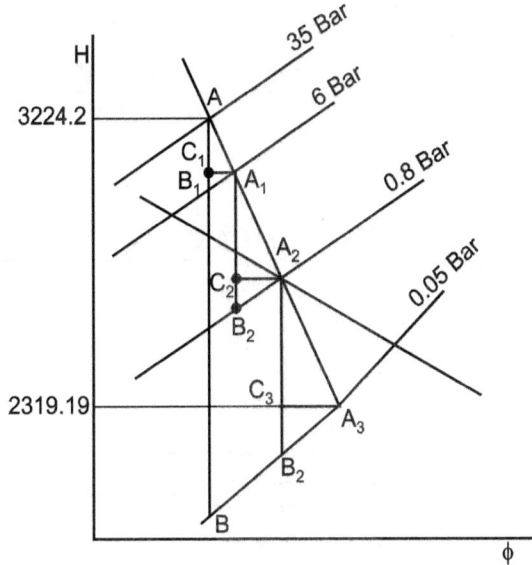

Fig. 6.34

From steam tables :

Enthalpy of steam at 35 bar and 400°C = 3224.2 kJ

Enthalpy of steam at 0.05 bar and 0.9 dry.

$$= 137.77 + (0.9)(2423.6) = 2319.19 \text{ kJ/kg}$$

Useful work = $h_A - h_{A_3}$ = 3224.2 − 2319.2 = 905.01 kJ/kg

This work is shared equally between three stages.

Hence Work done/stage = $\dfrac{905.01}{3}$ = 301.67 kJ

Stage efficiency, Stage I − $\dfrac{AC_1}{AB_1}$ = $\dfrac{301.67}{3224.2 - 2800}$ = 71.1%

Stage II − $\dfrac{A_1C_2}{A_1B_2}$ = $\dfrac{301.67}{2922.53 - 2530}$ = 76.8%

Stage III − $\dfrac{A_2C_3}{A_2B_3}$ = $\dfrac{301.67}{2620.87 - 2240}$ = 79.2%

(Values of enthalpy read from Mollier chart)

$$\text{Reheat factor} = \frac{AB_1 + A_1B_2 + A_2B_3}{AB}$$

$$= \frac{424.2 + 392.53 + 380.57}{3224.2 - 2080}$$

$$= 1.046 \qquad \text{... Ans.}$$

$$\text{Overall efficiency} = \frac{AC_1 + A_1C_2 + A_2C_3}{AB} = \frac{905.01}{1144.2}$$

$$= 79.09\% \qquad \text{... Ans.}$$

EXAMPLES FOR PRACTICE

1. Explain the difference in principle of action between impulse and reaction types of steam turbines.

2. The nozzles of the impulse stage of a turbine receive steam at 15 bar and 300°C and discharges it at 10 bar. The nozzle efficiency is 95% and the nozzle angle is 20°. The blade speed is that required for maximum work and the inlet angle of the blades is that required for entry of steam without shock. The blade exit angle is 5° less than the inlet angle. The blade velocity coefficient is 0.9. Calculate for a steam flow of 1350 kg/hour, (i) The diagram power, (2) The diagram efficiency.

   (Ans. 30.3 kW, 86.3%)

3. A reaction turbine is supplied with steam at 60 bar and 600°C. The condenser pressure is 0.07 bar. If the reheat factor is 1.04 and stage efficiency is constant throughout at 80%, calculate the steam flow required in kg/hour for a diagram power of 25000 kW. **(Ans. 75,600 kg/hour)**

4. A single row impulse turbine has a mean blade speed of 215 m/sec. Nozzle entry angle is 30° to the plane of rotation of the blades. The steam velocity from the nozzles is 550 m/sec. There is 15% loss of relative velocity due to friction across the blades. The discharge of steam is along the axis of the turbine. The steam flow through the turbine is at the rate of 700 kg/hour. Determine : (1) Inlet and exit

angles of the blades. (2) The absolute velocity of the steam at exit. (3) The power output of the turbine.

(**Ans.** (1) 46°, 49°, (2) 243 m/sec, (3) 19.8 kW)

5. At a particular stage of a reaction turbine, the mean blade speed is 150 m/sec. The exit angles of the fixed and moving blades are 20°. The inlet angles of the fixed and moving blades are 30°. The stage efficiency is 80%. The pressure at entry to the stage is 15 bar and the temperature is 200°C.

   Determine :

   (a) The specific enthalpy drop across the stage in kJ/kg.

   (b) The drum diameter and blade height if the blade height is one tenth of the drum
   diameter and the steam flow is 100 kg/sec.

   (c) Percentage increase in relative velocity across the blading as the result of pressure drop across the blading.

(**Ans.** (1) 127 kJ/kg, (2) 521 mm, 52.1 mm, (3) 46%)

6. In one stage of reaction turbine, both the fixed and moving blades have inlet and outlet blade tip angles of 35° and 20° respectively. The mean blade speed is 80 m/s and steam consumption is 22500 kg/hour. Determine the power developed in the pair. If the isentropic heat drop for the pair is 23.5 kJ/kg, find the efficiency of the pair.

(**Ans.** 127 kW, 86.2%)

7. At a certain pair in a reaction turbine, the blade velocity is 1.4 times the velocity of flow of steam and the blade outlet angles are 20°. The power developed in the pair is 4 kW at 500 rev/min and the steam consumption is 3 kg/sec. The steam flowing through the pair is 0.96 dry at 2 bar abs. Allowing a tip leakage of 8%, calculate :

   (1) Blade entry angles, (2) The mean diameter of the blade ring, (3) The height of the blades.

(**Ans.** (1) 36.6°, (2) 0.85 m, (3) 55 mm)

8. The following particulars relate to a two ring velocity compounded impulse turbine. Discharge, angles, Nozzles – 16°. First moving – 24°. Fixed ring 20°. Second moving 32°. Velocity of steam at exit of nozzle 540 m/sec. Velocity coefficient for each ring 0.9. Final discharge of steam is axial. Find (1) The mean blade velocity. (2) Specific steam consumption.

(**Ans.** 118 m/sec, (2) 30 kg/kWHr)

www.ingramcontent.com/pod-product-compliance
Lightning Source LLC
Chambersburg PA
CBHW060309240426
43661CB00059B/2704